March 1991

For Peggy, with continuing gratitude
and affectionate greetings,

Ken

# Austria in the Thirties: Culture and Politics

# Studies in Austrian Literature, Culture, and Thought

*Major Figures of Modern Austrian Literature*
Edited by Donald G. Daviau

*Introducing Austria. A Short History*
By Lonnie Johnson

*The Verbal and Visual Art of Alfred Kubin*
By Phillip H. Rhein

*Austrian Foreign Policy Yearbook*
Report of the Austrian Federal Ministry
for Foreign Affairs for the year 1988

*From Wilson to Waldheim*
Proceedings of a Workshop on
Austrian-American Relations 1917-1987
Edited by Peter Pabisch

*Arthur Schnitzler and Politics*
By Adrian Clive Roberts

*Quietude and Quest*
Protagonists and Antagonists in the Theatre,
on and off Stage
As Seen through the Eyes of Leon Askin
Written by Leon Askin with C. Melvin Davidson

# Translation Series:

*February Shadows*
By Elisabeth Reichart
Translated by Donna L. Hoffmeister
Afterword by Christa Wolf

*Night over Vienna*
By Lili Körber
Translated by Viktoria Hertling and Kay M. Stone
Commentary by Viktoria Hertling

*The Cool Million*
By Erich Wolfgang Skwara
Translated by Harvey I. Dunkle
Preface by Martin Walser
Afterword by Richard Exner

*Buried in the Sands of Time*
Poetry by Janko Ferk
English/German/Slovenian
English Translation by Herbert Kuhner

*Negatives of My Father*
By Peter Henisch
Translated and with an Afterword by Anne C. Ulmer

*Puntigam or The Art of Forgetting*
By Gerald Szyszkowitz
Translated by Adrian Del Caro
Preface by Simon Wiesenthal
Afterword by Jürgen Koppensteiner

# Austria in the Thirties:

# Culture and Politics

Edited by

**Kenneth Segar and John Warren**

ARIADNE PRESS

RIVERSIDE, CALIFORNIA

**Library of Congress Cataloging-in-Publication Data**

Austria in the thirties: culture and politics / edited by Kenneth
    Segar and John Warren.
        p.  cm. --  (Studies in Austrian literature, culture, and thought)
    Papers given at a symposium held March 14-16, 1988 at Oxford
    University.
                Includes bibliographical references.
                ISBN 0-929497-10-4 .-- ISBN 0-929497-29-5 (pbk).
                    1. Austrian literature--20th century--History and criticism-
    -Congresses. 2. Literature and society--Austria--Congresses.
    3. Austria--Politics and government--1918-1938--Congresses.
    4. Politics and culture--Austria--Congresses. I. Segar, Kenneth.
    II. Warren, John, 1935-    . III. Series.
    PT3818.A97   1990
    830.9'9436'09043--dc20                                    90-405
                                                                    CIP

Published with the assistance of the
Austrian Institute, London

# AUSTRIA IN THE THIRTIES: CULTURE AND POLITICS

Editors: Kenneth Segar and John Warren

EPILOGUE

# PREFACE

Authoritarian government, such as existed in Austria between 1933 and 1938, makes more palpable the ever-present interaction of culture and politics. Since it is frequently the minor writers of a period who best capture the tenor of their society (and sometimes little else), the 'culture' examined in this volume is largely of that order. At the Symposium it was also found that understanding the intricate patterns of cultural and political life in the Corporate State (Ständestaat) required continual reference to the whole period of the First Republic (1918–1938). Perhaps a brief summary would therefore be appropriate at the outset.

'German-Austria' (Deutschösterreich), as the founders of the Austrian Republic wished it to be called, was created in the aftermath of a crippling military defeat against a background of civil war and insuperable economic difficulties. The omens were hardly propitious and were even less so after the harshest terms had been imposed in 1919 by the Treaty of St Germain. By 1921 the broad spectrum coalition government had broken down and, despite the strength of the Social Democratic Party (which constantly polled 40% of the vote), the country was henceforth to be ruled by a series of right-wing coalition governments. Political tensions were further exacerbated by the formation on the right and the left of paramilitary organizations, whose violent confrontations became commonplace. Barely kept afloat by loans from the League of Nations, Austria experienced the misery of inflation and high unemployment, the latter reaching disastrous levels in the thirties. A much hoped-for way out of these troubles through union with Germany was blocked by the Allies. Vienna became a separate federal state in 1921, and its Social Democratic administration achieved miracles with its housing, welfare and educational programmes. But even though 'Red Vienna' had become a showcase for socialism, the pressure for authoritarian government grew ever stronger. This was spurred on by the right-wing paramilitary *Heimwehr,* whose members gained their inspiration from Italian fascism. Nor can one overlook the role of the Catholic Church in encouraging this move to the right, indeed in fostering one of its important ingredients, anti-Semitism.

Two landmarks on the road to the corporate state were the 1926 conference of the Social Democrat Party in Linz and the burning down of the Vienna Law Courts in 1927. The first produced a Programme which, despite Otto Bauer's clear hatred of force, introduced the idea of armed conflict into the political arena; its highly charged language gave the right-wing press a propaganda victory. The second led the police, under orders from the police chief Schober, to shoot down eighty-nine demonstrattors, who were protesting against the acquittal of three *Heimwehr* members charged with murder; and that caused many on the left to despair of ever achieving social justice. The ensuing debate in parliament only widened the political gulf. In 1929 constitutional changes weakened still further Austria's fragile democracy: the powers of the President were increased and his term of office lengthened; parliament was deemed to be no longer a permanent body but one called by the President twice annually; the powers of the National Council were reduced, as was the independence of Vienna, whilst the state police had their powers enlarged.

In 1932 and 1933 the National Socialist Party entered on the political scene and had considerable success in the elections for the federal states. Realizing that a national election would now prove disastrous, the right-wing coalition seized the opportunity presented by the resignation of all three speakers — parliament thereby being deemed to have suspended itself — to govern without parliament. Dollfuss ruled by means of an unrepealed Emergency Decree dating from the First World War. Urged on by his 'protector' Mussolini, he issued edicts (aimed more at the left than at the Austrian National Socialists) to begin the dismantling of democracy. He introduced censorship and the death penalty, banned the Communist Party and the socialist paramilitary organization (Schutzbund), and so created an atmosphere in which armed conflict was inevitable. The 'civil war' of February 1934 resulted in the abolition of all Social Democratic institutions, whether political or social, and the arrest of countless members of the party. The Mayor of Vienna, Karl Seitz, was forcibly removed from the town hall, and a Federal Commissioner was appointed in his place. On 1 May the corporate state was proclaimed, but the murder of Dollfuss on 25 July, when the Austrian National Socialists attempted a *Putsch,* revealed a more dangerous enemy.

Kurt Schuschnigg replaced Dollfuss as leader of the Patriotic Front (Vaterländische Front) and endeavoured, at first with the support of Italy, to maintain Austria's independence. As essays in this volume demonstrate, the odds were massively against him. Politically and culturally, Austrian life was permeated by the appeal of union with the new and vigorous Reich to the north. Germany capitalized on this. With efficient propaganda, an economic boycott, systematic infiltration at every level of Austrian public life, and the ruthless use of force, the Reich outmanoeuvred Austria at every turn. Even the July Agreement of 1936, which seemingly guaranteed Austria's independence, actually paved the way for greater penetration by Hitler's Germany. Once Italy had embarked on its Abyssinian adventure (1937) and needed German support in Europe, the survival of an independent Austria became highly unlikely. The final blow was the refusal of France and Britain unequivocally to guarantee support for Austria's independence. When the Anschluss came, it was broadly acceptable to the majority of the population.

*    *    *

In March 1988 the Oxford Austrian Study Group organized a Symposium to mark the fiftieth anniversary of the Anschluss. The essays in this volume, with the exception of the Epilogue, were given at that gathering, which took place at St Edmund Hall, Oxford (14–16 March). The Symposium consisted not only of the papers included in this volume; however, those by Professor Francis L. Carsten ('Austria seen through British Sources') and Dr

Hannes Hüttner ('Viennese Cabaret in the Thirties') cannot be published for technical reasons. Other events at the Symposium provided an opportunity to experience Austrian culture of the thirties at first hand. The Holywell Music Room lent its atmosphere to a concert by the Mozarteum Duo, Salzburg, whose recital included the first performance of the Suite for Violin and Piano, op. 56 (1937) by Egon Wellesz, who emigrated from Vienna to Oxford in 1938. Another emigré to Oxford in 1938, Bela Horovitz, the founder of the Phaidon Press, was commemorated by an exhibition (in the Old Library, St Edmund Hall) of many of the first Phaidon publications; our thanks are due to Hannah Horovitz for organizing this tribute to her father. Handsome tribute was also paid to Jura Soyfer, an early victim of the Anschluß who died in Buchenwald in 1939, by Milo Sperber's spirited and also moving reading from his works. Finally, participants were given the chance to see the film *Maskerade,* an example of the sentimental genre of the Austrian 1930s.

The organizers of the Symposium owe gratitude to many others: to the Austrian Institute, London, without whose financial support the whole venture would have been impossible; to Dr Ernst Menhofer, its then Director, for his enthusiasm and liaison work—not to mention his hosting of a splendid reception; to St Edmund Hall for providing a comfortable and hospitable venue; to our varied and enthusiastic audience for its whole-hearted participation; to our chairpersons, Professor Alan Bance, Miss Margaret Jacobs, Mr Brian McGuiness, Professor Peter Pulzer and Professor Norman Stone; and, finally, to our publisher, Professor Donald Daviau for his commitment to this volume and patience with its editors.

(N.B. Authors whose papers were given in English provided their own translations of German quotations. With the exception of Horst Jarka, his own translator, and Gerhard Renner, whose paper was translated by Jutta Renner and Murray Hall, the editors are responsible for translation of the papers given in German, namely, those by Klaus Amann, Friedbert Aspetsberger, Dieter Binder, Edda Fuhrich-Leisler, Helmut Konrad, Gisela Prossnitz, Anton Staudinger.)

# 'Austria' – The Ideology of Austrofascism

## Anton Staudinger

At no time during the short history of the First Republic had Austria's existence as an independent state been so clearly defended and officially propagandized as it was during the period when the Dollfuss government first dismantled parliamentary democracy, then destroyed it, and finally created a dictatorship. This brand of Austrian patriotism was similarly prescribed under Schuschnigg in the interests of the State. The continued existence of an independent Austrian state hostile to the National Socialist call for Anschluss was later to be seen as part of Austria's self-defence against National Socialism, and so the basis for her discovery of a democratic national identity after 1945. And the view is still maintained (or stated even more emphatically) that the 'Austria' ideology of the pre-Anschluss years created the democratic national identity which achieved broad acceptance only with the social developments of the Second Austrian Republic.

The Austrian Republic's image of itself had from the start been a 'German' one. The Social Democrats had conceived of a bourgeois, democratic German national consciousness. However, it must be admitted that this did not develop significantly in Austria. What did grow in Austria was, on the contrary, an anti-democratic, anti-socialist, anti-Semitic, racially based (völkisch) German nationalism, which in its anticlerical form led to National Socialism, and in a Catholic variant prepared the mould for the 'Austrian.' ideology of Austrofascism.[1] The first signs and early forms of this 'Austria' ideology can be traced back to the beginnings of the Austrian Republic, and were to be found most clearly on and around the right wing of the Christian Social Party, a good example would be Josef Eberle's journal *Das neue Reich* (New Reich), later *Schönere Zukunft* (Brighter Future),[2] where the polemic against the Republic, democracy, 'Marxism,' 'Liberalism,' the peace treaties of St Germain and Versailles was carried on in a language that was often anti-Semitic. The perspective was Christian, indeed Catholic, expressing belief in an Austrian mission to create a new 'Holy Empire' with an 'organic and corporate' structure. Closely linked to the universalist social concepts propounded by the circle around Othmar Spann, these early Austrian ideas of Empire (Reichsideologie) were to have influence on similar ideas on the Catholic Right in Germany.[3] The desire for Anschluss among Republicans (and by 'Republicans' I mean the Social Democrats with their goal of a socialist German state, also middle-class Liberal circles, and even some Christian Socials, particularly those in the regions outside Vienna) and the same desire among groups with anticlerical and racist ideas met with outright rejection from those advocating the 'Austria' ideology, or at best a certain ambivalent coolness with preference expressed for the idea of a 'Danube Confederation.' In the Christian Social Party, the 'Austria' ideology found most favour with those groups of Catholic intellectuals who in October and November 1918 had wanted to maintain the Habsburg monarchy as well as German dominance in the Austrian half of the Empire, and had therefore held out longest against the creation of an Austrian Republic.[4] Indeed, the first attacks on the democratic system in Austria between 1918 and 1920 came from the Catholic right-wing political groups around Ignaz Seipel. Of course, in the Christian Social Party as a whole, the idea of Anschluss clearly predominated.[5] The idea that Austria was part of the German nation was, with a very few exceptions on the fringes, undisputed by any political group, even if that idea meant something different to each group.

In 1927 and more particularly in 1930 the Christian Social Party suffered heavy electoral losses and found itself second in parliament to the Social Democrats. At this point we see coming to the fore within the Christian Social Party certain forces which were bent on rejecting the democratic, parliamentary system and working towards some kind of authoritarian, 'organic and corporative' (organisch-ständisch) political structure for Austria.[6] This change of direction is unmistakeable to anyone reading the commentary by Richard Schmitz on the 1926 programme of the Christian Social Party. That programme had been couched in very general terms, but Schmitz's commentary, written with the full agreement of the party, looks in a particular direction. The document, it is true, clearly aimed to win back lost electoral potential among the extreme Right, the paramilitary organizations (Heimwehr) and the National Socialists, and so in that sense had not yet abandoned a parliamentary democracy based on elections; and yet there are also platform points of a clearly anti-democratic nature, which were shortly to be brought into effect by the Dollfuss government. And here, in contrast to the 1926 programme, from which both the supporters of Anschluss and those of a 'Danube Confederation' could have taken their ideas, the party's official attitude towards the question of Austria as a nation reveals clear outlines of the 'Austria' ideology.

The Christian Social Party declares itself to be the 'natural (bodenständig) party of a Christian and German Austria . . . unswerving in its loyalty to that Greater Germany with which Austrian Germans feel indissoluble ties of blood, common language and culture, and a thousand years of history.' It is a party based on the idea of the German nation (nationalgesinnt) and so demands 'that German customs be kept up as part of our fine Christian heritage,' and that means not only 'cherishing our national traditions' (Volkstumspflege), but also 'submitting to the discipline so often lacking in present-day political life.' That discipline, of course, implied 'voluntary integration and subordination in the tradition of ancient Teutonic loyalty to the colours of the feudal overlord' (Heerbanntreue). But being German also means 'fighting against un-German and un-Christian influences,' indeed, mounting an 'anti-Semitic' attack on the 'superior forces of Jewish influence corroding intellectual and economic life.' Furthermore, the Christian Social Party is not content merely to declare its loyalty to the German nation, but actually demands revision of the 'unjust dictates' of the Treaties of St Germain and

Versailles, together with an 'acknowledgment of the right to self-determination of the German people . . . which has been denied to them alone.' The Christian Social Party thus particularly wished to see 'all relationships with the German Reich developing on the basis of its right to self-determination.' On this point Schmitz comments that some kind of 'coming together of the two states on equal terms (Zusammenschluß), given the right moment,' would be preferable to Anschluß, this latter being the 'no longer generally acceptable idea of making Austria into a province of Germany, or at best a federal state with little independence.' For Austria would be able to fulfill her 'mission as the Ostmark' only if it retained a sufficient measure of independence. Thus, maintaining the cultural and economic independence of German Austria (das deutsche Österreichertum) was 'in the interests of Greater Germany.'[7]

There is no doubt that this commentary was an attempt to win the co-operation of the young Catholic intellectuals who, from bases in Catholic organizations, were working for the union of Austria and Germany, but against parliamentary democracy and therefore against the Christian Social Party. These young people had been influenced at universities in Austria, particularly in Vienna, by the scholarly and educational work of pan-Germanists (Großdeutsche) like the philosophers Othmar Spann and Hans Eibl, the legal historian Karl Gottfried Hugelmann (a Christian Social member of parliament from 1921 to 1931), the geographers Machatschek and Hassinger, the historians Hans Hirsch and Heinrich Srbik, the Germanist Josef Nadler. Himself trained in this tradition, the historian Adam Wandruszka states that these academics 'were trying to create a synthesis: on the one hand there were the ideas on nationality stemming from Herder and the Romantics, the nation's experience of the First World War, the struggle on behalf of the borderlands and "extra-territorial Germany"; on the other hand, there were the universalist claims for the old Imperial ideal and the traditions of the Habsburg monarchy. A synthesis of these elements would, they hoped, be the blue-print for a supranational . . . order in Europe.'[8]

Let me cite the most important components of their vision. Srbik had the idea of a 'pan-German history' (gesamtdeutsche Geschichtsauffassung), which would, in historical terms, settle the controversies between the proponents of a Greater or a Lesser Germany, and would create a new concept of 'Empire.'[9] Nadler produced a 'tribal theory' (Stammestheorie),[10] which not only served as method for categorizing literature written in German but also gave its author an opportunity to derive principles governing the political order of a future German Empire. Hirsch[11] believed that Germany's capacity to lead the smaller nations of Central Europe in the Middle Ages could be adapted to suit the contemporary world. And in this connection there was a related idea that the major states had achieved their particular political organization and character because of their geographical position and political environment. And finally, there was Spann,[12] to whose Romantic, universalistic and anti-parliamentarian social philosophy I have already referred. He provides an important connecting link to Austria's 'authoritarian corporate state,' but his influence on the ideology of fascism in general cannot be overestimated.

It was in this spirit that a group of Catholic intellectuals set to work to strengthen the anti-democratic and racist tendencies to be found in Political Catholicism, especially in the Christian Social Party. This group was recruited from among high-ranking officials of the most important Catholic organizations, such as the League of German Christian Youth of Austria (Reichsbund der christlich-deutschen Jugend Österreichs), the German Christian Gymnastic League of Austria (Christlich-deutsche Turnerschaft Österreichs), the Austrian Catholic Student Fraternity (Österreichischer Cartell-Verband), the New Territory League (Bund Neuland), and others. In the group were to be found scholars, publicists, civil servants, priests;[13] and from 1932, they became in essence the German National Association of Austrian Catholics (Volksdeutscher Arbeitskreis österreichischer Katholiken) and played a leading role in setting up the General Assembly of German-speaking Catholics (Allgemeiner deutscher Katholikentag) held in September 1933. In the early summer of 1932 they joined with officials of the Christian Workers' Movement (Christliche Arbeiterbewegung)[14] and worked out a programme to develop the Christian Social Party along 'corporate' (ständisch) and 'racist' (völkisch) lines.[15]

Stressing its leaning towards the Catholic Church, this text shows elements of not only conservative but, indeed, fascist ideology: it claims to be 'anti-parliamentarian,' 'anti-liberal,' and – so it says – 'anti-capitalistic.' It is militantly 'anti-Marxist'; it espouses corporatism, hostility to the cities, a romantic attitude towards the countryside (Agrarromantik), expansionism, absolute sovereignty; it proffers ideas of community and folk based on biological principles as the path to harmonizing conflicts of interest within contemporary society – and conversely attempts to deflect attention from those conflicting interests by creating imaginary enemies, by making vague emotional appeals to the idea of Empire, and by encouraging anti-Semitism. According to this programme,[16] 'Catholic youth organizations were fighting a justified battle against a pseudo-democratic parliamentarianism,' in which 'the mere counting of heads and party political compromises,' always subject to fluctuation, had robbed the State of its capacity to pursue a single line in accordance with a dominant political philosophy. The battle was also directed against 'the erroneous selection of incompetents through the democratic electoral system.' We read: 'If what is wanted is a true People's State, then it is essential to remove the party system and an atomizing democracy.' Also: 'a short-term dictatorship would provide a reliable means of escape from democratic indecision and party compromise, and would promote the formation of a new, unified State,' and this, even though the proponents of a 'Christian State' with 'corporatist structure' were to remain in the minority.

This programme defines the 'people' (Volk) as 'in the first place, a spiritual community, one with a peculiar historical destiny, culture, language and religious outlook, but then also a community by the fact of blood and ancestry.' It is clearly no accident that 'Judaism' is rejected within this biological and racist position as 'something alien in blood and mentality,' whose 'disproportioate and substantial influence must be curbed by powerful measures, namely the withdrawal of political rights and a quota system in the professions.' And in keeping with these widely-held views, 'converting to Christianity would not alter the fact that one was a Jew.' On the question of nationality, the programme states:

> As Austrians, we declare our total loyalty to the German people and to a Greater German Reich, in which Austria would have an autonomous position befitting its special role. We view the Austrian task as one of leadership in the move to produce a new unified political structure for the Danubian lands and South East Europe. This restructuring will ensure for the ethnic groups and peoples of South East Europe both cultural independence and political freedom within the framework of a union of States and peoples [Völker- und Staatenbund], and will bring them at last into the sphere of German culture. This Austrian task is, however, only part of the Greater German task, and that is to reshape Central Europe, from the Baltic to the Black Sea and from France to Russia, as a union of free peoples. The Western idea of a centralist nation state is meaningless and inapplicable in the context of the Danubian lands and South East Europe.

Furthermore, the 'precondition and basis for any such political order, committed to the rule of law and the promotion of peace' must be 'full compensation for the injustice perpetrated by the Paris peace dictates.' Through their fight to 'restore justice, the German people will become leaders in the struggle to create a new Western civilization.'

These, then, were the political aims[17] of Catholic young professionals who thought of themselves as the inner circle of a new Catholic leadership. But whilst they were an élite, they were in no sense presenting the programme of a small, uninfluential clique of outsiders. All these members of the German National Association of Austrian Catholics lectured to practically every important conference of young Catholics; they went into schools, and they took part in all the preparations for the Catholic Assembly of 1933. And it was that gathering of Catholics which provided the religious legitimation for a dictatorship in Austria.

With the coming of the National Socialist state in Germany, however, Austrians had to modify their call for a 'pan-German' Empire. Shortly before, in 1932, the Austrian Government had accepted a loan at Lausanne and consequently had to accept from the League of Nations a renewed prohibition of Anschluss. From 1933/34 it found itself forced to combat the aggressive anti-Austrian policies of both the National Socialist government of Germany and the Austrian National Socialist Party, which was mounting terrorist attacks within Austria. Somehow the idea of a 'pan-German' Empire had now to be reconciled with the need of the Austrian state to preserve its autonomy. So the conception of such an 'Empire' became increasingly an Austrian one, and to that extent had little to do with the real world. The idea of creating a 'pan-German Empire' out of the Danubian lands, i.e., large areas of the former Austro-Hungarian Monarchy, was, to put it charitably, certainly not something that internal economic and political factors or the international context would permit in the foreseeable future.

Nonetheless, the historian Hugo Hantsch, a Benedictine monk, could still demand that the important lessons taught (as he saw them) by the history of the Holy Roman Empire and of the Habsburg monarchy should be applied. He argued that Austria, forming a 'geographical and climatological' transition zone, 'linked the German people with the peoples of the East and South, a mediating position of fateful significance.' Austria must always remain aware that its 'political and cultural activities are of vital importance to the whole German race.' It is 'German culture (Volkstum) that throughout the ages has been the element unifying the whole area, sustaining the Austrian idea there, fostering the development of all the many peoples living there;' it is 'German culture,' it is the 'German part of Austria' that created the Habsburg Empire, and the dissolution of that Empire was quite simply 'a blow against German civilization.' So the 'idea of the Austrian State' coming into being under the Dollfuss Government seemed to Hantsch to be 'capable of being developed . . . since it manifests all those elements which permitted the old Austrian State to grow into an Empire.' Austria is 'not just an area of so many square miles' but 'an idea, born of all that is German, since what is German demands empire and must perforce see its fulfilment in empire.' If, then, it is 'the nature of the German people to have a spiritual mission in the world,' there is logical significance in the idea of the Austrian State with 'its religious unity and its maintenance of unity with Rome,' since Austria has the capacity to bring about 'a Christian – more specifically, Catholic – regeneration in all the German lands.' Austria as constituted in 1918 could not 'come to terms with being a minor state, a role which it is forced to play in an area so fragmented into races and states as is South East Europe.' It has to 'think in terms of those larger contexts to which nature and history call it. This is not imperialism in the sense of prewar power politics, but rather in the sense of leadership: Austria must take the lead in the creation of an Empire where there will be peace and justice, for do not Christian principles and all objective truth point the way and lay the foundations? ' This is what is meant by 'restoring the dignity of the German nation,' and so it is that 'the way to a true idea of empire and to the true Empire itself must be via Austria.'[18]

Even more than in Hantsch the Austrian idea is clearly placed in a religious context by Kurt Schuschnigg, who spoke in his capacity as Austrian Minister of Education at the General Assembly of German-speaking Catholics in September 1933 as follows:[19]

> Since the source of the cultural power of the German people is to be found in the idea of Empire, it would be absurd to try to measure this great, far-reaching idea of Western civilization by the size of its proponent's power-political base, that is, by where present-day frontiers are drawn . . . what matters is not the physical size of our country at any given moment, but the great creative spirit working through the Western ideal of the 'Holy Empire,' for this is the earthly shadow of the mystic body of the

Church, and it is this which gives our Austrian homeland its permanent living significance. . . . Throwing the strength of Catholic Austria into the scales serves not only the interests of our own land, but equally those of Greater Germany and thus of the Western World . . . Without Catholic Austria, it becomes impossible for the German people to fulfil its mission on behalf of Western Christendom, namely to bring about a rebirth of the true Holy Empire and so restore peace to a Central Europe bleeding from a thousand wounds.

Schuschnigg was by no means the only person who used the Catholic Assembly to express commitment to that often theologically overblown ideology of the 'Holy Roman Empire of the German Nation.' On the contrary, this event created the general impression that the – predominantly younger – political activists among the Catholic intelligentsia were nearly all stamped with this 'ideology of Empire' (Reichsideologie). In this context one thinks of the lectures given by Alfred Verdross, but most particularly of that given by the former leader of the Austrian 'New Territorialists' (Neuländer), Anton Böhm.[20] However, the full significance of the Education Minister's statement lies in its demonstration of the fact that these ideas were not merely tolerated by the Government but actually formed an essential part of its own ideology and policy. This essentiality is further underlined by Dollfuss' proclamation of the principles – 'authoritarian, Christian and German' – according to which the 'authoritarian corporate state' was to be created: this proclamation occurred at the self-same Catholic Assembly, thus clearly revealing his acceptance of anti-parliamentarian Political Catholicism as the driving force of the emerging dictatorship.

This Austrian Catholic ideology of Empire was not simply the way people in the thirties interpreted their present, that is, by means of a kind of historical flashback: it was actually a programme to be put into effect, and it used religious and pseudo-scholarly ways of thinking to legitimize political action. As Kurt

Breuning expresses it, this ideology of Empire was a 'secularized prophecy looking backwards'; it was constructing a programme for future political action from a transfigured past via a misinterpreted present. Engelbert Dollfuss, albeit using the phrase 'Austria's mission,' never himself used the exaggerated slogans of these fantasies of Empire. It is true that in his student days Dollfuss, like the great majority of his colleagues who had been active in student organizations, supported the Anschluß movement.[21] He had been a member of the German Association (Deutsche Gemeinschaft), a Catholic secret society, organized along the lines of the illegal Freemasons, but made up of anticlerical nationalist groups. These had no truck with the usual ideological arguments found in Austrian universities in the pre-war period, and instead were concerned to combat jointly the 'threat to the German nation' posed by different international groups such as 'Bolsheviks,' 'Freemasons' and 'Jews.'[22] In keeping with this pan-German attitude, Dollfuss ignored the conditions attaching to the Lausanne loan forbidding any political links with Germany, and tried to establish close contact with the German Reich. Furthermore, after the National Socialists had come to power in Germany, and in the face of increasing conflict with the banned Austrian Nazi Party, Dollfuss went on trying to achieve, within Austria itself as well as through diplomatic negotiations with Germany, a settlement with the National Socialists[23] – this in marked contrast to his policy with respect to the Social Democrats.

Thus, unlike others in government, Dollfuss did not try to conjure the kind of 'Holy Empire' described above, but his view of Austria was nevertheless a 'German' (deutschnational) one, in the sense of an incorporation of Austria, at whatever level of autonomy or sovereignty this might be, into a German nation; it was also 'German' in the sense of 'Austria's German mission' (formulated in cultural terms) in Eastern and South East Europe; it was 'German,' finally, in the sense of a Catholic mission inside 'Greater Germany.'[24] The propagation of the 'Austrian idea' occupied a major place in the official publications of the regime. For example, the Home Public Relations Office (Heimatdienst), the first propaganda organization of the Fatherland Front (Vaterländische Front), produced a publication[25] explaining that the growth of a new Austrian self-confidence was a reaction to the 'craving for conquest' shown by the National Socialist regime in Germany. This regime is there described as 'truly fanatical in its attempts firstly to realize Bismarck's idea of "Lesser Germany" (Klein-deutschtum),' that is, completing Prussian centralization by destroying the last vestiges of federal rights, and then 'secondly declaring Anschluss with Austria to be a simple problem of annexation,' thereby intending to enslave Austria ('as the Soviet Union had enslaved its independent farmers') and reduce it to 'the status of a territory occupied by the German Reich.' But since National Socialism was seeking to degrade Austrians 'to the level of serfs,' these latter had 'risen in noble revolt' and shown renewed faith in Austria's 'mission on behalf of Western civilization.'

The 'Austrian mission'[26] is still felt to be valid, designating Austria as 'at the centre of a unified western world sheltered by the peace of Christ.' There is no need to emphasize that 'Austria will never allow itself to be taken out of spiritual attachment to the whole German world: nothing and no one will achieve this, not even the one-time Austrian citizen Adolf Hitler in his battle against his former fatherland.' It is, indeed, 'because of its very loyalty to the idea of a Greater Germany' that Austria is denied any constitutional relationship to the National Socialist German Reich. But the more the Germans, under the leadership of the National Socialists, lose themselves in ideas of 'national self-sufficiency and isolation,' the more 'the German peoples beyond the borders of the Reich – and that means in the first instance the Austrian people – must become trustees for the German task, that of bringing peace to all nations for the sake of the western, indeed the entire, world.'

In similar vein the successor organization, the Austrian Department of Propaganda (Bundeskommissariat für Propaganda), brought out a document shortly after the murder of Dollfuss stating: 'It is Austria's calling to be the heart of a new Central Europe. Her geographical position determines this; her history provides the appropriate qualifications.' It is as a 'border state looking east and looking south that Austria made its historical mark.' But this is not to be understood simply in terms of defence, as the National Socialists mistakenly wish to see it; rather these borderlands were 'sallyports from which a superior culture could ride out to make its moral conquest of the enemy.' Central Europe must be 'organized,' but it is useless leaving the Little Entente (Kleine Entente) under the leadership of Beneš the dominant power there, and it would be equally disastrous to gather moral support for Austria's Central European mission by entering into Anschluss with the German Reich.

The Austrians' gift, developed over the years, of being 'natural middlemen and mediators,' as well as the 'small size' of the country, make it possible for 'Austria to become the nucleus of an organic union of states stretching from the Black Sea to the North Sea.' But since Austria is also a tribe (Stamm) of the great German nation, it could, 'especially if that nation were to show understanding, claim sufficient moral weight to justify its role as leader, and it could do this even given the realities of the political situation.' But this means that 'Austria will be permitted to "return home" to the Reich only if the whole German nation can be educated into accepting responsibility for the idea of a Central European Federation.' And it is here that the author sees 'Austria's destiny,' for it is the nature of the Austrians to offer that 'better kind of German character which could heal Europe.' Only if the 'Austrian idea' conquers Germany will the 'injustice of 1866 be expunged.' Then Seipel's words will be fulfilled: 'We want both things: Anschluss and the Danube Confederation.'[27]

Here I should like briefly to interpolate one of the many sets of guidelines issued by the Fatherland Front to be used in training its officials.[28] The starting point is the concept of nationality, understood not in terms of the State but as relating to the German Classical and Romantic idea of 'belonging to the same culture' (Kulturzugehörigkeit). 'Being German' (Deutschsein) is described as 'not so much' a question of the one's spoken language but rather one of 'knowledge, acceptance and confirmation of German

cultural values, German traditions, the German way of life . . .'
Those who use the German language merely as a 'vehicle of
communication' are not on that account 'German in the cultural,
that is noblest, sense of the word.' It follows 'quite logically from
this . . . that anyone who is a parasite (Schädling der Gemeinschaft), a habitual offender, a traitor to the cause (Treuloser)
cannot be a German, nor can'—and this is clearly directed against
the 'Jews'—'anyone who has no feeling for the German cultural
tradition and whose life consists in striving for profit and power.'

The 'truly German conception' of the state is that it 'has
grown organically out of smaller associations, like the individual
community.' In this context 'German' has always meant 'co-
operative, federalistic,' and so 'in its truly German sense' the state
consists in 'co-operation of the different tribes (Stämme) and
regions (Länder)' in contrast to the centralism of the French
Revolution and the 'centralist State' of National Socialism. 'The
truly German community' is one 'in which each of the basic
communal structures—family, community, professional groups—
has its natural place, and where the people in their entirety are felt
to be one large union, respecting and preserving the historic individuality of all its members.' For this reason, 'what is truly
German has its home and its future in Austria.'[29] For this reason,
too, Anschluss must be rejected.

The positive 'idea of the Austrian State' presented in these
guidelines derives from: (1) the geographical position of Austria,
as 'the land destined by its place at the centre to be independent';
(2) Austria seen from the 'world historical perspective as the cru-
cible in which Europe's historical development is being formed';
(3) Austria's mission as a 'cultural empire' which is not 'bounded
by physical frontiers,' and so is able to have an impact beyond
these'; (4) the 'German substance of the Austrian idea,' since 'no
German colonization has had such lasting effects as those achieved
by Austria—indeed, the whole of South America might have become 'German' in the time of Charles V had it not been for the
'discord brought about within Germany by the Reformation';
(5) the particular view of life and society implicit in the Austrian
idea.[30]

The complex of ideas propagated by the State and described (somewhat summarily without attention to nuances) as the 'Austrian mission' remained unaltered in essentials after Austrofascism became established. The 'Guidelines for training leaders,' to which I have just referred, appeared in 1935, that is, in the period following Dollfuss' death, when Austrian foreign policy showed increasing antagonism towards National Socialist Germany, and its domestic policy was hostile to the Austrian NSDAP. The 'Austrian mission' at this point still had the same basic ingredients: it was 'German,' and there was the task of leadership in the Danubian Lands. Of course, since the National Socialists had consolidated their dominance in Germany, the ideology of the 'pan-German' Reich now had to be formulated more reticentl:', indeed covertly, as a task of 'European' or 'Western' leadership.

Expressly stating in the preamble to the May 1934 Constitution that Austria was a 'German' federal state could only have 'racist' implications for the political organization of the corporate state, since non-German groups formed part of the population. There were, for example, bizarre manifestations in the Fatherland Front organization known as 'New Life' (Neues Leben) — modelled on the German 'Strength through Joy' (Kraft durch Freude) and the Italian 'After Work' (Dopolavoro) — which was set up by the Austrofascists to organize cultural and leisure activities: here the officials tried to ensure that they had 'very German' titles, like 'Sachwalter' for agent and 'Treuhänder' for trustee.[31] But 'German nationalism' within the Austrian State is most clearly visible in the attitude of public institutions and officials towards the non-German population of the country. Nonetheless, it is not my intention here to give a sketch of all the strengths and weaknesses of the Fatherland Front regime,[32] but merely to establish the discrepancy between the topos of 'the Austrians' as 'supranational' in their whole outlook — often the subject of exuberant praise — and the actual 'German' mentality displayed in the Austria of the corporate state.

So what we have is the Austrofascist regime opposing the National Socialist ideology of the Third Reich with its own

'Austria' ideology: in this, the history of the Habsburg monarchy is interpreted from the standpoint of the contemporary political situation, as is the history of the Holy Roman Empire of the German Nation, and this all implies the future establishment of a 'Holy Empire' (Heiliges Reich). Austria had, of course, been reduced by the conditions of the Treaty of St Germain to the level of a petty state, but this was seen as only a temporary situation, and the creation of the 'true Empire' was declared to be part of the 'Austrian mission.' This Austrian mission was to be a 'German' one on two counts. Firstly, in foreign policy, it was to establish a 'pan-German' Empire to embrace territories beyond those with a German population, and so 'universal'–if not in the sense of 'Western,' at least in the sense of 'Central European.' And secondly, the principles of the internal organization of this Empire would be specifically Austrian, where 'Austrian' meant 'pertaining to German Austria.' So, it implied Catholic Austria as opposed to Protestant Prussia or heathen National Socialism; it implied federalism (permitting the most substantial possible autonomy to the states within the federal structure) as opposed to centralism; and most important, it implied Vienna and Austria rather than Berlin and Prussia as the centre of the 'Empire.'

Expressed somewhat differently, the 'German' mission of Austria imposed two different tasks. In the first place, there was to be missionary activity within the German world to convert the 'worse' (i.e., National Socialist) Germans by the example of the 'better' Germans (i.e., Austrians, who were Catholic, 'more flexible' and allegedly at a higher cultural level). Secondly, by right of these virtues, the Austrian Germans were to assume the leadership of pan-Germanism and demonstrate that their 'German mission' embraced the concerns of Europe, indeed of the world. A variant of Austria's 'German mission' often appealed to was the 'mission of the Ostmark': this came essentially from the Catholic ideology of Empire found in the German Reich, and cast Austria in the role of agent for the interests of the Reich in Eastern and South East Europe. Even when the National Socialist regime in Germany was consolidating its power and there was growing opposition to it in

Austria, the idea of a 'mission of the Ostmark' in no way lost all the support it had enjoyed in Fatherland Front circles.

The Austrians' view that they were self-evidently Germans was, literally, very far-reaching and was not confined to conservative circles and the Austrofascist leadership. The basis for this view was the Austrian variant of the German ideology of race (Volkstumsideologie), and at its centre was a longing to be a people in the sense of a holistic, organic entity embodying 'a true sense of community.' This proclamation of the 'people as community' (Volksgemeinschaft) was the demand for an 'ideology of integration' to pit itself against what was seen as the 'unnatural' division of the people into political parties, in particular the various organizations of the socialist Labour Movement; the claim of the integrationists was that they would remove the tensions that existed between the 'classes created by nature.' Any dissatisfactions arising from social disharmony could then be clearly placed at the door of internal and external 'enemies,' as in the creation of the 'Jewish enemy.'

Anti-Semitism never became government policy during the period of Austrofascism and was never used as a political instrument by either the Dollfuss or the Schuschnigg regime. Nevertheless, anti-Semitism of an Austrian stamp, inherited from the time of the Monarchy and comprising religious, economic and fascist elements, was having an effect in the corporate state.[33] This can be seen, clearly and concisely, in an exposition of the 'Jewish question' prepared for a meeting of leading officials of the 'Ostmärkische Sturmscharen,' one of the paramilitary units (Heimwehr), in September 1936.[34] Here the 'Jewish question' is discussed at length. Thus, the 'Jewish mentality,' which is to be combatted, manifests itself in 'materialism, Marxism, Liberalism and the like' and has 'made its appearance in very recent times in the most varied attempts to revolutionize society and the state.' But 'beyond the Jewish circles so infected, broad sections of the community have become gripped by these ideas.' In the 'fight against these ideas and those who propagate them,' it is 'the Jewish question which is the main problem.' This can be solved as far as personnel are concerned by 'giving preference to native Austrians, to indigenous people whose roots in Austrian soil go back generations.' The 'principle must remain unshakeable' that 'neither conversion to Catholicism nor membership of one of the Fatherland associations (vaterländische Verbände) can of itself without further proofs give someone rights in this matter.' The consequences are:

> 1. The need to promote cultural activity to replace alien ideas with the spirit of the Storm Company (Sturmschar).
> 2. Taking account of the above when appointing to office, giving commissions, establishing welfare institutions, buying and selling on the money market etc.
> 3. Ensuring that leadership in our political, cultural, economic and social life is conferred only on those who come from the indigenous population and alone are qualified for such office.

At the beginning of 1936, soon after the promulgation of the 'Nuremberg Race Laws' in the German Reich, Leopold Kunschak published the text of a draft bill which he had produced as early as 1919, and which might now be used to set up a special law governing the 'Jews' in Austria. The 'Jewish nation' was to be declared a national minority and separated off from the 'German majority'; a quota system would operate in public service, certain professions and business enterprises, limiting entry for 'Jews' to their proportion of the total population; they would have special bodies to represent them politically, and their culture would be served by their having their own schools.[35] This bill did not become law, but it is an indication of the anti-Semitic climate of the age that Kunschak published it precisely in 1936, when in 1919 Ignaz Seipel, despite thinking that the law was 'politically feasible,' had advised against its publication because this was 'the wrong momment.' What is also clear is the way in which the regime now tolerated the anti-Semitic activities of its paramilitary units, and the discrimination being surreptitiously practised against Jewish fellow-citizens. The hostility to Jews once again manifesting itself in Austria today can be explained as the continuation both of a more or less covert National Socialist tradition and of aspects of the 'Austria' ideology propounded by Austrofascism.

In 1918 the Austrians had lost their German domination in the Austrian half of the Austro-Hungarian Empire. The First Republic suffered from economic, political and military impotence. The prejudice inherited from the time of the Monarchy that 'German culture' was the superior culture continued. It is understandable given these circumstances that the 'Austrian mission' should become a 'cultural' one, to be understood in terms of a 'cultural imperialism.' This position is largely responsible for the appeal to legitimism, which was not, however, directly integrated into the 'Austria' ideology of the corporate state. The expansionism implicit in this 'cultural' German nationalism did not, of course, exclude political ambitions, however unrealistic these might have been. If we interpret this Austro-Catholic variety of pan-Germanism as an ideology of the dispossessed hoping to regain their lost position, we can see that this presented the Austrofascist regime with an insoluble problem: it supported an ideology and a political programme which it could not put into effect without the help of its declared foreign enemy, the National Socialist German Reich.

There can be no doubt that the corporate state intended to use the 'Austria' ideology to ward off moves towards Anschluss with the German Reich. In assessing the defensive power of this ideology, we must come to the conclusion that it could not hope to succeed. This is not simply another way of saying that the National Socialist policy of Anschluss won the day, but rather of recognizing the weaknesses of the Austrian position as a rival to National Socialism in pursuit of similar goals: social policy, the creation and organization of a great Empire, leadership of the German people (Deutschtum), fostering the 'German tradition' (deutsches Volkstum) at home and abroad. The fulfilment of such hopes must have made the power-political base of the German Reich appear vastly more attractive than the modest potential of the small Austrian state. Indeed, the 'Austria' ideology was not able to strengthen existing Austrian patriotic tendencies among its own supporters. The complicated intellectual formulations of the ideology of the corporate state did not exactly help to promote it on the broadest front. Furthermore, insistence on Austria's belonging to the German nation did not help early attempts (like those by Ernst Karl Winter) to give expression to an Austrian national identity, but rather, if anything, tended to suppress them. A further problem was using the 'Austria' ideology to create a combined front against National Socialism, since many who rejected National Socialism also opposed Austrofascism. That they did so was understandable, since the 'Austria' ideology simultaneously provided legitimation for the internal political take-over by the Fatherland Front, the event which excluded from all political involvement broad reaches of the population which before 1933 had been represented by the various parties of the Labour Movement.

This anti-democratic rivalry with the National Socialists was called 'Austrian' but was, in fact, 'German and racist' (deutschvölkisch). In emphasizing its Catholic orientation, the 'Austrian' position was certainly different from the 'neo-paganism' of the National Socialists, and it was this that maintained the short-lived Austrian dictatorship. But it was also this course which provided a kind of, albeit involuntary, preparation for the Anschluss and the establishment of National Socialist rule in Austria. Supporters of the 'pan-German' creed of the 'Austria ideology,' particularly those who were 'Catholic nationalists,' in fact played a role in the destruction of Austria's independence as a state in 1938, or at the least co-operated temporarily with German fascism. The suppression, internment and murder of representatives and officials of the Austrian dictatorship during the National Socialist regime's reign of terror did not occur because of absolute differences in their political goals, but because the National Socialist victors were pitiless in their cruelty towards their defeated rivals.

NOTES

1. This paper consists of a shortened montage of my essays: "Austro-faschistische 'Österreich'-Ideologie" in: E. Talos / W. Neugebauer (eds), *'Austrofaschismus.' Beiträge über Politik, Ökonomie und Kultur 1934–1938*, 4th edition (Vienna: Verlag für Gesellschaftskritik, 1988); "Zu den Bemühungen katholischer Jungakademiker um eine ständisch-antiparlamentarische und deutsch-völkische Orientierung der Christlich-sozialen Partei" in: E. Fröschl / H. Zoitl (eds), *Februar 1934. Ursachen –Fakten–Folgen* (Vienna: Verlag der Wiener Volksbuchhandlung, 1984).

2. St. Hanzer, "Die Zeitschrift *Das neue Reich* 1918-1925. Zum restaurativen Katholizismus nach dem ersten Weltkrieg," Diss., Vienna 1973. For the later period see H. Busshoff, *Das Dollfuß-Regime in Österreich in geistesgeschichtlicher Perspektive unter Berücksichtigung der 'Schöneren Zukunft' und 'Reichspost'* (Berlin: Duncker & Humblot, 1968 = Beiträge zur politischen Wissenschaft, vol. 6). In particular see P. Eppel, *Zwischen Kreuz und Hakenkreuz – die Haltung der Zeitschrift 'Schönere Zukunft' zum Nationalsozialismus in Deutschland 1934-1938* (Graz: Böhlau, 1980 = Veröffentlichungen der Kommission für neuere Geschichte Österreichs, vol. 69).

3. K. Breuning, *Die Vision des Reiches–deutscher Katholizismus zwischen Demokratie und Diktatur (1929-1934)* (Munich: Hueber, 1969).

4. A. Staudinger, "Monarchie oder Republik? Christlichsoziale Partei und Errichtung der Republik" in: "Aspekte christlichsozialer Politik 1917-1920," Postdoctoral diss., Vienna 1979.

5. For treatment of the debate within the Christian Social Party on this point of policy see A. Lüer, "Die nationale Frage in Ideologie und Programmatik der politischen Lager Österreichs 1918-1933," Diss., Vienna 1985.

6. A. Staudinger, "Christlichsoziale Partei und Errichtung des 'Autoritären Ständestaates'" in: *Vom Justizpalast zum Heldenplatz* (Vienna: Verlag für Geschichte und Politik, 1975).

7. *Das Christlichsoziale Parteiprogramm, mit Erläuterungen von R. Schmitz* (Vienna: Volksbundverlag, 1932), pp. 61-70.

8. A. Wandruszka, "Österreichs politische Struktur–die Entwicklung der Parteien und politischen Bewegungen" in: H. Benedikt (ed.), *Geschichte der Republik Österreich* (Vienna: Verlag für Geschichte und Politik, 1954), p. 411.

9.  H. Srbik, *Gesamtdeutsche Geschichtsauffassung* (Leipzig/Berlin: Teubner, 1932). See on this topic H. Dachs, *Österreichische Geisteswissenschaft und Anschluß 1918-1930* (Vienna/Salzburg: Geyer-Edition, 1974 = Veröffentlichungen des Historischen Instituts der Universität Salzburg).

10. J. Nadler, *Literaturgeschichte der deutschen Stämme und Landschaften,* 3rd edition (Regensburg: Verlag Josef Habbel, 1929-1932); Nadler, *Das Stammhafte Gefüge des deutschen Volkes* (Munich: Kösel & Pustet, 1934). On Nadler see S. Meissl: "Zur Wiener Neugermanistik der dreißiger Jahre: Stamm, Volk, Rasse, Reich – über Josef Nadlers Literaturwissenschaftliche Position" in: K. Amann / A. Berger (eds), *Österreichische Literatur der dreißiger Jahre. Ideologische Verhältnisse, institutionelle Voraussetzungen, Fallstudien* (Vienna/Cologne/Graz: Böhlau, 1985), pp. 130-146.

11. H. Hirsch, "Deutsches Königtum und römisches Kaisertum" in: H. Srbik / J. Nadler (eds), *Österreich, Erbe und Sendung im deutschen Raum* (Salzburg/Leipzig: Verlag Anton Pustet, 1936), pp. 43-60.

12. O. Spann, *Der wahre Staat. Vorlesungen über Abbruch und Niveau der Gesellschaft* (Leipzig: Quelle & Meyer, 1921). On Spann see K. J. Siegfried, *Universalismus und Faschismus. Das Gesellschaftsbild Othmar Spanns – zur politischen Funktion seiner Gesellschaftslehre und Ständestaatkonzeption* (Vienna: Europaverlag, 1974).

13. Among them Dr Wilhelm Wolf, Dr Joseph Pessel, Dr Josef Lehrl, Prof. Ernst Klebel, Dr Ernst Lagler, Dr Taras Borodajkewicz, Dr Karl Lechner, Dr Karl Rudolf, Dr Anton Böhm, Dr Eugen Kogon, Dr Fritz Flohr, Prof. Reinhold Lorenz, Walter Ternik, Dr Theodor Veiter, Josef Klaus, Ernst Marboe, Franz Riedl, Peter Graff.

14. Dr Karl Lugmayer and Karl Rehor.

15. On this point see A. Staudinger, "Zu den Bemühungen katholischer Jungakademiker," above n. 1.

16. "Grundlagen und Ziele völkisch-staatlicher Neugestaltung. Programm junger Katholiken," Sammlung Veiter, of which a photocopy exists in the Institut für Zeitgeschichte, Vienna.

17. These are extracts from a programme which was propagated in its entirety – albeit with occasional minor variation, toning down or camouflage – by members of the most important Catholic youth organizations. They wrote in the youth section of the *Reichspost* under the heading 'Der junge Strom' (tide of youth). This supplement was published first on 9 June 1932 and then once a month to begin with,

later every fortnight, but after 1934 no longer regularly and also much reduced in size. Its editor was Theodor Veiter, who was at that time an official of the Christian Social parliamentary party (Bundesratsklub) and held a leading position in the German Catholic Students' Union of Austria (Katholisch-deutsche Hochschülerschaft Österreichs). As already mentioned, he was active in the compilation of the programme under discussion.

18. H. Hantsch, "Österreichische Staatsidee und Reichsidee" in: *Österreichische Rundschau. Land – Volk – Kultur*, 1/1 (1934), 6–15. The piece was printed almost without alteration in: *Der katholische Staatsgedanke. Bericht über die katholisch-soziale Tagung der Zentralstelle des Volksbundes der Katholiken Österreichs am 29. und 30. April 1934 in Wien* (Vienna, 1934), p. 59–68. It also appeared in slightly modified form in: *Österreich. Volk und Staat* (Vienna: Österreichischer Bundesverlag, 1936), pp. 40ff.

19. *Allgemeiner deutscher Katholikentag Wien 1933, 7. bis 12. September* (1934), 59–64.

20. Breuning, above n. 3, *Die Vision des Reiches*, pp. 259ff.

21. G. Jagschitz, "Die Jugend des Bundeskanzlers Engelbert Dollfuß— Ein Beitrag zur geistig-politischen Situation der sogenannten 'Kriegsgeneration des Ersten Weltkrieges,'" Diss., Vienna 1967, pp. 140ff.

22. W. Rosar, *Deutsche Gemeinschaft. Seyss-Inquart und der Anschluß* (Vienna: Europaverlag, 1971), pp. 29ff. Among the members of the 'Deutsche Gemeinschaft' were the Christian Social politicians Emmerich Czermak, Viktor Kolassa and Richard Wollek; the university professors Niward Schlögel, Kurt Knoll, Wilhelm Czermak, Othmar Spann, Oswald Menghin, Alfons Dopsch; the aristocrats Aloys Schönburg-Hartenstein, Edgar Hoyos; the lawyers Arthur Seyss-Inquart, Gustav Steinbauer.

23. On this point see esp. D. Ross, *Hitler und Dollfuß. Die deutsche österreichpolitik 1933–1934* (Hamburg: Leibniz, 1966); also G. Jagschitz (with Alfred Baubin), *Der Putsch. Die Nationalsozialisten 1934 in Österreich* (Graz/Vienna/Cologne: Styria, 1976), pp. 56ff.

24. Many examples are given by E. Weber (ed), *Dollfuß an Österreich – Eines Mannes Wort und Ziel* (Vienna/Leipzig: Reinhold, 1935 = Sonderschriften der Berichte zur Kultur- und Zeitgeschichte, vol. 10).

25. *Österreichs Sendung. Unseres Vaterlandes Schicksalweg* (Vienna, 1933 = Schriftenreihe des österreichischen Heimatdienstes), p. 4f.

26. Ibid., pp. 14f.

27. A. Klotz, *Sturm über Österreich* (Vienna: Verlag der Wiener Zeitung, 1934), pp. 53ff.

28. *Richtlinien zur Führerausbildung,* published by the Vaterländische Front/Bundeswerbeleitung, Vienna, 1935.

29. Ibid., pp. 108–116.

30. Ibid., pp. 125–140.

31. Allgemeines Verwaltungsarchiv (AVA), Vaterländische Front, Karton 34, "Die Titelfrage im VF-Werk 'Neues Leben,'" 23 September 1936.

32. For the legal position and the norms laid down see Th. Veiter, *Das Recht der Volksgruppen in Österreich* (Vienna/Stuttgart: Wilhelm Braumüller, 1970). On the position of the Slovenes see Hans Haas / K. Stuhlpfarrer, *Österreich und seine Slowenen* (Vienna: Löcker, 1977), pp. 67–73. On the Czechs see K. M. Brousek, *Wien und seine Tschechen – Integration und Assimilation einer Minderheit im 20. Jahrhundert* (Vienna: Verlag für Geschichte und Politik, 1980 = Schriftenreihe des Österr. Ost- und Südosteuropa-Institutes, vol. 7).

33. S. Maderegger, *Die Juden im österreichischen Ständestaat 1934–1938* (Vienna/Salzburg: Geyer-Edition, 1973 = Veröffentlichungen des Historischen Instituts der Universität Salzburg).

34. AVA, Heimatdienst, Karton 14.

35. L. Kunschak, "Zur Judenfrage" in: *Neue Ordnung,* 1936, pp. 20–22. This draft bill is also published in: A. Pelinka, *Stand oder Klasse? Die christliche Arbeiterbewegung Österreichs 1933–1938* (Vienna: Europaverlag, 1972), pp. 297–300; also in A. Staudinger, "Christlichsoziale Judenpolitik in der Gründungsphase der österreichischen Republik" in: *Jahrbuch für Zeitgeschichte 1978* (Vienna: Löcker, 1979), pp. 40–42. It was this same Leopold Kunschak who in 1920, when he was Chairman of the Christian Social Party, demanded in the National Assembly that 'if the Jews could not be expelled and would not go voluntarily, they should immediately be interned in concentration camps.' Speech on 29 April 1920. See the typed record of the 'Konstituierende Nationalversammlung,' p. 2382. On anti-Semitism in the Christian Workers' Association see Pelinka, pp. 213–233.

# Anti-Semitism and the Austrian Nazi Party

Bruce F. Pauley

Peter G.J. Pulzer was undoubtedly correct when observing in his classic work, *The Rise of Political Anti-Semitism in Germany and Austria,* that the "main difference between the political anti-Semitism of the post- and pre-World War I periods lies not in its content but in its success."[1] Put another way, it changed quantitatively but not qualitatively after the Great War.[2] Nevertheless, there were new excuses for anti-Semitism during and especially just after the war and again after the onset of the Great Depression; anti-Semitic rhetoric became shriller and acts of violence against Jews became far more commonplace.

The Austrian Nazi party was far from having a monopoly on anti-Semitism in the First Austrian Republic, especially prior to about 1930. It was, however, ultimately the most successful party in exploiting traditional Austrian anti-Semitism as well as current events and problems in which Jews were associated or at least alleged to be associated. In doing so the Austrian Nazis employed mostly the traditional techniques of anti-Semites ranging from attacks on the alleged cultural influence of Jews to boycotts. Their solutions for the Jewish "problem" were equally shopworn and included such things as reducing Jewish representation in the professions and academic life to their proportion of Austria's (or Vienna's) population and expelling the Jews or at least the Jewish newcomers from Eastern Europe.

## Anti-Semitism in the German Workers' Party

The prewar Austrian Nazi Party or German Workers' party (*Deutsche Arbeiterpartei* or DAP), as it was known until 1918,

25

was not particularly vociferous in its opposition to Jews. Although the party had been founded in Bohemia in 1903, it was not until 1913, when its Iglau program was drafted, that anti-Semitism was even mentioned. Even then the program merely made the rather unexceptional assertion that the party would "'combat . . . the ever-increasing Jewish spirit in public life.'"³

During and immediately after the war the Austrian Nazis, who started calling themselves the German National Socialist Workers' party in May 1918, began to intensify their anti-Semitic message, as indeed did all of Austria's non-Marxist parties. Rudolf Jung, a Bohemian, the party's principal theorist, wrote an article during the war calling for the nationalization of monopolies, de-partment stores, and large landed estates that were not the prod-uct of 'honest work,' a disguised form of anti-Semitism.⁴ Jung was also most responsible for drawing up a new program for the party in August 1918 which opposed "'all alien influences, but above all . . . the parasitic power of the Jewish trading spirit in all spheres of public life.'" In particular the predominance of Jewish banks in Austria's economy had to be eliminated.⁵ Shortly after the war the party's leading newspaper, the *Deutsche Arbeiter-Presse,* put *Judenherrschaft* (Jewish domination) at the top of a list of evils the Party opposed.⁶

A major driving force behind the party's anti-Semitism, al-most from its founding, was one of its early leaders, Dr. Walter Riehl, who, like Jung, was from the party's original heartland in northern Bohemia. To be sure, anti-Semitism was not at the center of Riehl's political *Weltanschauung* the way it was for such bour-geois radical nationalists as Georg von Schönerer,⁷ the pan-German fanatic whose career in the Austrian *Reichsrat* peaked in the 1880s. Nor did Riehl resemble the adult Hitler in refusing even to associate with Jews socially.⁸ Still, as his early biographer, Alexander Schilling, noted, Riehl related almost all of Austria's problems, foreign and domestic, to Jews.⁹

Riehl's primary demand with regard to the Jews was one which could be found in all of Austria's interwar parties: the political, cultural, and economic "predominance" of the Jews had to be reduced to its proportion of the country's total population, roughly three percent.[10]

Even though Riehl's anti-Semitism was less extreme than that of either Hitler or Schönerer, he was far from being regarded as innocuous by Viennese Jews who bore the brunt of his fiery oratory. For *Die Wahrheit,* the organ of the capital city's liberal and acculturated Jews, Riehl was the "embodiment of wild street terror and violent racial anti-Semitism. . . . He was the personification of unredeemed hatred and bitter enmity toward Jews."[11]

## Nazi Demonstrations and Violence in the Early Republic

The minuscule size of the Austrian Nazi party in the early 1920s—its membership had reached only 34,000 by August 1923[12]—condemned it to relative obscurity in the anti-Semitic developments of early postwar Austria. Between the summer of 1918 and the spring of 1923 Vienna witnessed numerous anti-Semitic outbursts. These included mass demonstrations similar to those which occurred in Berlin and Munich at the same time.[13] In these demonstrations the Austrian Nazis play a leading role, or at least claimed to do so.[14] Angry demands were made at these rallies by politicians for the expulsion or incarceration of recent Jewish immigrants who had fled to Vienna from Galicia during the war in advance of the Russian Army. In 1915 there had been as many as 125,000 destitute Jewish refugees in Vienna, but by shortly after the war the number was down to no more than 25,000.[15] Nevertheless, as late as 1932 Austrian Nazis claimed in their election posters that there were over 300,000 Jewish immigrants who had been made Viennese citizens since the beginning of the war.[16] At one such rally in September 1920 Dr. Riehl asserted that Vienna's housing problem could be solved by the expulsion of 200,000 *Ostjuden.*[17] During the 1920s there were also assaults on Jewish-looking pedestrians and streetcar passengers. In none of these events were Nazis acting alone, however. Many of the participants came from the Greater German People's party (*Großdeutsche*

*Volkspartei*) or GDVP, which was founded in 1920 out of seventeen prewar pan-German and anti-Semitic organizations. Other demonstrators came from the 'non-partisan' League of Anti-Semites (*Antisemitenbund*) or AB, the paramilitary Front Fighters Association (*Frontkämpfervereinigung*), or FKV, and the right wing of the Christian Social Party (CSP), particularly its Workers' Association (*Arbeiterverein*) led by Leopold Kunschak. Not until 1923 when the Nazis first appeared at the Technical Institute (*Technische Hochschule*) in Vienna[18] and began their brutal assaults on Jewish students did they attract much attention.

One early instance of Nazi violence directed against Jews occurred in August 1923. Julius Streicher, the infamous Jew baiter from Nuremberg, spoke at a Nazi meeting in Vienna. In one two-hour speech he claimed that Jews alone profited from the World War, whereas all non-Jews had to be considered conquered peoples. Streicher furthermore repeated the medieval legend of Jewish ritual murder and warned the women and girls in the audience about the Jewish "white slave trade." Any German woman or girl who had any sexual contact with a Jew would be lost to the German people. The effect of one of Streicher's speeches was illustrated when one of his listeners hit a Jewish-looking pedestrian in the face following the meeting.[19]

The Nazis first succeeded in pushing their way to the forefront of the Jewish question in 1925. In that year Hugo Bettauer, a Jewish convert to Protestantism and author of the best selling novel *Die Stadt ohne Juden. Ein Roman von Übermorgen* (*The City without Jews. A Novel from the Day after Tomorrow*), as well as the editor of the allegedly pornographic magazine *Er und Sie,* was murdered in March by a young man named Otto Rothstock who until shortly before had been a member of the Austrian NSDAP. None other than Walter Riehl volunteered to defend the confessed killer because the latter had acted out of "purely idealistic reasons." After a sensational trial Riehl managed to gain a split verdict for the accused which prompted the *Deutsche Arbeiter-Presse* to call Rothstock a martyr for the German people. Rothstock's only punishment was to serve a mere two-and-a-half years in mental hospitals.[20]

The Austrian Nazi Party as a whole was first able to achieve real notoriety in the demonstrations which accompanied the holding of the Fourteenth World Zionist Congress in Vienna in August. Although the Nazis were far from being the only anti-Semites to protest against the Congress they did comprise the largest as well as the noisiest single group.

The pro-Nazi *Deutsch-Österreichische Tages-Zeitung* (*Dötz*) warned its readers that no fewer than 30,000 Jews, 25,000 of whom were despised *Ostjuden,* would be attending the Congress,[21] even though the organizers themselves expected no more than 6,000 delegates to attend.[22] The *Deutsche Arbeiter-Presse* was even more hysterical, at one time predicting that 50,000 Jews would attend the Congress, thus placing the Aryan girls and women of Vienna in great danger.[23] The *Dötz* claimed that 100,000 Viennese turned out to protest the Congress on 22 August; 6,000 policemen were needed to protect the delegates, thus turning the city into an armed camp. Walter Gattermayer, the leader of the Nazis' trade union and one of the speakers at the mass rally boasted that the anti-Semites had succeeded in reducing attendance at the Congress from 30,000 to only 4,000.[24]

What neither Gattermayer nor the *Dötz* mentioned was that the chairman of the Austrian Nazi party, Karl Schulz, as well as representatives of other anti-Semitic groups, had secretly promised the Vienna Chief of Police, Johannes Schober, that they would influence their followers not to disturb the Congress in order to prevent any damage to Vienna's economy and the good reputation of the city.[25]

## Academic Anti-Semitism

For Austria as a whole, the second half of the 1920s saw a definite decline in the number of outbursts of anti-Semitism. Not coincidentally these were also the years in which the Austrian economy made some modest improvements following the economically catastrophic breakup of the Habsburg Monarchy. The one major exception to this rule was Austria's institutions of higher education, where violent racial anti-Semitism, already strong before the World War and always stronger than in Germany, continued almost unabated.[26] In October 1925 *Die Wahrheit* reported that Nazi students had been covering so many walls of Vienna's *Hochschulen* with hate propaganda that the Chancellor's Office of the University of Vienna was finally forced to ban such notices as well as anti-Semitic books and pamphlets from academic property.[27]

During observances in November 1927 celebrating the founding of the Republic, Nazi students with the help of thirty SA men attacked the predominantly Jewish Socialist Student Association at the University of Vienna. After ten minutes eight Jewish students had to be carried away to receive first aid while the Nazi students triumphantly sang a party song. This episode was merely the first of a series of eight pitched battles (*Krawalle*) at the University in which Nazi students destroyed Jewish kiosks, disrupted lectures by Jewish professors, captured and held campus security agents prisoner for hours at a time, issued ultimata, and besieged Chancellor Theodor Innitzer's office.

Meanwhile, over a two-year period the National Socialist League of Students (NS *Studentenbund*) distributed 100,000 propaganda leaflets, held a dozen mass meetings, and organized countless "lecture evenings" (*Sprechabende*). By such "heroic" tactics the Nazi students attracted 2,000-3,000 followers by the beginning of 1930 and made themselves the "masters" (*Herren*) of one of the world's most distinguished universities.[28]

These developments were but a prelude to Nazi student activities during the 1930s. The Great Depression, which hit Austria harder than any other industrialized country in the world, only aggravated the already intense competition for virtually nonexistent jobs in the professions. By Jewish reckoning Jews in 1936 accounted for 62 percent of Vienna's lawyers and dentists, 47 percent of its physicians, over 28 percent of its university professors, and 18 percent of its bank directors. Ninety-four percent of the city's advertising agencies were also Jewish. (On the other hand, there were many areas where Jews were underrepresented, as in the civil service and school teaching.)[29] Thus gentile students were tempted to conclude that their passport to success was to join the Nazi Party and to help drive the Jews out of the country or at least reduce their "influence" to their proportion of the population.

Consequently, Austrian universities not just in Vienna, but also in Innsbruck and Graz became virtual battlefields during the 1930s with Jewish students being by far the most common objects of the students' demonstrations. One such episode at the University of Vienna in 1931 resulted in eighteen Jewish students being seriously injured. They were individually attacked by "students" armed with steel rods and rubber truncheons. Some female students were thrown down stairs. These attacks continued without interruption from 10:00 in the morning until 3:00 in the afternoon. Posters outside the University's main building read "*Juda verrecka*" (death to the Jews) and "Jews are forbidden to enter."[30] Another well-organized Nazi-led riot occurred at the University of Vienna and the *Technische Hochschule* after the Constitutional Court of Austria declared *Studentenordnung* (passed by the University of Vienna's Academic Senate), dividing students into "nations" (including one for Jews), to be unconstitutional.[31]

Nazi students did not bother to discriminate between which Jewish students they attacked. Consequently, American and other foreign Jews studying at the College of Medicine at the University of Vienna also fell victim to anti-Semitic outrages. The American League for the Protection of Foreign Studets in Vienna repeatedly protested attacks on American students, as did the American embassy and diplomatic representatives from Poland, Bulgaria, and Yugoslavia. After four American students of Jewish origins were injured in a student riot in October 1932 the University's chancellor issued a formal apology to the American ambassador.[32]

## The Great Depression and the Resurgence of the Austrian Nazi Party

Except for a few outbursts of street violence against Jews in the first five postwar years of high inflation and low employment, anti-Semitic outrages had been confined almost exclusively to academic corridors during the 1920s. By October 1929 *Die Wahrheit* had become so confident about the declining significance of Nazi anti-Semitism that in its 4 October issue it said that "we Austrian Jews have outlasted many anti-Semitic movements including the now finished Nazis."[33]

This relatively happy state of affairs proved to be all too short-lived. The Great Depression raised the already high number of unemployed to over 600,000 and caused the collapse of Vienna's two great Rothschild banks, the *Bodencredit* and the *Creditanstalt*. The crash undermined the belief that Jews were particularly gifted in financial affairs and encouraged anti-Semites to believe that anti-Jewish actions could be taken without harm to the economy.[34]

The economic catastrophe, combined with the impact of the impressive Nazi electoral victory in September 1930, helped the Austrian Nazis to garner over 201,000 votes in the municipal elections in Vienna compared to just 27,500 in 1930. By June of 1932 Nazi youths sometimes attacked people in the streets of Vienna who simply looked Jewish.

One particularly ugly incident occurred in October 1932 when forty Nazis, claiming they had been attacked by Jews while they were peacefully walking down a street, stormed a coffee shop which Jews used for prayers. Shouting *"Juda verrecka"* they destroyed window panes and furniture. Further damage was prevented when members of the recently organized League of Jewish Front Fighters (*Bund jüdischer Frontsoldaten*) came to the rescue.[35] Attacks by Nazis on Jewish individuals and businesses continued throughout the winter of 1932–33, until the Jewish jeweler, Norbert Futterwelt, was killed in June 1933,[36] one of the Nazi acts of terror which led to the outlawing of the Party on the 19th.[37]

The degree of violence, including homicide, which the Austrian Nazis were willing to employ and not simply discuss, surpassed the physical intimidation used by their bourgeois rivals and predecessors. Likewise, their anti-Semitic propaganda *as a whole* was more extreme in its content and rambunctious in its techniques than anything Austrians had seen before the World War.

On the other hand, there was little if anything new in the specific charges which Nazis leveled against the Jews nor even in their "solutions" to the Jewish "problem." The Nazis' opposition to "Jewish capitalism" could also be found in the country's Social Democratic Workers' Party or SDAP. The attacks on the Jewish leadership of the SDAP had long since been made by the Christian Social Party, and the paramilitary *Heimwehr,* the GDVP, and the *Antisemitenbund* had long been fond of accusing the Jews of materialism. All non-Jewish political groups in the Alpine republic charged that Jews dominated the Viennese press and cultural life. Even the Nazis' racism had for many years been a part of the programs of Georg von Schönerer, the GDVP, the AB, and parts of the *Heimwehr.* The Nazis merely combined all these existing forms of anti-Semitism and used them to hold together their very heterogeneous membership as well as to attract new followers.

As a matter of fact, the Nazis went out of their way to prove that their anti-Semitism was *not* something new or unique. The *Deutsch-Österreichische Tages-Zeitung* announced at least as early as 1926 that the greatest thinkers of all nationalities had been anti-Semites.[38] The Nazis' Office for the Handling of the Jewish Question sent out a long list of anti-Semitic quotations by great German intellectuals as well as statements by Jewish leaders which could be used by Nazi speakers and newspapers.[39] A disguised Nazi weekly newspaper, *Der Stürmer* (not to be confused with Julius Streicher's paper of the same name), which began publishing soon after the outlawing of the Austrian Nazi party in June, asserted that hatred of Jews dated back to ancient times and existed wherever Jews had lived. Even the American automobile manufacturer, Henry Ford, subscribed to the principle, as did the Ku Klux Klan.[40] *Die Wahrheit* pointed out that many of the Nazis' favorite quotations from Goethe, Herder, Luther, Moltke, Bismarck, Voltaire, etc., had been taken out of context and did not take into account temporary moods, historical circumstances, or even later changes of mind.[41] But few Nazis had such critical insight and even fewer read *Die Wahrheit*! Austrian Nazi newspapers also liked to publish false quotations from the *Talmud* and other Jewish works but would have to retract them a few months later.[42]

In a similar way the Nazis looked for confirmation of their anti-Semitic views in an authoritative source such as a pastoral letter by the bishop of Linz, Johannes Gföllner, written in January 1933, in which he claimed that Jews had a harmful influence on almost all aspects of modern culture, including law, medicine, the press, the theater, and the cinema. They were also responsible for capitalism, socialism, and communism. It was not just the right, but also the duty of Christians to stop the spread of this Jewish "spirit."[43] Nazis were careful to avoid mentioning that the bishop also said it was impossible to be both a good Catholic and a Nazi. Nor could they have been pleased when later in the same year the entire Austrian episcopate denounced Gföllner's letter for arousing social hatred and conflict.[44] Four years later, however, the Nazis' gained new ammunition for their propaganda when another Austrian bishop, Alois Hudal, wrote that Nazi racism was compatible with Christianity as long as fundamental Christian dogmas were not violated.[45]

### Scandalmongering: The Austrian Nazis, the Cinema, and the Press

The Nazis were particularly incensed about two aspects of cultural life in Vienna, where Jewish influence was especially strong: the cinema and the press. The percentage of Jews involved in these fields was undoubtedly high and thus gave a certain plausibility to the complaints of Nazis and other anti-Semites, as was also true in Germany.[46] For example, an estimated 70 percent of the city's cinemas were owned by Jews.[47] Nazi anger with American "Jewish" films and the Viennese Jewish cinemas which showed them reached its peak in the winter of 1930–31; several weeks of demonstrations by perhaps as many as 10,000 Nazis and other anti-Semites against the movie *All Quiet on the Western*

*Front,* which allegedly "ridiculed the memory of 2 million dead German soldiers," resulted in several people being injured, considerable property being destroyed, and the picture finally being banned.[48]

As for the press in Vienna, an English author in 1913 estimated that no less than 75 percent of the city's journalists were Jewish.[49] After the war the Nazis claimed that twenty-two of the city's newspapers were in Jewish hands and that "Jewish" newspapers had a daily circulation of 1.3 million compared to only 400,000 for the nine "purely German" papers.[50]

As usual, these Nazi allegations failed to tell the whole story. In reality only a few small Viennese newspapers such as *Die Wahrheit* and *Die Stimme* had an exclusively Jewish readership and supported issues of concern to their readers. The major Viennese newspapers which had Jewish editors or reporters, such as the *Neue Freie Presse,* for which the founder of modern Zionism, Theodor Herzl, worked around the turn of the century, simply ignored Jewish questions. They differed from "Aryan" newspapers only in (usually) refraining from supporting anti-Semitism.[51] Moreover, Jewish journalists were hardly monolithic in their political views. Some even wrote for newspapers that were notoriously anti-Semitic.[52] These considerations did not prevent one Nazi author from complaining that "at no time in history has so small a group of foreigners been able to exercise the unlimited domination the way the Jewish press has and does today."[53]

While railing against the "Jewish press" the Nazis privately fumed about the willingness of the Viennese to read the hated Jewish newspapers and were frustrated by their own financial woes, which in the 1920s made the purchase of a single typewriter a major expense and the payment of phone bills a constant problem.[54] Even in the (for them) more affluent 1930s their newspapers were poorly written and confined largely to party affairs. The rapid growth of dues-paying members meant better times for the party's press in the early 1930s. The NSDAP's social heterogeneity, which was far greater than that of any other party in either Austria or Germany, continued to be a serious problem, however, making it difficult for any paper to satisfy the literary and intellectual tastes of peasants, industrial workers, and professional people at the same time.[55]

A favorite solution to this dilemma was to report on crimes and scandals, especially those involving Jews.[56] Early examples of this can be found in the unofficial Nazi newspaper, *Der eiserne Besen*, which was published in Salzburg and Vienna. Its speciality was private sex scandals involving Jews. It frequently charged Jews with ritual murder and went so far as to implicitly call for the physical destruction of the Jews in Europe.[57]

In Graz, *Der Kampf*, the official organ of the NSDAP in Styria, accused a Jewish-owned clothing firm by the name of Rendi of failing to pay income taxes and investing the money in Switzerland. Stories about the scandal dominated the papers' headlines for several weeks.[58] Such articles could sometimes boomerang, however. When *Der Kampfruf*, the party's official mouthpiece in Vienna, warned its readers against patronizing the Phönix Insurance Company because it had Jewish directors, the newspaper was flooded with angry letters from the company's non-Jewish employees who complained that a boycott would threaten their jobs. The Austrian Nazi press chief soon advised the editors of the *Kampfruf* to publish an apology.[59] The Phönix Insurance Company was the focus of a genuine scandal a few years later, however, in 1936 when the business collapsed because of faulty speculations thus presenting anti-Semites with a propaganda bonanza.[60]

The *Deutsch-Österreichische Tages-Zeitung* in Vienna was still another Nazi newspaper which enjoyed relating horror stories about Jews. One article claimed that an "Aryan" country girl had just been lured into the house of a Jew and threatened with bodily harm. She was seriously injured after trying to escape by jumping from a second-story window. A whole Jewish band of abductors was at work but the authorities were silent about it, the headlines screamed.[61] Another piece told about the conviction of a Jewish child molester. "Jewry is conducting a systematic, tenacious fight against the morally upright German people. Sexual revolutionaries everywhere preach verbally and in writing Jewish morality and achieve it, at least with part of the Marxist *Untermenschen.* . . ."[62]

The ultimate Jewish scandal, so far as the Nazis were concerned, was the *Protocols of the Elders of Zion.* Written for the benefit of the Russian secret police in 1905, the *Protocols* were first published in German in 1920. The Nazis claimed that many of the *Protocols'* prophecies had already come true.[63] Despite numerous articles in *Die Wahrheit* showing that the *Protocols* were crude forgeries,[64] it was not until 1935 that a trial in Basel, Switzerland definitely proved their bogus nature.[65] Meanwhile, Nazi newspapers, especially *Der Stürmer* continued to maintain their authenticity, claiming the proof was in the content.[66]

An old tactic of anti-Semites which dated back to at least the time of Mayor Karl Lueger (1897–1910) was the boycotting of Jewish stores. Such attempts were particularly common during the Christmas season but had little success, at least before the end of 1932.[67] *Der eiserne Besen* began publishing the names of Jewish shops together with the names of "Aryans" who patronized them already in the early 1920s, a practice resumed by the illegal *Österreichischer Beobachter* in 1937. The Nazis also posted placards enumerating "Aryan" shops and pasted stickers on Jewish shop windows saying "Don't buy from Jews."[68] None of these actions, however, made much of an impression on Christian shoppers who still preferred Jewish stores because of their generally lower prices or because they were unwilling to break the habit. Moreover, even partially successful boycotts damaged the Austrian economy and cost Christians their jobs.[69] Not until Nazis began throwing small bombs into Jewish shops in late 1932 and early 1933 did non–Jewish shoppers become frightened.[70]

## Nazi Solutions to the "Jewish Problem"

When it came to actual solutions to the alleged Jewish problem, the Nazis had nothing whatsoever new to offer. Indeed, neither the Austrian nor German Nazis themselves had any preconceived plans about how to deal with the Jews once they came to power. The Nazis' anti-Semitic policies in Germany after Hitler's *Machtergreifung* "developed largely through internal ideological and political processes and continually caught the German Jews by surprise because it was not developed with any relevance to them save that they were hurt by it and ultimately killed by it."[71]

Austrian Nazi leaders, like those in Germany, issued statements at different times and in different places, which could be anything from blood curdling to fairly moderate. As early as June 1925 the *Deutsche Arbeiter-Presse* demanded that Vienna's second district, Leopoldstadt, be made a ghetto for all Viennese Jews as a prelude to their being expelled from the country.[72] Walter Riehl, when he entered Vienna's city council in 1932, demanded the expulsion of the Jews from the city.[73] On the other hand, the normally fire-breathing *Stürmer,* perhaps with an eye to the government's censors, stated in October 1933 that it rejected a violent solution to the Jewish problem.[74] One Nazi author, Dr. Erich Führer, writing in 1935, insisted that "no seriously-thinking anti-Semite who is familiar with the latest research wants the return of the ghettoes or the yellow star. A new time demands new viewpoints. From this [assumption] the Jewish problem of Austria can and will be solved in a satisfactory way."[75]

One solution which many Nazis as well as other anti-Semites sometimes supported was Zionism. The Zionist ideas that the Jews were a separate nationality which could not and should not assimilate into the non-Jewish population and that they ought to have separate schools and be allowed to emigrate to Palestine or Madagascar in order to establish a state of their own were all applauded by many Nazis.[76] *Der Stürmer* also warmly endorsed the idea of the Jews having their own schools and taxes as proposed by Emmerich Czermak, a former minister of culture and leading CSP member, and Oskar Karbach, a Zionist author, in their book, *Ordnung in der Judenfrage: Verständigung mit dem Judentum* (Vienna, 1933).[77]

Probably the favorite solution to the Jewish question which the Nazis and nearly all other anti-Semites advocated was proportional representation. If Jews made up 9.4 percent of the Viennese population, as they did in 1934, then they should be limited to that same ratio in such fields as commerce, law, medicine, banking, and higher education. Of course, the Nazis were willing to count as Jews only those who professed to be Jews and not the inflated number of "ethnic" Jews they estimated to be living in Vienna. Moreover, the ratio was to be imposed only where the Jews were unusually numerous, not where they were grossly underrepresented.[78]

After the Anschluß was consummated in March 1938 Austrian Nazis were no longer satisfied with such modest solutions. Robert Körber, one of the most prolific writers and speakers on behalf of "scientific" racial anti-Semitism who had already proposed in 1924 that citizenship be based on language and race,[79] renewed his demand in 1939 in a book entitled *Rassensieg in Wien:*

> Those states which are enemies of Germany and friends of the Jews appeal to our sympathy. But the Gauleiter of Vienna was right when he declared on 14 July 1938 that "this foreign press" was silent during all those years when we were tortured and cheated, sucked dry and raped. . . . They have no moral right to speak about things which concern only us.
>
> Sympathy for Jews means advancing the demands of the arch-enemy of the people. Whoever has taken a conscientious (*pflichtbewußten*) look into the . . . last five years knows that what is involved here is not normal people, but instead Jewish criminals, a criminal group of people who for hundreds of years have been seeking the destruction and death of our Volk by the most cruel and inhuman means, without actually declaring war. One can have no sympathy for criminals; criminals deserve a just punishment. And this punishment is restitution and separation (*Ausscheidung*)."[80]

### Anti-Semitism as a Unifying Element

Anti-Semitism was undoubtedly a major cause of the success enjoyed by the Austrian Nazi party after 1930. Walter Riehl, in commenting on the Nazi breakthrough in the local elections of April 1932 said that most bourgeois voters "did not understand the true nature of our movement. They valued only our anti-Semitic and above all our anti-Marxist positions. . . . The whole Aryan intelligentsia and a large part of the academic and higher civil servants have voted for us as well as many businessmen and architects."[81] These social groups all faced direct economic competition from Jews and were highly anti-Semitic.

Politically, the Nazis also enjoyed their greatest success with precisely those parties who were the most ardently anti-Semitic. In the same local elections of April 1932 to which Walter Riehl referred above, the Greater German People's Party, which at the very least equaled the Nazis in the intensity of its anti-Semitism, saw its vote in Vienna decline from 124,400 in 1930 to 8,800. In Lower Austria the combined vote of the GDVP and the Peasant League (*Landbund*) dropped from 70,100 in 1930 to 28,000 in 1932.[82] The other Nazi votes came mostly at the expense of the *Heimwehr* and the right-wing of the CSP, both of which were also highly anti-Semitic, if somewhat less so than the GDVP. Consequently, between 1930 and 1934 the Nazis absorbed virtually all of the pan-German and ultra-anti-Semitic Right in Austria just as they did in Germany.[83]

Although the conservative bourgeois camp had many differences with the Nazis, especially the CSP on church-state relations, anti-Semitism was not one of them. Not even Nazi brutality toward Jews was terribly disturbing to them except when it threatened the tourist industry.[84] On the contrary, anti-Semitism was a strong common denominator among right-wing groups in Austria and was a major part of the ideological glue which united the highly socially heterogeneous NSDAP in both Austria and Germany.[85] Anti-Semitism served a similarly unifying function in Poland between the wars.[86] It is doubtful whether any other single issue in Austria, even the hated Treaty of St Germain, appealed to so large a cross-section of the Austrian population as anti-Semitism.

In competing with other anti-Semitic organizations the most important advantage the Nazis enjoyed after January 1933 was that their comrades in Germany were actually doing something about the "Jewish problem" whereas Austrian anti-Semites had seldom done anything except talk. In the Reich Jewish influence had actually been eliminated from the civil service and cultural life of the country, and German Jews had been deprived of their full citizenship rights.

Of course, anti-Semitism should not be used as an all-encompassing explanation for Nazi electoral successes. Anti-Semitism had been part of the Austrian Nazi ideology since 1913 and a very important part since 1918; yet it was not until the Great Depression hit Austria, and the NSDAP began to enjoy an astonishing series of electoral successes in Germany, that the Austrian NSDAP began its rapid growth. Moreover, as Walter Riehl suggested, the party's anti-Marxism was also an important key to its success in a country with the largest (per capita) and most powerful Marxist party outside the Soviet Union.[87] Still, the Nazis' anti-Semitism found widespread support in interwar Austria simply because it was very much in accord with a long-standing tradition dating back to the Middle Ages.[88]

## NOTES

The following acronyms have been used in the notes:

| | |
|---|---|
| AVA | Allgemeines Verwaltungsarchiv; General Administrative Archive (Wien) |
| BKA | Bundeskanzleramt; Federal Chancellery (Wien) |
| *DAP* | *Deutsche Arbeiter-Presse* (Wien) |
| *Dötz* | *Deutschösterreichische Tages-Zeitung* (Wien) |
| K. | Karton; carton |
| NS-P | Nationalsozialistische Parteistellen, Gau Wien; National Socialist Party documents, Gau Vienna (located in the AVA) |

1. (New York: John Wiley & Sons, 1964), p. 300.
2. John Bunzl and Bernd Marin, *Antisemitismus in Österreich: Sozial-historische und soziologische Studien* (Innsbruck: Inn-Verlag, 1983), p. 40.
3. M. W. Fodor, *Plot and Counterplot in Central Europe* (London: Harper & Brothers, 1939), p. 163.
4. Rudolf Brandstötter, "Dr. Walter Riehl und die nationalsozialistische Bewegung in Österreich" (Ph.D. Dissertation, Universität Wien, 1970), pp. 137-138.
5. F. L. Carsten, *Fascist Movements in Austria: From Schönerer to Hitler* (London/Beverly Hills: Sage Publications, 1977), p. 35.
6. 16 October 1920, p. 1.
7. Andrew G. Whiteside, *Austrian National Socialism before 1918* (The Hague: Martinus Nijhoff, 1962), p. 104.
8. Willi Frischauer, *The Rise and Fall of Hermann Goering* (New York: Ballantine Books, 1951), p. 43.
9. *Dr. Riehl und die Geschichte des Nationalsozialismus* (Leipzig: Forum Verlag, 1933), p. 96.
10. Brandstötter, "Riehl und die NS Bewegung," p. 19.
11. "Er ist die Verkörperung des wüsten Straßenterrors, des gewalttätigen Rassenantisemitismus. . . . Er ist die Personifizierung unauslöschlichen Hasses und erbitterter Feindschaft gegen uns Juden." 8 April 1927, p. 1.
12. Gerhard Botz, "The Changing Patterns of Social Support for Austrian National Socialism," in Stein U. Larsen, *Who Were the Fascists: Social Roots of European Fascism* (New York: Columbia University Press, 1980), p. 204.
13. Theodore Abel, *Why Hitler Came to Power* (Cambridge, Massachusetts and London: Harvard University Press, 1986; originally published in 1938), p. 156.
14. See, for example, the *DAP* for 4 and 11 October 1919 and 4 September 1920, all p. 1.
15. "Die östjüdischen Kriegsflüchtlinge in Wien (1914-1923)," (Hausarbeit aus Geschichte, Universität Salzburg, 1978), p. 14.
16. "Deutsche Beamten und Angestellten," 4 September 1931, AVA, NS-P, K. 14 (Plakat Entwürfe), p. 2.
17. *DAP*, 4 September 1920, p. 1.
18. Helga Zoitl, "Kampf um Gleichberechtigung. Die sozialdemokratische Studentenbewegung in Wien, 1914-1925" (Ph.D. Dissertation, Universität Salzburg, 1976), p. 405.

19.  Letter of (Johannes) Schober to the BKA, Abteilung 14, 1 September 1923, AVA, BKA Inneres 1923, doc. 52.921, 4 pages.
20.  For details about the Bettauer case see Murray G. Hall, *Erotik und Hakenkreuz auf der Anklagebank. Der Fall Bettauer* (Wien: Löcker Verlag, 1978). The quotations are cited by Hall on pp. 95, 125.
21.  8 August 1925, p. 5. Nazi posters were less modest in their estimates claiming that 50,000 Jews were about to "invade" Austria. See *The Times*, 20 July 1925, Central Zionist Archives (Jerusalem), Z4/214/6.
22.  Letter of (Johannes) Schober to the BKA, Abteilung 14, 15 July 1925. AVA, BKA Inneres 1925, K. 32, doc. 103.533, 2 pages.
23.  25 July 1925, p. 2; 11 July 1925, p. 1.
24.  *Dötz*, 23 August 1925, p. 1.
25.  Letter of (Johannes) Schober to the BKA, Abteilung 14, 15 July, AVA, BKA Inneres 1925, K. 32, doc. 103.533, 2 pages.
26.  Pulzer, *Rise of Anti-Semitism*, p. 248.
27.  23 October 1925, p. 1.
28.  Letter of Leopold Tlimef (Wien) to Gauleiter Alfred E. Frauenfeld, 23 April 1930, AVA, NS-P, K. 5 (Gauleiter A. E. Frauenfeld, Korrespondenz, 1930-33), 5 pages. See also *Die Wahrheit* (Wien), 15 November 1929, p. 4.
29.  Sylvia Maderegger, *Die Juden im österreichischen Ständestaat 1934–1938* (Wien and Salzburg: Geyer Edition, 1973), p. 220. *Die Wahrheit* estimated in 1923 that 60 out of 230 professors at the University of Vienna were Jewish (15 July, p. 11).
30.  *Die Stimme* (Wien), 3 July 1931, p. 7.
31.  *Arbeiter-Zeitung* (Wien), 24 June 1931, p. 5; 25 June 1931, p. 4.
32.  Ibid., October 1932, p. 2; *Dötz*, 29 October 1932, p. 3.
33.  "Wir österreichischen Juden haben schon so manche antisemitische Bewegung überdauert — gerade der obige Hinweise auf unsere Hakenkreuzler, deren Macht heute erledigt ist, beweist die Stichhaltigkeit unseres Optimismus. . . . ," p. 24.
34.  Letter of J. H. Furth to the present author, 24 June 1979, p. 5.
35.  *Stimme*, 6 October 1932, p. 1. On the BJF see *Drei Jahre Bund Jüdischer Frontsoldaten Österreichs* (Wien: Selbstverlag der BJF, 1935).
36.  Letter of Braudi (Wien) to the BKA, Generaldirektion für die öffentliche Sicherheit, 4 November 1932, AVA, BKA Inneres 1932, K. 32 doc. 231.208, p. 5; Erika Weinzierl, "Antisemitismus in Österreich," *Austriaca* (July 1978), 316.
37.  *Arbeiter-Zeitung*, 13 June 1933, p. 1.

38. *Wahrheit,* 5 February 1926, p. 1.
39. Mitteilung für die Redner, Rednerbriefe, Presse und das Anschlagwesen, Amt für die Bearbeitung der Judenfrage, January 1933, AVA, NS-P, K. 5 (Gauleiter A. E. Frauenfeld, Korrespondenz, 1930-33), 3 pages.
40. *Der Stürmer* (Wien), 19 August 1933, pp. 1, 3; 16 September 1933, p. 3.
41. 5 February 1926, p. 1.
42. *Wahrheit,* 21 November 1929, p. 9.
43. Georg Glockemeier, *Zur Wiener Judenfrage* Leipzig/Wien: Günther, 1936), p. 106.
44. Friedrich Heer, *Gottes erste Liebe: 2000 Jahre Judentum und Christentum. Genesis des österreichischen Katholiken Adolf Hitler* (München: Bechtle, 1967), pp. 363-365.
45. Jonny Moser, "Von der antisemitischen Bewegung zum Holocaust," in Klaus Lohrmann (ed.), *1,000 Jahre österreichischisches Judentum* (Eisenstadt: Edition Roetzer, 1982), p. 257.
46. Donald L. Niewyk, *The Jews in Weimar Germany* (Baton Rouge/London: Louisiana State University Press, 1980), p. 4.
47. Glockemeier, *Wiener Judenfrage,* p. 109.
48. "diese Beschimpfung des Frontsoldatentums, diese Schändung des Andenkens von zwei Millionen Weltkriegstoten....," *Dötz,* 5 January 1931, p. 1; 10 January 1931, p. 1; *Stimme,* 8 January 1931, p. 1.
49. Henry W. Steed, *The Hapsburg Monarchy* (New York: Charles Scribner's Sons, 1913), p. 184. See also Robert Schwarz, "Antisemitism and Socialism in Austria, 1918-1962," in Josef Fraenkel, *The Jews of Austria: Essays on their Life, History and Destruction* (London: Vallentine, Mitchell, 1967), p. 446.
50. Pressebroschure von Gau Wien, AVA, NS-P, K. 16 (Propagandamanuskripte); *Wahrheit,* 15 July 1923, p. 11.
51. *Wahrheit,* 6 December 1929, p. 1.
52. Arthur J. May, *The Hapsburg Monarchy, 1867-1939* (Cambridge, Massachusetts, Harvard University Press, 1951), p. 177.
53. Dr Erich Führer, "Antisemitismus im neuen Österreich" in Robert Körber and Theodor Pugel, *Antisemitismus in Wort und Bild* (Dresden: M. O. Groh, 1935), p. 192.
54. *Der Kampfruf* (Wien), 2 May 1931, p. 1; *Arbeiter-Zeitung* (Wien), 28 January 1926, p. 1.
55. Karl Jung, "Die völkische Presse in Österreich" in Karl Wache (ed.) *Deutscher Geist in Österreich* (Dornbirn: Verlag C. Burton, 1933), pp. 345-346.

56. Roland V. Layton, "The *Völkischer Beobachter*, 1920-1938: The Nazi Newspaper in the Weimar Era," *Central European History* (1970), 377.

57. Ernst Hanisch, "Zur Frühgeschichte des Nationalsozialismus in Salzburg (1913-1925)" in *Mitteilungen der Gesellschaft für Salzburger Landeskunde* Bd. 117 (1977), 374-375; [Jakob Ornstein], *Festschrift zur Feier des 50 jährigen Bestandes der Union österreichischer Juden* (Wien: Union, 1937), p. 22.

58. 8 and 15 August, 26 September 1931.

59. Landespressechef Haintz (Linz) to J. Müller (Wien), 16 January 1933 and several attached letters, AVA, NS-P, K. 8 (*Der Kampfruf*, Redaktion).

60. Carsten, *Fascist Movements in Austria*, pp. 285-286.

61. 24 September 1932, p. 5.

62. "Das Judentum führt bekanntlich einen planmässigen, zähen Kampf gegen das sittliche hochstehende deutsche Volk. Sexualrevolutionäre predigen überall in Wort und Schrift die jüdische Moral und erreichen es, zumindest bei einem Teil der marxistisch verblödeten Untermenschen....," ibid., 7 October 1932, p. 8.

63. Pressebroschüre von Gau Wien, AVA, NS-P, K. 16 (Propagandamanuskripte).

64. Hermann Holzmann, "Antisemitismus in der österreichischen Innenpolitik 1918-1938. Der Umgang der drei politischen Lager mit diesem Phänomen" (Universität Wien, Diplomarbeit, 1986), pp. 81-82.

65. [Ornstein], *Festschrift der Union österreichischer Juden*, p. 14.

66. 14 October 1933, p. 5.

67. *Der jüdische Weg* (Wien), 28 December 1932, p. 1; [Ornstein], *Festschrift der Union österreichischer Juden*, p. 18.

68. Hanisch, "Frühgeschichte des Nationalsozialismus in Salzburg," p. 375; "Ihre Existenz ist in Gefahr," AVA, NS-P, K. 14 (Organisation, Prozesse), 4 September 1931; Carsten, *Fascist Movements*, pp. 284-285; *Stimme*, 22 December 1932, p. 1.

69. Maderegger, *Juden im österreichischen Ständestaat*, p. 244.

70. *Jüdischer Weg*, 28 December 1932, p. 1.

71. Herbert S. Levine, "The Jewish Leadership in Germany and the Nazi Threat in 1933" in Carole Fink, et al. (eds.), *German Nationalism and the European Response, 1890-1945* (Norman, Oklahoma and London: University of Oklahoma Press, 1985), p. 205.

72. 6 June 1925, p. 1.

73. *Kampfruf*, Sonderdruck, June 1932 (unnumbered page).

74.  14 October 1933, p. 1.
75.  "Kein ernst denkender und in den Ergebnissen neuester Forschungs-
     arbeit geschulter Antisemit wünscht eine Wiederkehr des Ghettos oder
     des gelben Fleckes. Eine neue Zeit erfordert neue Gesichtspunkte. Von
     diesen ausgehend kann und wird das Judenproblem Österreichs in
     zufriedenstellender Weise gelöst werden. "Antisemitismus im neuen
     Österreich" in Körber and Pugel (eds.), *Antisemitismus in Wort und
     Bild,* p. 204.
76.  Glockemeier, *Wiener Judenfrage,* p. 121; [Ornstein], *Festschrift der
     Union österreichischen Juden,* p. 29; *Stürmer,* 2 September 1933, p. 2.
77.  11 November 1933, p. 1.
78.  *Stürmer,* 30 December 1933, p. 2; 2 June 1934, p. 2; *Juden im öster-
     reichischen Ständestaat,* p. 197; Führer, "Antisemitismus im neuen
     Österreich," p. 202.
79.  "Richtlinien und Motivenbericht für ein Rahmengesetz zur rechtlichen
     Regelung und Lösung der Judenfrage" (by R. Körber), AVA, NS-P,
     K. 5.
80.  "Deutschfeindliche Mächte und Freunde der Juden rufen jetzt unser
     'Mitleid' mit ihnen an, da sie doch auch Menschen seien. Mit Recht
     erklärte der Gauleiter von Wien am 14. Juli 1938, daß 'diese Auslands-
     presse' geschwiegen hat, als wir all die Jahre hindurch vom Judentum
     gequält und betrogen, ausgesaugt und vergewaltigt. . . . Sie hat daher
     kein sittliches Recht, über Dinge zu sprechen, die uns und nur uns
     angehen. . . . Mitleid mit Juden, heißt die Erzfeinde des Volkes för-
     dern! Wer pflichtbewußten Einblick in die Dinge der Vergangenheit und
     der letzten fünf Jahre genommen hat, weiß, daß es sich hier nicht um
     normale Menschen, sondern um jüdische Verbrecher, um eine ver-
     brecherische Menschengruppe handelt, die seit Jahrhunderten ohne
     offene Kriegserklärung als heimtückisches Freischarlertum die Vernich-
     tung und den Tod unseres Volkes mit den grausamsten und unmen-
     schlichen Mitteln als Hauptzweck ihres Daseins anstrebte. Mit Ver-
     brechern hat man kein Mitleid, Verbrecher muß man der gerechten
     Strafe zuführen. Und diese Strafe lautet: Wiedergutmachung und Aus-
     scheidung." *Rassensieg in Wien: Der Grenzfeste des Reiches* (Wien:
     Wilhelm Braumüller, 1939), pp. 298–299.
81.  "Die meist bürgerlichen Stimmen genau genommen zum Teil irrtümlich
     abgegeben wurden, weil die Leute die wahre Natur unserer Bewegung
     nicht kennen und nur die antisemitische und vor allem antimarxistische
     Einstellung schätzen. . . . Nicht nur die gesamte arische Intelligenz und

gerade ein Großteil der akademischen und höheren Beamten uns gewählt hat, sondern merkwürdigerweise vom Gewerbe- und Kaufmannsstand besonders Architekten, Baumeister. . . .” Letter of Riehl (Wien)
to Alfred Proksch (Linz), 26 April 1932, Bundesarchiv in Koblenz,
Sammlung Schumacher, 305, II, p. 1.

82.  Gerhard Botz, “The Changing Patterns of Social Support for Austrian
     National Socialism (1918-1945)” in Larsen, et al. (eds.), *Who Were the
     Fascists?* p. 212.
83.  Heinrich Benedikt (ed.), *Geschichte der Republik Österreich* (Wien:
     Verlag für Geschichte und Politik, 1954), p. 405.
84.  Günter Fellner, *Antisemitismus in Salzburg 1918-1938* (Wien/Salzburg: Veröffentlichungen des Historischen Instituts der Universität
     Salzburg, 1979), p. 188.
85.  John Bunzl and Bernd Marin, *Antisemitismus in Österreich: Sozio.
     historische und soziologische Studien* (Innsbruck: Inn-Verlag, 1983), p.
     53; Hugo Valentin, *Antisemitism Historically and Critically Examined*
     (New York: The Viking Press, 1936), p. 120.
86.  Celia S. Heller, *On the Edge of Destruction: Jews of Poland between
     the Two World Wars* (New York: Schocken Books, 1977), p. 77.
87.  For comparisons with Germany see Ian Kershaw, “Ideology, Propaganda and the Rise of the Nazi Party” in Peter Stachura (ed.), *The Nazi
     Machtergreifung* (London: George Allen & Unwin, 1983), p. 168 and
     Niewyk, *Jews in Weimar Germany,* p. 80.
88.  Gerhard Botz, “The Jews of Vienna from the Anschluß to the Holocaust” in Oxaal, et al. (eds.), *Jews, Antisemitism and Culture in Vienna,*
     p. 202.

# Support for the Corporate State and National Socialism in the Socially Weaker Groups, 1934-1938

## Helmut Konrad

The four-year period in Austria prior to the Nazi take-over and the subsequent incorporation of the country into Germany can be viewed as a historical phase, during which society was fragmented into three groups of more or less equal strength. What this meant was that the ruling Austrofascists could not depend on a majority, since at most only one third of the country supported them. In numerical terms the balance was held by the opposition groups – the illegal Social Democrats, and the National Socialists, whose party was also banned for much of the period. Each grouping had roughly the same number of supporters without necessarily having the same chance of gaining power.

Although by no means homogeneous and certainly possessing strong regional variations, the social profiles[1] of the three 'camps' can be fairly clearly delineated:

(a)  The supporters of the corporate state recruited from the old ruling élite, from the bureaucracy (state and provincial), other sections of officialdom, the Catholic 'petite bourgeoisie' and the farmers.

(b)  The National Socialist camp drew a clear majority from students, minor employees, lower grade civil servants (who could either escape from the control of the corporate state or who were looking for a second string to their bow alongside the 'official' option), the new middle class, the rural proletariat and the unemployed.

(c)  The strength of the illegal Socialist Movement lay with the working class and certain sections of the unemployed, but it could count on higher than average support from intellectuals, many but by no means all of whom were Jews.

In broad terms this meant that in the period 1934–1938 the line dividing support for the corporate state from that for National Socialism is least clear among civil servants and small tradesmen; the line dividing support for National Socialism from that for the Socialist Movement is least clear among young activists and the unemployed. This explains the goals of Nazi propaganda, since it took them till after 1938 to make major inroads into the ranks of the farmers and industrial proletariat. In a country where there had been no recovery after the world economic crisis but where the economy had largely stagnated, the term 'socially weaker groups' covers a wide range and one whose boundaries are often fluid. These groups consist in the main of industrial workers, many of whom were unemployed, smallholders and the rural unemployed. At the same time, it must not be forgotten that many skilled workers actually earned more than white-collar workers and the self-employed, or that with the smallholders there were important differences within the group according to where they were living—a nearby town, for example, could change the picture. I intend to devote the major part of this paper to the two larger groupings, examining their political allegiances and their receptiveness or resistance to National Socialist ideas, and also to considering the extent to which National Socialism fulfilled their expectations after March 1938.

## The Rural Lower Classes

Between the wars Austrian Social Democracy was almost exclusively an urban movement.[2] If we ignore Otto Bauer's *Fight for Woods and Fields*[3] and the work of certain individuals like Laurenz Genner,[4] then the 'rural proletariat,' who were numerically significant even in the final decades of the Habsburg monarchy, remained a closed book for the socialist industrial proletariat. It therefore comes as no surprise that for those in country districts who were completely destitute the only political options available between 1934 and 1938 were to accept the corporate state or join the National Socialist opposition. To begin with, we have to note that in village life political behaviour has traditionally been determined by way of the Church. However, Catholicism did not run equally deep in all parts of Austria: there were, and still are, areas where reversion to Protestantism was, and is, possible – especially the Salzkammergut, but also areas only superficially reconverted to Catholicism during the Counter Reformation, such as Upper Styria and large tracts of Carinthia. (Tales of Lutheran bibles hidden in the walls of farmhouses in the 'Nockgebiet' of Central Carinthia[5] are still told today and may well have substance.) For the most part, however, it was the Catholic Church which determined life in the villages. If there was going to be opposition to the existing order (either at the level of the village or the state), its motivation would be anticlerical. It is no accident that in villages during the years preceding 1938 there was opposition between the schoolmaster and the priest, with the teacher representing the once liberal tradition of the Kulturkampf, which during the 1880s had turned into pure German nationalism with strong anti-Semitic overtones.[6]

Gains made by National Socialism among the rural socially weaker groups may be put down to at least seven factors:

1. In all those districts where the major upheavals of the inter-war period – the large debts acquired by many farmers, the increase in compulsory auctioning off of farms, the 'influx of the unemployed from other areas causing disruption in local working conditions'[7] – had shattered the old order, there was resistance to the rigid hierarchy of village life.

2. Dependent agricultural labourers, who had been overlooked by social law reforms, lived in exactly the same conditions as they had in pre-industrial times. For example, in the province of Salzburg only 6% of male farmhands and 4% of the women employed were married.[8] Living conditions were sub-human: sleeping quarters in the cowshed, attics without any form of heating etc. This provided considerable potential for social conflict.

3. The number of illegitimate children in rural areas was

particularly high. This was a direct result of the obstacles to marriage created by rural social conditions existing with the support of the Church. Unmarried mothers, in a society controlled by the Church, were disadvantaged, the children themselves had nothing like the opportunities open to farmers' children born in wedlock.[9]

4. It was mainly the smaller farmers and smallholders of the inter-war period who had first given in to the pressures of modernization, and then in the 1930s, finding the markets for their produce disappearing, could barely or no longer meet their debts. For them, National Socialism seemed to offer the chance of a new social status, of modernization in planned stages and of larger markets.

5. The close links between the state and the Catholic Church re-awakened dormant traditions of protest which were directed against Viennese centralism. Hans Kloepfer, the poet of Styria, still highly respected today, praised Hitler as a man 'you don't find better anywheres,' but particularly as the man who got rid of 'those big crooks in Vienna'[10] – a tone that was bound to appeal in Upper Styria.

6. As a result of occurrences in many country districts, particularly southern Austria, during 1918 and 1919, people there felt threatened by encroaching Slavs. Hermann Pferschy wrote in 1937: 'We stand where stood our forbear / so long, long ago / this land is German through our pains / and may it long remain so.'[11] Xenophobia was easy to whip up among these countryfolk, particularly in areas near the border or where two languages were spoken, and the peasantry with its own 'Blood and Soil' notions were very susceptible to certain aspects of National Socialist ideology.

7. In Austria there is a deep-rooted 'religious' anti-Semitism, which can be traced back continuously across the centuries and still exists today.[12] This traditional rural Christian prejudice then came to coincide with anti-urban attitudes ('Jewish' immorality of the big city) as well as with anti-progressive and anti-Marxist positions.[13] It is the reason for an 'anti-Semitism without Jews' found in many country areas of Austria before 1938.[14] This lack

of Jews was certainly no impediment to the success of National Socialism, even if the anti-Semitism which led to the holocaust possessed several further elements. However, that a form of anti-Semitism based on social Darwinism could be used for political purposes was possible only because of the long tradition stated above.

Yet clearly rural areas were not the main recruiting ground for Austrian National Socialism prior to 1938. The majority of the rural population remained adherents of Catholic and conservative standpoints until then. Even so, with a few 'progressive farmers' [Fortschrittsbauern],[15] a few farmhands and servant girls, plus a few from the minor artisan class and lower ranks of the educated middle class, a modest foothold was gained. After they had gained power in 1938, the National Socialists achieved broad support in rural areas, which they admittedly lost during the War. Despite the contradictions which characterize this support,[16] it must be recognized that the total number of NSDAP members drawn from among farmers and agricultural workers offers no real testimony to the party's popularity. The wave of support in country districts began when the party was already limiting membership.

In several economic sectors, National Socialism brought genuine improvement for a short period at least. The price that the individuals concerned had to pay was almost impossible for them to assess. This was all the more true for country areas, where political communication functioned in a very limited way. Since this remained the case after the Second World War, we still find stereotypical positive reactions to National Socialism on particular issues. The most important of these are:

1. The 'writing off of debts' [Entschuldungsaktion], as it is still called, even though it was in actual fact merely a rescheduling of debts. Here we must note that the world economic crisis, together with high interest rates in Austria, had created serious financial difficulties for farmers: between 1933 and 1937, 71, 135 farms (i.e. 16.7% of the total number) were auctioned, with 114,513 hectares coming under the hammer (equivalent to half the total agricultural land in Vorarlberg).[17] So rescheduling of

debts under National Socialism offered real hope. As soon as you had put in your request for rescheduling, you were safe from compulsory auction, and in many districts two-thirds of all the farmers applied.[18] All previous debts would then be transformed into long-term credits, usually scheduled for repayment over 51 years and to be paid off at the rate of one-half percent of the debt per annum at an interest rate of four-and-a-half percent.[19] This provided appreciable financial relief.

2. The 'law pertaining to property held in a family for a certain number of generations' [Reichserbhofgesetz], which applied to farms of between 7.5 to 125 hectares (i.e. the majority of Austrian farms, not including smallholdings), laid down that such farms could not be parcelled or mortgaged.[20] This meant that any children without rights of inheritance were grossly disadvantaged, their chance of receiving training and financial support, or of being offered a home if need arose, depending on the economic strength of the farm.'[21] In fact, the stability of so many farms depended on the unpaid work of the dispossessed children. Nonetheless, in general the security and self-confidence of farmers increased.

3. The incorporation of Austria into Germany increased the size of the market for Austrian farm produce, and also gave the benefit of increased prices, particularly in timber. Farmers today still tell you that 'when Hitler came, things were good for farmers ... You could sell every apple and every pig.'[22] 'Before, you had to try and sell a few cans of milk in the town. With Hitler things were different. You just took it all along to the dairy, and they bought every drop.'[23] It was not simply the size of the market but the improved market infrastructure that convinced the farmers, just as it created a picture of National Socialism that still exists in people's minds today.

4. The German Reich was also far ahead of the corporate state when it came to mechanization, and the Anschluss gave a boost to agricultural mechanization in Austria. In 1933 there were only 753 tractors in Austria, but between March 1938 and March 1940, 2,000 new tractors were handed over.[24] The trend was

halted by the War, but overall one can say that in 1939 the number of machines doubled. This was done at relatively low fixed prices, and because sales of agricultural produce were assured, the farmers could pay for the machines quickly:

> My neighbour . . . drove a few apples down and handed them over. They all went to Germany. On the way home he was able to buy an iron plough with the money he'd got for the apples . . . Today machines are so dear. Under Hitler they were cheap, really cheap. That'll never happen again, not for the farmers . . . Farmers'll never get the opportunities again that they had then.[25]

5. After March 1938, the poorer sections of rural society were given the chance to leave their villages and thus break free from their conditions of servitude. 'What was significant about this "flight from the land" [Landflucht] was the speed with which it happened and the level it reached within the space of a single year.'[26] The move to the towns, caused by the establishment of new industries, especially in armaments, sent up the price of agricultural labour, and even financial inducements could not slow the process down. Finally, particularly during the War, the problem had to be dealt with through the introduction of foreign or forced labour.

But despite all this, the NSDAP never became the farmers' party. In Catholic rural areas, resistance (in part caused by the hostility of the National Socialists towards the Church) always remained greater than in other social sectors, and was exceeded only by that of industrial workers, with their different tradition and quite different reasons for apathy towards National Socialism.

## Industrial Workers and the Unemployed

Austria did not experience that division within the working-class movement that occurred in many countries as a result of the

First World War. Certainly a Communist Party was founded, but whilst it was legally permitted up to 1933,[27] it was in terms of numbers of no real significance. It never, for example, won a seat either in Parliament or on the Vienna Municipal Council. The Austrian Social Democrats, on the other hand, could point to a membership of about 10% of the total population.[28] Almost every second person entitled to vote was thus an actual member of this the strongest political party in the country.[29] Higher still, after 1929, was the number of members of the Independent Trades Union,[30] and so it can certainly be said of the Austrian working class between the Wars that it was represented by Social Democratic organizations.

If we are to judge the political behaviour of industrial labour and the unemployed during the period of the corporate state, then we have to take into account the basic starting position of the Social Democrat Party – which was outlawed in February 1934 – because it was this party which had largely created the self-awareness and political culture of the working-class sector. Rival political groups could gain entry into the working-class milieu only by clearly defining and arguing their position with respect to the Social Democrats. In addition, we have to understand that a variety of regional conditions hindered or promoted the advance of National Socialism, and here we have to take material as well as political considerations into account.

The political battle for the support of industrial workers and the unemployed would be largely fought out between the Social Democrats and the National Socialists. For many reasons the Corporate State could only expect a rebuff in this sector:

1. Economic policy from 1933 to 1938 did little to solve the most pressing problems of the workers and the unemployed. For example, in January 1938 there were still 460,000 unemployed,[31] and this figure is based on statistics which did not properly take into account numerous problem cases (those not eligible for benefits, youngsters, women etc.). In contrast, then, to other industrial nations, Austria had seen no reduction in unemployment during the 1930s, and this was because for the Corporate State a stable

currency was more important.

2. The political situation was a further factor. In February 1934 the Social Democrats were defeated. Their organization was destroyed, their leaders were forced to flee, or were arrested and in some cases executed, with the executions given great symbolic significance by the regime.[32] All too often, getting a job depended on one's political allegiance, the condition being whether the applicant had a 'patriotic standpoint' [vaterländische Gesinnung]. What had formerly been positions of power within the labour movement were now taken over by functionaries of the Corporate State, who were not elected but imposed from above. Independent trades unions were outlawed and a single trades union was introduced, organized from above without really involving the ordinary workers. Works committees were now supposed to be responsible for 'joint aims and policy' [Werkgemeinschaftsziele] and not allowed to represent the interests of the workers alone.[33]

3. Between the Wars the working-class movement saw itself as the guardian of the democracy for which it had fought. Even if there are extraneous factors to be taken into account (like the Austrian defeats in the wars of 1866 and 1918), it is by and large true to say that the conservative section of the population was looking back to a happier time before 1918/19, whilst the labour movement was looking forward to a time beyond democracy: 'Democracy isn't enough, Socialism that's the stuff.'[34] The basic agreement of all political parties in present-day Austria that all conflicts of interest must be settled democratically simply did not exist in the 1930s. Democracy has taken time to find general acceptance in Austria, perhaps because there has been such a swift succession of different political systems: 1918, 1934, 1938 and finally 1945 brought in each case an essential change in political values and standards, and in addition, within only two decades, Austrians had found themselves living in three geographically very different states. Acting in an authoritarian manner which contained many traits of fascism, the Corporate State cleared away what it termed 'revolutionary rubble,' and that included the idea of democracy, which the workers thought worth fighting for, not

least because it was opposed by the conservative half of the nation.

4. The Corporate State proclaimed itself to be 'Austrian' but did not appear to know precisely what it meant by this. It seemed beyond doubt that Austrians belonged to the 'German nation,' especially if one was following the 19th-century tradition of equating nationality with language.[35] This was accepted by the labour movement as well, and apart from Otto Bauer's definition of 'nation' as 'history gone sour' [geronnene Geschichte], there seemed to be no difficulty about the idea of a 'nation of one culture' [Kulturnationsverständnis]. Stressing 'Austria' whilst at the same time claiming to belong to the 'German nation' seemed a simple trick to stay in power. It has been said that between 1934 and 1938 the democrats were bad patriots and the patriots bad democrats,[36] but from the workers' point of view this was not an acceptable equation since they, no doubt rightly, distrusted the patriotism of the Corporate State.

If, then, the Corporate State was unable to appeal to the workers and the unemployed, we must now consider what issues would influence the struggle between the Social Democrats and National Socialists for this sector of society. Here we have to remember that different local conditions would play their part in the outcome of that struggle. These differences in local conditions, which were more important in the well-established labour movement than in the 'youthful' National Socialist movement, are one level of explanation, and certainly do not cancel the effect of individual commitment and decision. So, what can be shown here are only the broad outlines, from which there will naturally have been deviation in individual cases:[37]

1. Industrialisation.

Austria has various kinds of industrial centres: well-established, of recent origin, dependent on one or on a variety of industries. Many industrial areas are rooted in the old artisan traditions of the region, whilst others have come into being only because of the excellent infrastructure available. Mining, for example, is mostly based on a long tradition. The different ways in which industrialization took place created different kinds of homogeneity in the working class. The collapse of the Habsburg monarchy resulted in cases of structural disequilibrium, whilst the world economic crisis had more serious effects in some sectors than in others. The more stable people's jobs were, and the more capable the labour movement proved itself in offering an acceptable response to unemployment (if only in emotional terms), the less people were tempted to defect to National Socialism. In traditionally closed industrial localities, anyone taking such a step would be stigmatized. And since the conditions in which they worked had persuaded most of them to participate in the struggles of February 1934, workers in these places usually saw the Dollfuss and Schuschnigg governments as their main enemy. Temporary alliances, even with the National Socialists, against these administrations might be formed, but there were rarely shifts of allegiance.

2. The industrial 'enclave.'

In Austria industrial 'enclaves' were and are more significant than continuous industrial regions. We find exceptions to this only in southern Lower Austria and in Upper Styria. In isolated industries in essentially rural areas, a high proportion of the workers always commuted. Workers who commute from surrounding agricultural areas experience, in the course of a working day or week, changes of milieu precipitating identity problems. And it was in contexts like these that the National Socialists found it easier to make progress than in areas where they met with a Catholic peasantry or well-established industrial workers.

3. Political opponents.

The Austrian Social Democrats did not find themselves confronted everywhere by clearly defined political and economic opposition. In politics room for manoeuvre is created not only by a party's own programme and beliefs, but also quite decisively by the ground occupied by political opponents. What stands out in Austrian history is the lack of homogeneity in the middle class. The large-scale entrepreneur is almost completely absent, and industrialization is carried out in an anonymous way by banks' providing the necessary capital. The middle class in smaller towns is largely drawn from trade, industry and the intelligentsia, but we often find that members of the 'petite bourgeoisie' with a social conscience, like teachers, play an important role in the socialist movement. We particularly find alliances between them and the nationalist bourgeoisie when it comes to fighting the Church. In smaller industrial communities in agricultural areas, the political opponents of Social Democracy were often wealthy farmers with right-wing Catholic views. The strong influence of the educated middle-class [Bildungsbürgertum] within the labour movement, more noticeable the further away from Vienna, eased the move over to National Socialism, and this was helped by the fact that the workers' cultural inheritance contained a strong nationalist element (the so-called 'deutsches kulturelles Erbe'). This kind of working-class movement, often labelled 'teachers' socialism' [Lehrersozialismus],[38] contained elements of socialism, nationalism and anticlericalism. It could in some areas of Austria so blur the dividing line between Socialism and National Socialism that the move from the former to the latter (and back again in 1945) was not felt to have made a decisive break in a person's life.

4. Organizational and ideological developments.

It was only because the programme and policy of the central Austrian Socialist Party were clearly recognizable as 'Austro-Marxist' that the party appeared so united. Yet Marxism was by no means the ideological basis of the provincial parties, whose positions could be defined in terms of political activism, left-wing liberalism, what remained of 'classical' anarchism, the teachings of Lassalle, and one or two other currents. Where there were actually cadres of workers who had been trained in Marxist thinking, there was less defection to National Socialism. In Vienna and traditional industrial agglommerations, where there was a well-developed alternative socialist culture, one which embraced the 'whole man' and sought political means of producing the 'New Humanity,' resistance to National Socialism was considerable.

5. Religion.

Austria was and is always considered to be a homogeneous Catholic country. Certainly the State between 1934 and 1938 considered itself to be Catholic. But alongside Catholicism there was a large Jewish community, and in certain areas Protestantism had reestablished itself. Even in some areas which appeared to be Catholic, the Counter Reformation had been only superficially successful. There are clear examples of the last two instances in the Salzkammergut, in the Ennstal and in large tracts of Carinthia. These places had developed a critical attitude over many years towards the centralized Catholic State, and were particularly susceptible to anti-Catholic ideologies. It was no difficult step in these parts to step from the Socialist into the National Socialist camp. (Even electoral results at the present day confirm this tendency.) It is also clear that anti-Semitism helped such a change of allegiance: in the labour movement anti-Semitism was a provincial phenomenon, and, especially among unionized workers, went hand in hand with criticism of an intellectualism far removed from day-to-day realities.

6. The question of 'nation.'

Within the labour movement there are various components to the question of 'nation.' Although after Hitler's seizure of power in Austria the Social Democrats decided to change the paragraph in the 1926 Party Programme favouring Anschluss with Germany,[39] Austrian patriotism did not capture rank-and-file members. They still belonged to a party which carried the concept of 'German Austria' in its name. The Communists had from the mid-thirties sought to establish that the Austrian nation was independent of and objectively different from Germany, but this idea was rejected by Social Democrats.[40] Thus the idea of 'nation' was no impediment to defection from Socialism to National Socialism. However, alongside this we must remember that Austria was by no means a country with only one language, and the frontiers imposed in ethnically mixed regions after the First World War had left the population somewhat traumatized on the question of nationality. Supposed threats from neighbouring states (with the ethnic minorities cast in the role of fifth columnists), this especially in Carinthia, allowed the political tenor of the country to appear conditioned by the idea of a national defence campaign. There was, of course, the added problem of German-speaking minorities in neighbouring countries, particularly the problem of South Tyrol, but also the question of the Sudetenland. The more an Austrian region was confronted with this kind of problem, the more receptive its Social Democrats would be to German nationalist ideas.

7. The centralist and authoritarian structure of the party.

Ever since they had overcome various autogenous and anarchistic tendencies at the end of the nineteenth century, the Social Democrats had been a centralized party, in which the leadership decided policy, which then quickly permeated all ranks. Even when this was not consistently the case, local leaders still exercised decisive influence on their followers. Losing one of those leaders would therefore cause a local Republican Defence Corps [Schutzbund] unit—even a well-organized one like that of Wiener Neustadt[41]—to become completely inactive during the fighting of February 1934. If a leader ceased to be politically militant and changed sides, this could cause a switch of allegiance by a whole organizational unit from, say, the Defence Corps to the National Socialist 'Austrian Legion' [österreichische Legion] on the other side of the Austro-German border after February 1934. This was, as will be shown, particularly true of Upper Austria.

Regional differences in tradition and policy existed not only among Social Democrats but also among Austrian supporters of National Socialism. In Vorarlberg, in particular Dornbirn, the most important social group were the textile manufacturers, who had been deprived of their main markets by the First World War; the resulting pressures on the workers in this industry naturally led to their falling under the influence of National Socialism. In Tyrol and Salzburg, the National Socialists aimed their propaganda particularly at those involved in the tourist industry. The dominant group in Styria and Carinthia was the educated 'petite bourgeoisie,' especially teachers, and they had been won over by the idea of a 'German cultural mission' in these borderlands. In Upper and Lower Austria the National Socialists targeted the urban 'petite bourgeoisie' and the self-employed, whilst in Vienna and other university towns they sought to attract students as well.

An important piece of National Socialist tactic was their 'Call for Action' [Propaganda der Tat],[42] with which they attracted young, militant members of the labour movement. Almost from Styria and Upper Austria alone they managed to recruit between 3,000 and 4,000 former members of the Republican Defence Corps. Leaving aside the activities of the SA, what was particularly significant here was the behaviour of various leaders of the Defence Corps, among them Richard Bernaschek, who had initiated the February uprising.[43] These actual shifts of allegiance were outnumbered by the cases of temporary alliances against the corporate state, of which Hans Schafranek has recently provided an impressive list of examples,[44] among them the particularly striking one of a town in which Nazis and members of the Defence Corps provided alibis for one another's illegal activities. Whilst the Nazis sat in the pub chatting with the police and playing cards, members of the Defence Corps would be pasting up and painting Nazi slogans. The next evening it was the turn of the Defence Corps to sit in the pub while the Nazis put up socialist propaganda.[45] Essentially it was young people coming from militant, more activist sections of the working class who moved over to National Socialism. The average age of the paramilitary formations of the NSDAP was considerably lower than that of the Republican Defence Corps.[46]

Once National Socialism came to power, it brought tremendous changes in the short term for both workers and the unemployed. In the one-and-a-half years between the incorporation of Austria into the German Reich and the outbreak of the Second World War, unemployment was effectively reduced to nil.[47] The section of the population involved did not understand the price that had to be paid, namely, rearmament and an aggressive foreign policy now that the old economic strategy of protecting the currency had been abandoned. The misery of the years prior to 1938 had so completely distorted people's views on these matters that in order to get work they were happy to be blind. Of course, once they had ceased to be taken in by National Socialism, those workers and the unemployed who came from the ranks of the inter-war

labour movement had the chance to recognize the connection between the social prosperity achieved on the one hand and war and
the holocaust on the other. This insight was, however, denied to a
new group of workers, 'first generation industrial workers,' who
came from the lower levels of rural society and had migrated to
the towns. Their feeling was that they had National Socialism to
thank for work and a decent form of existence. For them, the
question of what these brand new factories in Linz and Steyr produced was of little consequence. What mattered to them was that
next to these factories housing estates of remarkably good quality
– known to this day as 'Hitler housing' [Hitler-Bauten] – had been
built. To be able to move into those houses and to be given regular
work in the armaments factories meant for them a significant step
forward in their lives. As a result, it is difficult even today for such
people to relate their positive individual experiences of that time
to the horrible overall situation. 'But we were given work' –
whether by Hitler or National Socialism is unclear – is the stereotypical response, and one all the more insistent because it is based
on genuine experience, without any consideration of the more
abstract political picture.

These 'new' industrial workers really experienced National
Socialism as a workers' party, and that explains much about voting
patterns after 1945. For example, in Steyr-Münichholz, the Nazis
had built a housing estate alongside a factory producing aircraft
engines (where there had, of course, been forced labour). Of the
inhabitants – all of them workers of the older generation who had
been sent there during the previous five years – 70% voted for the
Socialist Party in 1945 because they felt themselves to be workers.
But in 1949, the Union of Independents [Verband der Unabhängi-
gen], a successor organization to the former National Socialists,
was allowed to put up candidates, and the result was that the
Socialist vote was halved, the Socialists and Independents running
neck and neck, each with about 35% of the vote.[48] Since then
these voters have practically all reverted to the Socialist Party.

So we see that the history of the years between 1938 and
1945 in Austria can be fully grasped only if we analyse the extent

to which National Socialism was rooted in the population well before the Anschluss. March 1938 was thus created not only by political and military aggression from beyond Austria's border, but also by latent or open civil war within its territory. It was Austria's fate in these years to be both victim and perpetrator.

## NOTES

1. The most successful attempt to provide a social profile of the National Socialists is that by Gerhard Botz, "The Changing Patterns of Social Support for Austrian National Socialism (1918-1945)" in: Stein U. Larsen et al. (eds), *Who were the Fascists? Social Roots of European Fascism* (Bergen/Oslo/Tromsø: Universitätsverlag, 1980).

2. Statistics to support this can be found in Josef Weidenholzer, *Auf dem Weg zum 'Neuen Menschen.' Bildungs- und Kulturarbeit der österreichischen Sozialdemokratie in der Ersten Republik* (Vienna: Europaverlag, 1981).

3. Otto Bauer, "Der Kampf um Wald und Weide," *Werkausgabe* (Vienna: Europaverlag, 1976), vol. 3, pp. 31-248.

4. Michael Genner, *Mein Vater Laurenz Genner. Ein Sozialist im Dorf* (Vienna: Europaverlag, 1979).

5. Conversations which the author has had with farmers from the region strongly support this possibility.

6. This is linked to the economic crisis of the 1870s, which both hindered the development of a strong parliamentary liberal party and limited the political scope of German nationalism. See Klaus Berchtold (ed.), *Österreichische Parteiprogramme 1868-1966* (Vienna: Verlag für Geschichte und Politik, 1967), pp. 76ff.

7. Karl Kaser / Karl Stocker, "Bäuerliches Leben in der Oststeiermark seit 1848. Vol. II: Die verspätete Revolution," typewritten MS, Graz, 1987, p. 196.

8. Ernst Hanisch, *Nationalistische Herrschaft in der Provinz. Salzburg im Dritten Reich* (Salzburg: Schriftenreihe des Landespressebüros, 1983).

9. The author's father was the illegitimate son of a servant in Preitenegg, Carinthia, and as a young man during the period of the corporate state suffered from every disadvantage of birth.

10. Karin Gradwohl-Schlacher et al. (eds.) 'Durch unsern Fleiß ward deutsch

dies Land und deutsch woll'n wir's bewahren.' *Steirische Literatur im Nationalsozialismus* (Graz: Strohalm-Verlag, 1988), p. 16.

11. Ibid., p. 27.
12. John Bunzl / Bernd Marin, *Antisemitismus in Österreich. Sozialhistorische und soziologische Studien* (Innsbruck: Inn-Verlag, 1983).
13. This is still to be found in rural anti-Semitism today (the 'Anderl von Rinn' cult).
14. Bunzl / Marin, op. cit., section on questionnaires.
15. Kaser / Stocker, op. cit., p. 203.
16. See Michael Mooslechner / Robert Stadler, "Landwirtschaft und Agrarpolitik," in: Emmerich Talos (ed.), *NS-Herrschaft in Österreich 1938-1945* (Vienna: Verlag für Gesellschaftskritik, 1988).
17. Ibid., p. 83.
18. Kaser / Stocker, op. cit., p. 198.
19. Mooslechner / Stadler, op. cit., p. 83.
20. Ibid., p. 75.
21. Ibid., p. 74.
22. Kaser / Stocker, op. cit., p. 202.
23. Ibid., p. 203.
24. Mooslechner / Stadler, op. cit., p. 80.
25. Kaser / Stocker, op. cit., p. 202.
26. Mooslechner / Stadler, op. cit., p. 88.
27. Helmut Konrad, *Widerstand an Donau und Moldau. KPÖ und KSC zur Zeit des Hitler-Stalin-Paktes* (Vienna: Europaverlag, 1978), p. 17.
28. Weidenholzer, op. cit., p. 19.
29. Ibid., p. 33.
30. Ibid., p. 21.
31. Emerich Talos, "Sozialpolitik 1938-1945. Versprechungen – Erwartungen – Realisationen" in: *NS-Herrschaft in Österreich,* op. cit., p. 130.
32. Examples of this are the prolongation of martial law until Koloman Wallisch, the leader of the Republican Defence Corps [Schutzbund] in Styria, could be caught and executed, and the execution of the seriously wounded Karl Münichreiter. See also Karl Stadler (ed.), *Sozialistenprozesse. Politische Justiz in Österreich 1870-1936* (Vienna: Europaverlag, 1986).
33. Emerich Talos, *Staatliche Sozialpolitik in Österreich. Rekonstruktion und Analyse,* 2nd edn (Vienna: Verlag für Gesellschaftskritik, 1981), p. 273.
34. This was the motto on banners carried by Social Democrats at demon-

strations during the First Republic. ['Demokratie, das ist nicht viel Sozialismus ist das Ziel.']

35.  Helmut Konrad, "Der Nationalismus" in: Anton Pelinka (ed.), *Ideologien in Bezugsfeld von Geschichte und Gesellschaft* (Innsbruck: Inn-Verlag, 1981).

36.  Coined by Gerhardt Botz at a conference of Austrian contemporary historians held recently in Salzburg.

37.  The following seven points match my presentation in an essay entitled 'Das Werben der Nationalsozialisten um die österreichischen Arbeiter,' to be published (autumn 1988 in Vienna) in a collection of essays entitled *Arbeiterschaft und Nationalsozialismus*, ed. Rudolf Ardelt.

38.  Helmut Konrad, "Zur österreichischen Arbeiterkultur der Zwischenkriegszeit" in: Friedhelm Boll (ed.), *Arbeiterkulturen zwischen Alltag und Politik. Beiträge zum europäischen Vergleich in der Zwischenkriegszeit* (Vienna: Europaverlag, 1986), p. 93.

39.  Helene Maimann, "Der März 1938 als Wendepunkt im sozialdemokratischen Anschlußdenken" in: Helmut Konrad (ed.), *Sozialdemokratie und Anschluß* (Vienna: Europaverlag, 1978), p. 63.

40.  Felix Kreissler, *Der Österreicher und seine Nation. Ein Lernprozeß mit Hindernissen* (Vienna/Graz/Cologne: Böhlau-Verlag, 1984), pp. 174–183.

41.  Karl Flanner, *Wiener Neustadt im Ständestaat. Arbeiteropposition 1933–1938* (Vienna: Europaverlag, 1983), pp. 75–85.

42.  Francis L. Carsten, *Faschismus in Österreich. Von Schönerer zu Hitler* (Munich: Wilhelm Fink Verlag, 1977), p. 230.

43.  For a detailed biography see Inez Kykal / Karl Stadler, *Richard Bernaschek. Odyssee eines Rebellen* (Vienna: Europaverlag, 1976).

44.  Hans Schafranek, 'NSDAP und Sozialisten nach dem Februar 1934.' Unpublished MS of a paper given at the symposium 'Arbeiterschaft und Nationalsozialismus,' held in Linz in March 1988.

45.  Ibid., pp. 21f.

46.  Gerhard Botz, *Gewalt in der Politik. Attentate, Zusammenstöße, Putschversuche, Unruhen in Österreich 1918–1938,* 2nd edn (Munich: Wilhelm Fink Verlag, 1983), p. 277.

47.  Talos, *Sozialpolitik in Österreich,* op. cit., p. 131.

48.  Helmut Retzl, "Steyr-Münichholz. Ein Stadtteil im Wandel der Zeit," diss., Linz, 1985, pp. 203ff.

# The Corporate State versus National Socialism:
## Some Aspects of Austria's Resistance

Dieter A. Binder

John Bunzl, writing in *Die Gemeinde*,[1] argues that it would be wrong to look at the Corporate State [Ständestaat] solely from the angle of resistance:

> You might say that the means used could never achieve their ends, perhaps because the regime was by its nature reactionary, and also because it had particular foreign alliances. The Corporate State suppressed both the Social Democrats and the Nazis, and so these groupings shared a feeling of hatred for its dictatorship, and both rose against the Government (in one case a revolt, in the other an attempted 'putsch'). As Bruno Kreisky put it: 'Hatred of Dollfuss was greater than fear of anything else.'[2] By the time that Hitler's army marched into Austria Social Democracy already had its confrontation with the regime behind it, and from this standpoint it was necessary to paint the Corporate State in the blackest possible colours and to see National Socialism in a relatively harmless light. For this reason it is often simplistically stated that one fascism merely followed another. No account is thereby taken of the difference that there were millions of dead, whilst the similarity, namely, repression and the abolition of democracy, is wildly exaggerated. It is only a logical extension of this thinking to call the internment camp at Wöllersdorf, where no one was murdered and which was half full of Nazis, a 'concentration camp' [KZ], even if it is not explicitly compared with Auschwitz. Of course, the position of the working-class improved after the Anschluss,

67

and provided that they were not Jewish, leading Social
Democrats either remained relatively untroubled (Renner!)[3] or were actually wooed by the Nazis – and so this
distorted perception of the situation came about and could
be said to continue to this day.

Let us begin by asking what the attitude of the Corporate
State to National Socialism actually was. In answer I should like to
catalogue the measures it took against the Nazis and Nazi Germany:

   – May/June 1933, the expulsion of the leading National
Socialist agitators of German origin [Reichsdeutsche], i.e. Hans
Frank, the Minister of Justice, and Theo Habicht, NSDAP General
Inspector in Austria [Landesinspektor].[4]

   – 19 June 1933, the banning of the NSDAP in Austria.

   – 23 September 1933, the establishment of an internment
camp for political prisoners.[5]

   – Police activity stepped up and the establishment of a
National Police Bureau in the Chancellery.

   – The ordinary penal code and martial law both strengthened, including the introduction of the death penalty for crimes
where explosives were used.

   – Introduction of special penalties for persons only periph-
erally involved in a Nazi 'putsch': committal to the internment
camp and confiscation of property.

   – Imposition of martial law following the 'putsch' of July
1934, including the carrying out of death sentences.

   – 2–14 March 1935, the trial on charges of treason of Anton
Rintelen and others involved in planning the 'putsch.'

   – Military planning in preparation for a possible attack by
Germany (the Jansa[6] plan).

   – 1936, the introduction of a law to safeguard the State
[Staatsschutzgesetz].[7]

   – 1937, the introduction of a law to safeguard public order
[Ordnungsschutzgesetz].[8]

   A different position is taken up by Ernst Hanisch. Whilst he sees the Dollfuss-Schuschnigg regime as part of the history of opposition to National Socialism, he also places it within the historical process by which an Austrian nation came into being [Nationsbildungsprozeß]:

> One can see in the resistance of the authoritarian state to National Socialism a link with the tradition of the Counter Reformation, as of the period prior to the March 1848 Revolution [Vormärz] and the period of neo-absolutism. Those who shouted 'Heil Hitler!' could be sent to prison for up to three weeks; those who left the Catholic Church could count on six weeks in prison. That shameful picture of the Hitler era which we often see in the press, depicting Jews being forced to wash the symbols of the corporate state off the pavements is, in fact, a humiliation invented by 'Austrofascist' officials and was first used against National Socialists and Social Democrats. In brief, petty tricks by the police against the Nazis were of little use, merely inflaming hatred in those concerned and resulting in ever more people joining the outlawed party ... And yet we must not forget that Dollfuss and Schuschnigg fought for Austrian independence, even if by the wrong means.[9]

Hanisch is very struck with his idea of the Counter Reformation – an idea, incidentally, which was part of National Socialist propaganda against the Corporate State.[10] In the article cited he uses the Counter Reformation two pages later to describe the period after March 1938 as well.[11] This certainly does not improve his comparison for the period before 1938: the Counter Reformation was directed against those who had different religious views, and these were bitterly persecuted by the stronger party. The measures taken by the Dollfuss-Schuschnigg regime were directed against the National Socialists, who supported a system which, even before 1938, was clearly criminal, murderous and warmongering. If today it is argued that the police measures referred to – about whose efficiency there could well have been more intensive discussion at the time – were directed against 'idealists,' then this is merely helping to propagate the 'obfuscation industry' which the National Socialists started. The 'idealism' of these 'victims' of the 'traditions of the Counter Reformation' cost the lives of six million Jews, for a start. Potential murderers have to be stopped; it is only the nature of the preventive measures that is open to discussion. And if Hanisch compares the 'scrubbing sessions' [Reibpartien] of the Nazis, who in 1938 made use of this ritual to humiliate their Jewish fellow-citizens, with those which the political opponents of Austrofascism had to endure, then in doing so he is ignoring the fact that it was not the officials of the Patriotic Front [Vaterländische Front] whom the Nazis persecuted, but a group specially selected on racial grounds. This is the kind of comparison which, alas, recalls those attempts to place the invention of the concentration camp in the Boer War or at Wöllersdorf in order to minimize Auschwitz or Treblinka.

Hanisch further states:

> Among its wrong methods we must also count the 'imitation fascism' which the regime practised: this ranged from the salute 'Heil Dollfuss!' to ceremonies in the schools which hardly differed from those in Germany . . . . People grew accustomed to a public life which was adorned by the symbols and forms of fascism, hence the change from February 1938 to March 1938 was scarcely noticed. In place of Austrian half-heartedness there was simply German radicalism.[12]

There is doubtless some truth in these ideas, but what gives the game away is the writer's conclusion: 'In place of Austrian half-heartedness there was simply German radicalism.' What we have here is the clubroom mentality [Stammtischmentalität] which speaks rather scornfully of the immature dictatorship of the corporate state but clicks its heels with a respect verging on awe when it is faced with Hitler's strong and ruthless dictatorship. Hanisch goes much too far in his efforts to 'understand' National Socialism.[13] The really serious problem when we consider the Corporate State is this: after abandoning a democratic constitution by means of what can only be described as a 'coup' staged over a period of time, it did use what were technically criminal methods against every opposition group. Those methods were entirely justified in the case of National Socialism, which was out to undermine the very existence of the state.

Nazi strategy against Austria used several methods, both from beyond its frontiers and within them. From 27 May 1933 Germany waged an economic war on Austria.[14] There was radio propaganda and the work of the leadership – in this period the Austrian Nazis were essentially controlled from Munich. Finally, financial and material support was  provided for terrorist groups of Austrian origin operating in Austria, and from 1935/36 military planning was stepped up.[15] From within Austria there were carefully targeted terrorist attacks, which increased in number after 1932. There were attacks on individuals, murders, damage to property, explosions, plans for a 'putsch' and an actual attempt to carry it out. People were denounced as police spies in so-called 'pillory columns' [Prangerecken] of the illegal press[16] and attempts were even made on such people's lives. The effect of all this terrorization on a population once it had openly declared its anti-Nazi feelings should not be underestimated. The ultimate goal was to destabilize the Government and the state.

The penal measures outlined above resulted in the fact that until 1945 no other country had arrested, tried, condemned or indeed executed as many Nazis as had Austria between 1933 and 1938.[17] However, on closer examination it transpires that these measures – leaving out of account their application to other opposition groups – were not in fact carried out with the full weight of the law. A comparison with other political trials shows that Nazis were often not given the maximum sentences possible. So the question requiring an answer is to what extent legal officials and members of the police had already secretly converted to Nazism, or, in other words, whether political considerations had played a decisive role.

Everhard Holtmann clearly addresses this problem of the 'justice of the age' [Tendenzjustiz], but in the above context it must be stressed that the Austrian Government did try to deal with the judicial consequences of February 1934, if only to achieve a broad basis of consensus at home and abroad.[18] In this context, one should also mention the 'Christmas Amnesty' of 1935, as well as the conduct of the 'socialist trials' of 1936, where international opinion clearly exercised a moderating influence on the intentions of the prosecutors. At this juncture a ministerial decree was issued 'chiefly against lenient treatment of members of the SA and the NSDAP.'[19] In connection with the Law to protect public order [Ordnungsschutzgesetz] of 1937, Kurt von Schuschnigg stressed that it was not a case of 'rabble-rousing' but that 'everything illegal must be prosecuted.'[20] And indeed, as Holtmann expressly states, 'open-court prosecutions . . . were maintained after the new Law of 1937 without favour to Right or Left.'[21] 'By the autumn of 1937 the police had uncovered dozens of local Nazi groups and regional organizations [Gauleitungen]; in many areas they had broken up Hitler Youth groups as well as SA and SS units.' The following successes for October 1937 were booked: 'Burgenland – "11 Hitler Youth groups dissolved." Lower Austria – "SS IX in the area between Vienna and Wiener Neustadt almost entirely destroyed." Carinthia – "a series of successes against the SA, and considerable material unearthed." Salzburg – "organization still holding, but 300 leaders arrested." Upper Austria – "brigade leader of the SA and HJ [Hitler Youth] leader dug out."'[22]

In view of the constantly claimed tendency of the police and legal authorities to favour the Right, I again refer to Holtmann's statement, which limits favour shown to NSDAP supporters to a specific recorded number: 'If one categorizes the total number of those sent to prison according to political status, then it is impossible to establish any bias in police prosecutions against the illegal Socialist movement. For example, of the 431 people who were imprisoned in 1936, 269 were National Socialists and 159 belonged to left-wing parties.'[23]

This analysis is in keeping with the statistics of those interned in Wöllersdorf.[24] The qualitative difference addressed by Holtmann was doubtless a question of the particular officials involved, for there certainly were police-officers and members of the legal profession who made no secret of their sympathy with National Socialism. Clearly, this must be tested case by case, because it is also true that after March 1938 we find attacks by the Nazis precisely on people involved in law enforcement, and many were accused of being demonstrably anti-Nazi in their professional conduct.[25]

In the face of Nazi aggression the Government tried to stabilize the situation by using the most varied and often contradictory methods. Sometimes in parallel with the criminal law, sometimes independently of it, they attempted to safeguard the state through foreign policy. There was, for example, as an attempt to calm 'nationalist opposition' at home, the Three Power Agreement guaranteeing Austrian independence – the 'fight against Marxism' banner of 1933 had also been for this purpose – and there were bilateral negotiations with the Third Reich, which were to lead to the disastrous 'July Agreement' of 1936 and thence to the real beginning of Anschluss, the Berchtesgaden Agreement. Efforts to pacify the 'nationalist opposition' at home and the bilateral negotiations show how badly the Government had misjudged the aggression of the National Socialists.[26] From the very beginning – and this is clearly stated by the German Government when discussing the imposition of a 'Thousand-Mark Visa' [Tausendmarksperre] – Hitler was interested only in an Austria that was fully integrated into the German system. Whether this integration [Gleichschaltung] occurred by giving Austria a puppet government and making it a satellite state of the Reich, or whether complete Anschluss was achieved – as happened in March 1938 – was of secondary importance. According to Gerhard Jagschitz:

> It seemed as if, after the events of July 1934, the old discredited policy of Chancellor Dollfuss towards the National Socialists could be reintroduced with greater chances of

success. At a cabinet meeting on 7 August 1934, the new
Chancellor, Schuschnigg, stated that Austria was without
doubt in a 'war situation,' and there were only two ways
out of it: their opponents could decide or be forced to
take a different line, or else Austria must ensure her safety
with the help of those powers interested in the preservation of peace. If the situation did not change fundament-
ally, the 'Austrian problem' would have to be looked at
again as an international, indeed European problem. In
trying to broaden their front at home, the Government
would have to enter into discussions with the workers, and
also try to incorporate nationalist circles into the Patriotic
Front.[27]

At the international level no state could be found that was interested in seeing the escalation of an Austro-German conflict, whilst
internally the Austrian Government failed in its approach to the
workers and misjudged the 'nationalist opposition.' Furthermore,
in the July Agreement of 1936, the Austrian Government was
making the same mistake which Britain had made in the Naval
Agreement of 1935: even as the treaty was being signed, Hitler
had no intention of honouring it beyond its usefulness as a tool of
day-to-day politics. The leading personalities of the somewhat
insecure Austrian NSDAP were informed on this point. It is also
massively documented in the plans of the German General Staff,
in the way the Austrian economy was being penetrated by German
capital, and in the infiltration tactics of the NSDAP. Despite being
banned, the party was active in Austria, particularly when it came
to making popular political speeches. Yet another error of judgment on the part of the Government was believing that basic
agreement on an anti-Marxist position could form the basis of co-
operation with Nazi Germany. The Nazis managed to keep ideological propaganda and practical politics separate with a cynicism
which it would be hard to surpass.

Because the dominant mood was anti-Marxist, Engelbert
Dollfuss failed to recognize that the leaders of the Austrian Social

Democrat Party (SDAP) had changed their attitude towards a government that had decreed a state of emergency appropriate to wartime conditions [Kriegswirtschaftliches Ermächtigungsgesetz], and was now ruling unconstitutionally. Until then their attitude had been that expressed by Karl Renner at the Social Democrat Conference on Frontier Provinces [Grenzländer] in September 1933: 'in Austria ... two forms of fascism ... are at war with each other ... It must be our policy not to let these two opponents unite. For that reason we have not taken sides. Against all expectations, this has worked to our advantage.'[28] As a result of that conference, Social Democrat officials made it clear that they were ready, in the face of a real threat from the National Socialists, to abandon their position of the 'smiling onlooker.' This led to the Social Democrats' making offers to negotiate with the Government right up to the shooting of March 1934. Basically anti-democratic attitudes, pressure from the Austrian fascists within Austria (the paramilitary organizations [Heimwehren]) and from abroad (Italy), together with powerful anti-Marxist feelings, prevented this offer of compromise from being accepted. Finally, the opportunity to achieve a broad basis for government was destroyed by judicial murder, and by the most petty and spiteful persecution not only of those who had taken part in the uprising of groups of the Republican Defence Corps [Schutzbund], but also of their families as well. So there was now a majority opposed to Dollfuss and to his successor Schuschnigg, an opposition within which National Socialist activism and anticlericalism could make their impression on the disappointed sympathizers with Social Democracy. Writing in 1945, Karl Renner expressed it thus:

> Robbed by clerico-fascism of their rights and their property, the working-class turned sadly against their own State and reached the conclusion that, if fascism was unavoidable, then better the German anti-clerical version than the Church-oriented Italian brand. From the point of view of foreign policy, this meant that the main body of the work force accepted without resistance the annexation

which followed four years later, and then allowed themselves to be blinded by Hitler's initial successes. Without
Dollfuss' actions in 1934, it would never – or scarcely –
have been possible for Hitler to subjugate Austria in 1938
with his usual remarkable speed.[29]

This was Karl Renner's rather hyperbolic analysis on taking office
in 1945. Ernst Hanisch points out the somewhat absurd position
of the Austrian Socialist Party [SPÖ], which would rather forgive a
leader 'for being weak in 1938 than for capitulating in 1934.'[30]
The fact that a 'fair number of workers' came to terms with the
National Socialists could be thought to have some sort of justification in their 'secret delight that the hated Schuschnigg Government was being seized by the scruff of its neck.' These currents of
thought are still around today and are responsible for the crass
attempts to label every discussion of the defensive role played by
the Corporate State as an apologia for Austrofascism.

　　With all this in mind we must stress that it was the officials of
the illegal Social Democrat Party and of the Trades Unions, as well
as representatives of the Communist Party, who in the crisis-
ridden weeks of 1938 demonstrated their willingness to cooperate
with the Government. Despite his hesitant reaction to the demands of these groups it is when Schuschnigg is making preparations for his plebiscite that we find the first examples of co-
operation between them and the Patriotic Front. This last-minute
mobilization makes very clear what potential the Government had
quite wantonly squandered in its defensive measures against
National Socialism. So, abandoning democracy, failing to come to
terms with the Social Democrats because of anti-Marxist attitudes,
and these constantly allowing thoughts of reconciliation with the
'nationalist opposition' to surface – all this produced that contradictory image of a government which on the one hand introduced
certain defensive measures and could be valued as a refuge from
the Third Reich, and yet on the other hand shied away from the
final steps necessary for the defence of the realm. Still, with its
stalling tactics, it could be said to have defied Hitler for four

years. Indeed, its stance on defence was actually praised by intellectuals who were opposed to the 'clerical fustiness' of the Corporate State.

It is the cry 'Anything but Hitler!' that explains people's readiness to take part in Austria's struggle, proclaimed by Dollfuss, against the ambitions of the Third Reich, and to make clear – for the first time in the inter-war period – their desire that Austria should remain independent. There may have sometimes been a lack of resolution, but in their relationship to the Third Reich these opponents sought to give a clear reply to the demands of the National Socialists. This attitude to defence – which in discussion of the Austrofascist system has generally been dismissed as no more than 'a piece of self-justification' [Legitimationsphrase] – actually impressed Karl Kraus,[31] as well as men like Joseph Roth and Walter Mehring.[32] Even Sigmund Freud accepted the defensive position taken up by the Corporate State as a response to National Socialism: 'Our Government is in its way worthy and courageous, defending itself even more energetically against the Nazis than previously . . . .' (6 February 1934). When he was faced with the events of 12 February 1934, Freud still applauded the Government's attempt to defend itself against National Socialism, and he now also tried to relativize the confrontation between the Government and the Republican Defence League:

> Naturally, the victors are the heroes and saviours of a sacred order, whilst the others are impudent rebels. But if the other side had won, things would not have been very pleasant and the result would have been a military invasion. One cannot judge the Government too harshly in this, since a 'dictatorship of the proletariat,' which seems to have been the aim of the revolt, would have been equally difficult to live with . . . The future is uncertain – either an Austrian fascism or the swastika. If the latter, we shall have to go; but from our own home-grown fascism we could put up with all sorts of things, for it would certainly not treat us as badly as its German cousin would . . . Our

> attitude to either political possibility on the Austrian
> horizon can only echo Mercutio's cry in *Romeo and
> Juliet:* 'A plague on both your houses.'[33]

To Karl Kraus one further thing mattered: he rejected Otto
Bauer's heroic phraseology, accusing him of trying retrospectively
to give meaning to the senseless deaths of the civil war. Furthermore, he distrusted the insurgents since, in his opinion, they had
withdrawn from a broadly based anti-Hitler coalition and in defeat
could well become partners of the illegal National Socialist party.
This whole phenomenon, which is increasingly attracting scholarly
attention, has a variety of causes, but two essential elements were:
German nationalism and the anticlericalism of the Social Democrats.[34]

What this system of government failed to produce during its
four years of power was a viable anti-Hitler coalition to protect
Austria, and it also failed to stimulate international interest in the
Austro-German conflict. Its attempt to reach agreement with the
'nationalist opposition' within the framework of the July Treaty
of 1936 destroyed a line of argument it might otherwise have used
in its foreign policy; instead of which, the Austro-German conflict
was internationally regarded as an internal German problem,
whose peaceful solution people were prepared to accept. Sensitive
observers in Austria – those, for example, associated with the
journal *Der Christliche Ständestaat* – had warned against this
development just as they had warned against the 'German Austria'
propaganda of the Corporate State.[35]

Now if we refer back to our opening quotation about the resistance, however limited, offered to Hitler by the Corporate
State, we are left with one further problem to consider. In contrast to the other fascist states of Europe – Italy and Franco's
Spain – and notwithstanding its efforts to achieve some kind of
settlement, Austria never entered into any comparable 'business
relationship' or partnership with Nazi Germany.[36] The loose
application of the term 'fascism' (coined in the course of day-to-
day political confrontation) too easily subsumes all the many

differing systems possible in the historical context we have sketched. As Rita Koch puts it: 'It has become fashionable to use the term "fascism" as a sort of euphemism for National Socialism, which then seems to appear more innocent.'[37] This means that a loudly proclaimed 'anti-fascism' is frequently used to cover up a missing 'anti-Nazism' in people's families. They all too often attempt to explain away the failure to oppose Nazism by pointing to their struggle with the 'fascism' of the Corporate State.

## NOTES

1.  John Bunzl, "Die erste und die zweite Lebenslüge," *Die Gemeinde* (Offizielles Organ der Israelitischen Kultusgemeinde Wien) Vol. 11, No. 355, 8 July 1987 (Tammuz 5747), p. 11.

2.  Bruno Kreisky, *Zwischen den Zeiten* (Berlin: Siedler, 1987), p. 207.

3.  On this problem see Ernst Panzenböck, "Karl Renner 1938 – Irrweg eines Österreichers: Ursachen und Verdrängung," *Österreich in Geschichte und Literatur*, vol. 32, nos. 1–2 (1988), 1–17.

4.  On these events see Dieter A. Binder, *Dollfuß und Hitler. Über die Außenpolitik des autoritären Ständestaates* (Graz: dbv, 1979); Gerhard Jagschitz, *Der Putsch. Die Nationalsozialisten 1934 in Österreich* (Graz/Vienna/Cologne: Styria Verlag, 1976); Gerhard Jagschitz, "Der österreichische Ständestaat 1934-1938" in: Erika Weinzierl / Kurt Skalnik (eds), *Österreich 1918-1938* (Graz/Vienna/Cologne: Styria Verlag, 1983), Vol. 1, pp. 497-515; Gerhard Jagschitz, "Illegale Bewegungen während der Ständischen Ära 1933-38" in: Erich Zöllner (ed.) *Revolutionäre Bewegungen in Österreich* (Vienna: Bundesverlag, 1981 = Schriften des Instituts für Österreichkunde, 38), pp. 141-162.

5.  For the earlier history of this decree (BGB1 No. 431/1933) see Gerhard Jagschitz, "Die Anhaltelager in Österreich" in: Ludwig Jedlicka / Rudolf Neck (eds), *Vom Justizpalast zum Heldenplatz. Studien und Dokumentationen 1927-1938* (Vienna: Verlag der österreichischen Staatsdruckerei, 1975), pp. 128-151, esp. pp. 131ff. Jagschitz emphasizes that the main target was the NSDAP.

6.  Erwin A. Schmidl, *März 1938. Der deutsche Einmarsch in Österreich*

(Vienna: Bundesverlag, 1987 = Veröffentlichung des Heeresgeschicht-
lichen Museums. Militärwissenschaftliches Institut), pp. 61-68; Peter
Broucek, "Die militärische Situation Österreichs und die Entstehung
der Pläne zur Landesverteidigung" in: Rudolf Neck / Adam Wandruszka
(eds), *Anschluß 1938* (Vienna: Verlag für Geschichte und Politik, 1981
= Wissenschaftliche Kommission, Veröffentlichungen, 7), pp. 135-163;
Erwin Steinböck, *Österreichs militärisches Potential im März 1938*
(Vienna: Verlag für Geschichte und Politik, 1988).

7.   Federal law to protect the State = Staatsschutzgesetz, BGB1.223/1936.
Since of all the illegal parties only the Nazis went in for bombings and
the like, this law actually represents an attack on the Nazis.

8.   Federal Law to safeguard public peace, order and security = Ordnungs-
schutzgesetz BGB1.282/1937. The opposition 'Nationals' managed to
effect changes during the draft stage, but once the bill became law,
police activity and prosecutions continued at a high level. Cf. Everhard
Holtmann, *Zwischen Unterdrückung und Befriedung. Sozialistische
Arbeiterbewegung und autoritäres Regime in Österreich 1933-1938.*
(Vienna: Verlag für Geschichte und Politik, 1978 = Studien und Quel-
len zur österreichischen Zeitgeschichte, 1), pp. 263f.

9.   Ernst Hanisch, "März 1938: eine Salzburger Perspektive" in: Eberhard
Zwink (ed.), *Der März 1938 in Salzburg. Gedenkstunde am 10. März
1988. Symposion Feindbilder am 6. November 1987* (Salzburg: Lan-
desregierung Salzburg, 1988 = Schriftenreihe des Landespressebüros
Salzburg, Diskussionen, 10), pp. 23ff. Here Hanisch gives a picture
similar to the one offered by Erika Weinzierl, "Der österreichische
Widerstand gegen den Nationalsozialismus 1938-1945," in: Erich Zöllner (ed.), *Revolutionäre Bewegungen,* see above n. 4, p. 163.

10.  Cf. *Die Gegenreformation in Neu-Österreich. Ein Beitrag zur Lehre vom
katholischen Ständestaat* (Zurich: Nauck, 1936). For the Austrian Nazi
background to this material see Gerhard Peter Schwarz, *Ständestaat
und evangelische Kirche von 1933 bis 1938* (Graz: dbv, 1987), esp. pp.
90ff.

11.  Hanisch, above n. 10, p. 26.

12.  Ibid., p. 24.

13.  Ernst Hanisch, "Ein Versuch, den Nationalsozialismus zu 'verstehen,'"
in: Anton Pelinka / Erika Weinzierl (eds.), *Das große Tabu. Österreichs
Umgang mit seiner Vergangenheit* (Vienna: Verlag der österreichischen
Staatsdruckerei, 1987), pp. 154-162.

14.  In cabinet discussion on 26 May 1933, Hitler acknowledged the 'anti-

German' attitude of the Austrian Government, which was trying to 'become a sort of Switzerland' [Verschweizerungsprozeß]. The imposition of the 'Thousand Mark Visa' [Tausend-Mark-Sperre] was to bring about the fall of Dollfuss, and thereby new elections. This would result in an internal Austrian 'conformism with Nazi Germany' [Gleichschaltung], without the need for an actual Anschluss. (Bundesarchiv Koblenz R 43/II-1475, fols. 292–297; ADAP Series C, vol. 1, 2, no. 262, pp. 481–485). Cf. Binder, *Dollfuß und Hitler,* pp. 120–135, see above n. 4; Gottfried-Karl Kindermann, *Hitlers Niederlage in Österreich. Bewaffneter NS-Putsch, Kanzler-Mord und Österreichs Abwehrsieg 1934* (Hamburg: Hoffmann und Campe, 1984), pp. 37f.

15.    For an outline of the economic and military situation see Norbert Schausberger, *Der Griff nach Österreich. Der Anschluß* (Vienna/ Munich: Jugend und Volk, 1978); Schausberger, "Der Anschluß und seine ökonomische Relevanz" in: Rudolf Neck / Adam Wandruszka (eds.), *Anschluß 1938* (Vienna: Verlag für Geschichte und Politik, 1981 = Wissenschaftliche Kommission, Veröffentlichungen, 7), pp. 244–270; Schausberger, "Ökonomischpolitische Interdependenzen im Sommer 1936" in: Ludwig Jedlicka / Rudolf Neck (eds.), *Das Juliabkommen von 1936. Vorgeschichte, Hintergründe und Folgen* (Vienna: Verlag für Geschichte und Politik, 1977 = Wissenschaftliche Kommission, Veröffentlichungen, 4), pp. 280–298.

16.    A good example is provided by *Der Angriff* [Attack], the organ of the Graz and district NSDAP. On 18 May 1934, we read: 'Official party news . . . We begin today with a public denunciation of informers, false friends and police spies. You are warned against the following persons: . . . To be continued.' In other articles, readers are called on to boycott shops, etc.

17.    What is meant by this is that the Weimar Republic had opportunities to tackle the NSDAP. It had at its disposal, for example, enough legislation and police regulations to deal quite decisively with National Socialism. We need only consider a memorandum of 1930 entitled 'The NSDAP as association hostile to State and Republic and guilty of treason' (para. 129 StGB, para. 4/1 RepSchGes-, para. 86 StGB). See also Robert M.W. Kempner (ed.), *Der verpaßte Nazi-Stopp. Die NSDAP als staats- und republikfeindliche Verbindung. Preußische Denkschrift von 1930* (Frankfurt am Main/Berlin/Vienna: Ullstein, 1983 = Ullstein Sachbuch 34159). Similarly, having prior to 1938 entered into a tacit agreement with Nazi Germany, Czechoslovakia was ready to prevent

Czech intellectual resistance to National Socialism in Germany, and certainly failed to take any strong line with the NSDAP. Cf. Hans-Albert Walter, *Deutsche Exilliteratur 1930–1950, Vol. 2: Asylpraxis und Lebensbedingungen in Europa* (Darmstadt/Neuwied: Luchterhand, 1972), pp. 151ff.; see also op. cit., *Vol. 7: Exilpresse I* (Darmstadt/ Neuwied: Luchterhand, 1974), pp. 38ff. and p. 75. Cf. Golo Mann, who in this context stresses the calamitous short-sightedness of Edvard Beneš, "'Ein Volk, ein Reich, ein Führer'– Hitlers Anschluß markierte den Anfang vom Ende des gemeinsamen geschichtlichen Weges von Deutschen und Österreichern" in: *Die Zeit* (4 March 1988), p. 3. Finally, a similar giving of ground occurred as a result of National Socialist terrorist activity prior to the plebiscite in the Saar.

18. Holtmann, see above n. 8, pp. 246ff.
19. Ibid., p. 257. Holtmann here gives details of the decree issued by the Minister of Justice to the senior State Prosecutors in Vienna, Graz and Innsbruck.
20. Meeting of security chiefs [Sicherheitsdirektoren] in October 1937, HHStA-NPA, Fasc. 286, Z1.44.651-13/1937, fol. 20.
21. Holtmann, above n. 7, p. 264.
22. See nn. 18 and 19.
23. Holtmann, above n. 7, p. 265.
24. See Jagschitz, above n. 5, pp. 148f. The following are the details of those interned at Wöllersdorf:

| Date of Survey | National Socialists | National Democrats & Communists | Total |
|---|---|---|---|
| 17.10.1933 .............. | 11 | | 11 |
| 9.11.1933 .............. | 32 | 3 | 35 |
| 15. 1.1934 .............. | | | 85 |
| 1. 2.1934 .............. | | | 173 |
| 15. 2.1934 .............. | | | 313 |
| 1. 3.1934 .............. | | | 372 |
| 15. 3.1934 .............. | | | 361 |
| 2. 4.1934 .............. | | | 267 |
| 16. 4.1934 .............. | 314 | 99 | 413 |

| Date of Survey | National Socialists | Social Democrats & | Communists | Total |
|---|---|---|---|---|
| 1. 5.1934 | 323 | | 508 | 831 |
| 15. 5.1934 | 255 | | 571 | 826 |
| 1. 6.1934 | 317 | | 627 | 944 |
| 15. 6.1934 | 397 | | 604 | 1001 |
| 4. 7.1934 | 548 | | 456 | 1004 |
| 15. 7.1934 | 558 | | 459 | 1017 |
| 1. 8.1934 | 690 | | 746 | 1436 |
| 15. 8.1934 | 1500 | | 682 | 2182 |
| 1. 9.1934 | 3404 | | 545 | 3949 |
| 15. 9.1934 | 4209 | | 551 | 4760 |
| 1.10.1934 | 4747 | | 555 | 5302 |
| 15.10.1934 | 4256 | | 538 | 4794 |
| 1.11.1934 | 4249 | | 468 | 4717 |
| 15.12.1934 | 3497 | | 462 | 3959 |
| 1.12.1934 | 2676 | | 387 | 3063 |
| 15.12.1934 | 1513 | | 311 | 1824 |
| 1. 1.1935 | 654 | | 171 | 825 |
| 15. 1.1935 | 626 | | 168 | 794 |
| 1. 2.1935 | 469 | | 156 | 625 |
| 15. 2.1935 | 507 | | 154 | 661 |
| 1. 3.1935 | 366 | | 143 | 509 |
| 15. 3.1935 | 340 | | 146 | 486 |
| 1. 4.1935 | 279 | | 142 | 421 |
| 1. 5.1935 | 255 | | 107 | 362 |
| 5. 6.1935 | 295 | 16 | 117 | 428 |
| 1. 7.1935 | 296 | 32 | 134 | 462 |
| 1. 8.1935 | 300 | 33 | 144 | 477 |
| 1. 9.1935 | 291 | 33 | 105 | 429 |
| 1.10.1935 | 295 | 31 | 78 | 404 |
| 1.11.1935 | 295 | 31 | 82 | 408 |
| 1.12.1935 | 292 | 32 | 76 | 400 |
| 1. 1.1936 | 276 | 17 | 63 | 356 |
| 1. 2.1936 | 227 | 8 | 49 | 284 |

| Date of Survey | National Socialists | Social Democrats & Communists | | Total |
|---|---|---|---|---|
| 1. 3.1936 . . . . . . . . . | 215 | 5 | 39 | 259 |
| 1. 4.1936 . . . . . . . . . | 220 | 8 | 42 | 270 |
| 1. 5.1936 . . . . . . . . . | 298 | 30 | 65 | 393 |
| 1. 6.1936 . . . . . . . . . | 325 | 31 | 73 | 429 |
| 1. 7.1936 . . . . . . . . . | 400 | 33 | 83 | 516 |
| 1. 8.1936 . . . . . . . . . | 360 | 37 | 96 | 493 |
| 1. 9.1936 . . . . . . . . . | 311 | 32 | 95 | 438 |
| 1.10.1936 . . . . . . . . . | 191 | 26 | 76 | 293 |
| 1.11.1936 . . . . . . . . . | 130 | 26 | 91 | 227 |
| 1.12.1936 . . . . . . . . . | 115 | 26 | 92 | 233 |
| 1. 1.1937 . . . . . . . . . | 75 | 21 | 82 | 178 |
| 1. 2.1937 . . . . . . . . . | 72 | 22 | 88 | 182 |
| 1. 3.1937 . . . . . . . . . | 52 | 20 | 88 | 160 |
| 1. 4.1937 . . . . . . . . . | 41 | 14 | 87 | 142 |
| 1. 5.1937 . . . . . . . . . | 27 | 14 | 68 | 109 |
| 1. 6.1937 . . . . . . . . . | 58 | 15 | 62 | 135 |
| 1. 7.1937 . . . . . . . . . | 83 | 22 | 74 | 179 |
| 1. 8.1937 . . . . . . . . . | 69 | 17 | 70 | 156 |
| 1. 9.1937 . . . . . . . . . | 64 | 16 | 61 | 141 |
| 1.10.1937 . . . . . . . . . | 53 | 17 | 63 | 133 |
| 1.11.1937 . . . . . . . . . | 49 | 16 | 62 | 127 |
| 1.12.1937 . . . . . . . . . | 45 | 11 | 58 | 114 |

## Numbers of Prisoners [Verwältungsstrafgefangene] and Internees [Anhaltehäftlinge] at Kaisersteinbruch

| Date | National Socialists | Social Democrats & Communists | Total |
|---|---|---|---|
| 22.1.1934 . . . . . . . . . . | | | 77 |
| 1. 2.1934 . . . . . . . . . | | | 393 |
| 15. 2.1934 . . . . . . . . . | | | 606 |
| 1. 3.1934 . . . . . . . . . | | | 634 |
| 15. 3.1934 . . . . . . . . . | | | 596 |
| 2. 4.1934 . . . . . . . . . | 516 | 113 | 629 |
| 16. 4.1934 . . . . . . . . . | 358 | 119 | 477 |
| 24. 4.1934 . . . . . . . . . | 149 | 119 | 268 |
| 27. 4.1934 . . . . . . . . . | 40 | | 40 |

## Numbers of Political Prisoners in Austria on 23.9. and 15.12.1934

(a) 23 September 1934:

| | National Socialists | Social Democrats & Communists | Total |
|---|---|---|---|
| Vienna . . . . . . . . . . . . | 629 | 610 | 1,239 |
| Upper Austria . . . . . . . | 598 | 303 | 901 |
| Lower Austria . . . . . . . | 906 | 219 | 1,125 |
| Carinthia . . . . . . . . . . . | 512 | 17 | 529 |
| Styria . . . . . . . . . . . . . | 3,215 | 41 | 3,256 |
| Burgenland . . . . . . . . . | 22 | 3 | 25 |
| Salzburg . . . . . . . . . . . | 689 | 13 | 702 |
| Tyrol . . . . . . . . . . . . . | 265 | 14 | 279 |
| Vorarlberg . . . . . . . . . . | 261 | 8 | 269 |
| Wöllersdorf . . . . . . . . . | 4,507 | 556 | 5,003 |
| Totals | 11,604 | 1,784 | 13,388 |

### Numbers of Political Prisoners in Austria
### on 23.9. and 15.12.1934

| (b) 15 December 1934: | National Socialists | Social Democrats | Communists | Total |
|---|---|---|---|---|
| Vienna | 172 | 135 | 189 | 496 |
| Upper Austria .... | 226 | 56 | 41 | 323 |
| Lower Austria .... | 102 | 6 | 47 | 155 |
| Carinthia | 75 | 3 | 16 | 94 |
| Styria | 245 | 19 | 53 | 317 |
| Burgenland | 19 | 2 | 3 | 24 |
| Salzburg | 158 | 1 | 17 | 176 |
| Tyrol | 102 | 4 | 14 | 120 |
| Vorarlberg | 28 | – | 28 | 56 |
| Wöllersdorf | 1,323 | 158 | 142 | 1,623 |
| Totals | 2,450 | 384 | 550 | 3,384 |

25.  Cf. Dieter A. Binder, "Einige Beobachtungen zur Geschichte von Justiz, Exekutive und Landesverwaltung während des Jahres 1938" in: *Historisches Jahrbuch der Stadt Graz*, 18/19 (1988), p. 122.
26.  A short compilation of these efforts by the Austrian Government can be found in Dieter A. Binder, "Die Ära Schuschnigg, der deutsche Weg und das Ende" in: Alfred Maleta / Horst Haselsteiner (eds), *Der Weg zum Anschluß 1938. Daten und Fakten* (Vienna: Karl von Vogelsang Institut, 1988), pp. 106-162.
27.  Gerhard Jagschitz, "Zwischen Befriedung und Konfrontation" in: Ludwig Jedlicka / Rudolf Neck (eds), *Das Juliabkommen von 1936*, above n. 15, pp. 161f.
28.  Cited by Anton Staudinger, "Die Sozialdemokratische Grenzländerkonferenz vom 15.9.1933 in Salzburg" in: Elisabeth Kovacs (ed.), *Festschrift Franz Loidl zum 65. Geburtstag* (Vienna: Verlag Brüder Hollinek, 1971), vol. 3, pp. 256f.
29.  Karl Renner, *Denkschrift über die Geschichte der Unabhängigkeitserklärung Österreichs und der Einsetzung der Provisorischen Regierung*

*der Republik Österreich* (Vienna: Österreichische Staatsdruckerei, 1945), p. 15.

30. Hanisch, above n. 13, p. 158.

31. See Dieter A. Binder, "Einige Überlegungen zu politischen Positionen von Karl Kraus," *Literatur und Kritik* 211/212 (February/March 1987), pp. 55–68.

32. See Klaus Weiß, "Walter Mehring als Mitarbeiter der Wochenschrift 'Der Christliche Ständestaat.' Ein Beitrag zur Literatur des Exils" in: Maximilian Liebmann / Dieter A. Binder (eds), *Hanns Sassmann zum 60. Geburtstag* (Graz/Vienna/Cologne: Styria Verlag, 1984), pp. 379–407. Weiß similarly portrays the attitude of Roth in an excellent paper: Paul Stöcklein, "Wirksame Gegner Hitlers" in: Schweizer Monatshefte, Vol. 69, No. 5 (1989), pp. 385–399. paper. The author thanks Dr Weiß for permission to read the MS.

33. Sigmund Freud, *Briefe 1893-1939* (Frankfurt am Main: S. Fischer, 1968), p. 457.

34. See Maximilian Liebmann, "Vom 12. Februar 1934 über den Antiklerikalismus zum Nationalsozialismus" in: *Neues Archiv für die Geschichte der Diözese Linz*, 3 (1984/85), pp. 49–55; Liebmann, *Theodor Innitzer und der Anschluß. Österreichs Kirche 1938* (Graz/Vienna/Cologne; Styria Verlag, 1988), pp. 57–59; Ernst Panzenböck, *Ein deutscher Traum. Die Anschlußidee und Anschlußpolitik bei Karl Renner und Otto Bauer* (Vienna: Europa Verlag, 1985 = Materialien zur Arbeiterbewegung); Helmut Konrad (ed.), *Sozialdemokratie und 'Anschluß'* (Vienna/Munich/Zurich: Europa Verlag, 1978 = Schriftenreihe des Ludwig Boltzmann Instituts für Geschichte der Arbeiterbewegung, 9). Dieter A. Binder, "Zum Antiklerikalismus in der Ersten Republik" in: Forschungen zur Landes-,und Kirchengeschichte (Graz: Institut für Geschichte, 1988), pp. 63–74.

35. Anton Staudinger's views on this matter, frequently repeated since 1976, seem to ignore the many differences of opinion which clearly existed within the Corporate State. Thus, alongside the continuing domestic view of Austria offered by 'German nationals,' we find a different viewpoint in periodicals like *Der Christliche Ständestaat, Berichte zur Kultur und Zeitgeschichte, Vaterland,* and others. Then again, Schuschnigg's often repeated formulation of 'Austria as a second, better German state' actually had its counterpart in the thinking of the Austrian Social Democrats. As they stated in May 1933: 'If we want Austria to maintain its independence from the fascist Third Reich, it is

not so that German Austria [Deutschösterreich] (!) can turn its back for ever on Germany, but so that German Austria (!) can fulfill its mission on behalf of the whole German people.' And in 1938, after the Anschluss, Otto Bauer thought it a 'reactionary position' to want to fight for an independent Austria. However, in the non-socialist anti-Nazi camp, the Austrian propaganda of the Corporate State seems to have been so effective that the struggle against National Socialism was still linked to the struggle for Austria's independence. See Anton Staudinger, "Zur Österreich-Ideologie des Ständestaates," in Ludwig Jedlicka / Rudolf Neck (eds), above n. 15, pp. 198-240; *Arbeiterzeitung* (13 May 1933), 1; Otto Bauer, "Nach der Annexion" in: *Der sozialistische Kampf / La Lutte socialiste* (2 June 1938), 2ff., cited in Otto Bauer, *Werkausgabe* (Vienna: Europa Verlag, 1980), vol. 9, pp. 853-860; for *Der Christliche Ständestaat* see above n. 32; for *Vaterland* see Jan Papiór, "'Vaterland' (1927-1938). Eine (groß)österreichische Zeitschrift" in: *Österreich in Geschichte und Literatur*, Vol. 32, Nos. 1-2 (1988), pp. 20-30.

36. Clearly the National Socialists had achieved massive infiltration in all kinds of areas long before 1938. But we must not on that account claim that the Austrian Government offered no resistance to the Nazis. For all the civil servants who illegally became Nazis we must also count those who did their duty in the fight against National Socialism. If some politicians failed in their duty to resist, there were others who were attacked by the Nazis as 'hard-liners.' Typical for me in this latter respect is the case of Karl Maria Stepan, whom the Nazis [brauner Sumpf] attacked before and after March 1938, and again after 1945, for he was one of their most determined opponents. See Dieter A. Binder, "Karl Maria Stepan. Versuch einer Biographie" in: *Zeitschrift des Historischen Vereines für Steiermark*, 73 (1982), pp. 161-181. For a first attempt at thorough documentation of this élite in its fight against National Socialism, see Maximilian Liebmann (ed.), *Gelitten für Österreich* (Vienna: Karl von Vogelsang Verlag, 1988). It would be equally sensible to set against the cultural advances of the Nazis the consciously anti-Nazi cultural policies of their opponents (cf. Edda Fuhrich-Leisler's article in this volume).

37. Rita Koch, "Das Bedenkliche am 'Bedenkjahr,'" in *Grazer Journal* (March 1988), p. 6.

# Youth Movement, Womb Fantasies, and 'Crystal' Maps:
## Arnolt Bronnen's Fascism around 1930

Friedbert Aspetsberger

## I

It should be made clear from the outset that I do not intend to discuss Arnolt Bronnen's development with reference to the two different possibilities of his parentage. It is well known that Bronnen's legal father came from Auschwitz in Galicia, was a dramatist, and like many Jews from the eastern provinces sought assimilation into the German culture of Austria. Such was Dr. Ferdinand Bronner, whose nom-de-plume was Franz Adamus. Secondly, there was the priest Wilhelm Schmidt; after a court-case —lasting from 1938 to 1941 — to establish Bronnen's Aryan status, Schmidt was declared his natural father. (Bronnen had raised the matter of his affiliation for the first time in 1930, after his 'hatred of the father' had led to a scandal in the press at the end of the twenties.) None of this will be given 'racist' interpretation in what follows, for that would expose us to the risk of repeating obsolete racist theories, and in any case Bronnen's 'hatred of the father' is simply one more thing making him typical of his generation. He is best understood in terms of the social and political situation of the generation born around 1900, especially in Vienna.

## II

There is good reason to begin with the novel that crowned Bronnen's career, *AEsop* (*Aisopos*). for here we have a covert depiction of his own path through life. Like his hero AEsop, Bronnen, albeit metaphorically, had his spine broken in youth with consequent effects upon the rest of his life. After his pursuers

have inflicted this serious injury upon the boy Æsop, he henceforth appears in two symbolic guises: he is crippled, unsightly,
diminutive, a misshapen dwarf; or, after his spine has been stretched,
an erect individual, an intellectual struggling on behalf of himself
and the oppressed, a writer of fables and a radiant hero, whose
altercation with the priests of Delphi ends in his death at their
hands. What his pursuers do to the boy Æsop as he flees from
slavery, Bronnen's family, his schooldays and the political situation in turn-of-the-century Vienna did to him. *Æsop* appeared in
1956, two years after Bronnen's autobiography, which had met
with the scorn and derision of most of the critics. It must have
seemed to Bronnen that he was back in the situation of 1910 and
that his life as a writer had come full circle. Clearly we need to
return to the main features of his early life.

## III

The younger generation to which he belonged – the 'generation of parricides'– felt it was under extreme threat, as we see
variously in the works of Wedekind, Kaiser, Hasenclever, Unruh,
Johst and others. The Austrian dramatist Ferdinand Bruckner,
who worked in Berlin like Bronnen, made this generation the subject of a cycle of plays entitled *Jugend zweier Kriege* (Youth of
Two Wars). These young men had, largely voluntarily, fled from
the constraints of their time into the First World War and then, if
they survived, returned to find that the (fatherless) democracies of
the post-war years still offered them no acceptable solution. The
hopelessness of pre-war days accompanied them into the inter-war
period, and so helped pave the way for the Second World War.
They were not always in tune with National Socialism, but they
shared many of the attitudes of the movement, for example, their
longing for total and final solutions to their problems, for 'deliverance.' Musil deals with this matter in several sketches for *The Man
without Qualities* (*Der Mann ohne Eigenschaften*), always pleading
for 'partial solutions.'

The first play of the Bruckner cycle is entitled *Sickness of*

*Youth* (*Krankheit der Jugend,* 1926). It shows 'young people' [junge Menschen]–a catchword in contemporary discussion, indeed the title of a magazine–as suffering from complete disorientation. In the second play, *The Criminals* (*Die Verbrecher,* 1928), Bruckner shows corruption, obsession with power and misery among young people, but equally the same condition in the older generation as it continues to manage affairs. The last play of the trilogy, *Races* (*Rassen,* 1933), shows the self-surrender of a generation that has been deeply affected by the crisis of late bourgeois individualism and now succumbs to or is vanquished by Fascism.

Bruckner pursued this theme during the Second World War. He wrote a play called *For His Days Are Not Long* [*Denn seine Zeit ist kurz*] (printed in 1945), treating the subject of resistance to Nazi rule in Norway. Here we see 'German youth' with its 'higher aspirations'–were they not once 'God's own longing'? – transformed into SS officers: they have rejected 'German inwardness' and embraced 'total power,' or in other words: murder. In the earlier piece *Races,* Bruckner shows the conscious destruction and renunciation of humane tradition, the false longings for deliverance which lead to catastrophe, a catastrophe brought about by themselves; no one and nothing alien is responsible, 'no, we have irrupted violently into our own world.' Bruckner, it must be said, was writing *For His Days Are Not Long* when Arnolt Bronnen had long since extricated himself from this kind of thinking. Bronnen had served with the anti-Fascist resistance movement in the Salzkammergut, was drafted into the Territorial Reserve Army [Landwehrersatzbataillon II/17] in Steyr and Znaim, and was more than lucky not to have found himself on trial for treason.

IV

In Bruckner's play *Races,* his character Tessow has been completely won over by the Nazis. He has found that bourgeois 'excess of intellect,' which is simply 'cultivation of one's ego,' has left him 'starving.' Where he has found release is in the hate-filled, fear-ridden Nazi League of Male Students [Männerbund]. This student association claimed to have created a new mass consciousness of historical significance. With its premiss of contempt for all traditional culture, it sought to 'murder the father' ('We had no fathers / Democrats cannot be fathers'). From this point it moved to feelings of personal insignificance ('I am nothing') and an abstract idea of 'the masses' i.e., 'being German.' The goal was to become part of the masses in this sense, and so find release from selfhood ('At last I am no longer myself' / 'If only I can cease to be the Tessow I once was').

We find a similar depiction in Musil's *The Man without Qualities,* where the Racist Movement is characterized through the figure of Hans-Sepp—in an early version called Hans-Depp [Johnny Blockhead]. His beliefs and aggressions are like those which Bruckner shows us in Tessow. Hans-Sepp talks of 'this hugger-mugger they call culture' but on the other hand cannot state his own position or goals with any clarity. When Ulrich asks him, he replies: 'I don't know. But I'm not alone. And when a few thousand people want something . . . .' So he too appeals to a new mass consciousness. He opposes the idea of individuals competing commercially, socially and culturally, and looks to a 'community of people who have completely renounced their individuality.' Musil has this 'young person' meet his death at the hands of the ruling system, thereby showing a certain sympathy with Hans-Sepp as martyr for a cause, characterizing him as follows: Hans-Sepp is a head that can't think properly, but he is defeated by nothing other than better heads, like Ulrich's.

Musil takes the question of youth and culture very seriously, even though he mocks it. He had already treated young people's intense feelings of vulnerability and hopelessness in *Young Törless* (*Die Verwirrungen des Zöglings Törless,* 1906). His point there was not racial but quite generally applicable to pre-1914 youth: in their sadistic and masochistic needs, they are a counterpoint to the order of society as evinced by the military academy. Musil highlights how society fails to respond to either the sexual or intellectual questionings of the young – an example of this failure is when Törless can get no satisfactory answer from his teacher on mathematical questions. In tormenting Basini Törless' fellow-pupil Reiting is motivated by his religious-cum-mystical leanings, but he also feels the need to show how manipulable a human being is, how the apparently firm shape of a personality can be altered so that the person is the same yet another. (The same thing happens to Bruckner's Tessow in *Races.*) Törless experiences the manipulations carried out by Reiting and Beineberg as something deeply part of himself. Musil later noted in his diary: 'Modern dictators *in nucleo.* It is there too in the idea of the masses as something to be coerced.' In *Törless,* he keeps politics out of the intellectual and sexual confusions of his adolescents, and limits his concern to the problem of being young. But the connection is still quite clear, as it is later in *The Man without Qualities* with the mass-murderer Moosbrugger. It is a connection made programmatically clear by Wilhelm Reich in *The Mass Psychology of Fascism (Massenpsychologie des Faschismus,* 1971), where we read that the 'coupling of sadistic brutality and mystic feelings . . . is commonly found wherever there is incapacity to achieve a normal experience of orgasm.' This was undoubtedly a particular problem for young people at the turn of the century.

Hanns Johst, who later became President of the Reich Chamber of Literature and a Brigade Commander in the SS, depicts the same kind of problem in his drama *The Young Man (Der junge Mensch,* 1916). For his hero, too, the 'façades' of culture and society collapse as though made of 'papier mâché.' There is talk of prewar Germany as a 'firm gone bankrupt,' in which young people are 'forced to live a lie.' The 'Young Man' longs for 'new words' like 'the Host,' but also for new priests who 'shed blood, blood, blood,' 'priests who slaughter.' This young 'murderer of the father' ('We are no longer sons; we are only comrades now') falls victim to prevailing circumstances, meets his death, is resurrected, and in the final scene of the play despairingly rushes towards the audience, cynically demanding their applause, appearing once again to sacrifice himself to society. Johst wanted to be a missionary, and his religious iconography is only too palpable.

It is this 'Young Man' who takes on the role of 'Aryan dynamite' in Hanns Johst's famous political drama *Schlageter* (1933). This new hero comes straight out of the Youth Movement with all its aggressiveness; his National Socialism is exaggerated to scandalous proportions, 'reaching for his Browning when he hears the word "culture."' The vocabulary of the Youth Movement contained many phrases like 'disgrace to civilization' [Kulturschmach] and 'manure heap of culture' [Misthaufen der Kultur]. These were not specifically Nazi, as this kind of negation had existed independently since Nietzsche. Contemporaries judged the turn of the century very differently from the way we do today. They did not shower praise upon its culture: Hermann Broch speaks for his time when he uncovers the cynicism lurking behind the decorative exterior, as does Musil when he describes his age as 'full of deception, like a quagmire' or calls its ideals 'those of police headquarters.' And so on.

Walter Hasenclever's *The Son* (*Der Sohn,* 1914) was seen by contemporaries as the work which gave voice to the protests of the younger generation. His hero demands, in terms similar to Johst's 'Young Man' that 'the ego should become more brutal in the world,' that 'you should kill what has killed you.' He gives the biological superiority of youth over age the status of a maxim. In the 'Club to Propagandize Life,' the 'son' appears as a redeemer 'sent by God,' a Christ who unclothes himself to reveal the stigmata of his youth. By creating a kind of mass hysteria, he gathers devoted supporters and disciples about himself. A constant feature of all these plays is the redeemer figure gathering mass support.

Hasenclever's 'son' states that hate not love is one's first experience of the parental home. The same applies to the State, as both the text of the drama and its contemporary reception show. Arnolt Bronnen wrote a parallel 'murder of the son' / 'murder of the father' play. In his autobiography he writes of these years: 'The State, the professor, the family—for me they were all a kind of brute force. I could achieve liberty only by destroying that force. I simply had to seek freedom, escape from constriction and unbearable coercion. At least, I thought that liberty was what I was seeking, but in fact it was nothing other than anarchy, destruction, conflagration.' Looking back on the time when he was involved with the Youth Movement, Bronnen cannot be other than critical, for he had not merely belonged to the movement but he had followed it into one of its political aberrations.

V

Bronnen was highly active in the Youth Movement in Vienna, and managed to engage on both its right and left wings. He moved in 'Wandervogel' circles of the Youth Movement around Müller-Guttenbrunn and Bruno Brehm, but more especially in the grouping led by Gustav Gugenbauer and Oskar Mahr. He was also active in the movement centred on the journal *Der Anfang* [New Departures], which was the creation of Siegfried Bernfeld (Vienna) and Georges Barbizon (Berlin), and edited by the well-known reformist pedagogue Gustav Wyneken. A good deal of work still needs to be done to reveal just how radical the movement was. The Vienna Secondary Schools' Discussion Groups [Sprechsäle Wiener Mittelschüler] spread from Vienna via Berlin to countless other towns in Germany. Bernfeld was in charge of the Archives of Youth Culture [Archiv für Jugendkultur], which among other things collected together writings of the younger generation. The Discussion Groups were divided into many Special Associations [Hetairien], each concerned with a specialist topic. Bronnen joined the one led by the brothers Eisler, and was actively involved in events surrounding a lecture by Wyneken which was banned by the police and gave rise to a political scandal. It was in the committee rooms of this Special Association in Vienna's Third District that, after locking out his comrades, he wrote his first dramatic works. We learn from his autobiography how in his youth he experienced such absolute contradictions that he could not decide between left-wing and right-wing tendencies. However, on neither wing did this reticent and inhibited young man manage, despite his eloquence, to take on the role of leader – 'Führer' was the title used by the Youth Movement.

In May 1913 Franz Pfemfert's *Aktion* press in Berlin published the first number of *Der Anfang*. At the same moment Bronnen completed his massive drama *A Right to Youth* (*Recht auf Jugend*), which remained unpublished and can be found among his posthumous papers in the Deutsches Literaturarchiv at Marbach/Neckar. In this work the recurring topoi of the Youth Movement find radical expression. The great sermons of the protagonist Hans Harder could be said to make the positive goals of the movement sound like the road to salvation; but what emerges most of all from the action of the play is the mass of contradictory attitudes seething beneath the surface. Bronnen characterizes the youth of his day in the round. There are the socially differentiated pupils of the academic secondary school, and in one of the acts we are shown working-class youth of two political kinds: socialist and proletarian on the one hand, gutter anarchists on the other.

All the existential, social and political confusions of the period are given focus in the chaotic sexuality depicted by the work, and this is very much in keeping with the significance ascribed to sexuality by contemporary writers like Freud and Otto Weininger. Bronnen's work shows clearly why the protest of the Youth Movement against a deadening environment had to be bound up with sexuality. It is because of attitudes of the older generation, which felt so in control of its rationally ordered world that it appeared to deny existence to anything outside that world, including the younger generation. Thus, fathers reacted to their children's perplexities with clever remarks, reducing the import of genuine problems by not taking them seriously. Harder's father can comfortably and cynically state that nothing is serious, especially one's children: 'But you can't take children seriously, my dear boy. Parents never take children seriously. Never. Let's be frank, what is a child? A sticky mess that could well have ended up in a condom. That's all. And a scientifically educated generation is supposed to take what it has spawned seriously!'

Everything the younger generation wants is put down to 'higher belly-ache,' part of bodily needs that have to be suppressed and controlled. 'Higher belly-ache as a result of lower belly-ache,' that is, everything the young want is really to do with their sexuality, which is here made to seem the sum total of their lives. The effect of this treatment is that their lives come to appear as something completely determined by the older generation — simply its own negative product, like the child as the sperm which was not caught by the condom. Life is something negative; it is chance or your parents, not you yourself. The school as institution stands at the centre of all this negativity. A school forced upon offspring by their parents is cynically viewed as 'a brothel, with pupils going in and out.' In Musil's *Young Törless,* the pupils visit a brothel on the river; in Bronnen's work, they can go to the school café and find a whore who will turn them all into 'filthy pigs' by offering them the sexuality of the adult world. As in Musil, the prostitute in the first version of Bronnen's drama is called Božena. She is 'well made, but a bit too Slav' — the class shows its 'friendly face' in this and countless other nationalistic and illiberal utterances.

The Jewish pupil Goldstein says that since the Christians have taken over in heaven even the weather gets neglected, and 'that's because 99% of tennis players pay the Jewish Community Tax — St Peter should remember that he too was once a dirty Jew.' When his German nationalist classmate Pavlovic sings, Goldstein would like to cry out, 'What a shame! What a shame!' Pavlovic says of a homosexual dance by some of the pupils that it is 'what the Jews call art,' and he introduces his classmate Törnök to the whore Božena as 'on the quiet side, but strong on anti-Semitism.' Božena asks the 'squirters' how often a day they masturbate, and there is a class song, to a well-known operetta tune, on the subject: 'Tiny little hand, shiny little hand / You are mine, don't decline / It's as plain as it can be? / You're a sweet little wife to me.'

The working-class young are no different. They may be socialist reformers missing out on their youth, or gutter right-wingers living out the sadistic fantasies of adolescence. Their songs, too, are similar, but much more vulgar. ('Cunt says I'm ready, prick goes in steady . . . Cunt says there's blood, prick says that's good.') Bronnen everywhere stresses the sexual component in all activity, because that is where the brutality of life imposed on the young most clearly shows itself. An example of this brutality – like that unleashed in the wave of violence against the Jews in Vienna after the German occupation of 1938 – is a scene in Bronnen's play where two youths relate how they spied on someone they knew, while he was having sexual relations, and then broke in on him:

> First we knocked him around the room like a football. Hey, that was great! He flew about and there was blood everywhere, and we just couldn't stop laughing. He got on top of the wardrobe to get a breather, but we soon had him down, and the wardrobe too – he crashed down so hard his legs nearly came out the top of his head. (Both laugh uncontrollably.) Then I took a knife and told him we were going to cut 'em off. He started hollering like a Red Indian. At the end we chucked him through the window. He was howling out there like a filthy Jew. (Laughs.) And we were howling inside the room. God, it was bloody good fun . . . I've never laughed so much! . . . Afterwards I slept with the girl all night. Good looker, bit hefty. I wanted to stick a knife in her, she'd got all that flab, but she chucked me out. I'll stick a knife in her one day, though . . . I like sticking it in people . . .

We saw in the case of the schoolboys how close the political and sexual spheres were; so, too, with the working-class young. The passage just quoted follows a depiction of the worker's sister, just out of school, who 'does for a Jew and has to clean up his muck.' The way she looks is put down to the fact that the 'Jew' is sexually abusing her, but this turns out not to be the real issue. What really matters is that she should not have a child and bring 'shame' on the family. This is because the worker is thinking of his own life, and how his parents married after he was born: 'I'd brought shame on the family and he would have to pay for it.'

Social and political problems which appear insoluble are transposed into sexual ones, turning sexuality into an analogous chaos. What results is a breakdown in communication, or complete isolation, or relationships which are perverse or sadistic. This is what characterizes life in the 'brothel,' that symbol of the adult world. This is the source of repression in the younger generation. The crassest example is the masturbation scene during the Greek lesson, when Springer slides under his desk and asks Hans Harder to help him gain relief, even by pricking him with a needle. It would be wrong to reduce the scene to Bronnen's exaggeration of sexuality, albeit the drastic presentation is unique to him. Musil, too, uses the image in *Young Törless,* when Törless watches Reiting and Beineberg torment Basini and gains an insight in which the limits of normal life are overstepped and his own needs are served: it is 'an incubation concentrated in the sharp pain of a needle prick.'

The intensity of sexual experience serves equally in Bronnen's drama *A Right to Youth* as the starting-point for aspiring to a different form of existence, here that of the God-sent prophet. After the scene in which he has helped his classmate find relief, Hans Harder begins his Imitatio Christi: at first he merely incites his fellows; then he preaches more and more powerfully, gathering his classmates around him like apostles; finally he turns his newly created community into rebels against the school. He has already killed his cousin, but alleges that the latter sacrificed his own life in youth's crusade against the older generation. In this way he creates, with the utmost cruelty, evidence for his apostleship, his teaching, his faith, his truth, his purity. All these things – like the Nationalists' 'sense of what it is to be German' – are hard to prove, and in moments of weakness Harder does not believe in them himself. But he knows that it is about a new way of feeling, an ideal of purity, a life that is described in words like 'sacred,' 'wondrous,' 'strange,' and one that stands opposed to the corrupt, sensual life imposed on the young by their parents:

> The day will come when youth will no longer be enslaved
> by you
> When we shall no longer suffer for being young
> Then we shall step out of the culture you teach
> And we shall establish our own existences.
> Then your power will be at an end.
> Then youth will stand high above you
> As I stand higher than all others . . .
> For my disciples, who fight in the vanguard for youth,
> must all possess an iron faith – to withstand the enormous
> pressure upon us all. They must possess an unbelievable,
> miraculous faith in our future – so that they can clear away
> all the dross . . . and their faith shall be as a miracle to
> shine forth upon all mankind.

Harder, like the programmatic journal *Der Anfang,* hopes to create
a new culture, the culture of youth. In this he is following albeit
with messianic claims, in the footsteps of Gustav Wyneken, who
read Bronnen's drama with enthusiastic approval. Bronnen was
very keen to meet, and did meet, Wyneken during the latter's visit
to Vienna in 1914. Harder's words, like the wish of the 'Young
Man' in Johst's work, are meant to take on the 'substance of the
Host.' The possibility of this kind of experience was in the air.
There are parallel examples in the posthumous papers of Wyneken,
to be found in the Archives of the German Youth Movement in
Burg Ludwigstein. One need only cite a letter to him from a
woman teacher in Hamburg: 'And then your words were there
again, the words I had from your lips, living words that were like a
call and a prophecy . . . Take leave of yourselves! Rise up! You
have the strength . . . so many of you hungering in our schools . . .
Jesus and his disciples! Come of one accord and follow the Master!'

Hans Harder's school revolt fails. He is thrashed all the way
home by his father. Of course, he does not give up. In the final
scene, we again have explicit portrayal of the connection between

youth's quest for purity and the corrupt sexuality imposed upon it by the older generation. Harder now murders his cousin Elise, who has fled her parental home with him and most clearly represents his sexual problems. As with his cousin Franz, Harder again uses the death to accuse the parent generation of creating a sacrificial victim. The scene is completed by the coarse comments of the crowd which gathers – much in the style of the young workers' depiction of the sexual act – giving Hans' 'pure' sacrifice of Elsie an 'obscene' frame.

Bronnen, we recall, wrote the drama in the committee-rooms of one of the groups associated with *Der Anfang,* but he does not appear to have shown or read the work to any of his comrades. All the groups were very keen on discussion, but Bronnen always felt inferior and criticized the 'quick-witted' Jews who formed the majority in these circles. (According to Wyneken's biographer, Kupfer, about one third of Wyneken's supporters in Berlin were of Jewish descent; in Vienna it was about 450 out of 500.) We find in a letter to Wyneken what, as far as I can see, are the only utterances of Bronnen to smack of anti-Semitism. And here it is important to remember that Bronnen is addressing his remarks to Wyneken, who at the Hoher Meissner Free German Youth Congress in 1913 had taken a strong line against attitudes of the 'Wandervogel' movement towards racial purity, anti-Semitism, anti-Slavism – attitudes which were particularly prevalent among Austrian members of the movement, like Professor Keil. So we are, in Bronnen's case, not dealing with anti-Semitic utterances in the modern sense. Bronnen subsumes his difficulties as follows: 'What is responsible? (1) the fact that there are too many of them, (2) the fact that there are too many good-looking girls ("Show your breasts! Show your wit!"), (3) just the fact that they're all Jews.' Quite clearly, he did not get very far with his apostleship in the intellectual circles associated with *Der Anfang.* Where he felt more at home was in the smaller 'Wandervogel' group around Gustav Gugenbauer. There he made contacts which he kept up after the World War.

And yet at the same time, Bronnen was hardly reticent about

his work. He sent it to Wyneken; he sent it to the Dramaturge of the Deutsches Theater in Berlin and also to people of his own age who might be expected to respond positively. Walter Benjamin found the manuscript 'very courageous, showing a lot of flair.' He considered Bronnen's letter to be 'among the most gratifying testimonies I could have received' and hoped that Bronnen 'without knowing me personally, will have heard enough from Berlin . . . to want to enter into correspondence with me, given that we both stand some way outside the main thrust of the Youth Movement.' The relationship did not, however, develop further, and Bronnen makes no mention of Benjamin in his autobiography.

## VI

It is not simply that Bronnen kept his drama secret in Austria and sent it to Germany; it seems that Germany, his mother's native country, was for him the great hope on the horizon. He wrote to Wyneken explaining how difficult things were for him in Austria: 'The Jews are not to blame. It's all the fault of this other damned race calling itself German Austrians [Deutsch-Österreicher] —to whom, thank God and thanks to my North German parentage, I do not belong.' The coda to this statement reveals his leap into a 'racial' ideal: his impulsion towards Germany presumably had something to do with 'hatred of the father' (whether this was Bronner from Galicia or Schmidt from Slovakia), since both were Austrian. But it was also, perhaps, part of the hopeless situation in Austria which Arthur Schnitzler so minutely documented in his novel *The Way into the Open* (*Der Weg ins Freie*, 1908). Young people in particular experienced their social and political frustrations as existential discontent. Bronnen writes in his autobiography: 'But we young people had already written off the State for which we were supposed to give our lives. Loyalty to the black and yellow flag of the Imperial house was seen as an old-fashioned caprice. The prevailing attitude among the sons of middle-class families was Pan-German, and if you took yourself seriously you wore a cornflower.' Käthe Leichter, who also moved in circles associated with *Der Anfang,* points out that the children of the liberal middle class felt their 'loss of roots' as well as 'revulsion at the sympathies for Old Austria shown by their fathers.'

Bronnen could find a good deal of support for his anti-Austrian feelings – for example, in *Die Aktion,* whose press produced *Der Anfang* and to whose editor, Franz Pfemfert, Wyneken had passed on the manuscript of Bronnen's drama. Bronnen is likely, then, to have read *Die Aktion,* which was at just this moment producing articles giving contemporary views of the Habsburg monarchy. In his own article of January 1913, 'Breaking away from Austria' ('Los von Österreich'), Pfemfert calls Austria 'an obstacle to our development,' 'a pillar of reaction,' 'an unnatural construct,' 'a compromising cultural dead weight.' Another article describes Austria as clerical, reactionary, Hungarian-agrarian, and so on. At the beginning of May, we read that Austria is not just toying with its own collapse but actively promoting it; the abscesses are bursting; the two-headed eagle is looking more and more like a bird of ill omen. Even Robert Musil, writing in *Die Aktion* in 1913, can say in his article 'Politics in Austria' ('Politik in Österreich'): 'Outwardly everything is so parliamentary that more people can get shot dead here than anywhere else . . . People challenge each other with a slap on the face, but everything has a half-conventional air, like a game with agreed rules . . . There is something uncanny in this obstinate rhythm without a melody, without words, without feelings . . . Austrian politics have no human goal, only an Austrian one.'

This description parallels those given by Schnitzler in his drama *Professor Bernhardi* (1912) and in *The Way into the Open* (1908). What comes over clearly are the powerful contradictions on the political scene, but at the same time the major concern of all political activity seems to be not to seek any kind of solution. All the ratiocination appears as a kind of compensation for paralysis, and this could well account for the radical nature of the scenes of Bronnen's drama, where ideas of messianic redemption look like the only alternative. A different solution, and one which Bronnen will try himself after the War, is offered by Nikodemus

(Heliogabal Schuster) in *Die Aktion:* 'The best among the German Austrians live abroad. This is because they can't stand having to listen to people singing out of tune all the time back at home.' Bronnen returned from captivity in Italy in October 1919, and in February 1920 he fled, with Wyneken's help, to Berlin.

## VII

Many contemporaries thought that the War offered them a way out of their difficulties. Bronnen immediately reported voluntarily and was turned down; he was finally called up, but only because he managed to hide his short-sightedness and to claim, falsely, that he knew Russian. In 1916 he was seriously wounded on the South Tyrol front and survived, according to an Italian doctor, because he was of 'good German stock' [buona razza tedesca]. His recovery seemed to him a kind of rebirth. From his Sicilian prisoner-of-war camp he kept up contact with Wyneken and 'Wandervogel' circles and so sustained his youthful attitudes throughout and beyond the War. In 1917 he wrote to one of his 'Wandervogel' contacts, Gustav Gugenbauer: 'The War was being run by old men . . . so it was reasonable, calm and apathetic. Not our war.' There was to be a special number of *Junge Menschen* (young people) for Austrians – not for 'Austria,' since there was already an Anschluss mentality – and Bronnen was planning a 'loud fart' for it. But his article did not appear; Gugenbauer's did.

On his return from captivity Bronnen reworked the four dramas he had now written. The play he had written in Italy, *Storm against God* (*Sturm gegen Gott*) was renamed *Storm Patrol* (*Sturmpatrull*). It shows a group of soldiers in a very exposed position who are ordered to mount an assault. But they are without any contact with their own troops and find their situation becoming desperate. The mental and physical traumas suffered are dramatically intensified to the point of near-hopelessness. The men's officer, Lecht, rises above a cynical and murderous attitude like Harder's in *A Right to Youth* and becomes a kind of Christ figure, taking the survivors in charge and procuring them an Ascension:

> From the earth arise those who are buried alive
> from the valleys come the dying
> from the wire entanglements crawl the putrefying
> dust and gas explode
> a mine tears the mountain asunder
> they stand aloft, hand in hand, encircling the One.

Bronnen's first version of the idea of redemption from the barbarity and dangers of life had, of course, been Hans Harder's unsuccessful Imitatio Christi in *A Right to Youth*. But he claimed that the idea for *Storm Patrol* had come to him as a result of mystical experience in the Carthusian nunnery at Calci. He had been taken there to convalesce, and as a Protestant had been peculiarly impressed by the religious rites of the nuns. The connection between Hans Harder and Bronnen's mystical experience at Calci again suggests the appropriateness of quoting Wilhelm Reich's *Mass Psychology of Fascism*. Reich notes the view held by those studying the economy of sexual life that religion can provide a fantasy gratification when physical gratification is absent: 'Vegetotherapy has demonstrated that mystical experience actually sets in motion the same processes in the autonomous life mechanism as do intoxicants. There are states of sexual arousal which are brought on by various kinds of intoxication and require the relief of orgasm.' Bronnen's religio-dramatic excursion, which he condemned with finality in his autobiography, seems to be in keeping with the above analysis, especially when one thinks of the place of sexuality in contemporary youth culture and its high profile in the psychological climate of Vienna. It is important to stress sexuality as a determining factor before passing on to Bronnen's 'parricide' drama as womb fantasy, which remained the mould for his fascist ideas until roughly 1930.

## VIII

It is possible to see Bronnen's fascism as taking a fairly straight line of development. But in view of the generally negative view of him as a political being psychology seems to offer a better basis for judging him. A good starting point for such a judgment is provided by Bronnen's best-known work, *Parricide* (*Vatermord*). Its content can be subsumed in a few words: the father, Fessel, is a despot as well as a failed social democrat functionary. He forces on his son Walter the career he wanted for himself. The mother is an able tactician; while appearing to be submissive to the father, she actually incites her aggressive son against him. She uses sexual attraction in her dealings with both. Following a series of arguments, the son locks his father out of the house, cohabits with his mother, kills his father, and finally frees himself from his mother, whom he taunts with 'being old':

> I have had enough of you / I have had enough of everything / Go and bury your husband you are old / I though am young / I do not know you / I am free / No one in front of me no one beside me no one above me father dead / Heavens I leap up to you I fly / It urges trembles groans cries must go upward swells gushes rushes flies must go upward
> I
> I blossom!

This phallic, orgasmic shape at the close corresponds to Hasenclever's figure of the 'Son' standing 'bathed in light'; it corresponds also to Johst's figure of the 'Young Man' ending his resurrection from the grave by leaping into the spotlight and towards the audience; it corresponds indeed to all the youth figures of the turn of the century, the most famous of which—so often sent as a postcard—is by the painter Fidus (Hugo Höppner), showing youths stretching their arms upward to the sun and entitled 'To God.' We might claim that the 'erect' Æsop of Bronnen also belongs here.

The figure of Walter Fessel soaring skyward shines brightly above the dark cave-like setting of Bronnen's play. In the stage directions of the 1915 version of *Parricide* the set is described as follows: 'Room of the Fessel family. Furnished like that of the poorest worker: three beds, three tables. Besides this room, a hole in the wall leading into the corridor and with just enough space for two beds and a sewing machine; a tiny dark kitchen and a closet. / Place: always the same; time: continuous.' In his 'Letter to My Father' ('Brief an den Vater') Kafka writes that 'the giant figure of my father' stretched across the last white patches on the map of the world leaving no space for his son to inhabit. Fessel keeps his son – who longs to break loose, become a farmer, perhaps go out to the colonies – locked up in the dark dwelling, forcing him to study, trying to make a politician out of him. At the same time, Fessel keeps his son locked away from his sexually attractive mother, thereby increasing the young man's sexual excitement. Fessel comes to realise that a plot has been hatched by mother and son, and when they lock him out, he breaks back in through the 'hole' that constitutes the marital bedroom (!). The son senses that his life is in danger: 'My murderer is here inside – he is tearing me apart / he is tearing me to pieces / he is impaling me . . . .' Clearly, the dwelling is to be seen as the mother's body before the birth of the child, and Walter's cry is the anxiety of the unborn child as the father's penis enters the mother. Birth is then interpreted as the attempt to escape the father and becomes a model for the son's behaviour, an attempt as it were to give birth to himself.

When he was reworking *Parricide*, Bronnen made clear in a letter to his friend Gugenbauer that he had no time for the modish idea of colonising and settling land, and so we may be fairly sure that the spatial vision in his drama is not about that but about the Oedipus complex. Even Walter's desire to be a farmer, or to go out to the colonies, is essentially a scheme intended to run counter to his father's professional hopes for him. He wants to break out of the prison-house of existing social and family tensions in which his father intends to keep him. And also, from a biographical point of view, Walter's flight from home doubtless reflects Bronnen's flight from Vienna to Berlin to escape the oppressive conflicts of his home town – exactly as in *A Right to Youth*.

In her work *Early Stages of the Oedipus Complex* (1985), the psychoanalyst Melanie Klein discusses how womb fantasies take on different spatial configurations within which symbolic acts occur. These constantly suggest to her ways of demonstrating the complex – such as using patients' drawings – in order to test the validity of her analyses. Her most instructive study for our consideration of the case of Bronnen is that of Richard, a child living in London during the Blitz. In the course of psychoanalysis, Richard executes a number of drawings. They show starfish, plants, cuttlefish and the like in water, and the boy shows his own spatial position in relation to all of these. There are also warships, whose manoeuvres clearly reveal his self-defensive fantasies. Over the period of treatment, he evolves a starfish which takes on a pattern and colouring symbolizing his father and siblings, so that the starfish becomes a map representing his more or less endangered selfhood. The starfish is clearly also a womb, and the events of the Second World War operate symbolically to characterize Richard's sense of self. Klein writes:

> The surface pattern shows an empire, and the different segments signify different lands. It is symptomatic that Richard's interest in the events of the War played an important part in his associations. He often used to look at the countries which Hitler had subjugated, and it was clear that there was a connection between those countries in the atlas and his own drawings of a great empire. These latter represented his mother, who was being encroached upon and attacked. His father frequently appeared as the enemy.

For Klein it is clear that 'the entire empire represents the womb.' The setting of *Parricide* – the dark dwelling with the 'hole' in the parents' bedroom, into which the father penetrates, endangering the son – can also be seen as a representation of the womb. Melanie

Klein reads the whole range of Richard's drawings as an indication of his inability to achieve the genital level; and this description could be used of the spatial organization in Arnolt Bronnen's drama too. The final image of the Youth, erect and bathed in light, is similarly suggestive.

Details of Bronnen's biography offer corroboration for this kind of interpretation. There are his problems as a private tutor during his schooldays, a period in which he considered himself to have been a pederast. He mentions strong urges which he felt in the Italian prisoner-of-war camps. And his friendship with Gugenbauer, the 'Wandervogel' figure, is equally part of the pattern.

## IX

For Bronnen the stage-set for *Parricide* of a symbolic womb (in Klein's terms the map of an empire) comes, after the First World War, to symbolize Germany. Perhaps the fact that his mother was Pomeranian played a part in this transposition. He had, we recall, in pre-war days tried to distinguish his 'race' from that of the German Austrians by stressing his descent from North German parents. Then there was the German nationalist ideology of Vienna's middle-class youth, but also Bronnen's growing despair in his Austrian home town. After the Versailles Treaty the remnant of Austria held no further interest for him. And we remember, too, how an Italian doctor had put his recovery from a dangerous war wound down to his 'good German stock.' When we put all this information into the context of Kafka's description of claustrophobia in the 'Letter to My Father,' as well as into that of Hans Grimm's novel of 1926 (when Bronnen knew Grimm), *People without Land* [Volk ohne Raum] – later to become a catchword with repercussions for mass psychology – we can begin to see these details of Bronnen's earlier life as having a more than personal significance.

Bronnen now gives a new sense to his womb image, that of an idealized Germany. Here he takes from his days with the Youth Movement the ideologeme that Germany is something pure and invulnerable. The frontiers drawn by the Versailles Treaty he feels as mutilations; he resents the vast political changes, even the revolutionary movements (for which his sense of being one of the oppressed ought to have elicited sympathy); he resents the speed with which wholesale capitalism is being unleashed and taking over every aspect of social relations, and so on. All these things now take the place of the father-figure, and become the new threats to the womb of Mother Germany. Once again he opposes to the chaos and excesses of reality the purity of the ideal.

In 1923 Bronnen's drama *Excesses* (*Exzesse*) reveals in its settings his new conception of the nation. The play shows the dangers threatening the inner and outer forms of a 'Reich.' The protagonists are two employees of a large bank, which is clearly intended to represent post-war Germany in all its corruptness. The two employees, who have fallen in love at first sight, are posted quite arbitrarily and against their wishes, to branches which are as distant from each other as they could be: one is in Stralsund, the other in Bozen (which had, in fact, recently been incoporated into the Kingdom of Italy). The northern and southern extremities of this 'Reich' — the annexation of Austria is tacitly deemed to have occurred — thus create frontiers and thereby real dangers for the integrity of the country. There is arbitrary separation of what (love decrees) should be together, and so there is danger to substance, particularly to the people involved. This is made clear in the behaviour of the protagonists, who live lives of continuous dissoluteness. The audience at the première in 1925 were shocked by the presentation of unbridled sexuality, alcoholism, constant brawling, and insurrection (in Bozen against the Italian Bersaglieri). The audiences's sense of shock even reached *The Times, The Morning Post, The Observer* and other foreign newspapers. However, contemporary critics recognized behind the excesses portrayed on stage things that were typical of the times, things of social relevance. The play was deemed to show how the theme of 'excess' had 'the widest possible implications and ought to be of general concern.' The *Berliner Zeitung* noted the play's treatment of primitive aggression in the social behaviour of the masses.

Stefan Grossmann wrote in *Tage-Buch:* 'Bronnen "drew" with truly prophetic eye a gang of racketeers . . . one of those credit institutes that, three years later, we read about in almost every issue of the daily press . . . What lives do they [the employees] lead? Deadening slavery at the till by day, dissipation by night . . . he has simply turned reality into fiction and given ordered form to what crawls about us in painful disorder.' One might find Bronnen's desire for 'order' suspect. However, it is not only the marginals who attract the brutal psychological and social realism of so many of his scenes. According to him, the crassness of detail is an emanation of the 'mythological' conception of his drama. In the preface to his play *Rhenish Rebels* (*Rheinische Rebellen,* 1925), he tells us that it is his intention 'to see and shape the crystal [by which he means Germany] around which a moment of history, its figures and their destinies form.' He claims that there is nothing intellectual in this idea, but nothing of traditional patriotism either; his 'crystal' drama will convince by its very form. Bronnen is equally irrational when he declares that his 'vision of the crystal' shows Germany as it really is, namely, the only country 'which has natural frontiers and fixes its own limits, like a solid foreign body, within the gently flowing contours of our continent.'

Against logic and experience – these are categories of the 'older generation'– Bronnen seeks in the pure solid form of the crystal an objective correlative for his ideal, or we might think of young Richard and say, with a certain exaggeration, that Bronnen is 'trying to achieve the genital level.' This applies equally to two further facets of his argument. *Rhenish Rebels* is to have the same effect on the audience as on its author, 'who saw on a huge globe this small, oppressed land lost in a vast wilderness of sea and rock, and could never forget that this was his country.' In this form of objectification we can see parallels to the author's womb fantasies: the same sense of danger and the same desire for flight are there. A parallel is there, too, in the choice of subject-matter: the revolt of the Rhenish Provinces and their attempt to form a Rhenish Republic independent of Germany. Bronnen is aware of the importance of this area in European history, and has the sense of a

'flux of ideas' within which the 'crystal' lies as though in a 'corro-
sive sea flowing around it'—the image of encirclement by hostile
forces.

Bronnen's treatment of this subject-matter underpins those
psychological components which reveal his nationalistic dramas
written during the Republic to be a continuation of his prewar
dramas, with their themes of 'youth' and 'murder of the father.'
The 'crystal' which is the country, like the 'crystal' which is a
people, is embodied by a woman, Gien, the unerotic, cool daughter of an industrialist (the name is presumably taken from the
Greek 'gyne'). 'She is the crystal which the author saw, contained
by its strict form, mathematically precise in its lines, closed upon
itself so that it returns constantly to its point of origin: bounded.'
It is this boundary, this closure against every intruder from without that is decisive. Gien is politically cunning and uses every
modern espionage technique on behalf of—naturally—the 'crystal.'
She refuses to give herself to the rebel Occc, whose deformed
body is mirrored in his illegible signature which has provided him
with a name. He has fallen madly in love with her, and she does
whatever she likes with him: she chastises him, humiliates him,
defeats him and his mistress Pola, who is a kind of counter-figure
to Gien as Madonna. Gien remains, whatever happens, virginally
pure, 'drinking in the land, intoxicated by its villages, raped by its
towns, her body enclosing our mountains.' The abstract purity of
this German woman becomes one with an abstract nationalism: 'It
is the nationalism of the sky, of language, of the ideal which floats
above the heads of eighty million people.' The significant exaggeration here of the number of Germans for the date in question reveals the aggressive nationalism hiding behind notions of purity. It
is a purity stemming from the same need which we have seen in
the adolescent Hans Harder of *A Right to Youth*, but also in the
desperate situation of Bronnen himself within his own family and
Viennese society.

Thus we see that Bronnen's dramas have their origin in his
psychological state but find further stimulus in historical and
political developments and finally conjoin with contemporary

nationalist opposition to the Weimar Republic. In 1927 Bronnen published in the *Frankfurter Zeitung* a declaration of his commitment to radical nationalism, or as he put it, 'a movement to the right.' He ended his close friendship with Brecht, made the acquaintance of Ernst von Salomon, the Jünger brothers and others. He met Goebbels and brought intellectuals together with leading members of the Nazi party. In all this he was hoping that he could discover a way of realizing the vision of the 'crystal,' Germany, in the context of National Socialism.

Furthermore, Bronnen travelled frequently to frontier zones and also found poetic stimulus in the idea of the 'frontier.' He planned a novel on South Tyrol but, realizing that industrial regions were more important, gave up his earlier idea to write a novel about the defence of Upper Silesia entitled *O.S.* [= Oberschlesien]. What really interests him is the defence of a borderland. It is for this reason that he goes to Carinthia, and this is where the abstract nature and absurdity of his idea—like those of nationalism generally at this time, indeed of National Socialism—become apparent. After 1918, the planned secession of Carinthian territory to the newly formed Kingdom of Yugoslavia and their occupation by southern Slav troops gave rise to a regional myth concerning 'defence of the realm.' Bronnen used the opportunity afforded by his trip to Carinthia to visit Hans Grimm, the author of *People without Land,* in his villa there. This linguistic frontier and the pockets of German-speaking people in Slovenia gave Bronnen the idea that the 'German hand' had stretched out towards the 'Southern Sea' (Südmeer), the Adriatic, but for some unaccountable reason had failed in its attempt. In the article he wrote for the *Münchner Neueste Nachrichten* in 1929, 'Going for the Southern Sea' ('Der Griff nach dem Südmeer'), we read how 'three fingers of the German hand' are trying to catch hold: 'the little finger reaches Görz, the ring-finger Trieste, the middle-finger stretches across Auersperg and Laas to Mitterburg. Is there not a geographical tragedy in the fact that Germany was denied access to the sea because of the presence of the coastal peninsula [Istria]? What might not have been, if at the point where the Trieste and Fiume railway lines part company there had been the sea? ' It is hard for him to take in that 'absurdly, the mountains offered resistance, the valleys, too, by running east to west, and so a massive energy was dissipated and exhausted.' Once he is on the heights of his 'geographical tragedy,' Bronnen is very generous with his idea: just as the rivers dried up in the limestone landscape of the Karst, so the Slav basin 'has swallowed up Goths, Longobards, Bavarians, Franks, German towns, German farming communities, German culture.' There lies one kind of 'acid' which eats away at the 'crystal.'

In 1930 Bronnen devoted an article in the *Kasseler Post* to the 'defence of Carinthia,' again mentioned in an article in *Die Woche* in 1931, when with a youth group he visited Hans Grimm in Lippoldsberg. He travelled to all the borderlands of the Reich, and in commentaries on his novel *O.S.* he mentioned 'frontier problems' in Burgenland, South Tyrol and elsewhere. Having worked for a Berlin radio station from 1928, he now projected his anxieties into a 'struggle for the air.' This provided the title [Kampf im Aether] for a novel which he published in 1935, albeit with different import. In his article 'Defence of the Air' ('Wehrfront im Aether'), published in the *Berliner Lokal-Anzeiger* in 1932, he argued for powerful radio stations able to transmit programmes to those wanting to preserve their German identity in Poland, Alsace, Southern Styria, South Tyrol, Sudetenland, Banat, the Baltic provinces, even Switzerland. It was tantamount to 'air cover' for the protection of the 'frontiers.' He referred to the 'battle' between Radio Graz and Radio Ljubljana (Laibach), to a 'radio battle in the east,' to the 'struggle to protect the western marches,' to a general 'battle of the air.' By 1932 all this was no longer quite so absurd as Bronnen's underlying 'frontier anxieties': it was indeed becoming part of real political activity, even if for the time being the frontiers would not be as far flung as he made them. In the mid-thirties, Austrofascism tried to give proof of its international standing by large-scale transmission of the Salzburg Festival — indeed, fighting a 'battle of the air' with Munich over the matter. Soon after this was not the only frontier that would be abolished by military power and then not at all in the sense intended by Bronnen.

If, following Melanie Klein, we interpret all Bronnen's attempts around 1930 to promote National Socialism as his attempt to 'achieve the genital level' of his own development, we must nonetheless recall Wilhelm Reich's study *The Mass Psychology of Fascism* and be very clear that Bronnen was no individual case.

X

Then again, Bronnen had in no sense securely achieved the genital level. His psychological state in these years of a very full life, the years of his successes and scandals in the Berlin theatre, was still a problematic one. This can be illustrated by a specific example. His nationalist and fascist thinking in images of maps and wombs, particularly in his play *O.S.*, produced violent reactions among liberal critics, both sensible and misguided. He was also attacked in the journal *Die Weltbühne* [World Stage] for being a 'half Jew,' as he was in the racist *Völkischer Beobachter* [German People's Observer]—a sufficient indication of the level of critical response. Bronnen wrote newspaper articles campaigning against the Amnesty, for a 'Führer,' against 'towns,' and was among those leading the disruptive activity at Thomas Mann's 'Address to the German People' ('Deutsche Ansprache') in October 1930. Shortly afterwards he married Olga Prowe-Förster, who acted on the Nazi stage and had also made quite a name for herself with her sexual conquests. At the time of her marriage to Bronnen she was Goebbels' mistress (if Goebbels' diaries are to be believed); she was no Gien, unless she too managed to indulge and remain 'pure.' This was the moment at which Bronnen set the wheels of his first affiliation case in motion. So we see that all the strands of a life that had been problematic since his youth were becoming terribly tangled. The hoped-for escape into a 'nationalism of the skies' seemed very distant. It is true that he enjoyed Goebbels' protection before and after the Seizure of Power, but as writer and

broadcaster Bronnen was constantly under attack. After Olga
Prowe-Förster's suicide, Bronnen remarried, this time Hildegard
von Lossow, who even declared that she was Bronnen's 'Aryan
alibi.' But the fact that he had to seek legal redress for dismissal
from his broadcasting post, and that he could do no more than
protest at the ban on his writings, is a truer indication of his
position.

Bronnen's new-found, apparently secure foundation in
nationalism became a matter of increasing uncertainty for him,
and this changed the import of his dramatic work. In his play
about Napoleon and Enghien, called simply *N* (which Bronnen
claimed stood for 'no' to National Socialism), we find no well-
rounded figure comparable to the parricide and offering a remedy,
nor is any geographically plausible 'Reich' presented. The play
about Elizabeth I of England, *Gloriana,* openly condemns the
queen's use of her power and her sexuality; and the single rounded
antagonist of his earlier works is here split into three: William
Shakespeare, Francis Bacon and Edward VI, who according to a
doubtful tradition are one and the same person. Without doubt
Bronnen is also attempting with his threefold antagonist to characterize his own situation and the range of his own problems. All his
strenuous efforts to get these two plays performed met with resistance. His political position was becoming more and more em-
barrassing, and he fled back to Austria to join the resistance movement in the Salzkammergut. (I have described this part of his life
in detail elsewhere.)

Bronnen's position, always a confused one, did not change
after the Second World War either. He might now be a communist,
but for everyone else – especially those returning from emigration
– he was still a Nazi follower. During the ensuing Cold War his
communism did not help to secure for him the kind of life which
his view of the poetic calling demanded. In his autobiography,
*arnolt bronnen states in evidence* (*arnolt bronne gibt zu protokoll,* 1954) he splits his own person – much as after the seizure of
power he had split the major character in his dramas – into prose-
cutor and defendant, one holding his head high, the other broken

in spirit. He does not actually defend himself, but merely gives details of his life and work; he does not put forward any redeeming 'idea,' but rather tells of his errors. Reacting to the contempt with which the biography was generally received, Bronnen created the figure of Æsop, the man with the broken spine who can stand erect: and that takes us back to the beginning of the present exposition.

In contrast to the figure of Æsop taken from a cultural tradition and laden with significance, the 'father' in Barbara Bronnen's novel *The Daughter* (*Die Tochter,* 1980) appears literally as 'no one.' This negative designation of the 'father' must, however, be seen to embrace a considerable number of leading National Socialists and 'fellow travellers.' In the case of the Austrians concerned, Klaus Amann has named them all in his well-documented work *Der Anschluß der österreichischen Schriftsteller,* 1988. The majority of them claimed after the war to have been 'no one.' But Bronnen in his autobiography confessed his complicity and gave a detailed account of his conduct up to 1945. It is the sub-title of the book, 'Thoughts on the History of the Modern Writer' [Beiträge zur Geschichte des modernen Schriftstellers], which gives the book its representative status, since it has a bearing on all those who later wished to have been 'no one.' In his complicity Bronnen was no great exception – and here we are back again with Wilhelm Reich's *Mass Psychology of Fascism;* but he is certainly exceptional in the frankness of his confession.

# Literary and Personal Responses to the Political Events of the 1930s in Austria: Stefan Zweig, Raoul Auernheimer, and Felix Braun

Donald G. Daviau

The political events of the 1930s from the appointment of Hitler as chancellor in Germany in 1933 to the Annexation (*Anschluß*) on 11 March 1938 affected the lives of all writers as well as all citizens of Austria, for everyone without exception was forced to take a position toward the political situation. After 1933 writers had three choices: to join the new National Socialist movement and follow its mandates, to remain an Austrian patriot and either go into exile or fall silent, or to withdraw into inner emigration and continue writing for a later time when the Nazi tyranny had ended. Jewish writers, like Zweig, Auernheimer, Braun, and many others, were not even offered this limited range of choices but were forced to flee into exile in order to save their lives. Once in exile the writers had the option of speaking out against National Socialism or of attempting to ignore it for whatever reasons. The three writers under discussion here illustrate three reactions to the turbulent political circumstances of the 1930s: Zweig, a positive-minded idealistic human being, preferred not to engage in polemical or political writings; Auernheimer, whose basic nature was also essentially idealistic and conciliatory, changed after 1938 into an outspoken opponent of National Socialism; Braun, the greatest idealist of all, lived in his own aesthetic world with total disregard of contemporary reality.

Zweig's initial reaction to National Socialism resembled that of the majority of other writers of the day, namely, the feeling that Hitler was merely a temporary phenomenon, who would soon self-destruct of his own excesses. Like other intellectuals, Zweig viewed Hitler in the context of the German sense of educational hierarchy; Hitler's lack of "education" (*Bildung*) made it impossible to take him seriously.[1] Since Zweig was the most cosmopolitan of all the Austrian writers and followed the European scene more closely than others, he soon rectified his initial misjudgment. He saw the ominous Nazi threat building early, but, as he always did when the outside world threatened his inner freedom and interfered with his literary endeavors, he withdrew into the world of his work—always his first priority in life—and attempted to block out unpleasant, depressing reality.

In assessing the favorable circumstances of his life in 1933 Zweig saw no reason to be concerned. Austria was still not part of Germany—indeed, the thought of annexation seemed absurd—and the protection of the Austrian legal system was still guaranteed. He was sufficiently wealthy never to have to work again if he chose not to do so, and he enjoyed an excellent international reputation as a writer. Nevertheless, his inner skepticism led him to consider moving to England in timely fashion, and consideration of this option changed to resolve following the book burnings by the German students in May 1933. For although these anti-Semitic and anti-intellectual demonstrations were purportedly not officially sanctioned, neither were they prohibited nor protested by the German government. The banning of his movie *Brennendes Geheimnis* (Burning Secret) in Germany to silence the public snickering following the burning of the Reichstag, and the *cause celèbre* over the performance of his opera *Die schweigsame Frau* (*The Silent Woman*) in 1934, which became an affair of state requiring resolution by Hitler personally, further contributed to his decision to leave Austria. Zweig felt unable even to continue to work with Richard Strauss, for even though Strauss had defended him and insisted that his librettist's name be listed on the program, Zweig worried that people might think he was collaborating with the Germans in order to receive special treatment for himself, since there was a general prohibition at this time in Germany against performances or publications by Jewish writers. When the opera was suddenly banned because of Strauss' incautious letter to

Zweig containing his frank opinion of politics in general and of the current regime, Zweig was relieved. He refused to write any further texts for Strauss to avoid compromising himself in the eyes of the other exiled writers.[2]

Precisely to avoid any hint of provocation and for his own peace of mind, Zweig for the rest of his life wrote little in literary periodicals or newspapers that could be construed as political. For example, he was invited by Klaus Mann to collaborate on the journal *Die Sammlung* (The Collection) and had initially agreed to take part as long as he believed that the journal was to serve as a bridge between the writers in Germany and those driven into exile, a periodical intended to overcome political boundaries and keep alive the humanistic ideas and values that Germany had always represented. When Klaus Mann insisted on making the publication into a political journal attacking the policies of National Socialism, Zweig withdrew from the project, explaining his reasons in a letter of 18 September 1933:

> I am not a polemical person. All my life I have always only written *for* things and for people and never against a race, a class, a nation, or a human being, and it is my conviction that people like Kerr do irreparable harm to our cause. One must approach such a great catastrophe in larger self portrayals, not with petty meddling.[3]

As will be seen, his biographical studies of *Erasmus* in 1934 and *Cicero* in 1938 were examples of what he considered proper responses.

Zweig was a pacifist and a moralist passionately devoted to humanistic and humanitarian values.[4] He aspired to be a moral leader, but only through his writings and not in person. Unlike writers such as Emil Ludwig or Romain Rolland, Zweig never enjoyed being in the limelight. On the contrary, he preferred anonymity to the extent that he claimed he would write all of his works under an assumed name, if he were given the opportunity to start his career again.[5] When he visited England in 1932, he compared his current stay with his visit as an unknown student a decade earlier, much preferring the earlier occasion, which enabled him to travel about unnoticed and in complete freedom, entirely according to his own free will.[6] Zweig was a socially responsible individual, an *Aufklärer* (enlightener), who sincerely wanted to make an impact on the world and improve it to the extent he could. However, at the same time he wanted to remain totally free as a human being rather than being hemmed in and encumbered by the public or even by friends. Furthermore, when he did occasionally make public statements in connection with his various speaking tours and readings, he deplored the way his remarks were twisted by the press, another reason why he preferred to refrain from holding interviews.[7] Even a personal letter that he wrote to the Insel Verlag explaining why he was withdrawing from *Die Sammlung* was published without his authorization, leading to misunderstandings with Klaus Mann. As a result Zweig withdrew his biographical study *Triumph und Tragik des Erasmus von Rotterdam* (Triumph and Tragedy of Erasmus of Rotterdam) from the Insel Verlag and gave it to Herbert Reichner, a small publishing company in Vienna. Zweig stood for high principles and abhorred compromise. His exemplary treatment of friends, such as Emil Verhaeren,[8] Paul Zech,[9] Raoul Auernheimer,[10] can serve as a model of behavior.

The turning point for Zweig in Austria resulted from a house search by the police in Salzburg on 18 February 1934. This invasion of the privacy of his home on the far-fetched pretext of looking for hidden arms so shattered Zweig's sense of security in Austria that he immediately fled to England to escape. Once there he quickly perceived how the British were being deceived about Germany's policy and intentions, but he still refused to speak out either personally or in his writings for several reasons: he wanted to avoid calling any attention to himself, he felt an obligation not to arouse controversy that could cause repercussions against his mother and other relatives and friends still in Vienna, and finally he felt that as a guest in England it was not his place to take a political stance that could cause his hosts embarrassment with the Germans. However, the main reason that he kept silent and refused to write for newspapers and magazines was his distaste for being in the public eye:

> The more the political tension mounted, the more I withdrew from conversations and from any public action. England is the only land in the old world in which I have never published an article on contemporary issues in a newspaper, never spoken on the radio, never took part in a public discussion; I have lived there more anonymously in my small apartment than I did thirty years ago in my student accommodations in Vienna. . . .[11]

This same attitude of withdrawal governed his behavior at the International P.E.N. Congress in 1936 in Buenos Aires, where he refused to stand for election as President or to hold any press conferences, preferring instead to remain quietly in the background as an observer. His contribution was limited to an homage to H. G. Wells. Similarly, when he toured South America, the United States, and Canada on extensive lecture tours carrying him to dozens of cities, he avoided political topics and spoke only on humanistic themes such as of "The Secret of Artistic Creation," "The Vienna of Yesterday," and "The Intellectual Unity of the World," even though this passive, non-political stance made him feel "useless," as he wrote in a letter to Felix Braun in 1939: "In the last war I could speak – could speak against the war, because I had my language, newspapers, journals, the possibility of contact. Our friends in neutral countries and in France have all those things. Here we are useless."[12]

His inner division is reflected in his hope that the BBC would discover him, and his feeling that he was not suited to delivering war propaganda. These ambivalent feelings of wanting to use his reputation for good purpose and yet unwilling to carry the weight of the responsibility accompanying a leadership role reveals the inner contradiction that eventually destroyed him. Physically and mentally he was unable to stand the strain of being an active visible leader. To Otto Heuschele and others he complained of how he suffered from the letters he received and how these continuous pleas for help, "almost always only pleas and complaints, outbursts of despair" corroded his creative energy.[13]

Initially Zweig genuinely tried to help to the maximum extent that he could, but the time-consuming nature of interceding on behalf of refugees by vouching for them and obtaining visas for them became so great that he could not continue. To Braun he lamented: "It is horrible what a burden these letters place on me."[14] He donated to the refugee fund and gave the proceeds from the performances of *Jeremias* in the United States to exiled writers, including Braun, but his time was another matter, when every trip to London cost him a day. To escape the pressure Zweig fled from England to the United States in 1940, only to find himself burdened with the same situation there: a constant barrage by telephone and by letter asking for help in placing manuscripts or in rescuing relatives or friends. Many of his old friends, now in exile, just wanted to see him for moral support and were offended when he avoided them. In a letter to Friderike he described his dilemma:

I have always had a profound sympathy for the refugees and have given them more help than almost anyone else. The fact is, I can stand only just a limited amount of sociability. It exhausts me to see five, six people a day and this prevents me (Paris was an instance) from seeing the people and things that *I* want to see. The telephone rang from early till late at night in New York and Buenos Aires; what I am afraid of is that people terribly overestimate what I can do for them: I am asked to get Huebsch to take this book or that, arrange about newspapers, etc., etc. Certainly when I *can* do something, I do it of my own free will. I now am acquainted with from 200 to 300 people in New York; all of them would be hurt if I didn't get to see them. I must, because of increasing exhaustion, salvage at least half of every day for my own affairs. After all I have business with my publisher, the dentist, other errands in New York — it's impossible to see everybody; and they call that snobbishness.[15]

Zweig was further burdened by his certainty that he could read the future better than others, and he suffered from what he foresaw: in 1937 he visited his mother briefly in Vienna and was appalled at the lack of concern he encountered there over the possibility of Anschluss. After trying to warn his friends and being chided as a Cassandra, he gave up any further attempts to bring the Viennese out of their delusions. He should have recognized how difficult it is to analyze a political situation up close, for he had been in Vienna during the Civil War in February 1934 and had seen nothing at all of the revolution.[16]

In a letter to Braun on 3 June 1938 he expressed his anguish at the fate he anticipated for the intellectual Jews in Vienna: "I suffer like a dog from the dozen letters, which I receive daily from Vienna, because I know that there are no possibilities for intellectual Jews—I would rather become a waiter or dishwasher than to tolerate the humiliations which await them."[17]

Zweig made his major literary reference to the political events of the 1930s in *Triumph und Tragik des Erasmus von Rotterdam* (1934), the aim of which he explained in a letter to Klaus Mann:

> I want to represent by analogy and develop in an unconfiscatable manner, with the greatest justice, in this man our type and the other. . . . Just as I took a position understandable to everyone in "Jeremias," without actually polemicizing, so too I am trying here to make a great deal of the contemporary situation clear and understandable by means of a symbol.[18]

Zweig then added an explanatory characterization of himself and his approach to his work:

> The purely aggressive does not suit me in terms of my character, because I don't believe in "victories" but in our quiet determined persistence, the stronger force lies perhaps in the artistic pronouncement. The others can fight too, they have proven that; thus one must strike them in

the other area, where they are inferior and wherever they bring out their Schlageter and Horst Wessel, show in artistically irrefutable form the pictures of our intellectual heroes.[19]

*Erasmus,* he felt, was a book for those who understand "in-between tones."

Zweig preferred reality filtered through the medium of literature. He praised a work like Hofmannsthal's *Berührung der Sphären* (Touching of the Spheres), which in his view contained more reality than could be found in all "Pseudo-Wirklichkeitsreferate" (pseudo presentations on reality) and he despised literature that he called a "Fotographie der Realität" (photograph of reality).[20] In a letter to Frans Masereel he complained about the hateful time and how difficult it was to maintain one's creative energies under such constant tension: "One simply must learn to resign oneself inwardly, live tougher, stricter, removed and perhaps even more indifferently."[21] His refuge was to flee into his work: "Forget, I said to myself, flee, flee into the thicket of your innermost self, into your work, into that part of yourself, where you are only your breathing ego, not a citizen, not an object of this infernal game, where solely your little bit of reason can still have a rational effect in a world become insane."[22] Had he been able to follow his own advice, quite possibly he would have survived. The fact that he was unable to do so, combined with other factors such as the irretrievable loss of his world, to which he devoted the loving eulogy *Die Welt von Gestern* (The World of Yesterday), the fear of never again finding the world in which he could relax and be himself while he was still young enough to benefit from it, led him finally to withdraw into the ultimate peace of a death of his own choosing.[23]

As in *Erasmus* Zweig touched upon the political situation in *Die Welt von Gestern* in his typical fashion of pure description without polemic and without bitterness. He also drew an analogy with the contemporary situation in the short narrative *Cicero,* which begins: "When a shrewd but not particularly courageous man encounters one stronger than himself, the wisest thing he can do is to turn aside and unashamedly wait until the road is clear."[24] Cicero did not follow this advice and found death, joining Zweig's other victors in defeat.[25] Similarly, the humanist is defeated in *Schachnovelle* (The Royal Game), Zweig's last published work, in which a humanist confronts a monomaniac representing the mentality of a dictatorship. This tale is primarily a psychological study of two opposing types, and the criticism of National Socialism again is implicit rather than direct. The protagonist does not forfeit his life in this instance, but the message emerges clearly that the humanist can never cope with the unfeeling, monomaniacal brute power of fascism.[26]

Although he preferred to restrict himself to literary topics, Zweig's avoidance of political questions was not absolute, and he dealt with such issues in a small number of essays and interviews. He spoke out particularly on behalf of the persecuted Jews, whose fate had awakened his own Jewish identity along with his normal human compassion. Of great concern to him was the fate of the Jews and particularly Jewish children in Germany. As early as 20 December 1933 he lectured on "The Jewish Children in Germany," appealing for aid to save them from the psychological damage being done to them in Germany by anti-Semitism: "Are Jewish children once more, in Germany of all places, in the heart of Europe, to become cowering and crippled souls, an anxious, terrified, broken generation?"[27] The children also need help to prevent them from reacting to their plight with hatred, "For I hate hatred as something unworthy of a spiritually-minded, of a religious-minded human being. . . . Hatred must never be directed at a whole community. A nation or a race must never be made responsible for the actions of its leaders."[28]

In 1936 in an open letter Zweig discusses Joseph Leftwich's book "Whither the Jews?," which suggests that Jews should be distributed around the world and not just in Palestine. In this view, a variant of a solution once proposed by the noted popular philosopher Joseph Lynkeus-Popper, Jews from Europe would be sent to underdeveloped countries to work the land, thus freeing Europe of its excess people – "Volk ohne Raum" (Nation without Space) was a favorite Nazi slogan – and also of its excess hatred: "The contrasts would be reduced – harmony spread, and by this means a moral task would be carried out along with an economic necessity."[29] This suggestion proceeds from the assumption that the Jewish problem is the result of economic *Mißstände* (bad conditions). To make his plan work Zweig calls for both a unified will among Jews to end the countless improvised schemes which have not produced helpful results. His own plan, however, was doomed to failure because it addressed only economic, not racial prejudice, which constituted the problem.

Other essays of these years address specific aspects of the Jewish question. In the essay "Eine Anrede" (An Address) in 1936 he argued against violent reactions of the Jews to persecution,[30] and in "Das Haus der tausend Schicksale" (The House of a Thousand Fates) (1937) he praised the work of the London East End Shelter for Jewish refugees.[31] In the article "Keep out of Politics" (1938) Zweig continued his quietistic approach urging Jews to adopt a lower profile: "Nothing has so promoted the anti-Semitic movement as the fact that Jews have been too much in evidence in various countries in various trends of political life, and in opposing parties, too often as leaders."[32] Jews should make their contributions through books, speeches and self-sacrificing devoted work, but not as visible leaders: "It is not the agitators, the zealots, and the politicians who are our true spiritual expression, but those who in a thousand different ways recreate the idea of the invisible God that we have brought into the world, and who does not belong to any party or to any class, but to the whole of mankind."[33] Such restraint will prove their moral strength and benefit all Jews, according to Zweig, a view which unfortunately opened him to attacks on all sides, particularly from fellow Jews.

In 1938 Zweig also drafted the beginning of an "Aufruf für die österreichischen Juden" (Appeal for the Austrian Jews), an appeal for assistance on behalf of Jews trapped in Austria: "A harder task faces Jewry than it has known in the two thousand years of its history,"[34] but the essay was never completed. A radio talk in Paris in 1940, entitled "Das große Schweigen" (The Great Silence), describes the fearful silence of the forty to fifty million people in central Europe, who were denied freedom of speech. It is the first duty of those who still have freedom of expression to speak for these trapped millions, whose only defense is the last weapon of the weak, hope and prayer. Zweig concludes that his life would mean nothing more to him, if he weren't convinced that eternal justice will hear this accusing silence.[35]

In 1941 Zweig contributed his thoughts on the topic "The Mission of the Intellectuals," stating: "Our moral duty was to show with patience and conviction that all the conflicts and contradictions which are raging today in Europe . . . could be resolved through a counter-action of the men of conscience and thought."[36] He felt that the intellectual's voice was drowned out by the loud voice of propaganda, and the P.E.N. Club had been weakened. The writers needed unity and a clear idea of their mission: "Our word should become, in spite of all the odds, stronger and stronger. The louder the shoutings of fanaticism, the stronger should be our word, the voice of reason. Some of us may be stifled, but governments cannot destroy all of us."[37] Despite his almost heroic stance here and his usual solution of portraying the victor in defeat, neither possibility proved viable for Zweig in his own life. Even though he was not threatened in any way except in his own black liver and dark thoughts, he lived in his mind and remained true to its dictates to the end. For all his high-mindedness, his moral and ethical principles, and his sincere humanitarian desire to improve the world, Stefan Zweig was ultimately not a good model of a humanistic defense against totalitarianism. Instead of acting, his personal need to stay free of involvement precluded any possibility of his taking a stand against fascism in direct polemical terms, and his sincere idealism failed to sustain him in his personal life. While he advocated opposition, although always in subdued or indirect terms, and while he glorified the victor in defeat, he was not mentally tough enough to follow either role himself. The flood of horror stories and pleas, the steady flow of negative news, the irretrievable loss of the only world in which he could be at home, and the unreasoning fear that Hitler might conquer South America, as he described in his essay "Hartrott und Hitler,"[38] combined to force his suicide. His uppermost goal in life had always been to live for himself in terms of his own free will, and he died true to himself and his ideals.

For the most part Raoul Auernheimer echoed the attitudes just described in the case of Stefan Zweig, but after 1938 he came to represent the opposite pole of his good friend and colleague. Auernheimer, a journalist/author, enjoyed an excellent reputation as a decent — *liebenswürdig* was the adjective universally applied to him — human being of great integrity, and as such he was accepted by all the major *Jung-Wien* authors. He led a good life in Vienna as a theater critic and Feuilletonist for the *Neue Freie Presse* and as an author following in the footsteps of Arthur Schnitzler and Zweig. Like Hofmannsthal, Auernheimer felt more at home in the eighteenth than in the twentieth century and, like Zweig and all the major *Jung-Wien* writers, literature and culture were the major concerns in his life. At the end of the 1920s, when National Socialism began to grow rapidly, Auernheimer devoted his attention to such aesthetic issues as the importance of using verse in drama as a means of heightening the poetic effect and to the Austrian past. In his autobiography *Das Wirtshaus zur verlorenen Zeit* (1948, The Inn at the Sign of Lost Time), a work that rivals Stefan Zweig's *Die Welt von gestern* in importance as a depiction of their generation, Auernheimer described how talent meant everything for their generation and politics nothing at all.[39]

Because of his reputation as a gentleman with high principles, Auernheimer was regarded as trustworthy by his peers and was often elected to offices in the various professional organizations. He served in the Österreichischer Schriftstellerverband in 1928 and in the writers' group, Concordia, only to resign because of what he regarded as the overly materialistic attitude of his fellow authors. He also served as secretary of the Vienna P.E.N. Club and as such was thrust into the political debate that wracked that organization in 1933.

The watershed event for all writers in Austria was the meeting of the P.E.N. Club at Ragusa from 26 to 28 May 1933.[40] Auernheimer was present at this meeting and was one of the signatories of the motion to protest the book burnings in Germany, since works by Austrian authors were among those being destroyed. The Austrian delegation split over this motion, and such representatives as Grete Urbanitzky, Felix Salten, Egon Caesar Corti, and Mirko Jelusich departed from the meeting with their German colleagues in protest against it. Both Urbanitzky and Salten later proclaimed that they did so in order not to endanger the livelihood of Austrian writers; they feared that Germany would retaliate by banning the publication of Austrian books and performances of Austrian plays. But in truth their defense of German behavior was indicative of their solidarity with the ideas of National Socialism, as Auernheimer documented later. Since nothing was decided at Ragusa, the debate was continued subsequently at a meeting of the P.E.N. Club on 27 June 1933 in Vienna, where again the deeply rooted political schism within the ranks of the P.E.N. Club surfaced. Urbanitzky, Salten, and twenty-five others resigned, splitting the organization, until it was banned after the Anschluss on 11 March 1938.[41]

While Auernheimer stood staunchly on the ethical side of protesting the affront to humanistic values and never gave a thought to personal economic advantage, the situation caused no personal alarm in him and no change in his writings during the next five years, that is, he continued to glorify the Austrian past in feuilletons, light comedies, and narrative prose works. Typical is his light comedy *Die große Leidenschaft* (The Great Passion), which was performed in the Akademietheater in 1936. Even the fact that he felt impelled to resign from the *Neue Freie Presse* in 1933 to protest what he termed "certain fascist leanings of the newspaper"[42] brought no alteration of the nonpolitical stance of his writings. He continued to publish the same style of books and reviews he always had, featuring elegant feuilletonistic style and nostalgic content. Such events as the civil war in Austria in February 1934, the heavy-handed Austro-fascist political actions of the Dollfuss regime, the failed *Putsch* of 1934 resulting in the murder of Dollfuss and the political maneuvering and manipulation under Chancellor Schuschnigg and his cultural Minister Guido Zernatto up to the Anschluß in March 1938, were all ignored. Like so many others, Auernheimer did not believe that the growing militance in Germany represented any threat to Austria, and even though half Jewish, he felt protected by the Nuremberg laws, since his father was a German from Nuremberg and he himself was raised as a Protestant. In addition he was totally assimilated and acculturated. So strong was his sense of security that he returned to Vienna in March 1938 immediately after the Anschluß from Switzerland, where he had been attending the première of his translation of Molière's *Le Misanthrope*. A week after his return, on 21 March 1938, he was arrested and sentenced to Dachau because of his role as an officer in the Vienna P.E.N. Club and also because he had sent a copy of his book *Wien – Bild und Schicksal* (Vienna – Portrayal and Destiny) to Schuschnigg in 1938 with a handwritten dedication urging resistance to the Anschluß.

This volume, which appeared in 1938 only shortly before the Anschluß, serves as an excellent example of how oblivious Auernheimer and many others like him remained to the Nazi threat to Austria right to the last minute. This nostalgic cultural survey consists of delightfully written feuilletons about various charming Viennese traits and customs and contains not a hint of any political or social difficulties or any possible dangers to the myth he is projecting of a pleasant carefree Austrian existence. The final chapter entitled "Und Österreich?" debates the relationship between Vienna and Austria, as if this were the most significant issue of the day, concluding:

> Is the Viennese a German? Hard to answer. He is a German; he is also not a German; he *is* a German. And all these stipulations and limitations the German has in common with the Austrian, Vienna with Austria. . . . Vienna the tall rampart profiled against the sky of a truly European Germanness. That is his role and at the same time the mission of Austria, seen from the tower of Saint Stephen's.

. . . For Vienna is Austria – even if Austria is not always Vienna.[43]

This book's tone contrasts sharply with the political reality in 1938, showing how Auernheimer remained willfully blind to all warnings to the very end, just as Zweig had lamented. He was willing to defend principles if confronted directly, as at Ragusa and as shown by his resignation from the *Neue Freie Presse,* but otherwise Auernheimer avoided any political responsibility and made little attempt to confront serious issues in his writings. For his negligence he spent five months in Dachau, until he was released through the efforts of the German writer Emil Ludwig and the American Chargé d'Affaires in Berlin, Prentice Gilbert, who had earlier translated two of Auernheimer's dramas into English.

Auernheimer was allowed to emigrate to the United States, where he was joined by his wife. Once there he believed that it was his moral obligation to alert the western world to the Nazi menace. Here is the major difference between Auernheimer and Zweig, for Auernheimer, sobered by his experience, now felt compelled to take a public stand, even though his reputation was nonexistent in the United States and did not provide him with the public forum that Zweig could have commanded. The change in Auernheimer is illustrated by their meeting in New York in 1939 following a performance of Zweig's pacifist drama, *Jeremias.* Auernheimer told Zweig that, while he greatly admired the play, he felt it should have a tenth scene added "to show how Jeremias was transformed from a convinced pacifist into a convinced 'warmonger' using all of his former arguments in the opposite direction."[44] He was totally unsympathetic now to the purely intellectualized type of victory in defeat that Zweig had portrayed. Zweig was not persuaded but accepted these remarks good-naturedly.

Despite his reputation in Austria, Auernheimer had never had any of his works published in English and therefore had no name recognition in the United States. Nevertheless, he enjoyed modest initial success with the historical novel *Prince Metternich, Statesman and Lover* (1940), which received reasonably good reviews but little attention by readers. Typically Auernheimer lavished more attention on the human side of Metternich as a lover rather than on the examination of Metternich's political career, which would have been more relevant to the time. He did, however, include a preface drawing parallels between the tyranny of Metternich and that of Hitler.

Auernheimer's other efforts to discuss his experiences as a warning were frustrated for the most part by indifferent publishers. He joined the P.E.N. Club in New York but could not establish a foothold there. He soon joined his daughter and son-in-law in Oakland, California, where he was removed from the mainstream. He wrote occasionally for the *Austro-American Tribune* but played little role in any of the Austrian organizations. Essentially he was reduced to delivering his message about National Socialism through such public lectures as : "War Guilt of the Victims," "I Was an Austrian," "Austria—A Symbol," "Thoughts About Austria," "There Was A Country Named Austria," "How to Get Along with Austrians," and "Vienna—not in Germany."[45] His most important achievement was to assist in establishing the view of Austria as Germany's first victim by urging in essays and talks that Austria be treated differently than Germany after the war. The Allied leaders, influenced by this view, which all of the exiled Austrian writers espoused, shaped the postwar policy accordingly at their summit meeting at Yalta in 1943 and in the Moscow Declaration.

Other contributions by Auernheimer, some of which were published, treated variations on the same themes, as can be seen from the titles: "A Graduate from the Concentration Camp," "Inside Barbed Wire," "Two Conquerors, Two Kinds of Men: Hitler and Napoleon," "Napoleon and Hitler," "The Shadow of Napoleon, History Repeats in Russia," "How to Live in Wartime," "Mark Twain and the Gestapo," "To Make Peace with Peace."[46] Ever the optimist Auernheimer liked to compare Napoleon with Hitler, drawing the parallel that Hitler too would overextend himself and self-destruct eventually. He had written an account of his five months in Dachau, entitled "Die Zeit im Lager"

(My Time in the Camp), but never succeeded in publishing his book. Even Auernheimer's friend, the agent Franz Horch, could not be persuaded that the account was worth publishing because it was considered not sensational enough for the American market. Auernheimer's response was to plead that he could not write about occurrences that he had not witnessed; but even without the description of atrocities he felt that the account provided a useful warning to Americans about the real character of the National Socialists. An excerpt of this manuscript was included in his autobiography under the title "Hitlers Gast" (Hitler's Guest).[47]

One of Auernheimer's most interesting and informative contributions to a retrospective view of the 1930s was a series of biographical essays that he prepared at the urging of his close personal friend Ernst Lothar.[48] Both men were greatly concerned about the task of rebuilding Austria after the war. To return quickly Lothar had joined the United States Army and was sent to Vienna after the war in American uniform to help revitalize the Austrian theaters, including the Salzburg festival. Auernheimer, unfortunately, never fulfilled his dream of returning home. In any event, because of his background and integrity Auernheimer was a good choice for the sensitive task of presenting the political history and evaluating the reliability of the authors he knew, so that Austrian and American authorities could establish the attitude of such writers towards democracy in the postwar period. Through his work in the various literary organizations and through his many years experience as a theater and book reviewer, he was well informed about the literary scene and knew personally most of the individuals he evaluated.

Auernheimer completed thirty-one reports,[49] but whether this number represents all that he wrote is not known. The questions he was asked to answer included date and place of birth, nationality and religion, family history, education and work history, political history, personal data, summary, the currentness of the information, and how well Auernheimer knew the subject. Since he had to research some of the information, these texts resemble encyclopedia articles, one to two pages in length typed in single spacing. In terms of his character Auernheimer was also a good source for such information because with few exceptions (Urbanitzky and Zsolnay) he harbored no hostility or personal grudges towards his contemporaries in Vienna, and his basic decency prevented him from seeking recrimination against anyone. At the time he wrote these reports in early 1945 before the end of the war Auernheimer was still planning to return to Vienna, although he died in 1948 without ever seeing Austria again. His views are worthy of attention because they provide a first-hand contemporary account that contributes importantly to under-- standing the actions of a number of writers to the events of the 1930s and provide a broader portrait of the general circumstances. The individuals Auernheimer evaluates include: Rudolf Hans Bartsch, Ernst Benedikt, Richard Billinger, Erhard Buschbeck, Egon Caesar Corti, Franz Theodor Csokor, Oskar Maurus Fontana, Franz Karl Ginskey, Josef Gregor, Paula Grogger, Hans von Hammerstein, Enrica von Handel-Mazzetti, Johannes Hollnsteiner, Edmund Glaise-Horstenau, Mirko Jelusich, Rudolf Jeremias Kreuz, Alexander Lernet-Holenia, Anna Tizia Leitich, Ernst Molden, Hermann Heinz Ortner, Hans Pernter, Karl Anton Rohan, Leon Schalit, Maximilian Schreier, Friedrich Schreyvogl, Michael Skubl, Heinrich von Srbik, Grete von Urbanitzky, Karl Heinrich Waggerl, Josef Weinheber, Josef Wenter, and Paul von Zsolnay.[47]

Of this group Auernheimer regarded the following writers as Nazi collaborators out of conviction: Corti, Gregor, Lernet-Holenia, Ortner, Hammerstein, Jelusich, Schreyvogl, Wenter, and Urbanitzky. In some cases Auernheimer attributed the collaboration to the dubious character of the individual, as in the cases of Gregor, Salten, Schreyvogl, and Urbanitzky. Concerning Corti, one of the P.E.N. Club members who had defected with Urbannitzky and Salten at Ragusa, he notes: "Corti was a great Nazi sympathizer and member of the Reichsschrifttumskammer." Such membership was necessary in order to be permitted to write in Germany and in Austria after the Anschluss. Auernheimer characterizes Corti as follows:

Corti belonged to the Urbanitzky – Salten section of the Austrian P.E.N. Club, whose majority in the International P.E.N. meeting at Ragusa, May 1933, had refused to sign the protest against the burning of books and sending writers to German concentration camps for racial or political reasons. When a few weeks later at Vienna the minority made up for it, Corti with five fellow travelers demonstratively executed a solemn exit, feeling deeply hurt by the belated protest action, and never returned to the P.E.N. Club. Politically Corti is to be labeled as a profascist Nazi sympathizer.

Another P.E.N. Club member who defected at the Ragusa meeting was Mirko Jelusich, whom Auernheimer describes as "editor of the anti-Semitic, pro-Nazi Viennese 'Deutsche Tageszeitung.' Essayist, historian, and short-lived literary artistic director of the Vienna Burgtheater immediately after the annexation of Austria in March 1938." Concerning Jelusich's activities in the Burgtheater, Auernheimer writes:

> What Jelusich was thinking of Austria may be read from the title of one of his printed lectures: "Ersatz Kultur and Kultur-Ersatz" (substitute culture and cultural substitutes) published in 1932. Hitler liked this political attitude and so did the Austrian Nazis. There were many of them even among the members and the staff of the Burgtheater and they made Jelusich their "Ersatz" director, a substitute for "Roebbeling, who was a German from the Reich" but, as director, kept to the business line without taking sides politically. Jelusich did. One day after the invasion of Austria by Hitler's legions Jelusich in his brand new stormtrooper's uniform appeared in Roebbeling's office, ordering him out. One year later he too was ordered out by Hitler and supplanted by Lothar Muethel, a true German Nazi from the "Reich."

Auernheimer's description of Alexander Lernet-Holenia reads differently than most accounts of this author and his role in the late 1930s and during the war. Lernet-Holenia is usually classified among those who went into inner emigration, continuing to write and publish against the grain of National Socialism and persevering, as it were, on thin ice. Auernheimer's assessment does not agree with this view. After naming several of Lernet-Holenia's successful tales and novels, *Die Standarte* (1934, The Standard Bearer), *Die neue Atlantis* (1935, The New Atlantis), *Der Herr von Paris* (1935, The Gentleman from Paris), *Die Auferstehung des Maltravers* (1936, The Resurrection of the Maltravers), *Der Baron Bagge* (1937, The Baron Bogge), and *Mona Lisa* (1937), Auernheimer notes: "The telling titles explain the growing success of the skillful and inventive writer with the Nazi reader. Lernet-Holenia did not wait for the Anschluß to join the ranks of the German national movement. It was years before that he, becoming 'illegal,' betrayed his homeland Austria." The report continues:

> As since the outbreak of World War II Lernet-Holenia's rich production did not subside and his books uninterruptedly were printed and reprinted by his Berlin publisher, one may conclude that his fertility seemed desirable to the Nazis. Otherwise the Nazi government would have silenced the 'officer in the reserve' by calling him to the colors. The conclusion is admissible that Lernet-Holenia became a complete Nazi in Naziland despite the fact that his address is still Wolfgangsee in Upper Austria.

Auernheimer concluded with the view that "Lernet-Holenia's political attitude was always anti-democratic and pro-fascist: This is to be read as well from his biography as from his books ... There is little hope that this buccaneer of sexual and facial greed ever will change into a decent human being."

Hermann Heinz Ortner was another writer who drifted into the Nazi camp, according to Auernheimer. He excused him to some degree by noting that Ortner was raised in upper Austria, where the atmosphere was impregnated with the German national movement of Schönerer. Auernheimer considers Ortner an opportunist who did not wish to miss the boat after the Nazis seized power in 1933:

> Ortner in 1934 showed distinct fascist and Nazi leanings which finally landed him in the Nazi camp. In 1938 after "Austria's return to the Reich" the position of Ortner's half Jewish wife at the now nazified Burgtheater had now become untenable. Nevertheless, Ortner, who hardly knew any foreign language, decided to stay in Vienna where he became a Nazi collaborationist probably, although to source nothing is known about his literary activities in the critical period between 1939 and 1945. He was a member of the German 'Reichsschrifttumskammer' and of the board of the 'Genossenschaft dramatischer Autoren' (guild of dramatic authors).

Auernheimer wrote one of his lengthiest and most negative reports on Grete von Urbanitzky, whom he had known for more than twenty-five years and with whom he had worked in the P.E.N. Club. When the P.E.N. Club was organized in Vienna by Urbanitzky, Arthur Schnitzler was named honorary president and Auernheimer chairman, with Urbanitzky as secretary and member of the board. Auernheimer makes it clear that her talents lay in promoting herself rather than in her literary ability:

> Mrs. Urbanitzky's heyday came when Mr. Felix Salten was chairman. Salten was an author of the Zsolnay Publishing House and so was very soon Mrs. Urbanitzky. She made the missing link between the appeaser Zsolnay and the growing up Nazi party, to whose 'ideology' she felt much attracted, overcompensating her racial minority complex by the strongest national — and soon enough — national-socialistic feelings. At the same time she published 'Durch Himmel und Hölle' (Heaven and Hell, 1932), 'Karen und

die Welt der Männer' (Karen and the Male, 1933), 'Ursula und der Kapitän' (Ursula and the Captain, 1934), 'Nina' (1935), and 'Einkehr zur Liebe' (Homecoming to Love), all of them with Zsolnay. She belonged to the group of P.E.N. Club members who left the club demonstratively after in June 1933 the majority of the membership had approved the protest against the Nazi methods concerning literature, burning of books, racial persecution, and so on. Not at all terrified by the atrocities Mrs. Urbanitzky in the last year before Hitler raped Austria became an assiduous commuter between Schuschnigg Vienna and Hitler Berlin, where she was persona grata if not gratissima.

Apparently Auernheimer did not learn that Urbanitzky also felt compelled to leave Austria and Germany to go into exile in Switzerland.

In several cases Auernheimer acknowledged the turn to National Socialism but blamed it on environmental conditions. For example, Karl Heinrich Waggerl, whom Auernheimer describes as modeling himself after Hermann Hesse and as a John Steinbeck minus Steinbeck's socialism, he regards as a regional writer possibly infected by the brownish tint of his region around Salzburg: 'Fortunately his inherited political indifference, the unity of his style and his sense of humor protected him against a serious Nazi infection.'

Josef Wenter also joined the National Socialist movement in Austria when it became expedient to do so, according to Auernheimer. Yet he suggests that the surroundings in which Wenter grew up might have influenced his political attitude, for the 'lovely valley of Meran, a famous Austrian health resort, was populated by one of the oldest and most Teutonic German tribes . . . German nationalist feeling always ran high among these red bearded, blue-eyed, slow men who looked and moved like the representatives of German mythology in a Wagner opera.' Auernheimer describes Wenter's career in Austria as follows:

Wenter's first play, characteristically titled 'Spiel um den Staat' (Gamble for Power), had its opening night in Klagenfurth in Carinthia, one of the hotbeds of this at that time still clandestine Austrian Naziism. The second play 'Der Traktor,' had its opening night in Braunschweig in 1933, when Hitler had seized the power in Germany. Finally, under the increasing pressure of Austrian Nazis, Wentner became the author of the Vienna Burgtheater in 1934 with 'Der Kanzler von Tirol' (Chancellor of Tyrol). Then came, 1935, 'Der nächste Heinrich' (Henry VI), a Hohenstaufen emperor of the twelfth century, and, 1936, 'Die Landgräfin von Thüringen' of the 13th. All these historical plays and some others, which were withheld from his Viennese audience, dealt exclusively with the German past. For these patriotic literary efforts of very mediocre taste Wenter was awarded the Austrian 'State Prize for Literature' in 1936.[50]

Auernheimer characterized Wenter's literary contribution in these terms:

The Nazis liked to accentuate their love for animals and so did Wentner. When tired of his medieval emperors, knights and princesses he wrote a novel on the cuckoo and one on the salmon. His increasing success was a watermark, from which one could read the rising fascism and Naziism in Austria. When he became her poeta laureatus, poor Austria was doomed.

Although Rudolf Hans Bartsch had joined the National Socialist movement, Auernheimer considered him more misguided than malevolent:

The book which has made Bartsch famous was 'Zwölf aus der Steiermark,' a novel published in 1905. Here too the German national trend was obvious, as in the description of Austrian provincial life lovingly depicted by the author. Graz, the capital of Styria with its purely German population was pitted against the imperial city of Vienna, whose progressive internationalism seemed dangerous to Bartsch and his followers as well in the field of literature as in other fields of Austrian culture. The issue was reaction against progress, past against present time, regionalism against Europeanism. In this way ingratiating himself with a wide, although mostly provincial readership, Bartsch supported by his remarkable narrative talent, became the head of the Austrian 'regionalist' writers, whose German nationalism paved the way for the approach of Naziism. But for this weakness and his Austrian 'Heimwehr' (home-guard) fascism, Bartsch always was and still is a lovable story teller and, especially in his historic miniatures ('Vom sterbenden Rococo' and so on) even an artist and poet.

Those whom Auernheimer praised as Austrian patriots included Erhard Buschbeck, Oskar Maurus Fontana, and Franz Karl Ginskey. Auernheimer had known Ginskey for thirty-five years and explained his situation in terms of his background. Ginskey belonged to the "German orientation of Austrian politics because of his ancestry and because of his belonging to the then ruling officers' caste, whose duty it was to favor the military alliance with Germany." Nevertheless, Auernheimer insists that Ginskey was a true Austrian, loyal to the emperor and to the Austrian Republic ten years later:

> It was no lack of character, merely political indifference that he was this way. He was no politician and too late became aware of the fact that his pro-Germanism had brought him dangerously near to the Nazi camp. When finally the Nazis invaded Austria and "germanized" it to extinguish all vestiges of Austrian culture and history, the cultured poet Ginzkey was bitterly disappointed as many of his equals were. Ginzkey could not emigrate, and simply had to stay and wait.

Paula Grogger was another writer whom Auernheimer considered a victim of circumstance more than political inclination:

> Although Grogger was living in a backward region where Naziism was endemic, purity and innocence of her character might have protected her against that poison. Educated for the use of an authoritarian government and by the equally authoritarian church, she belongs to the provincial type of Austrian conservatives if not reactionaries . . . She has neither political ambition nor understanding.

Enrica von Handel-Mazzetti was also excused because of her background, and Auernheimer pays her high praise, having believed at one point that she could develop into one of the most prominent women writers after Ebner-Eschenbach.

Auernheimer also defended Josef Weinheber:

> He followed the tradition of Austrian 19th century writers who sold themselves to the State for a governmental employment to buy the luxury of independent literary creation. The Nazis would have liked to reclaim this Viennese poet for their godforsaken "ideology," and there is but little doubt that staying in Vienna after the *Anschluss* and during the War Weinheber could not help getting along with them in one way or another. Nevertheless Weinheber may find his way back to human decency which in fact he never has injured as an artist. Miss Ruth Hofrichter, Associate Professor of Vassar College, in an essay on Weinheber she published in 1942 with The Oxford University Press quotes a letter he might have written her just before the war, in which he speaks of his "indestructible home" the house of his ancestors: Sappho, Marcus Aurelius, Schopenhauer, Hölderlin, Droste . . . This sentence does not ring as if a Nazi would have put it down. Neither does the poet's confession meet the Nazi ideology, that for him "the highest value is beauty of language. It is to be hoped

that after Victory Weinheber will reestablish himself as what he in the pre-Nazi-epoch has been: one of the very best of the contemporary Austrian poets.

If Auernheimer's assessment is correct, it places Weinheber's suicide a few months later to avoid capture by the Russians into tragic perspective.

If Zweig and Auernheimer represent opposing literary responses to fascism, Felix Braun represents a third variation, indeed, among exiles he is almost a variant unto himself. No other writer of that era was quite as *weltfremd* as Braun, who devoted his life single-mindedly to the pursuit of an aesthetic life to a greater extent than any of the *Jung-Wien* group and pursued this course through life without change until his death in 1973 at the age of eighty-five. His is a remarkable life and career in which the outer reality of existence was subordinated to a life lived for literature, regardless of the sacrifices that it entailed. He once said of himself: 'Nothing has as much power over me as beauty.' His works demonstrate the truth of this statement, but they also make clear that his interest was not beauty for its own sake but beauty for ethical purposes. Braun felt that human beings should live surrounded by beauty, echoing the idea of the Wiener Werkstätte, rather than having beauty remote from life and only touched upon on rare occasions. But underlying the aesthetic concern was always the ethical and moral basis, which gives his writings their significance and continued relevance. His works were dedicated to themes of life, Christianity, classical antiquity, mythology, fairy tales, and legends, in short, nothing with direct relevance to the modern world except in terms of their ethical and humanistic concepts and values. Braun's elegance of language and the concomitant slow pace of his writings along with his settings in the remote past have estranged him from modern readers. and even academics today pay little attention to his works any more than they do to those of Auernheimer. In an age devoted to social and political relevance, Braun was considered an adornment, a charming but somewhat boring relic from a previous era. With his gaunt, emaciated appearance he somewhat resembles Don Quixote, and his steadfast adherence to absolute values of truth, goodness, and beauty while most others had shifted to relative values characterizes him as such.

Because of his avoidance of reality, or more precisely his pursuit of a higher at the expense of pragmatic reality, Braun, as might be expected, never produced any commentary on the events of the 1930s or on the Anschluß. There was also another reason for the absence of such commentary, namely, he had left Austria in 1928 to accept a position as a Docent for German literature in Palermo and remained there until he found a better position in Padua in 1936. He lived a lonely life in Italy, with the pattern of teaching and writing broken only by rare visits from friends like Stefan Zweig, Hans Carossa, and Max Mell. In 1938 he had to leave Italy, and since he was unable to return to Austria and had been rejected by Switzerland for more than a temporary permit, he traveled to England. Braun adjusted to life in England better than did Zweig, and after a period of time was allowed to work, first as a private tutor and then as a Docent for literature and for art history at Durham, and finally in London. Unlike Zweig who avoided political writing in order not to embarrass his host country, Braun experienced no crisis of conscience, for it never occurred to him to write political statements. Instead, he devoted his time to polishing the language and style of his earlier writings. In England Braun continued to live his own quiet life, on the verge of poverty as in Italy, sharing his household with his sister Käthe Braun-Präger. He was totally self-reliant, and though he admired Rilke, Hofmannsthal, Zweig, Saar, and Hauptmann, he chose not to emulate any of them.

The unpublished correspondence of Braun with Zweig and Auernheimer – all three were mutual friends – shows their differing relationships to the events of the day.[51] It is apparent that Zweig held Braun in high esteem, but also that he felt more worldly than Braun and tried desperately to shake him out of his escapism and into the world of reality. It is somewhat amusing and ironic to see Zweig insisting to Braun that he should stop writing works about Classical antiquity and devote himself to current relevant themes, when he himself was attempting to avoid the unpleasant contemporary reality. In a letter of 1 June 1940 Braun, who was revising *Agnes Altkirchner,* his best known and most highly regarded novel, reworking some previous tales, and making a collection of his poems, complained to Auernheimer about Zweig's criticism: 'Stefan Zweig criticizes that and calls it a fruitless clinging to the past. But I think that we now possess the time to fulfill Horace's rule and that we must simply be serious about maintaining lost positions.'[52] Braun's failure to keep abreast of political developments, made easier by his being out of the country, caused a weakness in *Agnes Altkirchner,* which is generally recogniz'd as a forerunner of the major works by Musil, Roth, and Kraus that deal with the Austrian past, although not on the same level. When Braun attempted to treat the 1920s in the latter part of the novel, he was not familiar enough with the processes of the democratic and socialist movements to do the later years justice. The same criticism was leveled against Auernheimer's novel set in the late twenties, *Die linke und die rechte Hand* (1927, The Left and the Right Hand), even though he was present in Vienna and had witnessed the social changes at first hand. To ignore political occurrences in the 1920s and 1930s in order to live in a world of culture was a fatal weakness of their literary generation.

Braun wrote a second novel, dealing with Austria's decline, *Der Herbst des Reiches* (The Autumn of the Empire), but, like Auernheimer's *Wien—Bild und Schicksal,* without touching upon current problems. On 14 July 1939 Braun gave a lecture entitled *Klage um Österreich* (Lament for Austria), for which Auernheimer congratulated him, but like Zweig and Auernheimer, Braun devoted his efforts here to lamenting the loss of old Austria. In a second letter of 24 September 1939 Auernheimer calls Braun's eulogy of old Austria 'Österreichs Schwanengesang' and complains that Austrians under fifty do not read literature and that few Austrians of the World War I generation know or want to know anything about Austria, not to mention the postwar populace. Auernheimer in this letter mentions his own essay "Some

Words About Austria, Christianity, and Myself": "In this connection I presented with good effect several incidents with the Third
Reich that approached religious experiences."[53]

Both Braun and Auernheimer were distressed by Zweig's
decision to take his own life, feeling that this was a retreat in the
face of the enemy. It is one of the great ironies that Zweig, the
most widely traveled and most cosmopolitan of all Austrian writers, could not survive outside Vienna, while Auernheimer and
Braun could. In letters of 15 March 1942 and another of 21 June
1942 both friends insist that they must not emulate Zweig but
continue to live. True to his conviction Braun, who was the most
remote from politics and played no role in opposing fascism in the
thirties or in the postwar period, was able to return to Vienna to
general acclaim and respect. He was the first writer in the postwar
period to be awarded the 'Ehrenpreis der Stadt Wien,' which was
followed by the 'Staatspreis,' the 'Ehrenring,' and the 'Grillparzer-
preis,' among others. To the end of his long life in 1973 he never
confronted politics or the events of contemporary reality in his
writings.

This essay has attempted to show how three major writers
who were attempting to carry forward the Austrian tradition and
the literary legacy of the turn-of-the-century Impressionism reacted to the political turbulence of the 1930s. Although they were
close friends with a shared background and *Weltanschauung,* they
nevertheless exhibited differences in their responses to the same
set of causes. All three were idealists, noble spirits motivated by
the desire to maintain traditional humanistic and humanitarian
values in their world. Their differing ways of confronting adversity
resulted from their individual character, their inner resilience, and
their flexibility. The primary lesson to be learned from their experiences is that writers avoid a stance of social responsibility and
political concern only at peril to themselves and their society. As a
result of the 1930s authors and readers have changed in their
attitudes toward and expectations from literature. Unfortunately
these changes have resulted in the indifference of the contemporary world to the writings of Zweig, Auernheimer, and Braun,

whose works, while still eminently readable, for the most part all belong now to the world of yesterday.

## NOTES

*I wish to express my appreciation to Randolph J. Klawiter and Donald Prater for their valuable suggestions.

1. Stefan Zweig, *Die Welt von gestern. Erinnerungen eines Europäers.* (Frankfurt am Main: S. Fischer, 1952), p. 329.
2. Ibid., p. 340.
3. Stefan Zweig, *Briefe an Freunde,* ed. Richard Friedenthal (Frankfurt am Main: S. Fischer, 1978), p. 235.
4. Marion Sonnenfeld, ed. *The World of Yesterday's Humanist Today* (Albany, NY: SUNY Press, 1983). See also Donald A. Prater, *Stefan Zweig. Das Leben eines Ungeduldigen* (München: Hanser, 1981) and Joseph P. Strelka, *Stefan Zweig* (Wien: Bundesverlag, 1983).
5. Stefan Zweig, *Die Welt von gestern,* p. 297.
6. Ibid., p. 299.
7. "Aber es hilft nichts, noch so diskret zu sein, die Zeitungen verfolgen einen von früh bis nachts mit Photographien und Stories—in Riesenformat war ich abgebildet, wie ich bei der Rede Ludwigs *weinte* (!) Ja, so stand es mit Riesenlettern—in Wahrheit hatte ich mich so widerlich gefühlt, als man uns als Märtyrer hinstellte, das photographierten sie und erfanden den Text dazu." Stefan Zweig, *Briefe an Freunde,* p. 276.
8. Zweig devoted three years (1910-1912) to translating almost all of Verhaeren's works into German, an outstanding act of unselfishness of one author toward another.
9. Cf. Stefan Zweig/Paul Zech, *Briefe 1910-1942,* ed. Donald G. Daviau (Rudolstadt: ²Greifenverlag, 1987).
10. Cf. *The Correspondence of Stefan Zweig with Raoul Auernheimer and Richard Beer-Hofmann,* eds. Donald G. Daviau and Jorun B. Johns (Columbia, South Carolina: Camden House, 1983).
11. Stefan Zweig, *Die Welt von gestern,* pp. 356-357, 393.
12. Letter to Felix Braun, *Briefe an Freunde,* p. 304.
13. Stefan Zweig, *Briefe an Freunde,* p. 212.
14. Ibid., p. 292.

15. Ibid., pp. 322-323.
16. Stefan Zweig, *Die Welt von Gestern*, pp. 349-350.
17. Stefan Zweig's unpublished letter to Felix Braun of 3 June 1938. The unpublished letters are located in the Stefan Zweig Archive at SUNY Fredonia. Jorun B. Johns and I are presently preparing an edition of this correspondence with the permission of Ulrike Popović and Kurt Maschler, executors of the Braun and Zweig estates, respectively.
18. Stefan Zweig, *Briefe an Freunde*, p. 228.
19. Ibid., pp. 228-229.
20  Ibid., p. 213.
21. Ibid., pp. 227-228.
22. Stefan Zweig, *Die Welt von Gestern*, p. 391.
23. For a more detailed discussion of Zweig's suicide see Rosi Cohn, *Das Problem des Selbstmordes in Stefan Zweigs Leben und Werk* (Bern/Frankfurt am Main: Peter Lang, 1982).
24. Stefan Zweig, "The Head Upon the Rostrum," in *Twelve Historical Miniatures* (New York: Viking, 1940).
25. Donald G. Daviau, "Stefan Zweig's Victors in Defeat," *Monatshefte,* Vol. 51, 1 (January 1959), 1-12.
26. Cf. Donald G. Daviau and Harvey L. Dunkle, "Stefan Zweig's *Schachnovelle,*" *Monatshefte*, Vol. 55, No. 3 (Winter 1973), 302-316.
27. Stefan Zweig, "The Jewish Children in Germany," p. 4.
28. Ibid., p. 5.
29. "Stefan Zweig on Joseph Leftwich," in *Kraft aus dem Boden*, Organ der Freiland-Liga, Jüdische Territorial Organisation Österreichs, Jg. 1936, Nr. 3 (27 November 1936), 2.
30. Stefan Zweig, "Eine Anrede," in *Die schlaflose Welt. Aufsätze und Vorträge 1909-1941* (Frankfurt am Main: S. Fischer, 1984), pp. 211-226.
31. Stefan Zweig, "Das Haus der tausend Schicksale," *Mitteilungsblatt des Hilfsvereins deutsch sprechender Juden* (Buenos Aires), 1 March 1937.
32. Stefan Zweig, "Keep Out of Politics," *Query*, Book 2 (The Jews), London, 1938, p. 77.
33. Ibid.
34. Untitled text in Stefan Zweig's *Nachlaß* in London.
35. Stefan Zweig, "Das große Schweigen," *Das neue Tagebuch*, 8/18 (4 May 1940), 426.
36. Stefan Zweig, "The Mission of the Intellectuals," *Adam International Review*, Vol. 13, No. 152 (September 1941), 2.
37. Ibid.

38. Stefan Zweig, "Hartrott and Hitler," *Free World* (New York, 4 (December 1942), 224-225.

39. Raoul Auernheimer, *Das Wirtshaus zur verlorenen Zeit* (Wien: Ullstein, 1948), p. 69.

40. See Hilde Spiel, ed., *Die zeitgenössische Literatur Österreichs* (München: Kindler, 1976), pp. 19-25 and Klaus Amann, *P.E.N.* (Wien/Köln/Graz: Böhlau, 1984), pp. 23-38.

41. According to Csokor, there remained in the "Rumpf-Penklub" Fontane, Jacob, Fischauer, Robert Neumann, Sonka, and Robert Musil. Franz Theodor Csokor, *Zeuge einer Zeit* (München/Wien: Langen-Müller, 1964), p. 33.

42. Csokor mentioned that Auernheimer resigned to protest a cut in salary, but the one reason does not preclude the other. Felix Salten took his position. Ibid., p. 43.

43. Raoul Auernheimer, *Wien – Bild und Schicksal* (Wien: Otto Lorenz, 1938), p. 265.

44. Raoul Auernheimer, "Stefan Zweig" in *The Torch of Freedom*, eds. Emil Ludwig and Henry B. Kranz (New York: Farrar and Rinehart, 1943), p. 422.

45. Manuscripts in possession of the author. D.G.D.

46. "Inside Barbed Wire," *The Christian Science Monitor*, 26 September 1942; "Two Conquerors, Two Kinds of Men: Hitler and Napoleon," *New York Times Magazine*, 21 July 1940; "Napoleon and Hitler," *New York Times Magazine*, 2 February 1941; "Mark Twain and the Gestapo," *The Christian Science Monitor*, 10 October 1942.

47. Raoul Auernheimer, *Das Wirtshaus zur verlorenen Zeit*, pp. 223-272.

48. In a letter of 27 November 1944 Lothar explains the purpose of these profiles to Auernheimer:

> Aber das ist kein privater Brief, sondern eine Bitte, zu einer Kultur-Enquete beizutragen, die ich – auf Drängen Ferdinand Csernins – zu leiten übernommen habe. Er hat einer Österr. Kultur-Kommission gegründet, deren sogenannten Vorsitz ich führe. Zweck: dem State-Deptmt in Washington und den analogen Referaten in London und Moscow die Kultur-Bedeutung des Künftigen (u. gewesenen) Österreich und die Mittel und Wege vor Augen zu führen, die zur Wiederherstellung und dominierenden Stellung österr. Kultur im gesamten deutschen Sprachraum führen könnten. Es wird ein Memorandum vorgelegt werden, zu dem die hervorragendsten Repräsentanten österr. Kultur beitragen sollen.

Die österr. Nobelpreisträger werden die vier Fakultäten übernehmen; Prof. Tietze Kunstgeschichte; Schönberg und Bruno Walter die Musik; Lubitsch und Preminger den Film; meine Wenigkeit das Theater. Die Literatur soll von Dir, Werfel, Broch und Bruckner in voneinander unabhängigen Memoranden behandelt werden. Wie stellst Du Dir die Wiederbelebung des österr. Schrifttums vor? (Über Verlagswesen, Radio, Nachrichtendienst und Presse wird es besondere Gutachten geben.) Welche Wege sollen nach Deiner Meinung beschritten werden, um die österr. Literatur zu fördern und zu reinigen? Was kann der Staat (die Staaten) dazu tun? u.sw. Was immer Du beibringst wird von außerordentlichem Wert sein. Von Dir erwarte ich mir ausserdem jenen kurzen historischen Rückblick auf Österreichs Beitrag zur Dichtung (incl. Drama, Kritik, Essay) der der ignoranten Außenwelt den Star stechen würde. Deine Gutachten kann so lange oder so kurz sein—2-3 Maschinenseiten genügen—als es Dir beliebt. Jeder Beitrag wird dem Gesamtmemorandum unverändert eingefügt; mit Daten über den Author.   Letter in possession of the author. D.G.D.

49.  Manuscripts in possession of the author. D.G.D.

50.  Josef Wenter's *Die Landgräfin von Thüringen* was performed at the Burgtheater on 29 January 1938.

51.  An edition of the Braun/Auernheimer correspondence is in preparation. D.G.D.

52.  Letter in possession of the author. D.G.D.

53.  Here Auernheimer described his experiences at Dachau concluding: "I was put into a concentration camp, because I stood firm all my life for freedom, justice and democracy. Concerning you I only may beg you: Stand firm to the eternal ideas of freedom, justice and democracy and you will never have to get acquainted with a concentration camp, nor will your blessed country ever become so unhappy and tortured as Germany and all of Europe is today."
Manuscript in possession of the author. D.G.D.

# Everyday Life and Politics in the Literature of the Thirties: Horváth, Kramer, and Soyfer

## Horst Jarka

In 1936 Jura Soyfer answered the questions of what the public were looking for and what they found in Vienna's *Kellertheater:* "We are much closer to present-day life than the ordinary theater is. We are taking notice of the things that people are concerned with today."[1] If we are looking for such an immediate reflection of everyday life in the literature of the thirties and if by *Dinge* we mean the dreary daily round in the years of the Depression, of mass unemployment and extreme political tension, and if by *Menschen* we mean not only those who could still afford an evening in a *Kaffeehaustheater*), we will not find that kind of reality in the works of the most famous writers of the time—not in Kraus, Musil, Broch—nor in the writings of the state-approved authors like Schreyvogl, E. A. Mayer and H. T. Mayer, Wenter, Perkonig, Waggerl, or Strobl. Rather, the thirties, as they were experienced and endured by hundreds of thousands of Austrians, found their most convincing literary expression in the works of the three authors I shall discuss. If I link Horváth, Kramer, and Soyfer together, I do so not only because of their socio-critical realism, but also because of the very similar response their criticism evoked. During Austrofascism all three authors were more or less tolerated outsiders: the ensuing Nazi rule caused the non-Jew Horváth to start the wanderings which ended in his death, drove the Jew Kramer into exile, and the Jew Soyfer to his death in Buchenwald. After the war the three were gradually rediscovered and, finally, more or less reluctantly reappropriated as worthy sons of Austria. Here I shall deal with their works as documents of

151

the time, i.e., especially as reactions to the political situation; roughly categorised, each of the authors seems to exemplify a different degree of such literary reaction: from Horváth's diagnostic awareness I shall proceed to Kramer's compassion, and to Soyfer's activism. The works of all three writers provide a refreshing antidote of enlightenment to the nauseating racist mysticism that made much of Austrian literature in the thirties politically harmful and aesthetically boring. My conclusion, attempting to overcome a merely historical approach, will indicate the significance that the rediscovery of Horváth, Kramer, and Soyfer has for the literary and general intellectual climate in Austria today.

I

To speak of Horváth in this context is not without problems since after studies by Bance and Lechner[2] it is very questionable to what extent he can be considered an Austrian writer at all. In his work, especially his overtly socio-critical writings, his diagnosis deals far more with the Weimar Republic than with Austria in the thirties. And yet Horváth's change in outlook from satire in *Der ewige Spießer* (1931) to 'internalisation' in *Der jüngste Tag* (1937) also reflects his attitude to politics in Austria. Political references are particularly obvious in the two works written in 1931, the anti-travel novel I just mentioned and his anti-*Völksstück, Geschichten aus dem Wiener Wald.* The devastating exposure of "fadenscheinige Gemütlichkeit" (Nestroy) dramatized in the play is already manifest in the novel as a direct political attack:

> For barely fifty minutes Kobler shared his compartment with a *Hofrat* who had been in the civil service since monarchy days, and a so-called man of the people who buttered up the *Hofrat* because he hoped to use his influence to advance his career. This man was a corrupt foreman who, in order to get ahead of his fellow workers in an even more unscrupulous fashion, had joined the *Heimwehr,* an Austrian variety of Italian fascism. The point

being, his superior, the engineer, was Regional Commander of the *Heimwehr*.[3]

This commentary (it is Horváth's, not the protagonist's) may still be read as criticism of private, political opportunism; the ensuing dialog, however, exposes the brutality of the *Heimwehr* and at least one of their supporters in no unclear terms:

> The Austrians are very easy-going people. "I hope the good Lord will let me live long enough to see all the Reds hanged," said the *Hofrat*. "Just rely on him up there," the man said, "Berg Isel is right above us now," the *Hofrat* said. "Andreas Hofer," said the man and added: "The Jews are getting too fresh." . . . "The other day we beat up a Jew," the man said. "Did you really?" said the *Hofrat* gleefully. "The Jew was all by himself," said the man, "and there were ten of us. We sure beat the hell out of him, *Heimwehr*-style." The *Hofrat* snickered. (3:179)

In a variant of the novel the condemnation of the *Heimwehr* leads to an unequivocal partisanship with Red Vienna and "das arbeitsame, ehrlich Proletariat" (4:477) and on to an attack on the bourgeoisie, which (just as for Social-Democratic propaganda) for Horváth, was personified by the Christian-Social landlord, supposedly Christian but certainly not Social, who declares: "Whoever can't afford it should sleep under God's starry sky or in a shelter. Who needs an apartment if he can't pay for it?" (4:477).

In *Geschichten aus dem Wiener Wald* too we find overt political references if only sporadically. But although this is Horváth's only play with a specifically Austrian setting, the most obviously fascist character in it is neither a young *Heimwehrler* nor an *Altösterreicher* with fascist leanings; he is a German student who is not taken very seriously by the Viennese around him. When he reacts with a typically Prussian anti-Austrian cliché, he is put in his place—no doubt to the delight of an Austrian audience—by the Rittmeister who retaliates with an equally clichéd show of

Austrian superiority, a *Stammtisch*-bravado glorifying the *Habsburgische Mythos.* It will depend on the director of the play whether or not, in the nightclub scene, this monarchist succumbs like all the others to the symbolic stimulus of the Zeppelin, that pan-German, aereo-technological and phallic symbol of frenzied incestuous union with the virile "big brother."

In the novel the rabidly anti-Semitic *Hofrat* and the Jew-beating *Heimwehrler* reveal the historic continuity of racism from monarchy to *Ständestaat,* from Schönerer and Lueger to Starhemberg, Fey, and Henz. In the play the openly sadistic anti-Semitism exposed in the earlier work changes into a softer, more obligingly opportunistic form, and Horváth manages with inimitable acuteness and precise realism to catch its vagueness and tone quality: Valerie, after first having made a joke of Erich's racism, retreats in order not to spoil her chances of gaining a new sexual partner: "You don't think I like the Jews, do you?" (1:180) The most significant implication in *Geschichten aus dem Wiener Wald,* however, does not lie in rather obvious allusions or pronouncements but in the exposure of a collective consciousness ready to embrace fascism. I do not intend to repeat here things which are already well-known, but I would rather look at some instances of *Zeitgeschichte* and *Kulturpolitik* where Horváth's attitude becomes ambivalent.

Early in 1933 Horváth distances himself from politics, but his declaration of political abstinence is followed, a few months later, by a statement of obvious political implication; about his new play, *Himmelwärts,* he says in an interview in the *Wiener Allgemeine Zeitung* (14.9.1933): "I consider the fairy-tale farce especially suitable for the present time because in this genre one can say things which otherwise one would not be allowed to say."[4] But how much did Horváth actually "say?" To what extent did he pursue Nestroy's strategies of a hundred years before, strategies that Jura Soyfer practised in Horváth's own time? During the *Schutzbund* uprising in February 1934 Horváth is in Vienna, possibly still working on *Himmelwärts.* In one scene St. Peter says: "Yesterday, for instance, they again executed a bunch of innocent people down on earth—nothing but cases of a miscarriage of justice and yet all of them will go to hell anyhow" (2:299). If this passage was indeed written after February it is the only reference in all of Horváth's works and letters to the end of Austrian democracy — a far cry from the condemnation of the *Heimwehr* and the sympathies with Red Vienna so firmly stated in the novel three years before. In fact, the unspeakable truth uttered in *Himmelwärts* was not one of public but of private politics: The signer's pact with the devil for the sake of a career points to the pact Horváth was about to negotiate with the new rulers in Germany. Research has attempted to penetrate Horváth's attitudes in 1933–1935, the maze of his motivations, illusions, psychological twists, compromise, and remorse that surrounds what now, fifty years later, appears as an opportunistic sell-out or, viewed less harshly, an attempt at an *"innere Emigration"* forced by the need to make a living.[5] I shall comment only on those of Horváth's activities that are more or less related to Austria.

Keeping a low profile, Horváth assumed a pseudonym and wrote scripts for light feature films, four of them on "Austrian" themes: *Das Einmaleins der Liebe,* based on Nestroy's *Einen Jux will er sich machen, Der Pfarrer von Kirchfeld* (after Anzengruber's play), and *Das Fiakerlied,* ascribed to Hans Saßmann, one of the literary favorites of the *"Ständestaat,"* which hardly suggests subversive tendencies in the film. Finally, there was the script *Brüderlein fein,* a montage of motifs from Raimund's plays; it was not filmed until 1942—as entertainment for the home front as well as for those on leave from the real front. This suggests that it was one of those "typically Viennese" films that the Nazi authorities considered completely harmless and therefore welcome and that after the war were reassessed as examples of cultural resistance Austrian style. For the time being, however, it would be better to reserve judgment. Paul Hörbiger mentioned in his memoirs that strong criticism in the style of *Geschichten aus dem Wiener Wald* was smuggled into *Das Fiakerlied:* the *Schmalz* was to be served up as "a kind of kitschy novel but a pot-boiler."[6] But whether this intention was ever carried out, or whether *Das*

*Fiakerlied* and the other films for which Horváth wrote the scripts, in stark contrast to his *Volksstücke,* merely encouraged the deceptive and sentimental myth about Vienna (so much to the taste of Austrofascist image manipulators) can only be established through an analysis of the films. Horváth himself acknowledged that he abandoned working for the film industry because, in writing those scripts, he had acted against his conscience.

Conscience was to be the driving force behind Horváth's later plays, but it was not an openly political conscience. In *Der jüngste Tag,* for example, the question of guilt is so personal a matter (brought about by an unhappy marriage, flirtation, and jealousy) that the political relevance of responsibility ascribed to the play after the war can be maintained only at a rather remote symbolic level. Wolfgang Lechner has suggested that Horváth's plays after 1933 were quite consciously aimed at the needs and expectations of Austrian producers and critics.[7] If in fact Horváth wrote these works with such deliberations, then his calculations proved wrong as the reception, or rather non-reception, of his plays in Schuschnigg's Austria clearly shows; even his contacts, admittedly superficial, with circles close to the government did not lead to any support of his work.

To conclude: Horváth's reactions to politics in Austria were not those of a chronicler; he did not respond to specific events but to the social climate, i.e., to attitudes that also determine political behavior. His comments in *Der ewige Spießer* (only his exposure of the young *Heimwehrler* approaches what one might call a political character sketch) place him clearly on the side of the Social Democrats. In *Geschichten aus dem Wiener Wald* no such partisanship, neither for the left nor for the right, is evident. Unlike *Italienische Nacht,* this play, surprisingly enough for a realistic drama about Vienna in the early thirties, contains not even an allusion to a political party. None of the heated political battles of those years is mentioned. Again, in contrast to *Italienische Nacht,* none of the characters even reads a newspaper. The absence of politics in the play is one symptom of the absence of any social coherence, even the questionable one of political parties (be it only that of sheer political opportunism). Neither Marianne nor Alfred thinks of *Protektion* through a party when looking for work, as the *Heimwehrler* did in the novel. The characters in *Geschichten aus dem Wiener Wald* are beyond politics, public politics, that is. The unprincipled principle of looking out for one's own advantage as the basis of political or commercial inter-action, has become the principle of human relationships: "A purely personal relationship becomes genuine only if each partner gets something out of the other" (1:163), Alfred tells Valerie, summing up the way in which practically all human relationships in the play "work." Exploitation in an authoritarian family and in men's relation to women, sadism, religious sentimentality, bigotry to the point of murder, frustration, isolation, fragmented thoughts and language, helplessness, self-pity, intolerance – these are the ingredients that make up the collective "consciousness" of Horváth's Viennese in the early thirties. It is not a Nazi mentality he exposes but the value vacuum that was to be filled with the promises of the Nazi propaganda. Austrofascism – meekly – tried to fill that vacuum, and Horváth's prophetic flash in the nightclub scene anticipates who was to triumph over the Austrofascist *Parallelaktion.* Horváth is not on record as having made any com-ment on Austrofascism; he probably accepted it as the "lesser evil." After all, Austria under Schuschnigg, if she did not acknowl-edge his literary achievements, did not threaten his physical safety and in her indifference permitted him to write his late works, in-cluding *Jugend ohne Gott,* perhaps the most political work Hor-váth ever wrote: his condemnation of Nazi indoctrination of German youth. Whether the youth *with* God that the Austro-fascists trained in their paramilitary camps met with Horváth's approval, we will never know.

## II

For Horváth, the *petite bourgeoisie* in its readiness to accept fascism, was the *Volk* of the thirties. In order to link Horváth with Kramer and Soyfer, we may have to stretch this rather overworked concept, but not without making basic distinctions, also in the concept of *Volksnähe,* the affinity each writer felt to his *Volk.* Horváth's attitude was a paradoxical closeness from a distance which allowed him to view his characters not only as despicable, but also as pathetic in their hollowness and isolation. Horváth's *Volk* were also, we must remember, the socially weaker groups, in which both the *"Ständestaat"* and the Austrian Nazi Party, found most of their followers. For Theodor Kramer, the most important social poet of the interwar years, the *Volk* was the weakest group of all. His attitude was never harshly critical, it was an attitude of dedication, sympathy, and empathy. Kramer is still often thought of as the poet of those on the margin of society. Such a label, however, tends to restrict the socio-critical dimension of his work by relegating it to the bizarre and the exotic. But what was that margin really like? It is true, of course, that Kramer wrote numerous poems about pimps and whores and the demi-monde, and many of the jobs he depicted through individual representatives are so unusual that today one naturally assigns them to the very fringe – these *Rübenzupfer, Nußentkerner, Borstenzieher,* and *Aasgräber.* But with each different trade Kramer gave voice to, the "fringe" grew: with the workers in the brickyards or those in the limekilns or the migrant farmhands who came down from Slovakia, the *Saisontschuschen* of the day. And, after all, Kramer wrote poems about industrial workers and the unemployed (22 to 28 percent of the work force, not counting those who did not receive benefits anymore, the so-called *Ausgesteuerten,* many of whom ended up among the 27,000 Austrians who between 1927 and 1937 turned on the gas or drowned themselves in the Danube). Kramer is not the poet of the down-and-outs whose very far-out-ness surrounds them with the false aura of a hobo or hippy type of romanticism. Kramer's outsiders stood in rags on all the street corners and begged their way everywhere, not just through the *Weinviertel,* to which Kramer has been assigned as "local poet." Like Petzold, he was the poet of the victims and slaves of industrialization, discovering, in addition, the rural proletariat for poetry. He wrote countless *Rollengedichte* of the multitudes, the negligible mass of those, *die keine Rolle mehr spielten.* Fritz Achberger has drawn this conclusion:

> Theodor Kramer's language is a language of the margins of society, and it is for this very reason that his poetry is one of the few authentic voices which reflect the reality of the *Ständestaat;* because in this language we can hear the silence that was to come. In the main stream of Austrian society Kramer's language, even language itself, has become alienated; Kramer's exile is anticipated (he went to England in 1939).[8]

Is Kramer then an unpolitical poet of human misery? Sylvia Patsch finds in his extensive work "hardly one political poem . . . in the proper sense of the word . . . no call to resistance . . . resignation, rather, the apathy of people who got caught in the merciless wheels of history and are too weak to change anything on their own . . ."[9] It is true that Kramer wrote no activist poetry. But in a broader sense social poetry which offers no Christian consolation and presents misery without comment is certainly political, especially if it does not show "the merciless wheels of history" but rather the mercilessly grinding machinery of capitalist exploitation. And Kramer published poems of this kind. *"Des Volkes Groll"* ("the people's suppressed anger")[10] becomes even louder in those poems of Kramer's where the motif of revenge is sounded, the personal revenge of the outcast. In one of these calls for justice, bitterness is raised to the level of prophecy: the fall of the "have-nots" will drag the "haves" down after it; the sickness of society will be the death of the system (1:282).

Ecological concern—unusual in Kramer's time and as unpolitical then as it is political today—is the subject of the following poem which describes a nature that can no longer help man in his alienation and indeed can no longer help itself:

> The rivers all over the country
> are gripped by a terrible death.
> . . . . . . . . . . . . . . . . . . . . . . .

> the wastes are muddying the water,
> the trout and crayfish are dead.
> . . . . . . . . . . . . . . . . . . . . . . . .
> The landscape of brooks and of rivers
> is now almost everywhere gone;
> soon, in spite of abundance of rainfall
> only gutters will run to the sea. (3:218)

Particularly striking I find one of Kramer's early poems which combines ecology and socialism and ends in prophetic scepticism about the future of both. *Beerenlese* describes the plight of poor women who first have to beg a permit to gather berries from the landowner and then have to sell them at a price determined by him. Human exploitation is here accompanied by the exploitation of nature; the forest is being cut down. The poem ends with these lines:

> If ever, one day, working people hold
> the fruits of their own labors in their hands,
> who knows if towering forests will exist
> and if one bush with berries will yet stand. (1:170)

Apart from such indirectly political work, Kramer wrote a series of overtly political poems which I would like to examine more closely because they became accessible only last autumn with the publication of volume three of the Kramer edition. A complete register of Kramer's political lyrics from the thirties is not possible for political reasons: after the German take-over Kramer, "*in panischem Schrecken,*" ("in panic terror") destroyed all poems whose content seemed to him too dangerous. The value of the poems we have lies precisely in their supposed "innocence." They are not poems of party politics and not even political in the broader sense like Brecht's "Fragen eines lesenden Arbeiters" or "Es wechseln die Zeiten." They are poems *about* politics, about the impact of politics on private lives, its disruptive destructive effect, and after 1934 the effect politics had in separating men or bringing them together. It was typical of Kramer, who was born and raised in Niederhollabrunn, that he made the isolation of the industrial proletariat in the country a theme of poetry as in the lyric about the workers in a small factory somewhere in the *Wald-viertel* who are shunned by the farmers and not understood by the Viennese comrades. There are poems about those who, weary of politics and disillusioned, with all their political energy spent, refuse after 1934 to become involved again, like the brickmaker who tells his comrade from the city:

> Here in this village I must live;
> the farmers give me bread and milk,
> if they want to. What can you give me? (3:403)

Nothing political, nothing human is foreign to Kramer. The Social Democrat, pensioned off in 1934, slowly being hollowed out by enforced inactivity, appears in one of his poems, as does his son who, having endured the paralyzing silence at home, reasserts the rights of his youth and still promises in his heart, "to lead one day the cause / of the poor and beaten down" (3:402). It was the time when school children were obliged to wear badges with the motto "Seid einig!" ("United We Stand"), while families were being torn apart by political disagreement. Kramer makes us feel the conflicts within children subjected to the tensions – to them incomprehensible – between school and home, as for instance in the following poem:

### Question for Mother

> Mother, we don't live like other people,
> things are not the way they used to be;
> even the poorest have their little parties, ˙
> the guests we have are never really special,
> they come and go but hardly act like guests.

the appeal the teacher reads out to remind us
barely brushes by my ear and does not move me,
and I sense that I am forced to give.

I often see the others in the evening
as they go strutting in their uniforms;
yesterday at dusk beneath the bridge
I donned the tunic of the neighbors' boy,
my image in the water was not me.

Mother, something here at home is different
and I still can't make out what it is;
tell me, don't you see, I've got to know,
I've got to be on one side or the other,
I can't go on being torn between the two. (3:410)

Fascist *Gesinnungsterror* is a recurring theme in these poems, as is
the question of how to withstand it. *"Wie bleibt man sauber?"*
("How to Remain Honest?") is the title of one such poem which
ends in the passive acceptance of the situation at work and an
escape to a nature which preserves the only real truth.

If Horváth, as Alan Bance has shown, provides the dramatic
correlative to Siegfried Kracauer's *Die Angestellten* (1929), then
Kramer provides a lyrical one to *Die Arbeitslosen von Marienthal*
(1933) by Jahoda, Lazarsfeld, and Zeisel. The existential meaning
of work, the identification with it—even with the tools—the in-
security of waiting week after week to be fired, the deceptive
feeling of being on holiday for the first few days of unemployment, the panic and the terror of realizing the permanence of the
situation, the gradual alienation from oneself, the self-degradation
of the ever stronger pull downward, the morbid fascination of
letting oneself go to the dogs—all this Kramer knew how to bring
alive in moving situations and images of daily life. Many of his
poems are poems of politics suffered and endured, yet there is no
false pathos in them. Kramer's realism prevented him from any
idealization of the victims. Out of this truthfulness came a poem

in which the Social Democratic party member Kramer described an attitude quite unheard of in party lyrics: *Ein Krampenschlag vor Tag* pits the unemployed against the still employed; all solidarity acquired or commanded by the party is forgotten by the hungry. Demoralization through unemployment was one of the chief reasons for the debacle of the Social Democrats in 1934, and Kramer's indictment of a system that used a reservoir of starving people to undermine politically effective solidarity goes far deeper than many an activist tirade.

Apathy, avoiding politics out of caution, necessity, weariness are Kramer's themes just as much as revolt, the pent-up despair demanding and being denied release, the intolerable waiting, the temptation to use force. In a poem referring to Josef Gerl, a 23-year-old unemployed Social Democrat who blew up a railroad signal mast and was sentenced to death, we read:

> There is something so strange about violence
> even for those with least power.
> The thought of it is intoxicating and black
> and sends shivers up and down your spine . . .

and then the formula for terrorism:

> What rips the order apart
> gives life its order back again. (3:399f.)

Gerl's terrorism was an act of desperate frustration not that of a premeditated political strategy like that of the Nazis, and yet Kramer's poem is one in which the general political tension seems to overflow ideological boundaries.

No possible political reaction escaped Kramer; thus in the mass of poems dealing with political unrest, discouragement, and pent-up anger, we find a truly democratic one, which, considering that it was written in November 1933, is almost moving in its hopes for peaceful solutions. It is a poem in the spirit of those Social Democrats who, to the last, put their trust in negotiating. The speaker in the poem reflects on a meeting:

The door falls shut, the meeting's over now!
Amid small groups I drift home silently.
My pulses pound, my ears are ringing still,
the crowd is all around me in the hall,
before my eyes the lectern, table, wall,
and every word again is sharp and clear.

I hear the trembling in the speaker's voice,
I feel again what I must contradict,
I see me raise my hand up to object,
and suddenly with dreamlike intuition
I understand the words the other said
as if I'd found them deep within myself.

Much that I said I'd take back gladly now,
yet other things are too much part of me.
And could the others be thinking the same thoughts
as they at home now slowly draw the knife
through their loaf of bread?  Much would be easy then
and more than one had thought would be achieved. (3:391)

Kramer knew well why this hope was one in the subjunctive
mood. In October of the same year he published in Prague a poem
already anticipating the need of the party to go underground:

What will happen to us, when they outlaw our
                                    organizations,
arrest all our leaders, have our meeting rooms shut up
                                    and bolted,
when they take all our books and set fire to our very
                                    last pamphlet,
when each of us has to remove the badge from his
                                    buttonhole? (3:393)

Kramer's poems of solidarity with the German Socialists, persecuted since January 1933, began to gain an ominous relevance for

Austria. If in one poem Kramer pleaded for commitment to the old ideals in spite of oppression, in another he called to open battle, and in the next he already warned of dictatorship that would paralyze resistance:

> We are facing bitter years,
> every man will seem a spy,
> only anxiously, with fears,
> will we meet each other's eyes.
> . . . . . . . . . . . . . . . . . . . . . .
> All that makes our life worth living
> by tomorrow will be gone. (3:401)

Those poems Kramer wrote in Vienna after the Anschluss fulfill this prophecy in a most terrifying manner. They are poems of Horváth's *"große Kälte"* ("cold times") his *"Zeitalter der Fische"* ("Age of the Fish").

### III

Some of Kramer's political poems which I have mentioned were first published fifty years after they had been written and shared the contradiction inherent in all political poetry kept in the author's desk. And all the poems which he wrote for those "who are without a voice" (1:272) were hardly ever read by them. Equally limited was Horváth's impact on Schuschnigg's Austria; only two of his plays were produced in small theaters. Of our three authors only Jura Soyfer reached a wide public during his lifetime. Every week, from December 1931 to February 1934, the *Arbeiter-Zeitung* (then a paper of high standards with a large circulation) published "Jura's" political satires in which, with a verbal wit inspired by Karl Kraus, he ridiculed the forces of re-action in Austria and warned of German fascism and its militaristic policies.

It is illuminating to place Soyfer and Kramer side by side for a moment. Soyfer, too, wrote lyrics about the down-and-out, but

Kramer's poetry on this theme is grimmer. With Soyfer, the misery
is always overcome by "the sunlight dream of the poor" (279), not
as a mystical consolation (Rilke's "poverty is a great radiance from
within") but as a demand for realization in this world. Kramer
wrote a poem of boundless desolation in which one of the poorest
of the poor directs his prayer to heaven:

> You would not think your world looked right
> if you saw me – I'd spoil the sight,
> I beg you God, forget me! (1:283)

Soyfer's Lechner Edi (one of the *Ausgesteuerten*), too, is seized
with despair when he compares God's intentions and what man
made of them, yet his despair does not culminate in humility but
in an embittered cry:

> Do not touch the clay, O Lord!
> Adam will but wreck Your plan.
> Or if You've already made him,
> Cancel him! Unmake Your Man! (586)

And yet Edi finds a way back from his negating creation (*Schöp-
fungspessimismus*) to that affirmation of life with which Soyfer, in
his "Dachaulied," defies barbarism.

But let me return to the daily politics in the early thirties:
how far Soyfer's political temperament and literary engagement
differs from that of Kramer we see by comparing two poems
triggered by a police search for forbidden weapons, something
which was commonplace at the time and symptomatic of the
political climate. In Kramer's "Die letzten Gewehre" we see his
love of exact detail with which he describes, in long dactylic lines,
the rifles of the *Schutzbund,* their hiding place, the care with
which they were buried, the danger of neglecting them. It is only
in the last stanza that we see the workers and feel their anger and
their growing determination to strike back:

The hearts of the men in the factories, squares, and
                                                    the smoke-
filled huts beat now louder as for the tenth time in
                                                    the town
the search for the weapons is on, as floor-boards are
                                                    ripped up
and others are covered with rubble; they stare and they let
not a word escape through clenched teeth. And some of
                                                    them cramp
up their fingers as if they were round the trigger. (3:396)

And now Soyfer's poem, published in April of the same year,
1933: in place of description and indirect psychological observation, we find aggressive and sarcastic satire completely alien
to Kramer:

> Rock-a-bye, baby,
> Who's searching the nest?
> They're looking for weapons,
> The cops do it best.
> Comrades, we wanted to stand by
> The constitution, and guard it? Why?
> Leave that to our police chief Fey!
> He and his honest, green-coated mob
> Will do a bang-up job.

And the last verse:

> Dig on, worthy diggers of the State,
> Bury all compromise.
> We united the proletariat
> Against fascism's rise.
> And while you are digging lift your heads
> Past the cordon protecting your crew:
> You are surrounded by hundreds of Reds
> With fists clenched, all cursing you,

> See the unemployed enraged by their fate?
> Hundreds of mouths – one single cry!
> Is it really us who fan the hate?
> We leave that up to you, Herr Fey!
> You and your honest green-coated mob
> Will do a bang-up job. (111, 113)

There is a double irony in the poem. Alongside that intended by Soyfer there is irony in the fact that the poem appeared in the *Arbeiter-Zeitung* on 9 April 1933, four weeks after Parliament had been "closed" and after the party's failure to call for a general strike which meant in effect that the direction of things to come was already set. The tone and the date of publication of the poem indicate the contradictory position into which Soyfer was being driven. As a member of the left-wing of the Social Democrats he was fighting on two unequal fronts: against fascism on the one hand and against the defensive policies of his own party leaders on the other. The cry to arms, to which the poem steadily rises, and the revolutionary pathos of many of his other poems seem to match the *Verbalradicalismus* (the "talking big") of the party's propaganda machine, but, in fact, Soyfer was completely serious about his readiness to fight for the cause. In February 1934 one last irony awaited him. When he came to the meeting place, no one knew where the arms were hidden. The buried weapons – symbol of retribution and an unyielding spirit in Kramer's poem, in Soyfer's novel, and in Friedrich Wolf's *Floridsdorf* – had disappeared into thin air.

After February 1934 Soyfer not only changed his name and hid the well-known "Jura" behind various pseudonyms, he also changed his strategy, had to change it in fact from Agitprop to *Kleinkunst* for he was no longer addressing workers and unemployed who were party members but the left-wing intellectuals who attended the coffee-house *Kellertheater*. John Lehmann, Soyfer's English friend who lived in Vienna in the thirties, confirmed the documentary value of his plays:

His cabaret plays . . . are clever, full of topical wit against the police rulers of the country, but above all remarkable — to me — for their human warmth and the tenderness of their idealism. Jura was the poet of a ruined and dispossessed generation, the young men and women whose childhood had been the inflation and revolutionary aftermath of the war in Central Europe, and who had grown up to unemployment as a permanent condition of life around them. He expressed their half-despairing longings, the gentleness that remained in the midst of bitterness, the sense of civilized values so essentially Viennese (which penetrated right through the educated working class) with such truth of feeling that I have only to read the opening lines of one of his sketches for the whole atmosphere of that melancholy time to come back to me.[11]

In Lehmann's nostalgic emphasis on the emotional, the *Verklärung* tends to obscure the activist *Aufklärung* which was the very center of Soyfer's work. His *Zauberpossen* politicized the local comic tradition; as Edwin Zbonek has said: "Soyfer was a Nestroy who had read Marx."[12] Not just read, one must add, but made his teachings come alive — under the very nose of the censor — so skillfully, however, that a prosecuting attorney would have found it very difficult to prove the accusation in Soyfer's indictment of 1937 that his plays were communistic. The political message is clearest in Soyfer's *Astoria* (1937), a satire on the theme "*Ein Staat sucht ein Volk*"[13] ("A State is Looking for a People") and on the collective identity crisis in Schuschnigg's "second German state." Soyfer, although no native Austrian, countered this crisis with unquestioning patriotism: on the registration form for his last semester, for ethnic affiliation, he put down "Austrian" when even Socialists would have automatically written "German."[14] Soyfer's Austrianness, of course, had nothing to do with the *Österreichische Mensch* of Austro-fascist ideology but everything with the *Österreichische Nation* argued for by the Communists, whom Soyfer had joined after February 1934. Soyfer's concept of *Volk* changed, too. If before 1934 it had meant the industrial proletariat, he now extended the term, in keeping with the strategy of the Popular Front, to include the petite bourgeoisie – at least in his rather rare theoretical pieces, i.g., his essay on Nestroy, and in the one leaflet he wrote for the Communist underground. In his dramatic works, however, the satirist Soyfer often gets the better of the political strategist.

Some of Soyfer's best prose pieces after 1934 are satires on the petite bourgeoisie. In a sketch reflecting the reactionary climate at the University of Vienna, he shows how an innkeeper's son from the provinces turns into an opportunistic "intellectual"; in a short story he analyzes the frustrations of an "unpolitical" office worker. The first chapter of Soyfer's unfinished novel, *Thus Died a Party,* is a masterly psychogram of the authoritarian personality, just as T. W. Adorno characterized it years later: in Soyfer's Franz Josef Zehetner, Horváth's still apolitical *ewiger Spießer* has turned into a member of the *Heimwehr,* and together with the anti-Semitic *Hofrat* represents the *österreichischer Unmensch* even before *Der österreichische Mensch* was created as officially authorized model citizen. The figure of Zehetner is a significant antithesis to the "hollow men" in Soyfer's *Vineta,* that nightmare with which Soyfer hoped to awaken his contemporaries to the coming catastrophe. Soyfer saw not only the apathy which had affected many Austrians (an apathy which was to support the thesis of the "rape of Austria" in 1938), he saw only too clearly the Zehetners, by no means lethargic, whose frustrations drove them more than willingly towards the Anschluss:

> The fourteen years of the Republic had made the cup full, and the big hand on the clockface of History finally approached the hour of decision. Yes, he, Franz Josef Zehetner, was a German, an Aryan, an Austrian, a Christian; he was the prisoner of Versailles and Saint-Germain, he was the victim of Marxist terror and was the oak at whose root international Jewry gnawed. Even in him, most careful of the careful, something at last demanded a great

breakthrough, only he was not quite sure whether this
something was the call of the blood or the voice of the
Lord. In any case, he, Zehetner, had been awakened! No
one should reproach him any longer for being half-hearted!
(334f.)

This hodge-podge of clichés prohibits any thinking Zehetner already thinks only with his legs, his marching legs. More openly
satirical than Horváth in his exposure of a latent fascist consciousness, Soyfer allows for psychological nuances, drawing especially
on Alfred Adler's theories of inferiority. In the rest of the novel,
too, Soyfer combines psychological and political analysis, as he
describes the gradual hollowing out of the Social Democratic
Party, the schizoid conflict between revolutionary rhetoric and
defensive policy, between the wait-and-see strategy of the older
leadership and the activism of the left opposition in the party.
*Thus Died a Party* breaks off before the February fighting but
delineates the preceding developments so as to make the outcome
appear inevitable.

IV

When Soyfer's novel was finally published thirty-five years
after the war, it was hailed as a major work of political literature,
not only a document of the thirties but a work of immediate relevance in the eighties. Like the rediscovery of Soyfer, that of Horváth (which essentially started in the sixties) and of Kramer (his
*Gesammelte Gedichte* (Collected Poems) began appearing in 1984)
must be seen in a wider political and cultural context.

Wolfgang Lechner has shown the reasons why those Horváth
plays critical of society were accepted into the repertoire later
than the plays written after 1933: "The further back into the past
the historical facts moved, the less the theatergoer had to fear
being identified by Horváth with the guilty, the more willingly
those works by Horváth were received which more concretely than
others exposed petty-bourgeois bestiality and stupidity as the

breeding-ground of fascism."[15] It was this political relevance of Horváth's *Volksstücke* that decisively influenced the social drama of Sperr, Kroetz, W. Bauer, and Turrini. No other dramatist whose main work was produced in the thirties has had such an impact on postwar German-language drama as Horváth.

In the case of Soyfer, too, the political impact has gone hand in hand with the literary one. After decades in which Soyfer performances were few and far between, the socially conscious seventies saw a revival of interest in him. Since then scarcely a year has passed in which, in Austria and other German-speaking countries, Soyfer plays have not been staged. Censorship had forced Soyfer to raise the level of his plays from a topical to a general political significance; their relevance today is guaranteed by their universal themes: unemployment, the threat of world destruction, domination by the machinery of the state, big business imperialism. The appearance of the complete edition in 1980 (and one might well ask whether the financial support of this expensive undertaking by the Ministry of Science and Research would have been possible before the Kreisky era) brought about a literary revaluation of his works, especially his plays. Jürgen Hein corrected their previous classification as cabaret sketches by assessing them as *Volksstücke* and placing Soyfer between Horváth and Brecht; young scholars, taking Soyfer as an example, began to reexamine the question of anti-fascist drama opening up new areas for discussion. Donald Daviau, for example, has raised the understandable if problematic question whether Soyfer will be ascribed to the canon of German literature or placed in the fringe category of anti-fascist literature. Whereas the plays are of a wide political significance, Soyfer's novel has become a point of reference in a very specifically Austrian political controversy today. As W. Schmidt-Dengler has put it:

> Soyfer's left-wing criticism of Austrian Social-Democracy supplies arguments to those on the left who want to criticize the Socialist government today. Only the unchallenged SPÖ rule which now (1982) has lasted for more than ten

years seems to have created a situation favorable to the reception of an author who considered his party's readiness to compromise with middle-class values a betrayal of the old ideals which had inspired it from the very beginning.[16]

If Horváth's work had provided a starting point for the young dramatists in the sixties, twenty years later Soyfer and Kramer were discovered as forerunners whose tradition could be continued. Soyfer, who in his passionate demand for social change wrote literature and not propaganda, can provide a model for today's politically committed authors, as Heinz R. Unger's plays testify. Kramer's work, having undergone a revaluation, might very well inspire young talents to reexamine "realism" in poetry. Kramer is no longer assigned to the discredited *Heimatkunst;* "His poems, in their totality, are neither idylls of *Heimat,* like the works of Waggerl, nor dark anti-idylls, like the works of Bernhard, but preserve a kind of realism which is rare in our literature and surfaced again only in the literature of the 1970s, as for instance in *Alpensaga* by Peter Turrini and Wilhelm Pevny."[17] Kramer's aesthetic of the particular, his exactness in catching the language, especially the occupational language of lower classes not normally treated in literature, has been recognized not only as a contribution to social history, but also as a method of regionalism which preserves, "what has not yet deteriorated to the international uniculture of the monotonous."[18] With his awareness of ecology, Kramer has become a contemporary of a generation for which a poem about trees is no longer a crime but one without trees an act of irresponsibility. We are not just moved by Kramer's social lyrics but are discovering, alongside the sadness in his work, an affirmation of life, his poems on the joys of eating and drinking, his "demokratische Epikuräismus" (Konstantin Kaiser), which demands not just bread for everyone but "Brot und Wein" (1:337).

Naturally, the positive reception of Soyfer and Kramer is part of the process of political education breaking down the "great taboo" which for so long prevented an open discussion of the thirties and the Nazi years. K. Kaiser of the *Verein zur Förde-*

*rung und Erforschung der antifaschistischen Literatur* writes: "Not even the student generation of the 1968ers could relate to the dead of those years, their battles, their poetry. It was only the recurrence of the economic crisis, the resurgence of some neo-fascists and the even worse proliferation of fascistoid pseudo-thinking that brought those "lost years" closer to our present."[19] But it is not only this desire to throw light on Austria's "dirty thirties" which motivates this interest in Soyfer and Kramer; it is also indicative of the desire for new inspiration and a renewed sense of continuity. Thinking about the thirties is to think about an Austria different from that at the turn of the century which is constantly being celebrated in aesthetic terms, most recently as "dream" at the expense of "reality."[20] Kramer and Soyfer are becoming representative figures for young writers of the left. One of them, Erich Hackl, says:

> The task is to search Austria's past for republican, demo-cratic, socialist elements. The cultural heritage of this kind is especially vital for oppositional writers who are isolated in our social reality and are in danger of suffocating in it. This is all the more essential since the young generation of Austrian authors (the first generation that grew up in the Second Republic and has an historically, i.e., autobio-graphically unimpaired relationship to this state) lacks the great exemplary moralists that the Federal Republic of Germany has in Heinrich Böll and Switzerland in Max Frisch.[21]

What makes Horváth, Kramer, and Soyfer the spiritual contempo-raries of young, politically engaged writers today is their demand for ethical rigour, for social and political responsibility which, in spite of all their differences,[22] united them. Kramer overcame his self-pity, the temptation to drift, to cop out, the apathy so wel-come to ruling powers, by fighting his way through to an accep-tance of social responsibility, a process expressed with moving conciseness in the words: "Oh könnt ich doch noch sagen, / Es

kommt auf mich nicht an!'' (1:576). Moral and social responsibility is the force that liberates the teacher in Horváth's *Jugend
ohne Gott* who, setting an example, creates, if only in a modest
way, a spirit of resistance. The urgent need of collective resistance
against the forces of destruction was the message in Soyfer's plays,
most powerfully stated at the end of *Vineta:*

> Sure, there really is no city in the world that's like this
> Vineta, but if one day a tidal wave should come, some big
> barbaric outbreak, I wonder if the whole world might not
> turn into a Vineta. And if that's not just in my imagina-
> tion, then it's pretty serious business, isn't it? In that case,
> all of us would have to put all our energies together, all of
> us and right now, and even then there might not be much
> time left, because no one would know when it might
> come, that flood. (647)

With these words Soyfer dismissed his audience in the ominous
autumn of 1937. Many Austrians were afraid of the tidal wave,
others tried to stop it, but all too many welcomed it enthusiastically, among them many authors who had presented the so-called
*Literarisches Leben im Austrofaschismus.*[23] Those celebrities have
faded into oblivion. The great writers, however, Musil or Kraus,
can be less directly associated with the thirties than with the preceding decades back to the monarchy. It is in the works of Horváth, Kramer, and Soyfer that the Austrian thirties, so different
from the decades before and after, find their most specific and
valid literary voice.

## NOTES

1. Jura Soyfer, *Das Gesamtwerk,* ed. Horst Jarka (Wien: Europaverlag,
   1980), p. 483. In the following all page numbers after Soyfer texts
   refer to this edition.
2. Alan F. Bance, "Ödön von Horváth: Kasimir und Karoline," *Forum
   for Modern Language Studies* 13, pp. 177-189. Wolfgang Lechner,
   *Mechanismen der Literaturrezeption in Österreich am Beispiel Ödön*

*von Horváths* (Stuttgart: Akademischer Verlag, 1978), pp. 83–114.

3. Ödön von Horváth, *Gesammelte Werke*, eds. D. Hildebrandt, W. Huder, T. Krischke, 4 vols. (Frankfurt am Main: Suhrkamp, 1970–1971 3, p. 178f. Page numbers after Horváth texts refer to this edition. See also Horváths more extensive, very critical characterization of the *Heimwehr* in 4, p. 477.

4. Quoted in Traugott Krischke, *Ödön von Horváth. Kind seiner Zeit* (München: Wilhelm Heyne, 1980), p. 184.

5. See especially Alexander Fuhrmann, "Zwischen Budapest und dem Dritten Reich. Horváths Umwege in die Emigration," *Horváths Stücke*, ed. Traugott Krischke (Frankfurt am Main: Suhrkamp, 1988, st 2092), p. 184.

6. Quoted in Traugott Krischke, *Ödön von Horváth*, p. 190.

7. Wolfgang Lechner, *Mechanismen der Literaturrezeption in Österreich am Beispiel Ödön von Horváths*, p. 396.

8. Friedrich Achberger, "Österreichische Literatur," *Deutsche Literatur. Eine Sozialgeschichte*, ed. Horst Albert Glaser, vol. 9, p. 337.

9. Sylvia M. Patsch, "Der Dichter im Exil: Theodor Kramer," *Illustrierte Neue Welt* (Wien), März 1983, p. 11.

10. Theodor Kramer, *Gesammelte Werke*, ed. Erwin Chvojka (Wien: Europaverlage, 1984–1987) 3 vols. 1, p. 288. Page numbers after Kramer texts refer to this edition.

11. John Lehmann, *The Whispering Gallery, Autobiography I* (London: Longmans, Green and Co., 1955), p. 295.

12. Gespräch E. Zbonek–Heinz Lunzer, Dokumentationsstelle für Neuere Österreichische Literatur, 2 May 1978. Tonband: DST 355. A.1.

13. Cf. Wolfgang Bauer, *Und Österreich? Ein Staat sucht ein Volk* (Paris: Streitschriften des europäischen Merkur, 1933). Whether Soyfer knew this book, which was forbidden in Austria after 1934, is not known.

14. The form distinguished between *Staatsbürgerschaft* (citizenship) and *Volkszugehörigkeit* (ethnic affiliation). In Austrofascist terminology *Volksstum* and *Nation* were often used interchangeably meaning that Austrians shared both with the Germans.

15. Wolfgang Lechner, *Mechanismen der Literaturrezeption*, p. 397.

16. Wendelin Schmidt-Dengler, "Die Zeitgeschichte im Spiegel der Literatur der Ersten und Zweiten Republik," *Österreichs Erste und Zweite Republik*, ed. Erich Zöllner (Wien: Schriften des Instituts für Österreichkunde 1985), p. 186.

17. Alfred Pfoser, "Dichter der armen Leute," *Salzburger Nachrichten*, 5

April 1983, p. 8.

18.  Karl-Markus Gauß, "Natur, Provinz, Ungleichzeitigkeit. Theodor Kramer und einige Stereotypien der Literaturwissenschaft," *Theodor Kramer 1897-1958. Dichter im Exil,* ed. Konstantin Kaiser (Wien: Dokumentationsstelle für neuere österreichische Literatur, 1983), p. 20.

19.  Konstantin Kaiser, "Lyrik einer 'verschollenen' Zeit," *Kulturkontakte* (Wien) No. 16 (April 1983), 15.

20.  See the critique of the Viennese exhibition *Traum und Wirklichkeit,* Künstlerhaus, 1985: Manfred Wagner, "Wien und sein Fin de siècle in der Gegenwart. Was bleibt, ist Ornament-All," *Ornament und Askese im Zeitgeist des Wien der Jahrhundertwende,* ed. Alfred Pfabigan (Wien: Verlag Christian Brandstätter, 1985), pp. 297-311.

21.  Erich Hackl, "Das Glück beim Schreiben," *Theodor Kramer 1897-1958* (see note 18!), p. 10f.

22.  Since Horváth's attempt to compromise with the Nazis has become known, associating him with Kramer and Soyfer seems impermissible. But even if we do not know how Horváth would have acted had the Nazis accepted his offer of collaboration, we do know that in *Jugend ohne Gott* he took a definite stand against them.

23.  Friedbert Aspetsberger's *Literarisches Leben im Austrofaschismus. Der Staatspreis* (Königstein/Ts.: Hain, 1980) gives an in-depth analysis of Austrofascist *Literaturpolitik* and for that reason has to exclude Horváth, Kramer, and Soyfer from discussion.

# Political Attitudes and the Book Market: Special Features of the Austrian Literary Scene between 1933 and 1938

Klaus Amann

## Literature and society: general conditions

Unlike Germany's National Socialist literature, Austria's was illegal. The radical change in the function of racist and National Socialist literature in Germany after 1933, when at a stroke the violent changes in the political order turned it into an officially promoted State literature, holds good for Austria only with certain reservations.[1] In the year in which the NSDAP came to power in the Reich, such literature was banned in Austria, and as a result National Socialist writers in Austria found themselves without political legitimacy. Moreover, the introduction of the 'Thousand Mark Visa,' the attempted Nazi 'coup d'état' and murder of Chancellor Dollfuss in July 1934 were the beginning of an 'ice age' in relations between Austria and the Third Reich, and that meant that all Austrian writers, including National Socialists, lost the German market, which had always been economically vital to them.[2] However, in the long term, the rupture between the culture of the two countries produced by Austrian political measures merely strengthened the spirit of resistance and the encouraged inventiveness among Austrian National Socialists. Since things did not happen simultaneously in Germany and Austria, there was at first no systematic, outward attempt to produce ideological conformity (Gleichschaltung) in Austrian literature. This process was, however, begun through the founding of illegal associations and through reformulations of what constituted the Austrian tradition. The process of cultural infiltration characterizes the Austrian situation more than that of any other country bordering Third Reich Germany, and this situation calls for a depiction of the institutions which conditioned the production of fascist literature in Austria.

## The 'Militant League for German Culture' (Kampfbund für deutsche Kultur), the 'Circle of Nationalist Writers' (Ring nationaler Schriftsteller) and the 'Reich Association of German Writers' (Reichsverband Deutscher Schriftsteller) in Austria

It was as though the dress-rehearsal were following the première: the founding of National Socialist cultural organizations in Austria mirrored the party political struggles and disputes among those responsible for cultural policy in Germany. Designated by Hitler as the leader of the Militant League for German Culture, Alfred Rosenberg could nourish the hope at the end of the 1920s that he would exercise a decisive influence on the cultural policy of the coming Reich.[3] He very quickly used his organization, founded between 1927 and 1929 and seen as the 'beginning of organized National Socialist "cultural activity,"'[4] to gain a foothold in Austria. As early as 1931, a committee consisting of nationalist figures – including a former Director of the Burgtheater, Max Millenkovich-Morold, as well as the founder of the Vienna Criminological Institute and former Rector of Vienna University, Wenzel Count Gleispach – set up an Austrian section of the Militant League for German Culture.[5] This group adopted the guise of a non-political cultural organization, and was decisive in the early 1930s in bringing Austrian nationalist and National Socialist artists and intellectuals together. The highly popular writer Mirko Jelusich ran the local Vienna group, and Josef Weinheber acted as its literary adviser from the spring of 1933; others involved were Franz Nabl, Robert Hohlbaum and the lawyer Arthur Seyss-Inquart, who later became Reich Governor (Reichsstatthalter) of the 'Ostmark' and, from 1940, Reich Commissioner (Reichskommissar) for the Netherlands.

The Militant League was officially disbanded in 1933, but it still managed to set up a secret information service with the Reich, by means of which it was able to receive political directives from Germany, as well as banned publications and propaganda. The Reich party propaganda machine also used this channel to gain information about Austria and Austrians. The declared aim of the Militant League was quickly to initiate the process by which the cultural changes imposed with state powers on the Third Reich would come about in Austria. It used every possible means to this end: public defamation or denunciation of particular individuals, outright conspiracy – in fact, anything that brought advantage to Militant League members or their sympathizers. One of its strategies was to infiltrate the press and publishing so that its members could publicly laud one another, and at the same time destroy the reputations of politically or racially undesirable colleagues by denunciation or crude anti-Semitic attacks. In this way openings would be created for 'writers of German blood.' Once the party had been banned, party members and sympathizers were continually being recruited into official positions with the aim of creating a network of political conspirators.

An example of this is given by Egmont Colerus von Geldern, a successful writer and high-ranking official in the Statistics Section of the Austrian Chancellery. In his *curriculum vitae*[6] of 1938, he states that he has 'done everything possible' to support his National Socialist comrades: in 1933–1934 he 'entered into an illegal arrangement' with Jelusich to conduct the official disciplinary investigation into the doings of one Karl Wache, the National Socialist official responsible for transmitting political directives in the District of Vienna, who had been brought to book for engaging in activities incompatible with his status as an Austrian civil servant. 'In my department, my own secretary reproached me for lacking objectivity and favouring Dr Wache; and, at the risk of being denounced myself, I refused to examine hostile witnesses from the Fatherland Front who had come forward of their own accord.' Wache was given a 'sentence for the look of the thing, since the case would otherwise have been taken out of our hands and . . . Wache, a party member, would have been dismissed from his post,' which actually happened in 1934.[7] Colerus, who was at the centre of things in the Chancellery, recalls: 'It goes without saying that I warned party members whenever I could.'[8]

The attempt to organize Austrian writers at the beginning of the thirties started almost from nothing. This was because National Socialist cultural policy came on the scene in the Reich relatively late, and also because of peculiarities of the Austrian situation. Before 1933, Nationalist and National Socialist authors in Austria were distributed fairly evenly across P.E.N. Club, Nationalist, Catholic and regional associations – they were even to be found on the executive committee of the leftish Union of German Writers (Schutzverband deutscher Schriftsteller). All this changed radically after the Nazis seized power in 1933, establishing 'ideological conformity' and disbanding the most important German associations (P.E.N. Club, Union of German Writers).[9] The result of this was that sister organizations in Austria would no longer promote members' interests in the Reich, a life-and-death matter when it came to marketing their books. In point of fact, even before the political polarization which culminated in the attempt by Nationalist and Catholic writers – abetted by officials in the Reich – to split the P.E.N. Club (June 1933),[10] both the P.E.N. Club and the Union had lost their attraction for those Austrian writers who wanted to continue publishing in Germany. Nationalist and National Socialist writers were evidently too weak and disunited to bring one of the larger writers' associations under their control before 1933, and there was in any case as yet no need whilst the German market remained open to all comers. Thus, when the Nazis came to power in Germany, these Austrian writers had no real organization of their own apart from the Literary Federation (Fachschaft Schrifttum) within the Militant League. But they certainly reacted swiftly to the change of political power in the Reich.

As early as May 1933, the Literary Federation of the Militant League responded to recommendations from their Nazi colleagues in the Reich by founding an Austrian writers' association, the Circle of Nationalist Writers (Ring nationaler Schriftsteller). This was to have the function, its founders proclaimed, of 'preparing writers of a nationalist persuasion for things to come.'[11] However, the Circle had too little time before the Nazi party was banned in Austria to bring all the nationalist writers into its fold. But it clearly played a certain role, for we find that, years later, in their proposals for party membership and statements to party tribunals, people make reference to their membership of the Circle, and this is clearly intended to be evidence of their involvement in National Socialism.[12] In the end it was neither the banning of the Party nor internal quarrels that caused the disappearance of the Circle; it simply ceased to attract people when, at the beginning of June 1933, the German Ministry of Propaganda set up the Reich Association of German Writers (Reichsverband deutscher Schrift-steller = RDS)[13] under the patronage of Goebbels.

It was Goebbels' intention that the RDS should replace all existing writers' professional associations. The RDS had emerged from the Union of German Writers (Schutzverband deutscher Schriftsteller) after this had been forced into 'ideological con-formity,' and it now took on the status of an official professional association, preparing the way for the work of the later Reich Chamber of Letters (Reichsschrifttumskammer).[14] It was a mere few weeks after its foundation that the first attempts were made to extend the RDS to include Austria, where its initiators were the Austrians who belonged to the Circle of Nationalist Writers.[15] In the new situation, it was clearly more promising to belong to an enterprise launched by Goebbels than to remain attached to Rosenberg's Militant League, which was increasingly losing its status and influence in the Reich.

And it seemed even more promising than attaching oneself to the now 'ideologically conformist' German P.E.N. Club. Hanns Martin Elster, the German P.E.N. Club official, wrote to the Vienna correspondent of the *Berliner Tagblatt,* Erwin Stranik, assuring the Austrian writers 'who had withdrawn from the Vienna P.E.N. Club because it was dominated by Jews' that they would be 'very welcome' members of the German P.E.N. Club, but only a few Austrians took him up on this. According to Elster, there were fewer than ten authors, among them Egon Caesar Conte Corti, Hans Hammerstein, Karl Hans Strobl and Wladimir Hartlieb.[16] Prominent P.E.N. Club dissidents like Mirko Jelusich, Robert Hohlbaum, Hermann Heinz Ortner, Franz Nabl, Bruno Brehm, Franz Karl Ginzkey, Paula Grogger and Max Mell, it seems either could not or would not commit themselves. Such commitment meant, of course, deciding for one or the other competing power blocks within the Reich NSDAP. Thus, behind the 'ideological conformity' of the Prussian Academy stood the German Education Minister Rust; behind that of the German P.E.N. Club was the Militant League; and Goebbels was responsible for disbanding the Union of German Writers. It was only when a Ministry of Propaganda had been set up and when moves were afoot to establish a Reich Chamber of Culture (Reichskulturkammer) – i.e., Goebbels' creation of a single, inflexible apparatus with which to control culture – that the outside world could see that Rosenberg was about to lose out in this particular internal power struggle. As Rosenberg's fortunes waned, the rising star in the firmament was the RDS under Goebbels, and with only a brief delay Austrian authors also followed the rising star.[17]

The threat was soon made public in Germany and Austria that 'in future . . . membership of the RDS will be the criterion for deciding whether an author can or cannot be published in Germany.'[18] The result was that the organizers of the RDS drove Austrians in great numbers into this unequivocally National Socialist association, which required of every applicant a declaration that he would 'unreservedly and at all times promote German literature in the sense understood by the nationalist government.'[19] It is true that in December 1933 there was a legal clarification to the effect that only writers resident in the Reich could be forced to join the RDS; but in point of fact even after this date many publishing houses, newspapers, journals and theatre managements demanded a declaration of loyalty to the German government as well as membership of the RDS. In October 1934, barely a year after its foundation, the director of the Austrian branch of the RDS claimed that it had 450 members[20] and was thus probably the largest writers' association in Austria.

This is somewhat surprising in that not only had the RDS never been formally constituted as an association in Austria, but it was actually illegal there. However, given that a broad section of the population regarded the government itself as 'illegal,' the question of the association's illegality was hardly a basis for decision where it was a matter—and not just in people's minds—of economic life or death. The RDS, on the other hand, knew how to make itself appear to be the only route into the German market. More than that, it helped greatly to strengthen and consolidate the grouping of National Socialist writers in the eyes of the outside world. It was through membership of the RDS that so large a number of Austrian writers became known quantities in the Reich. By the end of 1934 the RDS had collected several hundred completed questionnaires in which its Austrian members gave detailed descriptions of their personal circumstances, the names of associations to which they belonged, the nature of their literary activity and their political stance.

This provided the Reich Chamber of Letters and the Ministry of Propaganda with a great deal of information, which made it much easier to extend their political measures to Austrian writers publishing in the Reich. The RDS thus became the instrument by means of which the regime could institutionalize and bureaucratically manage public 'separation of the intelligentsia into two groups'—*de facto* the case since the book-burnings and P.E.N. Club scandal. Through it the regime could organize boycotts and ban the group to be persecuted, whilst granting the other group the benefits of association membership and political support.

### The Illegal Austrian Bureau of Culture (Landeskulturamt) and the League of German Writers of Austria (Bund der deutschen Schriftsteller Österreichs)

Nonetheless, the failure in July 1934 of the Austrian National Socialist 'putsch' was a distinct set-back in the creation of a group of Austrian National Socialist writers. On the one hand there was Hitler's newly declared policy of 'non-intervention' (Nichtein-mischung), which had the effect of isolating the Austrian NS-DAP;[21] on the other hand, strict surveillance by the Austrian authorities hindered the work of the illegal party. Even though the Austrian branch of the RDS continued to exist, the reconstruction of party organization, which had taken such a battering following the 'putsch,' required a good deal of personal and strategic re-thinking even in the sphere of cultural politics. In May 1935, therefore, the Nazi Austrian Bureau of Culture was set up. Its task was to work in closest cooperation with Franz von Papen, the new German Ambassador to Austria, to whom Hitler had given pleni-potentiary powers. The Bureau would attempt to monopolize and control every aspect of cultural relations between Austria and the Third Reich.

But clearly the Bureau was also to exercise responsibility for political supervision and disciplinary action. At least, that is the conclusion one might draw from what happened when Hermann Heinz Ortner joined the NSDAP. On his becoming a member – he claimed that this was in 1933, but other sources give 1934 – objections were raised in the National Socialist camp because of the 'widely known fact . . . that Ortner's wife, the Burgtheater actress Elisabeth Ortner-Kallina, was a Person of Mixed Race (Class I).'[22] For this reason 'Ortner was summoned to the resi-dence of the political head of Vienna's writers' association, Party Member Professor Josef Weinheber. The Director of the Austrian Bureau of Culture, Party Member Stuppäck was also invited to attend . . . Weinheber and Stuppäck together conducted the hearing.'[23]

This somewhat bizarre situation, in which officials of the illegal Bureau of Culture could put Ortner on trial, with all the legal niceties of summons, charge, testimony, defence and sentence, reveals the extent to which this group claimed to have political authority, indeed to be able to impose sanctions. And at the same time, the situation described shows how writers who had voluntarily taken up a political stance were fully prepared to accept consequent coercion, even when this affected the most private aspects of their lives.

Our necessarily brief resumé of the attempts made by the National Socialist writers of Austria to organize and consolidate their grouping may have given the impression that this was achieved without a hitch. The opposite is the case, as the above difficulties experienced by Ortner make clear – he was, after all, one of the most frequently played German-language dramatists of his day. In fact, the whole history of how the Austrian National Socialist writers came to form a group is one of endless disputes, denunciations, struggles for leadership, inquisitorial tribunals, conflicts of loyalty, strong animosities and reconciliations. The official and private utterances of these writers always suggest that they are in the front line of battle, and this is no mere political rhetoric of the period: they really do feel as though they are engaged in a military struggle, that they are surrounded by enemies and have no alternative but to express themselves in the language of destruction and decimation. And yet, curiously, their sense of the superiority of what they somewhat monolithically called 'the enemy' did not strengthen their group consciousness. There are perhaps two determining factors at work here.

In the first place, writers work in isolation, and compete with one another to get published. The writers of the inter-war years were no different from those of other periods in experiencing mutual estrangement and rivalry, that is, they too were subject to a market mechanism which simultaneously united and divided them.[24] Because, however, between 1933 and 1938 there were specific conditions determining whether Austrians would get their works on to the German market, political organization for these writers meant essentially putting a correct political attitude before the laws of the marketplace. They might, no doubt rightly, have feared literary competition, but, since they did not control the market, they had to be more worried about the political competition which existed prior to the question of book sales: in other words, defeating their literary rivals was less important than proving that they were politically beyond reproach. It is for this reason that their 'political leaders' constantly found themselves sitting in judgment (Blockwartmentalität), and, whenever they were in doubt about a writer's political attitude, conducting an enquiry. Thus, in the report on the case against Ortner, we read: 'Both [Stuppäck and Weinheber] were convinced of Ortner's clear National Socialist position.'[25] The numerous appeals for and against Austrian writers sent to the various official institutions of the Reich (the Ministry of Propaganda, the Chamber of Letters, the German Embassy in Vienna), just like the German press denunciations and calls to boycott Austrian left-wing or Jewish writers, were no doubt in one sense forms of literary rivalry — either more legitimate or less so; but they were also an almost inevitable consequence of the political autonomy of Austrian literature, with its relatively small group of appointed, or self-appointed, 'leaders.' We can see the decisive power of sanction enjoyed by this group from an anonymous denunciation of some of its members made to the Vienna police in 1935: the circle around Jelusich, the denunciation runs, 'has its own secret court [Femeabteilung], which poses a threat to recalcitrant writers by blocking their access to the German market, and has even been known to intimate to proscribed writers that their very lives are at risk.' The anonymous informer swears the 'truth' of every detail, claiming that he would have put his name to the document but for 'the rigour with which the secret court pursues those it suspects — as I well know from several cases — and thus the danger from that quarter to which I should be exposing myself.'[26]

This connection between competition in the literary field and the political stance of a writer is the underlying cause of the enormous increase in public confessions accompanying the success of

Austrian National Socialist writers. These confessions were largely a public-relations strategy with an eye to the book market. So it is no accident that the desire to confess fell off dramatically after the Anschluss, when the Nazis had destroyed their literary opponents and now had the market to themselves.

The second reason why National Socialist writers often failed to produce a sense of solidarity and were constantly divided by malice and denunciation can be found in the military-style hierarchy and chain of command now found in the cultural sphere. The 'literary' leaders in Austria owed their status less to their literary reputations than to their better connections with whichever party cliques happened to have most influence in the Reich at a given time. Since between 1933 and 1938 the Austrian National Socialists did not have the power to shape public opinion in any decisive way, it cannot surprise us that the work of the political hierarchies which they set up to control cultural life foundered on the imponderable nature of public response. The inevitable result was that these artificially created hierarchies could not prevent the formation of cliques, whose cohesiveness might spring from any one of a number of causes: friendships, hopes of special concessions, political advantage. Whilst the National Socialists might hope that the political organization of literary and cultural affairs could be strictly controlled, these often not precisely locatable sub-cultures were to be found everywhere and led to uncertainties on both sides. For a start, this situation completely obscured the, admittedly never very clear, dividing line between Austrofascism and National Socialism. But it also produced the social conditions in which self-styled 'non-political writers' could emerge, i.e., those who were party to everything without official membership of anything. Another aspect of this world of uncertainties is that political capital could be made of it after 1945: individuals could point to the many squabbles and denunciations among the different cliques to get themselves exonerated from the charge of complicity in Nazism, and some would even use the obscurities of the situation described to claim that they had been politically persecuted. Hermann Heinz Ortner, one of the most active Nazis among

Austrian writers, did just this after 1945, and succeeded in establishing himself as a former resistance fighter.

In his skillful promotion of 'evolutionary policies,' the German Ambassador to Austria, Franz von Papen, sought public acceptance and political integration of the National Socialist camp in Austria. His truly momentous achievement was the July Agreement (Verständigungsabkommen) of 1936 between Austria and the Reich. National Socialism regarded being 'German' as identical with being National Socialist,[27] and so the fact that Austria acknowledged in the Agreement that it was a 'German state'[28] was tantamount to giving up its independent identity, and every future presumption of independence could be interpreted by the Third Reich as reneging on the Agreement. In the cultural negotiations following the July Agreement the Germans cleverly used a mixture of diplomatic deference, appeals to the new-found partnership and straight blackmail, and it soon became clear that in this dialogue the Austrians were no match for them. Out of a misunderstanding of the idea of a common German culture, the Austrians gave ground in areas where, even after the Austrian Chancellor Schuschnigg had accepted some kind of cultural Pan-Germanism, there was and could be no common cause.[29]

Von Papen's persistence in attempting to have the National Socialist Party made legal and then to have it infiltrate every aspect of public life became, after the July Agreement, the goal of National Socialist writers. In the autumn of 1936 the illegal Austrian Bureau of Culture took the initiative in a third attempt – following the founding of the Circle of Nationalist Writers and the RDS – to create a specifically Austrian National Socialist writers' association, namely the League of German Writers of Austria (Bund der deutschen Schriftsteller Österreichs). In the changed political situation following the July Agreement, it was now possible to constitute the association legally. The Catholic writer Max Mell, who enjoyed great esteem in Austrian government circles, was able as Chairman of the League to unite in his own person the Catholic and nationalist camps. His name lent respectability to the practices of an association which aimed at the sup-

pression of all writers branded as racially and politically 'undesirable.' So, within a few months the League achieved what its
predecessors could only take the first steps towards: that is, it
established in Austria by entirely legal means a covert outpost of
the Reich Chamber of Letters, which – well before the Anschluss –
put into practice the racist principles of National Socialist policy
and essentially held the monopoly of literary contact with Germany.[30] Membership of the League soon became the only means
of access to the literary market of the Reich.

The entry of German troops into Austria in March 1938 met
with the wholehearted support of the members of the League,
among whom were Richard Billinger, Bruno Brehm, Paula Grogger, Robert Hohlbaum, Mirko Jelusich, Max Mell, Josef Friedrich
Perkonig, Franz Tumler, Karl Heinrich Waggerl and Josef Weinheber. The League produced its infamous 'Declaration of Support
by Austrian Writers' (Bekenntnisbuch österreichischer Dichter), in
which the 'leading nationalist writers of Austria' acknowledged to
themselves and the world that they had used 'unselfishly, courage-
ously, tirelessly and unflinchingly . . . the power of their personalities and their literary works to help create the climate in which
their people would ultimately be liberated.'[31]

Official recognition of this action was not slow in coming.
The German troops had not yet set foot in Vienna when the
former President of the Reich Chamber of Letters, Hans Friedrich
Blunck, informed its executive officer, Wilhelm Ihde, that the
League was known to have been 'a covert National Socialist
organization,' and therefore the future work of the Chamber
would 'probably be best passed through the hands of Mell and
Jelusich – particularly the latter, who had been the Party liaison
officer':

> Many people will now want to make contact with the
> Chamber of Letters. The best course is probably to consult
> the official literary body of the Party, the League of
> German writers, regarding such persons' political attitude
> during the difficult years, their Aryan extraction, their

position on the Pan-German question. The organization in question was set up a good two years ago by the Chamber of Letters to sift out reliable from unreliable writing.[32]

And so it came about. The executive officer of the League, Max Stebich, became the executive officer of the Austrian branch of the Reich Chamber of Letters. Under consideration for its director were Max Mell, Karl Heinrich Waggerl and the illegally appointed Head of Cultural Affairs in Austria, Hermann Stuppäck. The position actually went to Karl Hans Strobl, who had written with all speed on 13 March 1938 to Hanns Johst, President of the Reich Chamber of Letters, offering himself for the job on the grounds that it would undoubtedly be necessary 'to entrust the selection of loyal colleagues to someone who knows the Austrian situation.'[33]

We can here only allude to the fact that the idea of the Anschluss as the great moment for reward turned out to be correct for a large number of Austrian writers. Many enjoyed huge increases in income as a result of the Nazis' political guarantee of their right to work and publish. The top earners among them, like Jelusich, received six times what was paid to the highest rank in the army and to area commanders (Gauleiter), and this was eighty times what the majority of their 'fellow Germans' could expect to earn.[34]

## A New Function for Aesthetic Forms and Literary Genres: The Historical Novel as Example

The illegal situation in which Austrian National Socialist writers were working provides a key to our understanding of the aesthetic structures of Austrian fascist literature prior to the Anschluss. Before 1938 in Austria, any declaration of support for a National Socialist Greater Germany was forbidden, and that fact actually shaped Austria's racist literature in the thirties. Thus, an enormous number of historical novels and biographies so often used a past epoch, particularly an Austrian one, as a barely disguised prefiguration of National Socialist modern Germany. In many cases there was actual allusion, quotation or clear-cut analogy. Certain technical appurtenances were commonplace: metaphorical use of dreaming or remaining silent to suggest what may not be uttered but what, against all political reason, the heart must hold sacred; the notorious imagery of light to figure the dark Austrian night yielding to the bright day of modern Germany; the use of stock religious motifs drawn from the Passion of Christ to adumbrate the German path to salvation.

Of all the attempts to use literary genre to promote contemporary ideological and political objectives the most striking and effective is that of the historical novel, which had again become fashionable in the early years of the century. Here, almost obsessively, the racist type of historical novel 'uses any fictive tale to make a substantive point about the eventual Coming' of a National Socialist Germany.[35] Discontent with their present causes these authors to turn to history, from which a better future is extrapolated. History is not so much turned into fiction as reinterpreted; it becomes simply a source of costumes and settings in which to clothe contemporary conflicts and hopes; it shows the past as 'instinct with the problems of the present day' and shapes 'the past into a symbol to rouse men to the kind of action required by our own present circumstances.'[36]

The political function of such historical novels lies in their programmatic literary opposition to the 'destructive' critique of society in Heinrich Mann's novels or to the psychological analyses in the historical biographies of Emil Ludwig; and it also lies in the voice given to the promotion of anti-modern, anti-republican, fascist 'resistance.'[37] That such writing sought to combat the present by using the past as an arsenal of weaponry was stated clearly by Robert Hohlbaum at the first Pan-German Writers' Congress, which was held in the presence of Goebbels at Weimar in 1938: 'Their blood coursed with longing for past happenings; it was this longing which made history seem so near, indeed nearer than a present which had only ghostly reality for these writers. It would be a mistake, however, to think that they were running away from the present—they were, in fact, amassing arms with which to combat their hostile contemporary world.'[38]

According to Heinz Kindermann, an Austrian spokesman for National Socialist German studies, the historical novel is akin to war literature in making people receptive to the 'meaning of great sacrifice,' to the 'development of a creative personality'—i.e., in the historico-political context, that of the 'Führer'—and to the 'altruistic deed,' thus preparing the way for an age which will have a 'strict and resolute sense of duty.'[39]

National Socialist literary propagandists saw the historical novel, First World War literature and the products of the 'Blood and Soil' writers as a kind of opposition to the work of Vienna's Jewish writers—Schnitzler, Hofmannsthal, Werfel, Zweig, Kraus— and as such represented a continuation of the true, i.e., racist, Austrian literary tradition. They also made clear the well-nigh paradigmatic status of the historical novel as the genre in which National Socialism could best camouflage its message. Heinz Kindermann, who more than any other academic critic of the period gave weight to the historical and political context in which a work was produced, saw that the predominance of the historical novel in the Austria of the thirties was related to the illegal situation of the Nazi party. Illegality produced 'secret meetings of all the outlawed and disbanded groups, secret publication and distribution of pamphlets and journals to replace what had been banned.' But it also demanded 'from writers a kind of code language, whose merest suggestions would immediately be picked up by blood-brothers and those of a similar outlook.' That is why we look to 'this strange period for the beginnings of a Pan-German National Socialist literature in Austria, when in the guise of the historical novel we find a struggle going on against those who would suppress the reality of the contemporary world, just as we find an expression of common cause with "Führer" and "Reich."'[40]

Norbert Langer said of Jelusich—whose *Cromwell* (1933) was on its author's own admission a 'barely disguised biography of Hitler'[41] that his works in the thirties were a 'source of inspiration for the people who discovered in the disguise of historical subject matter all those contemporary problems and solutions which could scarcely have been addressed publicly in any other form.'[42]

'Blood and Soil' literature and First World War writing have less directly practical application than the historical novels of Bruno Brehm, Hermann Graedener, Robert Hohlbaum, Karl Itzinger, Mirko Jelusich, Erwin Guido Kolbenheyer, Theodor H. Mayer, Karl Hans Strobl and Josef Wenter. For the reader who is familiar with the code language of these racist writers, and whose 'ear has become attuned to the subtlest hints and tones,'[43] it is easy to ignore the play with historical detail and to read these novels as political statements complete with directives for action. This is a literature for the initiated, who essentially already agree. It is a literature intended to rally and fortify the faithful. The reader's reactions are carefully guided by this propagandistic material,[44] which reduces historical specifics to the one teleo-logical model, where the end-goal of history is seen to be the modern National Socialist world. The political slogans inserted into these novels confirm how close we are to contemporary examples of political agitation.[45]

Josef Nadler characterizes the situation with a precision one associates otherwise only with Heinz Kindermann: what the literary mode reveals with regard to political action is that the 'path from the Old to the New German Reich is an act of spiritual transformation, in which the Ostmark dies only to be reborn.' It is a radical change in one's experience of life and view of the world: 'Literature has set all this in motion and attested its valid-ity. The statesman has completed the venture.'[46]

## The 'Temper of the Age' and Literature.
## The 'Frontier' as Topos

Nadler perceived a connection between the temper of an age and political activity, and this can be seen most clearly in the Austria of the thirties whenever the question of political and historical legitimacy is raised. In literature the dream of a Reich was con-stantly provoked by the ratification in the Versailles Treaty

(Friedensdiktat) of the frontier between Austria and Germany. If one is looking for an absolutely characteristic topos in the racist literature of the thirties, it would have to be the wholesale use of 'the frontier.' In this topos, a range of historical experience is fused with hopes for the future in a way that expressly legitimizes political action. By pointing to a common language, a common history, a common duty regarding Eastern and South East Europe, writers could describe the existence of an Austro-German frontier as 'unnatural' or at best a temporary phenomenon.[47]

The problem of the frontier always called into question the independent status of Austria. However, this acquired a new political significance when the Austrian government under Dollfuss tore up Austria's constitution and destroyed its democracy, thus radically undermining the legitimacy of the state. The opening lines of Josef Weinheber's poem 'Austria 1934' reflect this situation: 'Guilt begets and gives life to War. / Merest chance was their victory. / The victor takes with brutish force, / gives his wrong the form of law. / Trampled rights cry revolt / for theirs is misery no madness knows. / From despairing depths the spirit climbs, / and points the path from pain to dream. / Dream like a flame sears with longing / for a new, a better Reich.'[48] The 'merest chance' is Parliament's momentary incapacity on 4 March 1933 giving Dollfuss victory; the 'coup d'état' is the result of 'Jewish chicanery in interpreting details of the Constitution'[49] – these were the essential happenings which caused the National Socialists to 'cry revolt' and dream of a 'better Reich.'

It is no longer the makers of the Versailles Treaty but a clique of 'illegal usurpers' and 'political criminals' who, in their own country, are most responsible for 'trying to destroy the German will of the Ostmark.'[50] In the eyes of National Socialists it was a cynical and 'unparalleled reversal of all accepted political standards' that a government which had torn up the Constitution and now based its claim to power on force should, following the ban on the Nazi Party in June 1933, refer to the National Socialists as 'illegal.' It was surely those in power who were 'unlawful,' lacking all legal, political or moral standing, in contrast to the

National Socialists, who claimed that they had 'always acted within the Constitution in their publicly avowed struggle to overthrow that Constitution.'[51] In this the Austrian National Socialists had the support of the Reich, whose propaganda described the 'radical reorganization' in Germany as the legitimate overthrow of parliamentarianism by means of a plebiscite, and as such part of the organic development of the German people; whereas the 'radical reorganization' in Austria was designated a despotic act performed to legalize a violation of the Constitution.[52]

In the novel 'The Military Oath' (*Der Soldateneid*) by Franz Tumler, the young star among Austrian National Socialist writers, the problem of the legitimacy or otherwise of the Austrian state becomes a matter of life and death for the hero Toni. The novel begins with the fictional situation that the Austrian government may decide to offer military resistance if Germany attempts to annex Austria. This would place officers in the Austrian army in a dilemma, since their oath of allegiance to the Schuschnigg state could force them to 'fight against Germany.'[53] The labourer Toni, whose first reaction is to ignore the call-up of all those born in 1915, talking to two such officers, explains his intended desertion as follows: "I don't want to enlist because I don't want to go through what you're going through. You're soldiers and have taken the oath, and now you've got to obey orders. If you didn't, you'd be dishonoured. But if you obey orders, you're just as much dishonoured, because you're letting them use you to fight against Germany (p. 114).

Count Eisenwörth, a lieutenant and friend of the protagonist, Lieutenant Roman Gürtler, cannot solve this problem in his own case. He is a man with 'sad features and fear in his eyes' (p. 78), but he comes from old aristocratic stock and has a 'greater sense of honour, it would appear, than anyone else' (p. 100). He shoots himself. Another figure is a major who, for the reader of the time, lacks 'insight' and 'qualities of leadership,'[54] breaks his oath of allegiance and gives up his command. A third, Captain Zankitsch, represents the ideology of blind obedience: 'You don't think about things and act before you're told if you're a soldier' (p. 102), as he puts it. After the major steps down, Zankitsch assumes command of the company and is ready to follow orders and defend his country should the need arise. This is when the hero has his moment of glory. He happens to be on the spot in civilian clothes; he has the captain arrested, takes over command of the company and marches on Vienna with the express purpose of securing the airport at Aspern.

The hero's 'coup de main' is, in fact, only the culmination of his growing awareness, which Tumler has been describing for the last two hundred pages. When we first meet the protagonist, he is described as a 'man slow to react,' who believes that 'it is an officer's duty to remain loyal and keep the oath he has sworn' (p. 7). He is, it is true, convinced from the outset 'that the government in Vienna' is hardly worth all the 'honesty' he devotes to trying to solve his problem – a problem which so many of his comrades have already solved with the formula: 'the law of Race knows no law of State' (p. 8). It is only when he finds himself on the Czech border near Deutsch-Altenburg that he realizes 'for the first time what the frontiers of his Reich have meant to a German over the last twenty years, as never to another people: whenever he comes to such a frontier, the German finds on the other side people of his race speaking his language. Lieutenant Gürtler had suddenly woken up to the situation. He now had the keenest sense of everything that secured a German's freedom, as of everything that deprived him of it or threatened it' (p. 33).

This experience of the 'frontier' is the basis of a broader understanding, which Tumler now permits his hero to formulate. And here we have the programmatic poetics not only of this story, but also of so much of the racist fiction of the thirties: 'How is it,' Roman Gürtler asks himself, 'that wherever we are and whatever is happening to us, everything always has political significance? ' (p. 33). 'Our misery' has simply 'changed the way we see everything. Nowadays we are incapable of letting our minds take in things just as they are' but we have to read them 'politically,' and it does not matter 'whether the things are landscapes or works of art' (p. 32).

The novel uses this 'new' way of seeing landscape, history and individual motivation to map out a kind of general basis for political action in the concrete situation just prior to the Anschluss. It is in this sense a work of great literary ambition, clearly drawing on the language and descriptive manner of the Austrian classic writer Adalbert Stifter. The hero wins over to his vision even the sceptical labourer Toni, who is the same age as the hero and has the function in the novel of voicing the doubts of readers who saw things differently from the way the author sees them:

> It doesn't help just to conquer a country [says Roman Gürtler]. In the long run, soldiers can't maintain a frontier; it's people who must be there, and they must build and have children.
> But, Toni asked, if we have no work, what are we supposed to do with children?
> You would have work, Roman answered, if the land here were Germany.
> Toni remained silent for a while. Then he said: And that is why you are breaking your oath?
> So that you can have work, replied Roman hesitantly, — yes, so that you can have children, and so that through your children Germany will move eastward!
> So it's for Germany, then? Toni asked.
> Yes, for Germany, replied Roman, because if Germany is to survive, it must be larger. We're opening a gateway to its future.
> Now I understand, said Toni, now I know what you are doing (p. 114).

It is the charitable reading of a later age that allows even these fascist writers to claim that they did not know what they were doing.

## NOTES

1. See Uwe K. Ketelsen, *Völkisch-nationale und nationalsozialistische Literatur in Deutschland 1890-1945* (Stuttgart: Metzler, 1976), esp. pp. 79f.
2. See Murray G. Hall, *Österreichische Verlagsgeschichte 1918-1938*, 2 Vols (Vienna/Cologne/Graz: Hermann Böhlaus Nachf., 1985), esp. Vol. 1, pp. 102ff. Up to 90% of all Austrian writers published in Germany, and the few belletristic publishing houses in Austria sold up to two-thirds of their books there. Between 1929 and 1936 Austria's book exports to Germany fell by 67%.
3. See Reinhard Bollmus, *Das Amt Rosenberg und seine Gegner* (Stuttgart: Deutsche Verlags-Anstalt, 1970), pp. 27ff.
4. See Hildegard Brenner, *Die Kunstpolitik des Nationalsozialismus* (Reinbek bei Hamburg: Rowohlt, 1963), pp. 7ff.
5. On the following, see my study *Der Anschluß österreichischer Schriftsteller an das Dritte Reich. Institutionelle und bewußtseinsgeschichtliche Aspekte* (Frankfurt am Main: Athenäum, 1988 = Literatur in der Geschichte – Geschichte in der Literatur, Vol. 16), pp. 25ff.
6. Berlin Document Center (BDC), Personalakte Egmont Colerus.
7. See BDC/Karl Wache.
8. See above n. 6.
9. See Ernst Fischer, "Der 'Schutzverband deutscher Schriftsteller' 1909-1933" in: *Archiv für Geschichte des Buchwesens* 21 (1980), Cols. 1-666; see also *Der deutsche PEN-Club im Exil 1933-1948. Eine Ausstellung der Deutschen Bibliothek Frankfurt am Main* (Frankfurt am Main: Buchhändler-Vereinigung, 1980).
10. See Klaus Amann, *P.E.N. Politik, Emigration, Nationalsozialismus. Ein österreichischer Schriftstellerclub* (Vienna/Cologne/Graz: Hermann Böhlaus Nachf., 1984), pp. 23-59.
11. Quoted by Gerhard Renner, "Österreichische Schriftsteller und der Nationalsozialismus: Der 'Bund der deutschen Schriftsteller Österreichs' und der Aufbau der Reichsschrifttumskammer in der 'Ostmark.'" Diss. (typescript), Vienna 1981, p. 17.
12. As examples, see BDC/Colerus and BDC/Max Stebich.
13. See Dietrich Strothmann, *Nationalsozialistische Literaturpolitik. Ein Beitrag zur Publizistik im Dritten Reich,* 4th edition (Bonn: Bouvier, 1985), p. 31; see also Fischer, above n. 9, Cols 625-638.
14. See Josef Wulf, *Literatur und Dichtung im Dritten Reich. Eine Doku-*

*mentation* (Frankfurt am Main/Vienna: Ullstein, 1983), p. 113; cf. also Klaus Siebenhaar, "Buch und Schwert. Anmerkungen zur Indizierungs-praxis und 'Schrifttumspolitik' im Nationalsozialismus" in: *'Das war ein Vorspiel nur . . .' Bücherverbrennung Deutschland 1933. Voraussetzungen und Folgen. Ausstellung der Akademie der Künste vom 8. Mai bis 3. Juli 1983* (Berlin/Vienna: Medusa, 1983), pp. 81–96, esp. p. 86.

15.   See Gerhard Renner, "'Hitler-Eid for österreichische Schriftsteller?' Über österreichische Schriftstellerorganisationen der dreißiger Jahre" in: Klaus Amann/Albert Berger (eds.), *Österreichische Literatur der dreißiger Jahre. Ideologische Verhältnisse – Institutionelle Voraussetzungen – Fallstudien* (Vienna/Cologne/Graz: Hermann Böhlaus Nachf., 1985), pp. 150–163, esp. p. 153.

16.   Elster to Stranik, 26 September 1933, Institut für Zeitgeschichte, Munich, Fb 215. This file is an incomplete copy of Vol. R561/102 in the Bundesarchiv Koblenz. See also Amann, above n. 10, pp. 37f.

17.   On the question of the power struggle between Rosenberg and Goebbels see Bollmus, above n. 3, and Günter Hartung, *Literatur und Ästhetik des deutschen Faschismus. Drei Studien* (Berlin [Ost]: Akademie-Verlag, 1984), pp. 169ff.

18.   Quoted by Renner, see above n. 11, p. 71.

19.   Cf. 'Aufnahme-Erklärung,' Reichsverband Deutscher Schriftsteller E.V. (in several personal files of Austrian writers; held by the BDC).

20.   BDC/Franz Löser.

21.   See Norbert Schausberger, *Der Griff nach Österreich. Der Anschluß* (Vienna/Munich: Jugend und Volk, 1978), pp. 298ff.

22.   Supplement 1 of 'Stellungnahme [Ortners] zu dem Erkenntnis des Obersten S.A. Führers vom 28. Juli 1934,' BDC/Hermann Heinz Ortner.

23.   Ibid.

24.   See Franz Schuh, *Das Widersetzliche der Literatur. Kritische Kritiken* (Vienna/Munich: Jugend und Volk, 1981 = protokolle 4/1981).

25.   See above n. 22.

26.   The Federal Chancellery and Vienna municipal authorities accepted the charge in August 1935. See Allgemeines Verwaltungsarchiv Wien GD1/GD2, Z1. 327.726/1935, "Nationalsozialistisch getarnte Kulturorgani-sation." This file contains the results of police enquiries concerning an anonymous denunciation of illegal National Socialist cultural organizations and their officials. I have commented more fully on this denuncia-tion in my article "Die literaturpolitischen Voraussetzungen und Hintergründe für den 'Anschluß' der österreichischen Literatur im Jahre

1938," *Zeitschrift für deutsche Philologie* 101 (1982), 216-244; see esp. 227ff.

27. See Rudolf Ebneth, *Die österreichische Wochenschrift 'Der Christliche Ständestaat.' Deutsche Emigration in Österreich 1933-1938* (Mainz: Mathias Gründewald-Verlag, 1976 = Veröffentlichungen der Kommission für Zeitgeschichte, Reihe B. Forschungen; Vol. 19), p. 154.

28. These are the actual words used in the official communiqué. Published in: *Akten zur Deutschen Auswärtigen Politik 1918-1945. Serie D: 1937-1945* Vol. I (Baden-Baden: Imprimerie Nationale, 1950), p. 234.

29. See above n. 5, pp. 108ff.

30. See ibid., pp. 152ff.

31. See *Bekenntnisbuch österreichischer Dichter.* Published by the 'Bund deutscher Schriftsteller Österreichs' (Vienna: Krystall-Verlag, 1938), p. 7.

32. Letter from Blunck to Ihde, 12 March 1938, Bundesarchiv Koblenz, R 56 V, Vol. 57, p. 112. Printed in: Wulf, see above n. 14, pp. 221f.

33. Letter from Strobl to Johst, 13 March 1938, Bundesarchiv Koblenz, R 56 V, Vol. 57, p. 111.

34. See above n. 5, pp. 164ff.

35. Johann Sonnleitner, *Die Geschäfte des Herrn Robert Hohlbaum. Die Schriftstellerkarriere eines Österreichers in der Zwischenkriegszeit und im Dritten Reich* (Vienna/Cologne: Böhlau, 1989 = Literatur in der Geschichte—Geschichte in der Literatur; Vol. 18).

36. Erwin Stranik, *Österreichs deutsche Leistung. Eine Kulturgeschichte des südostdeutschen Lebensraumes,* 2nd revised and enlarged edition (Vienna/Leipzig: Wiener Verlagsgesellschaft, 1937), p. 286.

37. See Ketelsen, above n. 1, p. 74. See also Friedbert Aspetsberger, "Metaphysische Grimassen. Zum biographischen Roman der Zwischenkriegszeit" in: Klaus Amann/Albert Berger (eds.), *Österreichische Literatur der dreißiger Jahre,* above n. 15, pp. 247-276.

38. Robert Hohlbaum, "Die deutsche Dichtung und die Welt der Geschichte" in: *Weimarer Reden des großdeutschen Dichtertreffens* (Hamburg: Hanseatische Verlagsanstalt, 1938), pp. 17-30. Quotation p. 27.

39. See Heinz Kindermann, *Kampf um die deutsche Lebensform. Reden und Aufsätze über die Dichtung im Aufbau der Nation* (Vienna: Wiener Verlagsgesellschaft, 1941), p. 271.

40. Ibid., pp. 408f.

41. See Jelusich in: Kurt Ziesel (ed.), *Krieg und Dichtung. Soldaten werden Dichter—Dichter werden Soldaten. Ein Volksbuch,* 3rd edition (Vienna: Wiener Verlag, 1943), p. 248.

42.  Norbert Langer, *Die Deutsche Dichtung seit dem Weltkrieg. Von Paul Ernst bis Hans Baumann,* 2nd enlarged edition (Karlsbad/Leipzig: Adam Kraft, year not indicated), (1941), 303.
43.  Franz Koch, "Die großdeutsche Idee in der deutschösterreichischen Dichtung" in: *NS-Monatshefte* 9/100 (1938), 596–609. Quotation 608.
44.  See Friedbert Aspetsberger, *Literarisches Leben im Austrofaschismus. Der Staatspreis* (Königstein/Ts: Hain, 1980 = Literatur in der Geschichte – Geschichte in der Literatur, Vol. 2), p. 140; see also Johannes Sachslehner, *Führerwort und Führerblick. Mirko Jelusich. Zur Strategie eines Bestsellerautors in den Dreißiger Jahren* (Königstein/Ts: Hain, 1982 = Literatur in der Geschichte – Geschichte in der Literatur, Vol. 11), pp. 174f.
45.  See Uwe K. Ketelsen, "Nationalsozialismus und Drittes Reich" in: Walter Hinderer (ed.), *Geschichte der politischen Lyrik in Deutschland* (Stuttgart: Reclam, 1978), pp. 291–313, esp. pp. 294f.; see also Alexander von Bormann, "Vom Traum zur Tat. Über völkische Literatur" in: Wolfgang Rothe (ed.), *Die deutsche Literatur in der Weimarer Republik* (Stuttgart: Reclam, 1974), pp. 304–333, esp. p. 322.
46.  Josef Nadler, *Literaturgeschichte des deutschen Volkes. Dichtung und Schrifttum der deutschen Stämme und Landschaften,* 4th completely revised edition, 4 Vols. (Berlin: Propyläen-Verlag, 1939–1941), Vol. 4, p. 438.
47.  See Klaus Amann, "Die Brückenbauer. Zur 'Österreich'-Ideologie der völkisch-Nationalen Autoren in den dreißiger Jahren" in: Klaus Amann/Albert Berger, above n. 37, pp. 60–78, esp. pp. 67ff.
48.  Josef Weinheber, "Österreich 1934" in: *Das Innere Reich* 5/2 (1938/1939), 226–229. The poem, which was written in 1934, is quoted on p. 226 of this Special Number of the journal devoted to 'The Return of German Austria to its Home in the Reich.'
49.  Reinhold Lorenz, *Der Staat wider Willen* (Berlin: Junker und Dünnhaupt, 1941), p. 51.
50.  See Wladimir von Hartlieb, *Parole: Das Reich. Eine historische Darstellung der politischen Entwicklung in Österreich von März 1933 bis März 1938* (Vienna/Leipzig: Luser, 1939), p. 59 and p. 187.
51.  Lorenz, see above n. 49, p. 61.
52.  See Ralf Richard Koerner, *So haben sie es damals gemacht . . . Die Propagandavorbereitungen zum Österreich-Anschluß durch das Hitlerregime. 1933–1938* (Vienna: Ges. zur Förderung wiss. Forschung, 1958), pp. 136ff.

53.  Franz Tumler, *Der Soldateneid. Eine Erzählung* (Münich: Albert Langen / Georg Müller, 1939), p. 105. Further page references appear in brackets immediately following the quotation.
54.  Cf. Hermann Pongs, "Soldatische Ehre in der Dichtung der Gegenwart," *Euphorion,* 42 (1942), 89–129, esp. 94f.

# Publishing in the Thirties:
## The Paul Zsolnay Verlag

Murray G. Hall

Asking how many people today live off the word 'poet' is like seeking infinity . . . You could begin with literary chairs and seminars and go on through the whole university industry, with all the functionaries, janitors and others supported by the system. Or you could begin with publishers and all the many employees of a publishing house, with printing works, paper mills and machine factories, with the railways, the postal service, the tax authority, newspapers . . .; all these thousands of people make their living, a good one, a bad one, full-time or part-time, from the existence of poets, even though no one knows what a poet is . . .

Despite the self-irony inherent in the text – the quote is taken from Robert Musil's feuilleton "Eine Kulturfrage," which appeared in 1931 – it nevertheless outlines the wide range of field for a literary scholarship which does not merely restrict itself to the "reine Dichtung," to the literary product itself. If one attempts to render Musil's amusing observations in a more scientific language, then a definition provided by Herbert Göpfert would seem to do the trick. Göpfert writes that it is 'clear that the conitions and processes of publication with all their technical, economic, social, legal, political and organizational – i.e. historical – determinants help to condition not merely the reception but also the very production of literature . . .'[1]

Recent scholarship dealing with the history of Austrian literature in the inter-war years with special consideration being given to the specific development in Austria has, in part, already proved the thesis that the reception and production of literature are widely determined by non-literary factors.

Using one Austrian publishing house as an example, I would like to show how such a history can contribute to our understanding of German literature in the 1930s. The book and publishing trades are, as banal as it may sound, prerequisites to the entire process of literary communication. The trades are also closely tied to business life in general and thus subject to economic parameters. As far as the period in question is concerned, it would almost be an understatement to say that the "historical determinants" were largely a result of the political system in Nazi Germany after 1933.

The Paul Zsolnay Verlag was founded in 1923 and published its first work – Franz Werfel's *Verdi. Roman der Oper* – in the spring of the following year. It was to become the biggest, financially most successful and most prestigious (three Nobel Literature Prize recipients!) publisher of *belles lettres* in Austria. And the acceptance of the Paul Zsolnay Verlag especially in Germany was a feat no other Austrian company before or after it achieved. Zsolnay became the heir of the Kurt Wolff Verlag in Germany, which like its competitors long laboured with the uncontrolled inflation. He took over a number of established and popular writers including Franz Werfel, Heinrich Mann, Max Brod and Carl Sternheim. Coming from a wealthy family, the young publisher Paul von Zsolnay, who was a successful flower grower by profession, did not have to worry too much about the financial viability of his fledgling operations. He was born in Budapest in 1895 and was a Slovakian national, a detail not worth mentioning if it were not for the fact that it saved his life in March 1938 while his colleagues were being tracked down and sent to concentration camps. As far as the authors were concerned, Paul Zsolnay was able reliably to offer them royalties in the (stable) currency of their choice which no German publisher at the time could afford.

With the family wealth behind him he could risk flops and publish hitherto unknown authors out of the goodness of his heart. A survey of Zsolnay's programme during the first ten years of production shows a penchant for European and international literature without entirely neglecting young Austrian writing.

The early financial and literary success of the Paul Zsolnay Verlag was based on three prominent writers: Heinrich Mann and Franz Werfel – both of whom signed lucrative general contracts with the young publisher – and John Galsworthy of whose works the Verlag printed no fewer than 1.4 million copies in German before 1938. By comparison Zsolnay printed almost 660,000 copies of Werfel's works and 250,000 of Heinrich Mann's oeuvre. The emphasis among the literature in translation was on English, American, French and Russian. Not until 1934 did Zsolnay begin to publish Scandinavian literature systematically. This "Ausländerei" began to upset German booksellers who were leary of so much foreign literature. Paul Zsolnay was not opposed to contemporary Austrian literature; he had simply not established his company with the intent of creating a base for Austrian writers per se or to serve as the long-awaited Austrian publishing house which would, after the decade-long export of literary manuscripts and import of the finished product, repatriate Austrian literature. Indeed, the scope was primarily European. When literary production and reception began to be dictated by the Nazi authorities in Germany so too did the Zsolnay programme take on a German nationalist flavour. The issue of an "Austrian publishing house" is neither chauvinistic nor provincial nor an attempt artificially to justify the existence of an Austrian literature. It raises a fundamental question in literary history, namely that of the existence or non-existence of a national cultural identity. For as long as Austria and Germany got along with one another the question was insignificant. Whether the country had its own more or less autonomous and commercially viable publishing trade was not a matter of life and death, not a question of survival in the spiritual sense, at least as long as Germany took no action which was essentially directed against the very existence of Austria.

The fact that authors such as Franz Grillparzer, Marie von Ebner-Eschenbach, Peter Rosegger, Arthur Schnitzler, Robert Musil and so on published their works in German houses was periodically bemoaned but not viewed as a threat. It was only when Hitler came to power in 1933 that people came to realize Austria's almost exclusive cultural dependence on Germany. 1933 marked the true beginning of a process of cultural annexation from within and without. Be that as it may, the Paul Zsolnay Verlag production programme took on an Austrian flavour of a completely different kind as a result of the Nazi-dictated market parameters after 1933. Production, distribution, sale, and reception of literature were now to become dependent on extra-literary factors.

The key event of the year 1933 for the further development of Austrian literature or literary life in Austria in the 1930s was without doubt the 11th International P.E.N. Club congress in Ragusa, Yugoslavia at the end of May 1933. Because so much has been written in the past decade about the conference from an Austrian standpoint, I shall restrict myself here to the repercussions on the Paul Zsolnay Verlag and its literary programme. The conflict and later split within the Vienna P.E.N. Club arose from the heated debate over the position to be taken by the official Austrian delegation vis-à-vis the question of persecution of writers in Germany. The spectacular book burnings had taken place in a number of German cities only two weeks prior to the Ragusa congress. It was decided, by no means unanimously, that the official Austrian representatives, the president Felix Salten and the founder Grete von Urbanitzky, would not participate in any such debate against Germany or the "nazified" German group of the P.E.N. Club. With minor exceptions the protagonists were all authors of the Paul Zsolnay Verlag. Indeed, Paul Zsolnay himself and his literary director Felix Costa were influential members and benefactors of the Vienna club.

The split in the aftermath of the Ragusa meeting, during which the Austrian delegation abided by its resolution to maintain "strict neutrality" (Salten) and, if at all, to stick to "internal

criticism," was more or less an anti-climax to the Vienna prelude.
It was the Nazi party member and Zsolnay author Friedrich
Schreyvogl who had brought the message of an impending exodus
of the "nationalist" members. A hitherto unknown and unpublished "Protokoll über die vor dem Kongress im Haus von Felix
Salten abgehaltene Sitzung" of the club on 21 May 1933 supports
the thesis that the later exodus of Catholic-nationalist writers from
the Vienna club was pre-programmed. The minutes bear the
signatures of the founder Grete von Urbanitzky and the "dissi-
dent" Hugo Sonnenschein-Sonka, both Zsolnay authors from
opposite ends of the political and ideological spectrum. Because
the text sheds new light on the turmoil within the club and hints
at the material motives influencing the stand in Ragusa, I would
like to quote briefly from it here. The P.E.N. Club president Felix
Salten, who was to be poorly rewarded for abstaining from criticism of the Nazi German actions against his writing colleagues,
argued, for example, in the following manner:

> No government in Germany can be allowed to accuse us of
> having fought against Germany in the battle . . . An Aus-
> trian protest could only be directed against the German
> P.E.N. Club in Berlin, but we ought not to use the Con-
> gress to protest against Germany itself . . . It is better to
> remain silent than to show disapproval. If we protest, we
> shall provoke an international squabble . . . Enough na-
> tions will oppose Germany. It is for us to remain neutral
> and silent.[2]

Whether Salten and the others who sided with him by remaining
"neutral" really expected to be spared from the repressive measures against "Jewish" and/or other "undesirable" writers in
Germany is difficult to say. At any rate, their "brotherly love"
was to remain unrequited. Following Salten's credo "silence is
golden," the spokesman for the nationalist authors placed his
cards on the table: 'If the Austrian delegation were to turn against
Germany, all nationalist and Catholic writers would immediately

resign from the Club.' Understandably, several of the members attending the meeting in Salten's home protested against what they saw as a veiled threat in Schreyvogl's words: 'The Vienna P.E.N. Club cannot be dictated to by any group . . . Schreyvogl has spoken only for a small number of people who happen to have communicated with him. The Vienna P.E.N. Club draws its membership from all political parties – isn't Sonka, for example, a Communist?!' So much for the members of the policy-making meeting prior to the Ragusa conference. The exit of Catholic and nationalist-leaning P.E.N. members did not take place on one single day as Schreyvogl had predicted, but the split was a "fait accompli." Incidentally, the publisher Paul Zsolnay and his director Felix Costa also decided it was advantageous to leave the club. The importance from an historical perspective lay not only in the split in the Vienna club itself or down the middle of the Paul Zsolnay Verlag, but also in the consequential division of Austrian writers into two camps, those who would profit from and those who would suffer from the Nazi policy on literature. Seen from a wider perspective, the decision to remain in the club or to leave it was open to an eminently political interpretation. The events in Austria provided Nazi authorities who were at no time particularly familiar with the literary scene in Austria with an initial opportunity to distinguish the desirable from the undesirable.

The measures introduced in Nazi Germany from 1933 onwards with the aim of "Gleichschaltung" of all fields of cultural, social and political life, the book burnings, and the unofficial "black lists" of proscribed authors and books forced numerous Austrian publishers to revise their literary programmes. For someone as politically abstinent as Paul Zsolnay, pragmatism seemed the best path to follow. Following several financially disastrous years Zsolnay was now confronted with a politicized publishing trade. Whereas the law of supply and demand had hitherto ruled the book trade, the free market forces were now out of commission. Whereas hitherto various literary currents vied with one another for readers, "undesirable" literature was to be eliminated through an administrative procedure and the invisible censor of literary book production in Austria sat in Germany.

To appreciate the extent of the remote control of production in Austria it is important to recall various statistics showing that something like 90% of Austrian authors published their works in German publishing houses and that the Paul Zsolnay Verlag, for instance, sold three quarters of its production in Germany. The ban of an individual work or several books meant a financial loss for the publisher in the short and long term, but for the author effected the immediate loss of the market for two thirds and more of his book sales. Economic dependence on the German book market was thus extremely great both for the publisher and for the now undesired author.

Even Paul Zsolnay's declared political disinterest did not impress the Nazis in the least. For them he was a liberal Jewish publisher, and it was questionable that as such he should be permitted to publish and sell "German" literature at all. Zsolnay was forced to make the best of a bad job and try to restrict damage to his company and his authors to a minimum. It is definitely to his credit that he made every possible effort under the circumstances to soften the blow for the many authors whose works had, in whole or in part, been banned from the German market. Zsolnay, like his friend Franz Werfel, was convinced that once the dust had settled the situation would return to normal. Some authors voluntarily withdrew and turned to emigrant publishers in Holland, aware that there was then no return. Other authors, although black-listed in Germany, continued to be published, and it was here that Paul Zsolnay took advantage of a firm he had established in Switzerland in the autumn of 1929 under completely different circumstances and for an entirely different reason. "Paul Zsolnays Bibliothek zeitgenössischer Werke" was established first in Bern and was then moved to Zürich. It was the Vienna publisher's answer to a new trend on the German book market. In an effort to reach wider sections of the reading public and to open up a new market, a number of German publishers began to follow the lead taken by Thomas Mann's

*Buddenbrooks* and introduce so-called "Volksausgaben," special cheap editions of popular\contemporary works at a price more or less dictated by the big department stores in Germany. RM 2.85 was the magic new price. But the *Bibliothek,* originally intended to further popularize successful Zsolnay publications such as the works of H. G. Wells, Franz Werfel, or John Galsworthy, offered Zsolnay a solution to the problem of what to do with authors who could no longer be sold in Germany. Even if the printings in what after 1933 was falsely regarded as a "ghetto publishing house" were limited to between 3,000 and 5,000 copies, it meant at least some financial support for otherwise homeless writers.

But not all Zsolnay authors felt they were being dealt with correctly. Heinrich Mann, whose correspondence with Zsolnay (and others) reveals a constant wrangling over money, was one example; Emil Ludwig, who had been brought from the Ernst Rowohlt Verlag was another. Both were early victims of Nazi literary persecution, both prominent in the first book burnings in May 1933. Since that time it was utterly hopeless to place their works on the market, something which did not prevent the two writers from blaming the publisher. Whereas Emil Ludwig chose to air his displeasure in an interview with a Vienna paper, Heinrich Mann was less restrained in letters he wrote to his brother Thomas. He called Zsolnay a "cowardly traitor" and a "scoundrel." Understandably there was little contact between Mann and Zsolnay after 1933. Indeed, among his papers in the Heinrich Mann Archives in East Berlin there are copies of only two Mann letters. Not until the Zsolnay Verlag sent him a statement of account did Mann break his silence to accuse his publisher of breach of contract. In a letter of 1 October 1934 from Amsterdam Mann described the statement as unacceptable and made a further charge: 'I refuse to enumerate all your many sins of commission and omission in our contractual dealings . . . This letter requires no answer, particularly since you have taken great pains to avoid any written correspondence with me since February 1933.' Mann's final letter to the Paul Zsolnay Verlag dates from April 1935. Again, Zsolnay has sent a statement of account, 'which does not concern me [Mann] in the slightest. You can keep your manipulations with book returns to yourselves . . . There will be no further business dealings between us . . . You will herewith "take cognizance" that I intend henceforth not to open, read or reply to any further communication from you.' Mann did not reconcile his differences with Zsolnay until 1947. But Mann was an exception among the many authors whose works could no longer be sold in Germany. Others showed more understanding for the predicament Zsolnay was in. Zsolnay did not then altogether cease to publish and sell the books of authors who because they were Jewish or liberal were in one way or another undesired in Germany. Franz Werfel's works, for instance, with the exception of the monumental novel *Die vierzig Tage des Musa Dagh*, were distributed in Germany until a sweeping confiscation by Leipzig police in April 1936. Zsolnay retained and published new works by Franz Werfel, Felix Salten, and Leo Perutz in his Vienna company. They were merely not exported to Germany. This practice became part of the contracts between author and publisher in order to rule out later disagreement. The relevant passage reads as follows:

> Concerning the sale in Germany of the work in question, author and publisher are in accord that such sale will in all probability meet with difficulties immediately upon publication or soon after, and that there is even the likelihood that sale will prove impossible. Publisher and author have therefore agreed that it shall be for the publisher to decide whether an attempt should be made to put the book on the German market or not.

The contract in question with Leo Perutz (*Der schwedische Reiter*) is dated 3 July 1936. Like the attempts to publish his authors in the Swiss firm, this again was another form of co-existence with the closed German market despite the prohibitive financial risk involved. The extent to which the above-mentioned assessment of the situation on the German market was correct is evident from a letter which Zsolnay's attorney Paul Neumann wrote to the former author Robert Neumann in March 1937:

> I hardly need tell you that the problems with authors of non-Aryan extraction writing in German are now almost insuperable. We have an example in Perutz' splendidly written novel 'The Swedish Cavalryman,' which despite the most intensive publicity has barely found a market. Had the same novel been published in 1929, I estimate that 10,000 copies would have been sold in no time at all.

Whereas earlier first printings of Perutz's works were around 8,000 copies, under the present circumstances the figure had dropped to 2,000.

The forced disappearance of a number of authors from Zsolnay's programme had been a passive reaction to the politicized literary market. But the publisher was also compelled to seek support in National-Socialist circles to maintain its acceptance on the all-important German market. Because of his close association with the P.E.N. Club Zsolnay at first turned to two writers. One was Grete von Urbanitzky, one of his own authors and the lady at the centre of the controversy within the Vienna club. She had left Austria for Berlin from where she led a campaign of denunciation against her colleagues in the Zsolnay Verlag and other P.E.N. dissidents. Zsolnay's second "attorney" for interventions with Nazi authorities was the German P.E.N. delegate in Ragusa, Hanns Martin Elster who was a pronounced National-Socialist. They were to counter the propaganda campaign against the Paul Zsolnay Verlag in Germany and recruit new and "reliable" authors for the house in Vienna, who, if at all, Zsolnay accepted for artistic reasons only. Later, the Austrian author Erwin Rainalter who had also gone to Berlin to work among other things as a correspondent for the *Völkischer Beobachter* was active in maintaining the acceptance of the Zsolnay Verlag.

Zsolnay's second option after 1933, apart from throwing in the towel, was to open his puhlishing house systematically to Nazi writers in Austria. This process of "nazification" began in late 1933/early 1934. All of a sudden a group of authors decided to leave the highly unsuspicious L. Staackmann Verlag in Leipzig. But the most visible outward sign of this development was the unofficial appointment of a contact man, a confidant of the illegal Nazi organization in Austria. His name was Hermann R. Leber, and it was his task to provide a link with Nazi authorities in Germany and with the German Embassy in Vienna. The latter was the actual "headquarters" for the quiet process of cultural annexation with Germany. Leber was to recruit "nationalist" authors, the majority of whom were so mediocre, as Josef Weinheber put it, that they would have otherwise stood no chance of being accepted. Gone now were writers such as Heinrich Mann, Max Brod, and Emil Ludwig, only to be replaced by over a dozen new writers whose only real claim to fame or recognition was that they were members of the illegal Austrian Nazi party.

In a later account of the events up to the mid-1930s written in 1941, one of Zsolnay's authors, a key functionary in the Nazi cultural organization in Austria, Albert von Jantsch-Streerbach summarized as follows: 'As early as 1934 Mr Paul von Zsolnay reached agreement with the Reich Ministry of Propaganda that he would delete Jewish authors from his list and henceforth publish only the works of Aryan writers.' Although this statement is not correct as it stands, the "Aryan" authors—and Jantsch-Streerbach was one of them—did come to dominate the Zsolnay Verlag. As of 1935, the company had taken on sixteen new "nationalist" authors. When the time came for writers to mix facts with fiction in order to embellish their curricula for membership in the *Reichsschrifttumskammer* or the NSDAP the "nationalization" of the Zsolnay Verlag—described in June 1935 as 'at the time the only large-scale cultural organization in Austria truly to have been brought into line with National Socialist policy [gleichgeschaltet]' —came to have many fathers. .One of the species was the very popular Zsolnay author Egmont Colerus, who described his rôle as a service to the Nazi movement before 1938. In a lengthy confession of May 1938 entitled *Mein Lebensweg als Deutscher*

Colerus wrote that he had 'then established relations between the party agents designated to me [viz. Erwin Rainalter, Hermann Leber, Franz Spunda and Otto Emmerich Groh] and the publishing house of Zsolnay. The intention was to destroy international influence in the publishing trade to whatever extent possible and to secure the services of a large publishing house for Austrian National Socialist writers.' No matter to whom credit should be given, the transformation within the Zsolnay Verlag provides a prime example of the way literary and cultural life was being "nazified" from within. The new reader and recruiting man, Hermann R. Leber, did not represent the company in an official capacity, but instead pulled the strings from the privacy of his own home. Taking control of the Zsolnay Verlag had top priority within the Nazi party itself in Austria. Their leaders had 'quite clearly given the order that nationalist writers in Austria, who had no access to a large publishing house, should take control of the firm of Zsolnay with its substantial means of publicity and distribution.' This was even more plausible in view of the fact that, according to the same source, Paul Zsolnay 'in spring 1934 approached nationalist Austrian writers, offering to place his publishing house at their disposal.' Although the publisher Zsolnay and his literary director Felix Costa were not willing to sign on just any German writer cherished in Nazi circles in order to improve their acceptance in Germany, there is no evidence to support the thesis that Zsolnay as a "Jewish" publisher being viciously attacked from all sides was not fully aware of what he was doing. But this seemed to be the price he was willing to pay. A brief glance at the roster of Zsolnay authors in the 1930s shows the extent of the change. Scarcely any of the newcomers were not already or soon to become members of the illegal Nazi party in Austria. Even the main book illustrator and graphic artist Rudolf Geyer had been a member of the S.A. and NSDAP since early 1934. At the same time the situation in the country's largest literary publishing company is paradigmatic for the exchange or exclusion of literatures which had begun in 1933. To give a further example, roughly 30% of the contributors to the now legendary

*Bekenntnisbuch österreichischer Dichter,* which came out just
after the annexation of Austria and which is widely regarded as an
indication of support for Hitler and the Nazi movement had been
Zsolnay authors prior to 1938. The figure rose to 35% after 1938.
An analysis of the list of members of the "legal" Austrian branch
of the *Reichsschrifttumskammer,* the *Bund der deutschen Schriftsteller Österreichs,* would be likely to produce similar results.

Not surprisingly, the transformation of the Paul Zsolnay
Verlag over the years did not escape public notice and was viewed
with deep suspicion by the liberal Vienna press, by Nazi circles
in Germany and Vienna, and by the Jewish and liberal authors in
Austria. As an example, I should like to quote a couple of brief
entries in the unpublished diaries of Leo Perutz. Because of their
private nature they provide overwhelming evidence in support of
often self-serving claims made by nationalist authors. On 8 March
1935 Perutz noted: 'Had a row with Zsolnay over Scheibelreiter
and his Nazi views . . . Dr Neumann (from Zsolnay) treated me to
a long justification of their Nazi policy, and I sent him packing.'

Police and government records first uncovered and evaluated
by Klaus Amann show the extent to which politics and literature
were closely intertwined in the 1930s. They demonstrate how the
transformation process in the Zsolnay Verlag became tied up in
domestic politics and involved the government all the way up to
the Chancellor himself.

It all began in April 1935 when the state police in Vienna
(Generaldirektion für die öffentliche Sicherheit) received an
anonymous letter full of information and allegations about the
clandestine activities of the nationalist authors and their cronies.
The well-informed source also charged that the Paul Zsolnay
Verlag had become or was now a 'concealed National Socialist
cultural organization.' Police at various levels began to investigate.
The police department in Vienna, generally blind in one eye when
it came to matters concerning illegal National Socialist activities
found nothing to support the claims. The state police, on the
other hand, were able to substantiate them. The investigation
proved to be a particular embarrassment for the Chancellor Kurt

von Schuschnigg who was a good friend of both Paul Zsolnay and Franz Werfel. Schuschnigg demanded that his officials get to the bottom of the matter, rejecting reports by the Vienna police as "useless." Paul Zsolnay, who was subsequently questioned by police, pointed out, and rightly so, that he was not in a (financial) position to continue to publish the works of authors banned from the German market and that not one of his books paid homage to National Socialism or was directed against Austria. And that was where the affair ended.

Viewed in perspective, the case of the Paul Zsolnay Verlag shows at what early stage the process of cultural penetration by the Nazis set in and to what extent the internal cultural annexation was a virtual *fait accompli* long before 1938 and to what degree this gradual process was legalized by the so-called July Agreement of 1936.

In conclusion, one can say that a number of external factors or historical determinants force us today to re-assess what is widely considered to be *the* Austrian literature representative of the inter-war years. One can also conclude that the biggest publishing house in the country not only failed to resist the exchange of literatures beginning in the early 1930s, but also promoted such a development. The external factors influencing both the production and reception of German and – in light of its specific parameters – Austrian literature were many and varied. All of them – essentially non-literary – were responsible for abolishing the free market system. They included import quotas imposed by the Germans on Austrian publishers, book bans, a clearing system which made it almost impossible to make regular payments to authors or obtain the release of frozen assets in Germany, the policy compelling Austrian publishers to have printing done in Germany to the detriment of local printers, the system of book dumping ordered by Propaganda Minister Joseph Goebbels in 1935, which put Austrian publishers at a disadvantage, and finally the sporadic unofficial boycotts of Austrian publishing houses in various parts of Germany.

The history of the Paul Zsolnay Verlag in the 1930s, of

which only a few highlights have been presented here, is a stunning example of how the political annexation of 1938 had long been preceded by the Anschluss of the publishing trade. Whether the path taken by Paul Zsolnay and others was dictated by economic reasoning or opportunism is open to debate. Contemporary reports speak of the swastika flag flying on the publishing house headquarters as early as 12 March 1938. The gesture appears to have been purely symbolical . . .

## NOTES

1.  Herbert G. Göpfert, "Verlagsbuchhandel," *Reallexikon der deutschen Literatur* (Berlin 1979), Vol. 4, p. 651.
2.  *Nachlaß* Grete von Urbanitzky (Geneva). Since these documents were first consulted, the literary papers of Grete von Urbanitzky have been transferred to the Wiener Stadt- und Landesbibliothek.

# 'The Miracle of Survival' — The Theater in der Josefstadt under Ernst Lothar (1935–1938)

Edda Fuhrich-Leisler

It is impossible to talk about the Theater in der Josefstadt without thinking about its complete transformation in the hands of Max Reinhardt.[1] Although he so often directed the theatre from afar, he created a house style and spirit which long survived his period as Director.[2] His theatre, modelled on that of La Fenice in Venice, had an atmosphere which is palpable to this day. In it one immediately thinks of festive drama, of intimate theatre and the cultivated style of a select ensemble. All this was inaugurated by Max Reinhardt when he took over the theatre in 1924.[3] He was to remain there as lessee until 1929, and then until 1935 as a shareholder in 'Wiener Schauspiel AG,' the limited company which took over the theatre. When he resigned his post, it was for purely material reasons: by giving up his shares to Camillo Castiglioni, he was able to keep possession of Leopoldskron, his Salzburg 'palace.' After the political events of 1933, this was to be a refuge, from which he hoped to carry out all his future plans for film and theatre work in Europe and the United States. Unfortunately, the place was saddled with a tax debt running into millions, and although the money was owed to Hitler's treasury it could be collected in Austria. Reinhardt settled his debt, ironically, just six months before the annexation of Austria.[4]

The legal agreement signed by Reinhardt and Castiglioni in 1935 tells us much about the relationship between artistic direction and commercial operation at the Josefstadt. It reads as follows:

Castiglioni assumes full responsibility, financial and legal, for any obligations entered into by Reinhardt, director and lessee of the Theater in der Josefstadt, towards 'Schauspielhaus AG.' Reinhardt agrees that, should Castiglioni so wish, all posters, programmes and other advertisements of the Theater in der Josefstadt shall bear the same designation as previously ['The Players of the Josefstadt Theatre under the direction of Max Reinhardt.'] It is again stressed that Reinhardt shall in no way be legally liable for any contract or other agreement using his name for artistic or similar purposes. Reinhardt further declares his readiness to continue acting as artistic adviser to the theatre on the understanding that he has the right to direct two productions at the Josefstadt each year. All negotiations, settling of dates, selection of plays and other artistic matters shall be personally handled by Reinhardt jointly with Castiglioni. The former shall in no way be dependent upon whoever is Director at any given time. In return for the above-mentioned duties Reinhardt shall receive an honorarium of 10% of the gross receipts of any play produced by him. 'Schauspielhaus AG' undertakes to ensure that each new lessee accepts the above-mentioned commitments. In return Reinhardt declares that, so long as all obligations with respect to him continue to be fulfilled, he will not direct plays or be otherwise involved in the production of plays at any other Viennese theatre for the period of the agreement. Exception shall be made, however, in the case of performances of a kind hitherto not given at the Josefstadt, in particular, opera, operetta, festival productions and the like. If Reinhardt is dissatisfied with the artistic standards of the Theater in der Josefstadt, he is entitled to communicate this in writing to Castiglioni. If any legitimate demand in such a matter is not speedily met, the use of Reinhardt's name in connection with the theatre shall necessarily be discontinued.[5]
Ernst Lothar—writer, theater critic of the *Neue Freie Presse*

and producer at the Burgtheater from 1933 to 1935 – became a shareholder in 'Wiener Schauspielhaus AG.' He paid 130,000 Austrian schillings and had Max Reinhardt's active support. On 1 September 1935 he became Director of the Josefstadt. He found that the theatre he had taken over could compete on artistic terms with the Burgtheater, but that, as a private enterprise saddled with a mortgage to the tune of a million schillings, it would have to be run for profit. Nonetheless, as he later tells in his autobiography, during the short period which lasted until his enforced resignation and emigration, he discovered in the Josefstadt 'a theatre that cared little for commercial practice but believed with heart and soul in the primacy of artistic values.'[6]

Lothar's own contribution was a highly praised cycle of festival performances: Grillparzer's *A Loyal Servant of His Master* (*Ein treuer Diener seines Herrn*) in 1935, his *Jewess of Toledo* (*Die Jüdin von Toledo*) in 1936; also in 1936 Lessing's *Nathan the Wise* (*Nathan der Weise*) and Anzengruber's *The Fourth Commandment* (*Das vierte Gebot*); in 1937 Goethe's *Brother and Sister* (*Die Geschwister*), Max Mell's *Apostle Play* (*Apostelspiel*) and Gorki's *The Lower Depths* (*Nachtasyl*). Production, sets and casts were first-rate in every case. Lothar's choice of plays was intended to create more than mere highspots in the repertoire: they were a humane statement and patriotic affirmation at a time when collapse threatened. In his autobiography 'The Miracle of Survival' (*Das Wunder des Überlebens*), he writes of 'the times beginning to cast a distorting shadow' and of events which one could register but consciously refused to accept: 'on our island, where massive waves were already beating against the shore, we still felt secure. The Swiss press was constantly sounding the alarm, but we were still crying, "Hitler will never come," when he was almost there. In this uncanny position, between euphoria and apocalypse, we performed plays as though the future of the world depended upon it. This could happen only in Vienna.'[7]

In questions of repertoire Lothar for the most part conformed to the cultural norm laid down by Schuschnigg's authoritarian government, but he never sacrificed his personal artistic standards. His productions of the classics were certainly made topical, but were not instruments of state propaganda. Of course, in the latent crisis of national identity it was easy to read Grill-parzer's poetic message in *A Loyal Servant of His Master* as bolstering confidence and helping to give new meaning to the Austrian state. The *Illustrierte Kronen-Zeitung* of 8 December 1935 wrote: 'The considerable interest shown in this festival production was very clear from the composition of the audience, amongst whom were to be found President Miklas and his family, Cardinal Innitzer with members of the clergy, the Minister of Justice Dr Winterstein and his family, the Secretary of State for Education Dr Pernter, and many other leading members of the government.'

The première clearly acquired a kind of official status from the presence of so many leading members of Church and government. Aesthetic value within the cultural ideology of the Doll-fuss/Schuschnigg era essentially meant the lack of anything controversial in things religious, ethical, political or literary; and it was certainly the nature of *A Loyal Servant* to permit this ideal to be taken to absurd lengths. This was more surprising in the case of Lessing's *Nathan the Wise,* which hardly lent itself to similar ideological treatment.[8] Indeed, Emil Geyer, who once deputised for Reinhardt as Director at the Josefstadt, wrote the following corrective:

> Courage and idealism – by no means emblazoned on every director's coat of arms – were needed to stage this pro-duction. Hofrat Lothar clearly has the highest ambitions for the theatre, and his desire to make it serve noble and humane ends has led to productions like the present one of Lessing's *Nathan the Wise.* At such a moment, he is nailing his colours to the mast, revealing his belief that the theatre may be timeless in its poetry, but is also bound up with the thoughts and deeds of its age. In the context of the debate in progress, Lessing's *Nathan* rings out as a hymn to mercy, tolerance and universal brotherhood. There is sim-

plicity and greatness in its allegorical poetry, but I doubt if it was ever before possible, whether one was reading or watching the play, to experience these words as powerfully as in this present phase of European civilisation.[9]

And of course, an attentive first-nighter could scarcely have failed to notice the absence of both government and clergy in the case of *Nathan,* whereas, a few months earlier, distinction had been conferred on Emmet Lavery's popular religious play *The First Legion* (*Die erste Legion*) — the story of a quarrel in the Jesuit movement — by the presence of Cardinal Innitzer at its première. A similar 'for and against' can be seen in the theatre reviews of the Christian Social *Reichspost,* which expressed wholehearted support for the government's cultural policy. As one would expect, the greatest praise goes to Anzengruber's *The Fourth Commandment* and Max Mell's *Apostle Play.* In the latter case, particularly, the reviewer used every nuance of the officially prescribed vocabulary: 'Simple and clear as a mountain stream, like a true folk-tale, the "message" proclaimed by this poet of Austria embraces all the doubts of the age, but again and again offers consolation . . . In the whole of German dramatic literature there is scarcely another example of such a "miracle play." '[10]

   If, then, Lothar succeeded with his 'Festival cycle' in creating a topical theater, this was even more true of contemporary dramas which he selected with programmatic intent. Here, too, his interest was primarily social and humanitarian, as with Schönherr's *Carter Folk* (*Karrnerleut*) and *A Child's Tragedy* (*Kindertragödie*). Above all, he gave voice to an unreserved pacifism, putting on the first performance of Giraudoux's *The Trojan War Will Not Take Place,* and inviting the author to the première. At the party following the opening performance, Giraudoux offered the following memorable toast: 'To Vienna, which has the grace of an innocent child and, perhaps for that reason, the wisdom of an old man.'[11] The actor Rudolf Frank describes in his memoirs the effect which this production had on the audience. It must have affected him deeply, too, as he had only shortly before been released from the custody of the Gestapo in Berlin.

> It was like being at a play within a play. In his box to the right sat Dr Kurt Schuschnigg, the Austrian Chancellor, and there on stage was his prototype, Hector of Troy. Yes, Schuschnigg could have played the role – hadn't he in fact been playing it for several years? Wasn't he, like Hector, gambling everything on offering these Boeotians no pretext to attack? He had kept silent and averted his gaze from infringements of the law, border violations, economic boycott, tear-gas attacks, terrorist bombing and assassination attempts. The Giraudoux was being performed under the aegis of the French Embassy; otherwise the police or the 'Kunststelle' [a euphemistic term for the Viennese censorship] would certainly have banned it. Or perhaps they failed to notice what was hidden beneath the antique garb? The Viennese audience did notice, and kept throwing stolen glances at the Chancellor's box. It was as though Giraudoux had written the play just for him.[12]

In addition to Giraudoux's *The Trojan War Will Not Take Place,* Emmet Lavery's one-act play *Monsignore's Great Hour (Monsignores große Stunde)* was also performed. In this play we find the Pope facing a question of conscience: should he, in the threatening situation, call on the faithful to pray for peace and thereby essentially let things take their course, or should he not rather use all the means at his disposal to prevent a European armed conflict? This topic was only a short while later to become a burning issue for the Austrian Church when it had to decide upon its attitude towards the National Socialist régime. In November 1936, the critics simply commented on the concern with pacifism: 'The Theater in der Josefstadt has declared its faith in the theatre as a moral institution. An Austrian has brought together an American and a Frenchman, and the three of them have spoken out against war and for world peace.'*13*

Lothar himself contributed to the contemporary drama with his stage version of Schnitzler's *Miss Elsa* (*Fräulein Else*, 1936) about which the critics were divided in their opinion.[14] It achieved, however, a certain notoriety in the annals of the theatre because of a tragi-comic, even grotesque, episode that belongs to that short chapter of theatrical history about the 'Theatre in Exile in Austria.'[15] This episode concerns the Jewish actor Leo Reuss, an Austrian who was forced to leave Germany in 1933 and who, once back in his native land, found that his racial origins prevented him from acting there too. Fearful for his livelihood, he hit on the idea of camouflaging his identity (which meant his Jewish appearance). He grew a beard, dyed his hair blond and sought a job in the theatre, claiming to be a Tyrolese peasant named Kaspar Brandhofer, who had discovered an irresistible vocation to act. His new persona was so successful in both appearance and speech (he managed the local dialect to perfection), that he was engaged by Lothar to make his début in the important role of Herr von Dorsday in Schnitzler's *Miss Elsa*. The right-wing press was full of praise: 'Brandhofer, a son of the soil, adds real substance to an otherwise phony piece of theatre' (*Völkischer Beobachter*).[16] Indeed, it had just been announced that Brandhofer would have a part in the forthcoming production of Schiller's *William Tell*, when the whole deception was revealed by Schnitzler's son, Heinrich. Lothar felt that he had been tricked and reacted with incomprehension and insensitivity to an incident that was so clearly created by times that were out of joint. Reuss left for the United States, where he was able to make a highly successful career for himself in films.[17]

In November 1937 Lothar invited Walter Firner's company, the 'Austrian People's Theatre' (Österreichische Volksbühne)[18] to make a guest appearance at the Josefstadt. The company gave the first Austrian performance of Gerhart Hauptmann's *Hamlet in Wittenberg* on the occasion of the dramatist's seventy-fifth birthday. At Lothar's invitation the same company also gave a special late-night performance of a youthful work by Giraudoux, *The Unnamed Soldier*. The performance was under the patronage of the French Ambassador, of the Minister Puaux and the President of the Pan-European Union, Richard Coudenhove-Calergi. In January 1938 another guest performance is worthy of note, namely, that by the recently revived association of the 'Friends of Contemporary Theatre' (Freunde neuzeitlicher Dramatik), who performed Ferdinand Bruckner's *Napoleon 1*. This too was a special late-night presentation whereas the proceeds went to the hospital of the Brothers of Charity. The 'Friends' had been created by the Principal Dramaturge of the Vienna Volkstheater, Professor Heinrich Glückmann, in conjunction with the 'Circle of Austrian Stage Actors' (Ring Österreichischer Bühnenkünstler), and the resulting union led to the proclamation of an 'Austrian National Theatre' (Österreichische Nationalbühne), which would make its principal aim 'to perform, irrespective of genre, works whose authors are still unknown to the general public.'[19] A further function would be 'to perform plays of merit which cannot be performed elsewhere for theatrical or extra-theatrical reasons.'[20] If such a formulation seems worthy of note in January 1938, then how much more so the review of Bruckner's play by the well-known critic and historian of the theatre Rudolph Lothar:[21]

> When he wrote his play *Napoleon I*, Ferdinand Bruckner clearly intended to present in tragic form Napoleon's marriage to the daughter of the Austrian Emperor . . . It was probably the author's intention to show that this marriage was the tragic turning-point in Napoleon's life. He fell in love with Maria Luise and frittered away his time, instead of choosing the right moment to march against Russia. The delay led to his downfall, for it was with the catastrophic Russian campaign that his inexorable decline began. This was surely the drama Bruckner intended to write, but he was evidently frightened by his own audacity and ended up merely hinting at his original purpose . . .

Bruckner is proffering a warning from his American exile about the nature of power that has over-reached itself. Yet our reviewer,

who comments prophetically on Bruckner's theme, appears not to
see the topicality of the play's coded message: 'One can actually
have a sense of going towards one's downfall, of being just about
to discover the abyss behind the highest pinnacle of power, and
yet continue along the path.'[22]

Lothar naturally found that he had occasionally to lower his
sights, and as well as his ambitious programme of highbrow drama
(Theater der Dichtung) and contemporary plays, he had to offer
works of light entertainment (Boulevardstücke) to meet the tastes
of a broader public. These light-hearted, unproblematic plays,
often full of catchy tunes, had names like *Enjoy Life* (*Freut
euch des Lebens*), *The Tilted Hat* (*Der schiefe Hut*), *Marriage
Blossom* (*Blumen der Heirat*), *Fried Chicken* (*Backhendl*), *High
Society* (*Feine Gesellschaft*). Many of them were not performed in
the Josefstadt Theatre itself but in the 'Kammerspiele,' which had
been used as a smaller sister-theatre since 1925. Special    summer
productions were mounted, like Ralph Benatzsky's *The King with
the Umbrella* (*Der König mit dem Regenschirm*) and *Parisiennes*
(*Pariserinnen*) – both 'officially banned for young people.' What
the public found so attractive in this genre and gave the plays
named such long and successful runs was the incomparable elegance and assurance of the acting, even when the content was of
the most trivial. 'A little bit of nonsense, but beautifully wrapped,'
as Alfred Polgar once pithily described it. Whilst Lothar was
Director, it was always virtuoso performance at its most perfect,
with an ensemble that had largely been trained by Reinhardt and
comprised names that were famed throughout the German-
speaking world: Tilla Durieux, Adrienne Gessner, Paula Wessely,
Lili Darvas, Albert Bassermann, Ernst Deutsch, Anton Edthofer,
Hans Jaray, and Attila Hörbiger, to name but a few.

Every production, after it had run for three or four weeks,
was given in matinée performances at specially reduced prices
(from 1 to 10 Austrian schillings, or from 80 groschen to 8 schillings). Subscription series, with four price levels, were first introduced in September 1937, and we find the following advertise-
ment in the Viennese press: 'New scheme! Subscription tickets at

reduced price now available from Gerngross —easy method of payment.' The links between the Josefstadt and the subscription system run by the State through one of its agencies (the 'Österreichische Kunststelle'), which was increasingly monopolising subscription schemes and thereby gaining enormous influence on theatre repertoires, requires further research.

After handing over the directorship to Lothar, Max Reinhardt returned only once more to the Josefstadt. This was in October 1937, when he produced Franz Werfel's play for All Souls' Day, *One Night* (*In einer Nacht*). The critics were unanimous in their praise for the 'overall creativity' in Reinhardt's production. There was also mention of how he had studiously toned down everything problematic, treating contemporary issues by raising them to the level of pure art. On the first night a reception was given in Reinhardt's honour,[23] and those present in the Sträussel Suite included senior members of the government and diplomatic corps, as well as numerous influential society figures. When Reinhardt gave an interview in Paris a few days later, just prior to his leaving for the United States, he could not know that it was his final leave-taking from Europe. But the words he chose were prophetic: 'My recent stay in Vienna will remain unforgettable. I have always been fond of that city, but this time it seems to have affected me as never before. Vienna is without doubt the cultural and artistic centre which turns every artist's work into an experience for him.'[24]

On the morning of 23 January 1938 there was a ceremonial matinée at the Josefstadt with the title 'Austria in Its Poetry' (Österreich im Gedicht). Lothar explained in his introductory address that he had selected 'only the most beautiful and most characteristic from the rich store available.'[25] The press almost unanimously agreed that the event had a strange atmosphere. In retrospect, it seemed more like a 'danse macabre': poets whose patriotism would not prevent their shortly being ostracized, persecuted or simply passed over in silence in the self-same land they had praised in their poetry. But there were other poets in the programme who would only too happily step forward to serve the country's new masters. The audience heard poems by Grillparzer, Lenau, Rilke, Hofmannsthal, Werfel, Beer-Hofmann, Trakl, Saar, and Wildgans, but also Weinheber, Mell and Ginzkey. When, at the end of the matinée, Ernst Lothar recited Grillparzer's poem 'These green banks of Danube they shall not take' (Sie sollen ihn nicht haben, den grünen Donaustrand), Schuschnigg, who until then had sat out of sight, moved to the front of his box and led such a storm of applause that—as Lothar recalled in his memoirs—'it seemed as though the Thousand Year Reich was about to make way for thousand-year-old Austria.'[26]

On 4 March 1938, in recognition of his services to the Josefstadt, Lothar's contract was renewed by the theatre administration for a further five years. By this time he had managed to put the house's finances in order. A week later the 11th of March began in the Josefstadt as a normal working day. Carl Zuckmayer reports in his autobiography as follows:

On the morning of 11 March I experienced something that seemed to have less to do with politics than with a fantasy world, and when I looked back on it, I found that it took on a tragi-comic air. It was an early rehearsal of my new play [*Bellmann*], which Lothar was directing with a fine Viennese cast—Paula Wessely, Attila Hörbiger, Anton Edthofer. On the morning of that catastrophic day, in the subdued light of an empty theatre, a handful of people managed to forget the world outside and the crisis which could affect all their lives, and for a few hours succumbed to the magic of the stage. We argued over cuts, movements, alterations, as though there were nothing of greater moment in the whole world. When we left the theatre in the afternoon . . . everything was over, and two hours later, Schuschnigg broadcast his farewell message: 'I am yielding to force. God protect Austria.'[27]

On 15 March the newspapers announced that 'in keeping with the spirit of the new order in Austria' there would be 'a wind

of change' in the affairs of the Josefstadt Theatre too. 'The actors
have asked Erik Frey and Robert Horky to represent them. The
Zuckmayer play already scheduled will not now be performed.'[28]
On 18 March it was announced in the press that Lothar had
resigned from the Directorship of the Josefstadt the previous
day. At his request and on the recommendation of the National
Socialist group which had taken over the running of the theatre
(Betriebszellenleitung), Robert Valberg,[29] a well-known actor, had
been officially appointed Director until instructions came from
higher authority. The announcement concluded with an indication
of how things were to continue: 'Following the appointment of
Robert Valberg as Director of the Josefstadt, there are to be no
changes in personnel.'[30] At any rate, that was the official version.
The truth is, however, expressed by the emigration, for political
reasons or on racial grounds, of the following actors and actresses
who had been engaged either for the whole season or for particular
productions: Albert and Else Bassermann, Mady Christians, Lili
Darvas, Ernst Deutsch, Tilla Durieux, Else Eckersberg, Adrienne
Gessner—who left with her husband, Ernst Lothar—Hans Jaray,
Oskar Karlweis, Karl Paryla, Ludwig Stössel, Helene Thimig-
Reinhardt, Rosa Valetti and Gisela Werbezirk.

Valberg's directorship lasted barely six months. As early as
the following October, in response to the wishes of most of the
ensemble,[31] Heinz Hilpert, a former pupil of Max Reinhardt's and
now Director of the Deutsches Theater in Berlin, became the new
Director of the Josefstadt as well. Running the two theatres as
part of one operation, Hilpert continued to work in the humane
spirit of his respected teacher, and that helped keep the Josefstadt
buoyant through and beyond the stormy years of 1939 to 1945.

NOTES

1.  See Anton Bauer, *Das Theater in der Josefstadt zu Wien* (Munich:
    Manutiuspresse, 1957); Fritz Klingenbeck (ed.), *Max Reinhardts
    Theater in der Josefstadt* (Salzburg: Residenz-Verlag, 1972).

2.  See Gustav Kropatschek / Wolfgang Mika (eds.), *175 Jahre Theater in der Josefstadt, 1788 [bis]1963* (Vienna: Theater in der Josefstadt, 1963); Otto Basil, "Die dreistufige Entwicklung des Josefstädter Theaters" in: *Maske und Kothurn*, 7 (1961), 131ff.

3.  See Joseph Gregor, *Das Theater in der Wiener Josefstadt* (Vienna: Wiener Drucke, 1924; Robert Musil, "Das neue Theater Reinhardts in Wien," *Deutsche Allgemeine Zeitung*, 8 April 1924; Bertha Zuckerkandl in: Reinhard Federmann (ed.), *Österreich intim. Erinnerungen 1892-1942* (Frankfurt am Main/Berlin/Vienna: Propyläen), pp. 149ff.

4.  See Gottfried Reinhardt, *Der Liebhaber. Erinnerungen seines Sohnes an Max Reinhardt* (Munich/Zurich: Droemer-Knaur, 1973), pp. 200ff.

5.  Max Reinhardt-Nachlaß. Österreichische Nationalbibliothek, Sig.: MR 28/604/8,9.

6.  Ernst Lothar in: *175 Jahre Theater in der Josefstadt* (see above n. 2); see also Helmuth Waldner, "Das Theater in der Josefstadt von Lothar bis Steinboeck," diss., Vienna, 1949.

7.  Ernst Lothar, *Das Wunder des Überlebens. Erinnerungen und Ergebnisse* (Vienna: Paul Zsolnay, 1961), p. 83.

8.  The same applies to Lothar's production of *The Jewess of Toledo*, which had its première on 10 February 1937 even though—or perhaps because—Germany and Austria had signed the July Agreement in the previous year. Ernst Deutsch played King Alphons, and was either praised or condemned according to the political colour of the paper or periodical concerned. He was, of course, banned from appearing in Germany on racial grounds.

9.  Emil Geyer, *Die Stunde*, March 1935 (review of the première on 17 March).

10.  *Reichspost*, 18 June 1937.

11.  Ernst Lothar, *Das Wunder des Überlebens*, above n. 7, p. 89.

12.  Rudolf Frank, *Spielzeit meines Lebens* (Heidelberg: Lambert Schneider, 1960), pp. 343f.

13.  *Der Wiener Tag*, 8 November 1936.

14.  The historical significance of the performance can be properly grasped only in the light of the scandal surrounding Schnitzler's *Carousel* (*Reigen*, performed in 1921), since when Schnitzler's entire literary work had been subjected to varying degrees of censorship.

15.  See *Theater im Exil 1933-1945. Ausstellung 1973* (Berlin: Akademie der Künste [Catalogue], 1973); Curt Riess, "Exil-Theater in Österreich" in: Lothar Schirmer (ed.), *Theater im Exil 1933-1945* (Berlin: Akade-

mie der Künste, 1979), pp. 58ff.

16.  See Ernst Lothar, *Das Wunder des Überlebens* above n. 7, p. 86.

17.  See Hans Thimig, *Neugierig wie ich bin. Erinnerungen.* Recorded by Edda Fuhrich, Gisela Prossnitz and Renate Wagner (Vienna/Munich: Amalthea, 1983), pp. 180ff.

18.  The actor and producer Walter Firner had left Germany for Austria in 1933 and founded this company, which gave Jewish exiles, among others, the chance to continue their acting profession. The ensemble made guest appearances in theatres and adult education centres, always maintaining the high standards for which it was famous. See Horst Jarka, "Theater für eine 'Jugend in Gefahr'" in: Franz Kadrnoska (ed.), *Aufbruch und Untergang österreichischer Kultur zwischen 1918 und 1938* (Vienna: Europaverlag, 1981), p. 582.

19.  *Der Wiener Tag,* 15 November 1936.

20.  *Wiener Zeitung,* 23 January 1937.

21.  In 1934, Rudolph Lothar's work *Das Wiener Burgtheater* was published with a Preface by Dr Kurt von Schuschnigg, the Minister of Justice and Education.

22.  *Neues Wiener Journal,* 26 January 1938.

23.  See Ernst Lothar (Rede über Max Reinhardt) in: *Neues Wiener Journal,* 7 October 1937; on the relationship Ernst Lothar–Max Reinhardt, see also Ernst Lothar, "Bekenntnis zu Max Reinhardt," *Süddeutsche Zeitung,* 9 September 1953; and Ernst Lothar, "Max Reinhardt" in: Alfons Übelhör/Richard Wolf (eds.), *Große Österreicher* (Vienna, 1946), pp. 5ff.

24.  *Neues Wiener Journal,* 10 October 1937.

25.  *Neue Freie Presse,* 25 January 1938.

26.  Ernst Lothar, *Das Wunder des Überlebens,* above n. 7, p. 91.

27.  Carl Zuckmayer, *Als wär's ein Stück von mir. Horen der Freundschaft* (Frankfurt am Main: Fischer, 1966), pp. 70f.

28.  *Neues Wiener Journal,* 15 March 1938.

29.  The actor Robert Valberg was a member of the association 'German Stage' (Deutsche Bühne), which had been formed the previous November by Mirko Jelusich. In its programme it proclaimed that 'a frank belief in racially pure art and resistance to all perversions of art practised by aliens in no way constitute a political statement' (*Wiener Neueste Nachrichten,* 12 November 1937). At the same moment as the Nazis officially took over the Theater in der Josefstadt, Valberg was placed in charge of the 'Circle of Austrian Artists' (Ring österreichi-

scher Künstler).

30.  *Neues Wiener Journal,* 20 March 1938.

31.  See Hans Thimig, *Neugierig wie ich bin,* above no. 17, pp. 186ff.

# 'Salzburg: Perhaps Art's Last Existing Sanctuary from the Political World' –
## The Salzburg Festival in the Thirties

### Gisela Prossnitz

In 1930 the Salzburg Festival celebrated an anniversary. Ten years had passed since its memorable opening, with Hugo von Hofmannsthal's *Everyman* (*Jedermann*) being performed in the Domplatz in Max Reinhardt's production. The Festival was founded specifically as a 'first act of peace' at the end of the war and following the collapse of the Austro-Hungarian Empire: its purpose was to 'use the conciliatory power of art to help bring the peoples of Europe together.'[1] The Festival was to betoken faith in the future as well as in the age-old mission of Austria. Despite the difficulties of the post-war years and the period of inflation, the organizers used their remarkable energies to build on the foundations laid by that first performance of *Everyman,* developing the rich and varied programme that made Salzburg into an international centre of culture.

The spiritual fathers of the Festival were Max Reinhardt, Hugo von Hofmannsthal, Richard Strauss, Franz Schalk and Alfred Roller.[2] The world reputations of these founders ensured a great deal of publicity for the Festival. But they were also backed by a politician who was aware that the Festival had both cultural significance and also economic value: it would play a part in the survival of Salzburg and the whole of Austria. This great advocate of the Festival, as well as its counsellor, was Dr Franz Rehrl, the Christian Social Provincial Governor (Landeshauptmann) from 1922 to 1938.[3] His undogmatic views on finance and economic policy allowed him to rescue the Festival from disaster more than once, and thanks to some unconventional reorganization he placed the Festival on a firm financial footing. A clever negotiator, he persuaded the provincial government, the Salzburg city authorities and the Fund for the Promotion of Tourism (Fonds zur Förderung des Fremdenverkehrs) – a registered organization and his brain-child – to make equal annual contributions to the Festival.

The tenth anniversary of the Festival was celebrated with all due pomp and circumstance: honouring individuals, gala performances and all manner of social events. The great names of the artistic world were there, as were the political and industrial leaders, at their head the Austrian President, Wilhelm Miklas, and the Austrian Chancellor, Johannes Schober. It was the first time that the Festival showed a financial profit. But if at the start of the thirties things seemed to be getting ever better, disappointment quickly followed, as the Festival was at the mercy of economic changes and political developments in Germany. Just as Salzburg was finding its financial feet, the world economy was becoming destabilized. The depression and uncertainties on the international money market had repercussions for the festival city. Austria was seriously affected by the Emergency Decrees (Notverordnung) which came into effect in Germany on 22 July 1931, three days before the opening of the Festival. The Decree required that every German travelling abroad pay a tax of 1000 Reichsmark.[4] This ensured that visitors from across the border in Bavaria, who often made the trip just for a performance and then usually purchasing only the cheaper seats, did not attend that year's Festival.

Ironically, the 1931 programme was the most substantial yet. The 175th anniversary of Mozart's birth was celebrated in his birthplace with performances of five of his operas; there were also productions of Richard Strauss' *Der Rosenkavalier,* Beethoven's *Fidelio,* Gluck's *Orpheus and Eurydice;* and for the first time La Scala Milan came to Salzburg on tour, bringing three productions.[5] In addition to his *Everyman* there were three more brilliant productions by Reinhardt: Goldoni's 'commedia dell'arte' piece *The Servant of Two Masters,* Hofmannsthal's *The Difficult*

*Man* (*Der Schwierige*) and Goethe's tragedy *Stella*. There were orchestral concerts, serenades, performances of religious music. In short, it was a sumptuous offering in keeping with the already established – and still continuing – policy of catering to a public able to afford it.

The artistic success of the 1931 Festival is attested to by a great many press reports. No fewer than 231 journalists had attended, and 'for the first time, even the Viennese press, which to date had behaved somewhat churlishly towards the Festival, unanimously proclaimed Salzburg's grandiose success.'[6] Financially, things were not nearly so happy: the season ended with a net loss of 51,000 schillings. Furthermore, the outlook for 1932 was bleak. This was the year in which the world economic crisis was at its worst, unemployment was continuing to rise fast, and foreign travel – particularly from England and the United States, both of which suffered falls in their currencies – fell off. The Festival management realized that there was likely to be a serious loss of income from box-office receipts, and felt the need for caution. The Austrian government, itself facing the greatest financial difficulties, demanded prudent planning. Its lapidary comment on the budget estimate presented to the Board of Directors on 9 November 1931 was: 'Salzburg is living in Cloud Cuckoo Land!'[7] Nonetheless, it was agreed to go ahead with planning the 1932 Festival and to maintain high artistic standards come what may, for 'the worse the economic situation, the more splendid the Festival must be in order to attract the largest number of visitors and so overcome all our difficulties.'[8] Despite all the warning signs the 1932 Festival did not fare as badly as predicted, and the only complaints came from hoteliers and restaurateurs, who noted that the tourists were being more careful with money.

Performances of Weber's *Oberon* played, in fact, to 87% capacity, followed by *Everyman* with 86%, the latter gaining in interest because Paul Hartmann had taken over in the leading role. And here we must consider the reason why Alexander Moissi, who had for so long played Everyman, could not be engaged for this season. There was public pressure not to engage him because he had seen fit to be present, in the guise of a doctor, at a birth in a Salzburg maternity clinic. It was publicly stated that he had done this in preparation for a book he was writing. The Salzburg branch of the NSDAP used a mass meeting it was holding to make capital of the incident, and this action led to weeks of emotional debate in the press and between factions. The attacks were primarily on the 'Jew'–which Moissi in fact was not –and only secondarily about his presence at the birth. There was still no end to the harassment when Moissi's wife, the actress Johanna Terwin, sent an open letter ('To the Women of Salzburg!') to the *Salzburger Volksblatt* on 2 October 1931. She wrote as follows:

> As the wife of Alexander Moissi I feel it my duty to defend my husband in the face of unjust attacks levelled against him; the more especially since it was I who prevented him (as he is abroad) from defending himself. As for his presence at a birth, people who do not know my husband as, after twenty years, I know him may be excused for finding fault with his behaviour if they have read only the malicious representations given of it. Indeed, I am convinced that their severe condemnation of him results largely from such distortions. These appear to impute base motives to him, but in reality have nothing to do with how he acted and are simply a means of attacking the 'Jew' Moissi. I have in front of me a number of such attacks taken from different German-language newspapers. They are headed as follows: 'The Jew Moissi enjoys himself!'–'A Jewish actor is allowed to watch a birth!'– 'Incredible obscenity! Moissi-Moses as obstetrician!'– 'A Christian woman gives birth to entertain a Jew!'– 'Who gave Everyman-actor Moissi-Moses access to the maternity ward?'–'A woman giving birth should not provide entertainment for a lewd and sordid Jew!' etc. As is clear from the above selection, the real cause for anger

is the 'Jew' and only incidentally his presence at a birth, about which there could be differences of opinion. It is well known that Moissi, a man of intellect, refuses to be dragged into racial and religious disputes, and that even the *false* accusation that he is a Jew would not affect him. Purely to set the record straight and to correct the misrepresentation which people have not hesitated to put about, may I state categorically that both Alexander Moissi and I are of pure Aryan extraction, and that this can be proved by recourse at any time to the relevant documents. In particular, Alexander Moissi's baptismal certificate shows that he was baptized by the priest of St Nicholas's Church in Trieste in the year of his birth.[9]

Ticket sales had risen by 4% in 1932, giving the Festival management the courage to announce its long-awaited production of Goethe's *Faust* by Max Reinhardt for the 1933 season. This was a chance to popularize 'the greatest work of the greatest German poet' by presenting a faithful version to as broad a public as possible.[10] Further plans for 1933 included *Der Rosenkavalier,* whose undiminishing popularity made it into a standard repertory work of these years, and a revival of Strauss' *Woman without a Shadow,* which had been astonishingly well received. But perhaps the most daring project, given the financial situation, was the world première of a new version of Strauss' *The Egyptian Helen.* A Wagner opera was to be given for the first time in Salzburg: this would be *Tristan and Isolde,* conducted by Bruno Walter, and was intended to vie with Bayreuth as a fiftieth anniversary commemoration of the composer's death. Walter himself had his greatest successes with Mozart, but he constantly pleaded for an enlargement of the repertoire. In December these plans for the Festival were published, and the organizers looked forward to the coming year with confidence.

So far it had been the general economic situation that had put the Festival at risk, but from 1933 it was primarily political happenings which threatened its existence. From 1933 Salzburg mirrors the power conflict between Hitler's Reich, which sought Anschluss, and an Austria struggling to retain its independence. Both sides used art to political ends. In bringing their illegal, violent and sometimes terroristic manoeuvres into the artistic arena, the Germans could be said to be trying out their 'cultural policy' in Salzburg. Thereafter, no holds would be barred in suppressing undesirable art and enforcing cultural conformism (Gleichschaltung). Hitler and Goebbels learned between 1933 and 1937 how much disturbance they could create abroad in the cultural sphere. But these years also taught Austria just how much resistance could be put up. When, however, Austria's political leaders capitulated, the Salzburg Festival was forced to capitulate too.

On 30 January 1933 Hitler was elected Chancellor of the Reich. From 13 March, Goebbels was in charge of the newly established Reich Ministry of Public Education and Propaganda (Reichsministerium für Volksaufklärung und Propaganda), which had power over press, radio, film, theatre and music. The new cultural policy bit quickly. The law passed on 23 March 1933 'to eliminate the danger to the Reich and its people' (Gesetz zur Behebung der Not von Volk und Reich) gave Hitler legal freedom of action, indeed full dictatorial powers. One of his first measures was to decree a 'general boycott of Jews.' Large-scale purges followed, in which Jewish artists and others sympathizing with them were denied employment, or had their contracts terminated, or were forced to take extended leave of absence.

Max Reinhardt had already left Germany before this law came into effect, in fact immediately after the première of Hofmannsthal's *Great World Theatre* (*Das große Welttheater*), given on 1 March at the Deutsches Theatre in Berlin. Bruno Walter had also left Germany. He was to have conducted a concert by the Gewandhaus Orchestra in Leipzig, but both this concert and one with the Berlin Philharmonic due to take place a little later were officially banned 'in order to forestall a breach of the peace.'[11] Richard Strauss took Walter's place in Berlin but stipulated that he would accept no fee and that the sum which was to have been paid to Walter should go to the orchestra. Shortly before this Otto Klemperer had been the victim of anti-Semitic attacks in Berlin. In Dresden Fritz Busch was boycotted: 'Although an Aryan, he was said to have associated too freely with Jews and to have been responsible for the engagement of Jewish and foreign artists at the Dresden Opera.'[12]

For many of those not tolerated in the Reich, as for those actually driven out, Austria became a stepping-stone to emigration. These people placed their hopes in the Corporate State (Ständestaat) of Engelbert Dollfuss, its Chancellor. The state was authoritarian in constitution, but it had deported Dr. Hans Frank, the Reich Law Commissioner (Reichsjustizkommissar), on 15 May 1933 and had declared the NSDAP illegal shortly after, on 19 June. Hitler's sanctions followed without delay. His first act was to pass the 'Law concerning travel to the Republic of Austria' (Gesetz über die Reisen nach der Republik Österreich), the so-called 'Thousand Mark Visa' (Tausend-Mark-Sperre), which came into effect on 1 July 1933. This was tantamount to closing the border, with disastrous consequences for the Salzburg Festival just about to begin.[13] Salzburg had welcomed 15,681 visitors from Germany during the Festival month of August 1932, but in 1933 this figure was reduced to a mere 874. Besides this, many foreign visitors were put off by the increasing number of disruptions engineered by the National Socialists.

As in 1931, the new crisis turned the Salzburg Festival into a symbol of Austrian independence, and to make this point, it was vital that the Festival take place. The Austrian government gave large special subsidies and stepped up publicity: President Miklas, Chancellor Dollfuss and Kurt von Schuschnigg (who had become Education Minister in May 1933 with consequent responsibility for the Festival) appeared regularly at performances. But the press boycott imposed by the Third Reich as a further measure against Austria was a serious blow. Not one of the German journalists registered for the 1933 Festival came. Even after the Austro-German July Agreement of 1936 and the abolition of the Thousand Mark Visa, we find the German Government Cultural Press

Association (Kulturpolitische Pressekonferenz der Reichsregie-
rung) instructing journalists to 'exercise restraint in reporting the
Salzburg Festival.'[14] A third decree of Hitler's Reich made it very
difficult for the Festival to engage appropriate artists. The substance of the decree, to which frequent recourse was made, is
reproduced in the following statement by the official Reich
committee set up to promote German life and culture (Lektorat
zur Förderung des Deutschtums): 'No moral or economic support
of any kind may be given to the Dollfuss regime. Such support
includes participation in the Salzburg Festival by artists from the
Reich. Since these artists are themselves a great draw, they can
only make the Festival more attractive, and for that reason must
be prevented from appearing there.'[15]

Just before the opening of the 1933 Festival, Wilhelm Rode,
Sigrid Onegin and Eugen Klöpfer withdrew from the leading roles
they were contracted to perform.[16] Either the German government had made clear that they should keep away from the Salzburg Festival, or it had gone so far as to refuse them the necessary
exit permits. Of course, there were artists who needed no order
from the government but declined to come to Salzburg from
personal conviction. Hans Pfitzner is an example. He withdrew,
offering the following explanation in his letter of 13 July to the
Festival management, which was, incidentally, pointedly published
by several daily papers:

> To my deepest regret, the attitude towards the German
> people shown by the Austrian government under Dollfuss
> forces me to withdraw from participation in the Salzburg
> Festival. You will permit me to avoid going into details
> concerning my decision; suffice to say that every German
> is indignant at the way the Austrian government is be-
> having in the face of an awakening commitment to Ger-
> man ideals. My own total commitment to such ideals
> prevents my fulfilling my Salzburg engagement. When I
> entered into the contract, I naturally understood it to
> imply that I was thereby serving the cause of German art.

242 Gisela Prossnitz

That understanding is contradicted by the official attitude of the Austrian administration to everything that Germany stands for, and that includes its art. I am on that ground unable to fulfill my contract.

My action is, however, in no way intended to disturb my affectionate relationship with Germany's Austrian brothers. I shall always remain grateful to that part of the Austrian public, especially in Vienna, which has responded so warmly to my artistic work.[17]

Richard Strauss reacted differently. Bayreuth wanted him for its festival, but his fame gave him a free hand. He would 'attend the Salzburg Festival come what may, since he wished to ensure that his name and work remained associated with Salzburg.'[18] But in 1934, when the Salzburg Festival was mounting a cycle of his works in honour of his seventieth birthday and the new power structure in Germany was paying him court, Strauss was forced into line. On 7 May the General Inspector (Landesinspektor) of the National Socialist Party of Austria, Theo Habicht, wrote to Goebbels from Munich as follows:

I have learned today that the Salzburg Festival, which is usually directed by the notorious Max Reinhardt, is planning to make extensive use this summer of the services of Richard Strauss and Professor Furtwängler. As far as I can discover, discussions between the Festival management and those I have named are in train at this very moment ... It is a matter for concern whether, given the present political differences between the Reich and Austria, such prominent persons as Strauss, Furtwängler and, in a different sphere, Werner Krauss (who are, I believe, either Prussian Councillors of State (Staatsräte) or members of the most important cultural institutions in the Reich[19]), should participate in cultural activities in Austria. A further cause for concern is that the Festival plays a significant part in Austria's publicity for its tourist in-

industry, and for that reason is boycotted by all our party members in Austria. I send you this information with the request that consideration be given to making clear to the persons concerned that they should take all possible steps to withdraw from cultural involvement in Austria until further notice.[20]

Following this notification from the Austrian National Socialist Party, the Ministry of Propaganda sent instructions on 25 May to Strauss and Furtwängler in the terms proposed by Habicht: 'It has been brought to the attention of this Ministry by the National Socialist Party of Austria that you intend to participate in the Salzburg Festival during this coming summer. The Minister, Dr Goebbels, has instructed me to inform you that this runs directly counter to the Führer's policy. The Minister consequently requests that you withdraw from the Festival in the political interests of Germany.'[21]

This veto from Berlin, and also the bomb attack of 17 May on the Festival Theatre there, persuaded Strauss to cancel his appearance. The Festival management accused him of 'breaking faith with his own child.'[22] In a 'confidential' letter of 2 August, Strauss replied from Bayreuth to this charge:

> I did not of my own free will give up the chance to be present at the Festival. I had so looked forward to the fine performances of my works with which you intend to honour me this year. My very real fatigue and my family's concern about my life and health are only part of the reason for my not coming to Austria at this time of political unrest there. In point of fact, you must see that even I am powerless against orders from 'on high.'[23]

In mid-August, however, after repeated audiences with Goebbels, Strauss was given a short-term travel permit and was able at least to be in the audience for a performance of his *Elektra*, conducted by his friend Clemens Krauss.

Even though he was unwilling to sign its Statutes because of a clause concerning race, Strauss had been President of the Reich Chamber of Music since November 1933. At the same time he had discovered in Stefan Zweig a worthy successor to Hugo von Hofmannsthal and fought a long, hard-won battle against the Nazi regime to keep him as his librettist. Of Strauss's somewhat indifferent attitude towards the new men of power his biographer Heinrich Kralik has the following to say: 'He had so little understanding of political ways of thinking and speaking that he was utterly surprised and indignant when people abroad interpreted his actions as a compromising partisanship.'[24] In a letter to Zweig of 17 June 1935, which incidentally the Gestapo intercepted, he offered the following self-justification:

> Who told you that I have taken a serious political step? Is it because I conducted a concert for Bruno Walter? I did that for the sake of the orchestra. Or is it because I filled in for another 'non-Aryan,' Toscanini? [25] I did that for the sake of Bayreuth. All this has nothing to do with politics. I don't care what the gutter press makes of it, and you should not concern yourself either. Is it because I play at being President of the Reich Chamber of Music? I took that on in order to do good and prevent worse! I would have taken on the irritations of this honorific post under any government, but neither Kaiser Wilhelm nor Herr Rathenau offered it to me.[26]

The opening of the 1934 Festival was overshadowed by the July 'Putsch' and the murder of Chancellor Dollfuss. But it began only sixteen hours late on 29 July with performances of the Funeral March from Beethoven's *Eroica* Symphony and his *Fidelio*. But ticket sales collapsed, with masses of cancellations following the terrible events of the day. Things changed decisively towards the end of the Festival with the first Salzburg appearance of Toscanini, who conducted three concerts with the Vienna Philharmonic. Toscanini was a violent opponent of all forms of dictatorship, refusing to conduct after 1931 in Mussolini's Italy[27] and turning his back on Bayreuth after Hitler's seizure of power. In acquiring Toscanini not only had Salzburg engaged the world's most famous conductor, but also the man himself 'soon became the symbol of resistance to fascist tyranny, an exemplary figure committed to and showing solidarity with the victims of racism.'[28]

For the 1935 Festival Toscanini was asked to conduct not only orchestral concerts but *Fidelio* too. He agreed on condition that he could also conduct Verdi's *Falstaff* with an Italian cast. The Festival management made some objections, fearing that damage could be done to the 'idea of Salzburg,' whose musical essence was Mozart and Strauss, not Verdi. Toscanini's response was: 'No Falstaff, no Toscanini.' The final decision was taken by Chancellor Schuschnigg: 'Falstaff and Toscanini.'[29] The Maestro also won the artistic power struggle with Clemens Krauss for pride of place at Salzburg. For years Krauss had shared the majority of the Festival performances with Bruno Walter. But in December 1934 he left the Vienna State Opera to succeed Wilhelm Furtwängler in Berlin, and with this move he also gave up Salzburg for the time being. In the years following, Toscanini was the reigning monarch in Salzburg. In 1935 he created sensations with his performances of *Fidelio* and *Falstaff;* in 1936 followed Wagner's *The Mastersingers of Nuremberg,* and in 1937 Mozart's *The Magic Flute.* Of course, the stringent discipline he imposed in rehearsal, his fiery temperament and his proverbial belief in his own wisdom led to constant friction with orchestra and management. But always people finally gave in: the Maestro had to be kept at Salzburg at all costs. On 1 June 1936, when Toscanini was once again showing his displeasure, Bruno Walter wrote to him:

> I can't imagine Salzburg without you. Salzburg needs you, we all need you. I know that your reasons are valid, but I am equally certain that the failure of Kerber or others is just part of the casual Austrian manner — this is without question unacceptable, but it is, I assure you, in no sense a token of ill will, and certainly does not imply a lack of

sympathy for your work or disrespect towards you personally. I beg you to let me know what must be done to satisfy you, and I will take it upon myself to ensure that it is done . . . You know better than I do, particularly after the events of last summer, that Salzburg is perhaps art's last existing sanctuary from the political world. Don't leave us in the lurch – I can only repeat, we need you.[30]

Salzburg was anything but a 'sanctuary from the political world.' Those who came in droves from all over did so not only to admire Toscanini's conducting, but also, like the Maestro himself, to demonstrate their faith in Austria and their belief that it must remain politically independent. Salzburg was full of visiting celebrities: Crown Prince Umberto of Italy, the Duke of Windsor, the wife of Winston Churchill, the mother and son of President Roosevelt, Marlene Dietrich. Public lectures were given by Thornton Wilder, Sacha Guitry and Thomas Mann. The press was directed to write in ecstatic tones of the Festival's many triumphs. The actual number of visitors (increasing annually) and the names of prominent people (showing greater exclusivity from year to year) were used to demonstrate that the Festival was going from strength to strength. Stefan Zweig in his *The World of Yesterday* (*Die Welt von Gestern*) described Salzburg as the 'artistic shrine of Europe'[31] and – at least to all appearances during those few weeks of summer – an 'Isle of the Blessed.' In his autobiography, *Als wär's ein Stück von mir,* Carl Zuckmayer wrote that after 1933 'the Salzburg fairy-tale lasted for another half-decade.'[32] Its fame and glory were expected to take people's minds off the appalling economic conditions, the uncertain political situation and, most of all, the constant threat of Anschluss.

Max Reinhardt once said, 'The best thing about these Festival summers is that each one could be the last. You can taste transience.'[33] He had applied for American citizenship in 1935, and from then on came to Salzburg just once a year to touch up his *Faust* and *Everyman* productions. It is true that he had new plans for 1938: a production of Johann Strauss' operetta *Die Fleder-*

*maus* under Herbert von Karajan, and a new staging of Hofmannsthal's *The Salzburg Great Theatre of the World* (*Das Salzburger
große Welttheater*). Toscanini was planning to conduct Wagner's
*Tannhäuser.*

But things turned out differently. On 12 February 1938
Chancellor Schuschnigg met Hitler on the Obersalzberg near the
Austrian border. He hoped to make concessions and thereby preserve the independence of the Austrian state. Two days later, on
14 February, Reinhardt telegraphed Toscanini's daughter Wally
from Hollywood: 'From here events in Austria are still difficult to
interpret, but many experts think the situation serious. May I
presume on our friendship to beg you to let me know in good time
your father's intentions and any definite decisions he makes, as I
should like my own dispositions to accord with his. Devotedly,
Max Reinhardt.'[34]

On 16 February Toscanini sent a telegram to the Festival
management and to the Provincial Governor Dr Rehrl: 'The present political events in Austria force me to cancel my engagements
at the Salzburg Festival. Arturo Toscanini.'[35] From Salzburg
attempts were made to change Toscanini's mind, urging him to
await clarification of the situation by the Austrian Foreign Ministry. But Toscanini, as always, remained firm in the face of fascism.
To Bruno Walter he sent a telegram on 21 February, stating
characteristically: 'My decision is final, albeit painful. I am capable
of only one way of thinking and acting. I hate compromise. I have
chosen the path of honesty and always will – that is what life is
about for me. Sincerely Arturo Toscanini.'[36] Immediately following the entry of Hitler's troops into Austria on 12 March 1938,
and the proclamation of the 'Law pertaining to the Reunion of
Austria with the German Reich' (Gesetz über die Wiedervereini-
gung Österreichs mit dem Deutschen Reich) on 13 March, a great
deal changed for Salzburg and its Festival. 'There was not a
moment's delay in starting a campaign against everything that was
considered un-German.'[37] Austria's only experience of a public
book-burning occurred in the Residenzplatz in Salzburg on 30
April. Then on 6 May the newspapers reported that Reinhardt's

property Leopoldskron had been confiscated on the grounds that its 'private ownership was inimical to both the State and the national interest.' However, Hitler's adjutant, Captain Wiedemann, reported that the Führer later ordered 'the immediate return of all personal possessions to the former owner of Leopoldskron, Professor Max Reinhardt.'[38]

On 12 May 1938 the Cultural Press Association of the German Government (Kulturpolitische Pressekonferenz) issued a directive: 'It is a matter of urgency that we pay far more attention to the Salzburg Festival than in previous years.' Clearly the Third Reich now intended to use all the distinction and aura of the Festival for its own propaganda purposes. In the record of this session of the Association we read further 'that Jews must no longer be permitted to dominate the Festival programme. Whilst stress should be laid on German values, it is equally important to emphasize the international character of the Festival. There must be full press coverage of attendance by visitors from abroad . . . The Salzburg Festival is to be treated as the most important in the immediate future.'[39] The following report on the programme appeared in the *Salzburger Volksblatt* on 11 July, just two weeks before the opening of the Festival:

> Regarding the performance of plays, the repertoire has been completely re-thought. A definite change of direction was required here. The new Festival wants no truck with *Everyman*,[40] or the existing *Faust* production, which has so little to do with the authentic *Faust*. We shall be seeing *Egmont*, that prelude to the liberation of a nation; and also Kleist's *Amphitryon*, that clear proof of how a superficial French comedy can be deepened by a German master to reveal a nobler humanity and truly Olympian serenity. These specimens of German theatrical art will be created for us by Heinz Hilpert and Erich Engel.[41]

The new rulers accused 'the Jews and the clerical party of misusing culture for their business interests: the Jews turned it into cash, the clerical party reduced it to a tourist attraction . . . Salzburg has had a false Jewish-cum-cosmopolitan atmosphere, but the stage will now be held by Germanic ideals in all their perfection.'[42] The musical offerings would be: several orchestral concerts, *Don Giovanni*, *The Marriage of Figaro*, *Fidelio* and *Tannhäuser*. The Festival opened with a performance of *The Mastersingers of Nuremberg*, conducted by Wilhelm Furtwängler. The other conductors would be Hans Knappertsbusch, Karl Böhm and Vittorio Gui. The opening performance on 23 July was attended by Joseph Goebbels, Edmund Glaise-Horstenau, Reich Governor (Reichsstatthalter) Arthur Seyss-Inquart and Area Commander (Gauleiter) Rainer, the last now given charge of the Salzburg Festival by the new Statutes. Thus was ushered in the new era at Salzburg.

There was a complete change of ethos. From the cast lists of 1938 to 1944, it is easy to work out who had gone, who had stayed, the latter either 'doing their duty' or simply furthering their careers. Artists of stature still participated and ensured performances of high quality. But the flavour which Jews bring to art was missing in performance, and there were no Jews in the audience either. The Germans had excluded them from both functions, and not all the art of Böhm, Knappertsbusch and Clemens Krauss could prevent the Festival from losing in status. It had been created as something 'Austrian,' but once Salzburg had become simply a small town in the Ostmark, it was no longer a match for Bayreuth, where Hitler played host to the world.

Salzburg had more or less to begin from scratch in 1945, and in getting underway again only shortly after the end of the war provided further evidence of the Austrian will to survive. At first it could boast very few prominent artists: these had to be people who had remained in the country but were not incriminated by a Nazi past. Within a few years, however, the famous returned, and with them Salzburg's former glory. The misrule of the thirties had shown how especially vulnerable an institution of the rank of the Salzburg Festival was. But like the new Bayreuth, it rose phoenix-like from the ashes, perhaps to teach us that art outlives dictators.

## NOTES

1. Cf. Max Reinhardt, "Denkschrift zur Errichtung eines Festspielhauses in Hellbrunn," 1917. Max-Reinhardt-Nachlaß in der Theatersammlung der Österreichischen Nationalbibliothek Wien. Sign.: Re 30/679/3.

2. In 1918 Max Reinhardt (1873-1943), Richard Strauss (1864-1949) and Franz Schalk (1863-1931) were elected to the Board of Artistic Advisers (Kunstrat) by the Patrons of the Salzburg Festival Theatre (Salzburger Festspielhausgemeinde), a body constituted in 1917. The existing members of the Board were joined in 1919 by Hugo von Hofmannsthal (1874-1929) and Alfred Roller (1864-1935).

3. On the subject of Franz Rehrl (1890-1947) see Wolfgang Huber (ed.), *Franz Rehrl. Landeshauptmann von Salzburg. 1922-1938* (Salzburg: SN-Verlag, 1975).

4. See *Salzburger Volksblatt,* 20 July 1931.

5. The 'Stagione d'Opera Italiana' of La Scala Milan was presented by the impresario Max Sauter-Falbriad with Arturo Lucon as musical director and Mario Ghisalberti as producer. Between 25 July and 7 August 1931, the company performed Rossini's *The Barber of Seville,* Donizetti's *Don Pasquale* and Cimarosa's *The Secret Marriage.*

6. Report of the Patrons of the Festival Theatre to the Salzburg City Council on 2 November 1931. Archiv der Salzburger Festspiele, Salzburg.

7. Minutes of a meeting of the Board of the Patrons of the Salzburg Festival, 9 November 1931. Verwaltungsarchiv Wien. Sign.: 3392-I.

8. Ibid.

9. *Salzburger Volksblatt,* 2 October 1931.

10. Cf. "Festspiele. Ein Gespräch mit Max Reinhardt" in: Erwin Kerber (ed.), *Ewiges Theater. Salzburg und seine Festspiele* (Munich: R. Piper, 1935).

11. See Fred K. Prieberg, *Musik im NS-Staat* (Frankfurt am Main: Fischer, 1982).

12. Ibid., pp. 41f.

13. The Thousand Mark Visa was abolished on 24 August 1936 by the 'Law concerning travel to Austria' (Gesetz über den Reiseverkehr mit Österreich).

14. Minutes of the 'Kulturpolitische Pressekonferenz' on 1 July 1937. Bundesarchiv Koblenz. Sign.: ZSg 02-62.

15. Copy. Lektorat zur Förderung des Deutschtums (signed Oskar Jölli) to

the Reich Chamber of Culture (Reichskulturkammer), Berlin-Charlottenburg, 28 April 1934. Bundesarchiv Koblenz. Sign.: R55-1184.

16. Wilhelm Rode was to sing Pizarro in Beethoven's *Fidelio,* and Sigrid Onegin Orpheus in Gluck's *Orpheus and Eurydice;* Eugen Klöpfer was to take the title-role in Goethe's *Faust.*

17. *Neues Wiener Journal,* 17 July 1933.

18. *Die Stunde,* 20 July 1933.

19. Richard Strauss was at this time President of the Reich Chamber of Music (Reichsmusikkammer); Werner Krauss was Vice—President of the Reich Chamber of Theatre (Reichstheaterkammer).

20. Letter from Theo Habicht to Joseph Goebbels, Munich, 7 May 1934. Bundesarchiv Koblenz. Sign.: R 55-1184.

21. Funk, State Secretary in the Reich Ministry for Public Education and Propaganda, to Richard Strauss, Berlin, 25 May 1934. Bundesarchiv Koblenz, Sign.: R 55-1184.

22. Franz Hadamowsky, *Richard Strauss und Salzburg* (Salzburg: Residenz Verlag, 1964), p. 52.

23. Letter from Richard Strauss to the President of the Festival, Heinrich Baron Puthon, Bayreuth, 2 August 1934. Archiv der Salzburger Festspiele, Salzburg.

24. Heinrich Kralik, *Richard Strauss. Weltbürger der Musik* (Vienna: Wollzeilen Verlag, 1963), p. 302.

25. Press reports of 6 June 1933 revealed that Toscanini had finally decided that he could no longer conduct at Bayreuth. Richard Strauss conducted the performances of *Parsifal* in his place. See Harvey Sachs, *Toscanini. Eine Biographie* (Munich: R. Piper, 1980), pp. 308-313.

26. Letter from Richard Strauss to Stefan Zweig, 17 June 1935. Quoted in Fred K. Prieberg, *Musik im NS-Staat,* op. cit., p. 207 and p. 423, n. 7.

27. Toscanini had refused to conduct the fascist 'Giovinezza' anthem at a memorial concert for Giuseppe Martucci given in Bologna in May 1931. A pro-fascist group thereupon physically assaulted him. The incident received international attention and acutely embarrassed the Mussolini regime. Toscanini refused to conduct in Italy from then on.

28. Harvey Sachs, "Salzburg, Hitler und Toscanini. Unbekanntes Briefmaterial aus den dreißiger Jahren," *Neue Zeitschrift für Musik,* vol. 14, nos. 7/8 (1987), 18.

29. Harvey Sachs, *Toscanini. Eine Biographie,* op. cit., p. 300.

30. Ibid., p. 339.

31. Stefan Zweig, *Die Welt von Gestern. Erinnerungen eines Europäers*

(Frankfurt am Main: Fischer, 1987), p. 396.

32.  Carl Zuckmayer, *Als wär's ein Stück von mir* (Stuttgart: Lizenzausgabe für die Evangelische Buchgemeinde, 1966), p. 72.

33.  Ibid., p. 72.

34.  Telegram from Max Reinhardt to Wally Toscanini, Hollywood, 14 February 1938, quoted in: Harvey Sachs, *Salzburg, Hitler und Toscanini*, op. cit., p. 20.

35.  Telegram from Arturo Toscanini to the Festival management and to Landeshauptmann Dr. Franz Rehrl, New York, 16 February 1938, quoted in Harvey Sachs, *Salzburg, Hitler und Toscanini*, op. cit., p. 20.

36.  Telegram from Arturo Toscanini to Bruno Walter, New York, 21 February 1938, quoted in Harvey Sachs, *Salzburg, Hitler und Toscanini*, op. cit., p. 22. The documents quoted in notes 34, 35 and 36 are held by the New York Library and Museum of the Performing Arts and were published for the first time by Harvey Sachs.

37.  Gert Kerschbaumer, *Faszination Drittes Reich. Kunst und Alltag der Kunstmetropole Salzburg* (Salzburg: Otto Müller, 1988), p. 94.

38.  Attestation signed by Capt. (retd) Wiedemann, Berlin, 24 November 1938. Bundesarchiv Koblenz. Sign.: NS 10-118.

39.  Record of the 'Kulturpolitische Pressekonferenz' session held on 12 May 1938. Bundesarchiv Koblenz. Sign.: ZSg 102-62.

40.  The Salzburg Festival was initiated on 22 August 1920 with a performance of Hugo von Hofmannsthal's *Everyman* (Jedermann). The work was again performed in 1921, and then annually from 1926 to 1937. Since 1946 it has been continuously part of the programme.

41.  *Salzburger Volksblatt*, 11 July 1938.

42.  Gert Kerschbaumer, *Faszination Drittes Reich,* op. cit., p. 115.

# The Anschluss of the Film Industry after 1934

## Gerhard Renner

My interest in the medium of film grew out of research into the culture of the thirties and forties, the era in which artists found that they were facing a moral crisis. The centre of my concern was the literary market, especially the problems confronting Austrian authors in the German book market.[1] In delving into this matter, I discovered – as banal as it may seem – that these problems were not restricted to the literary field, but applied to all the arts which needed a larger market to survive.

One of these arts was the film. The film industry, understandably, had a different economic base in different countries. Everything depended on the size of the market in which the films could be distributed. Whereas the silent film had been practically an international medium, Austria soon discovered that the advent of the sound film limited its motion pictures essentially to German-speaking countries, or at least to those with a large German-speaking minority. But Austria by itself was too small a market for film-making to be economically viable, and box-office receipts did not match enormously increased costs of production. There were too few cinemas and too few filmgoers. The capital which was essential for the creation of sound-film studios could be obtained only with the greatest of difficulty. Sascha, a well-established company, took over the former Vita Studios in Vienna in 1932, but they had to call on the German company Tobis AG to finance renovation and modernization. Tobis, which had begun as a company patenting sound-films, became within a very short time the largest film-production company in Germany.

In 1933 Tobis gained possession of one half of the capital stock of the Sascha company, and the most important Austrian film company was from then called Tobis Sascha Filmindustrie AG. The person responsible for the immediate success of the new company was the Jewish lawyer Oskar Pilzer. Oddly enough, Pilzer has been completely overlooked by Austrian film historians. Born in 1882, he received his Doctor of Laws degree from the University of Vienna, and worked from 1913 as a lawyer in industry and public finance. Except for a brief interruption, he managed the Sascha company from 1932 to 1936. From 1933 on, he and his brothers (known as the 'Pilzer Group') owned half the share capital of Tobis-Sascha. After the Anschluss, the Pilzer brothers emigrated via Paris to the U.S.A.[2] Little more is known about them.

Unlike its silent films, Austrian sound films could live off the Austrian theatrical and musical traditions, and this promised a substantial development of the industry.[3] In 1933, Willi Forst's film about Franz Schubert, *Leise flehen meine Lieder,* was an international success. Forst had written the screen-play together with Walter Reisch. The film's producer, Gregor Rabinowitsch, had worked for the German film company UFA in Berlin until 1933 and then, like Reisch, emigrated to Austria, giving up all film work in Germany. Forst, on the other hand, continued to work in Germany as well as Austria. *Leise flehen meine Lieder* created the highly successful genre known as the 'Viennese film,' of which *Maskerade* might be considered the best example.[4] The scene appeared to be set for Austrian films to enjoy a huge international success. Indeed, film historians have tended in retrospect to view the Austrian cinema of the thirties almost entirely as a success story. But they fail to note the other side of the coin: the Austrian film industry became willy-nilly caught up in National Socialist film policy, and this had serious consequences for its independence.[5] It was in this same year, 1933, that Goebbels made his first attempts to gain control of the German film industry.[6] His first act was to segregate film artists and technicians along ideological and racial lines: one could hardly expect emigrants who had fled Germany for Austria and other countries now to be allowed to re-enter Nazi Germany via the medium of the film. This Nazi film legislation clearly affected other film industries besides that of Germany, namely, Austrian, Czech, Hungarian and, to a certain extent, American.

## The Control of Scripts and Casting

Early in 1934, a new Motion Picture Law (Lichtspielgesetz) was passed in Germany, giving legal status and new powers to the so-called Reich Film Dramaturge, a post in the Ministry of Propaganda since November 1933. The position was held by Willi Krause, a former editor of *Der Angriff,* the Berlin newspaper of the National Socialist Party. It was his job to examine screenplays submitted by film producers to determine whether they were compatible with the provisions of the new Motion Picture Law.[7] All films had to be approved by the Reich Film Dramaturge if they were to have any chance of being passed by the Board of Film Censors (Filmprüfstelle). The Austrians, with an eye to the German market, also had to worry about these regulations, and tried to get Austrian production plans examined by the Reich Film Dramaturge in the same way as the German ones. In discussions with Germany primarily devoted to mutual film import quotas, the Association of Austrian Film Producers (Bund der Filmindustriellen Österreichs) felt obliged to raise the question of having Austrian films inspected. The Austrians obtained this permission, and passed off their success as the result of their negotiating skills. However, it soon became known that the result of the negotiations was, in fact, an agreement to demands made by the Reich Chamber of Film (Reichsfilmkammer).[8] Nazi control over Austrian film production was not restricted to the contents, but involved the casting too. As early as 1934 the aim was to keep emigrants, who were numerous, out of Austrian films. The agreement on German-Austrian film exchange, which had been renewed every year since the end of the 1920s, did not mention the matter in so many words. But there was a memo to the effect that: "the production of films with German nationals and German firms banned from participating in film production in Germany is inadvisable. This also applies in general to all non-German persons and firms previously employed in the German film industry but no longer granted this right."[9]

The Austrians leading the negotiations had thus left all the prominent Germans who had emigrated to Austria more or less in the lurch. The Vienna Chamber of Commerce deeply regretted the loss of highly qualified personnel 'because it is precisely among these emigrés that so much in the way of talent and international reputation is to be found.'[10] The negotiators also sacrificed those Austrian actors and directors who had worked in Berlin before 1933, and had now re-emigrated to Austria. Austrian Jews who had remained in Austria – in later discussions referred to as 'native non-Aryans' (bodenständige Nichtarier) – were not, or at least not yet, affected by these negotiations. Soon, Austrian film producers were to have great difficulty getting scenarios and cast-lists approved. Whereas in Hungarian films even the leading actors could be Jews, with Austrian films there were objections to a Jew being third cameraman. It gradually became almost impossible to employ Jewish film people in any capacity whatsoever. It was no longer just the large number of German Jewish emigrés who were to be eliminated from the film industry, but also the native Austrian Jews.

### Austria 'Imports' Germany's Nazi Legislation

The Nazi film administration very quickly produced measures to control casting. Most of these measures dated back to the Weimar Republic, but they were now given more force. In the long term the most important of these measures was the one referring to the Quota Office (Kontingentstelle), an agency which during the Weimar Republic had served as a registering office for foreign films. It now classified films into 'German' and 'foreign.' However, the classification did not refer simply to the country in which the film was produced. For a film to be accepted as 'German,' it was necessary for the writer of the script, the composer of the music, the producer, the director and most of the cast to be Germans.

Under the terms now obtaining, a 'German' was defined as a person of German (excluding Jewish) descent possessing German citizenship. These requirements had to be fulfilled if a film was to be shown in Germany under the heading 'German film'; in all other cases the distributors were forced to pay enormous 'quota-fees' (Kontingentgebühren). This produced a simple method of excluding Jews from film-work in Germany, and within a very short time in Austria as well.[11]

It is unclear whether the above regulations applied to Austrian films in 1934. But they were certainly incorporated in the German-Austrian film-trade agreement which was renewed in 1935. There it was stipulated that Jews were to be barred from participation in all Austrian films intended for the German market, which meant 90% of Austrian annual film production. No similar restrictions were imposed on films not intended for showing in Germany. And it must be noted that no express reference was made to extras, musicians, technicians and similar employees who did not actually appear in the film.[12]

## Finding a Line of Argument

In 1934 a number of individuals, among them the director Richard Oswald, who had emigrated to London, lodged protests against the exclusion of emigrants from film work. But once the trade agreement of 1935 had been signed, Austrian film policy came under increasing pressure to conform. Parts of the Austrian press and certain political functionaries, as well as the existence of a Nazi film policy, forced the Ministry of Trade and Commerce to outline a specifically Austrian film policy. In a memorandum, Egon Lanske, who was responsible to the Ministry for everything connected with the film industry, reported on developments after 1934 and contrasted these with the original German demands.[13] These latter were defined as follows:

— observance of the 'Aryan Clause' (Arierparagraph) for the entire cast and crew;

- closing down of all film production not intended for the German market (i.e., banning all so-called 'independent' films);
- acquisition of the major holding in Tobis-Sascha (this final point being of the utmost significance).

Lanske compared the German regulations with what the Austrians had been able to achieve at the negotiating table. He stated that the 'Aryan Clause' would not be applied to extras or technical staff. He also wanted it to be possible for native Austrian Jews – not for emigrants, since that would have been impossible – to work in capacities other than as extras or technical staff. The segregation that had already been made into 'native' and 'non-native' Jews (terms which referred to Austrian and foreign Jews respectively) may have given Lanske a certain latitude, but it did not represent a genuine political alternative.

Lanske attached particular importance to the fact that, since its Austrian shareholders were the Jewish Pilzer brothers, non-Aryan influence on Tobis-Sascha had been preserved. On this point the Austrian administration had in fact managed to contain Nazi German expansion, but pressure soon became too strong to resist. Lanske pointed out the potential economic effect on the film industry and its large number of employees. He feared that any embargo on films intended for the German market would create stagnation in the Austrian film industry. He tried to curb his annoyance at harshly critical newspaper reports. From his point of view it was obvious that 'continuing to produce films for Germany would produce discontent among about twenty non-Aryans, who would find themselves out of work and would naturally want to see changes made which would disadvantage the non-Jews.' Lanske used two central arguments. First, it was important to follow Nazi German film policy in order to maintain the economic viability of the Austrian film industry. Secondly, he stressed the promotional value to Austria of internationally successful films, which could hardly be produced without German capital. Nonetheless, he tried to make clear that he was not advocating total acquiescence in the Nazi German demands, and he mentioned in this context – to a certain extent rightly – the continuance of Jewish influence in Tobis-Sascha against the wishes of Germany.

At the end of 1935 this line of argument came to lose its basis in fact, and the room for manoeuvre became more and more restricted. There was no longer any trace of compromise with the Nazi film bureaucracy, as had occurred in the watering down of the 'Aryan Clause' in favour of Jews of Austrian nationality. The inspection of Austrian film production was conducted through a semi-institutional body, known in the jargon of the Reich Chamber of Film as the Otzoup Combine (Kombination Otzoup). What had happened was that the National Socialists who had fled to Germany were now back, with the intention of controlling the casting of Austrian films and ensuring the total exclusion of Jews. This was done from within a German film company, Otzoup and Gaik, which had been set up for precisely that purpose.[14] It was now impossible to give work to either a Jewish actor or a Jewish extra.

In the second half of 1936, the Nazi film bureaucracy was to deal a further severe blow to the Austrian film industry, which had already lost a good deal of its autonomy.

## The Removal of the Pilzer Brothers

It was in 1934 that Tobis in Germany made its first attempts to gain the majority shareholding of the Austrian Tobis-Sascha company.[15] Because of heavy investments in its studios, Tobis-Sascha had large debts and was faced with the need to increase its capital. Its plan was to consign one-sixth of its shares to the Dutch parent company of Tobis (Germany), two-sixths to Pilzer, and the remaining 50% to Tobis (Germany). The Pilzer Group acted to prevent the German company from becoming the major shareholder, but an arrangement to have the rights of the Dutch company controlled by Tobis (Germany) was still effected. The whole transaction turned out badly. The Austrian Chancellor's Office allowed an increase in capital, but insisted that 50% of the shares remain in Austrian hands. Tobis (Germany) wanted to fulfill the Government's conditions, but tried to exclude Pilzer. The company was informed by Fritz Hirt – who at the time was working for the Waldheim-Eberle printing house and later became the managing director of Tobis-Sascha and Wien-Film – that permission had been refused because of the attitude of the Pilzer brothers. They had sought Government protection against the major shareholder, Tobis (Germany), because that company refused to countenance their – as Hirt put it – 'pure' Austrian films, i.e., films made by emigrants. Tobis declared that Pilzer had acted from 'selfish motives' – without specifying – and stated its intention of ceasing to cooperate with Pilzer. The Austrian Creditanstalt Bank and its Governor, Josef Joham, were used to find some other way of eliminating Pilzer. The plan was to get the Creditanstalt to call in the loans which it had made to Tobis-Sascha. This was thought a possible course because the bank had arranged to turn the loans into shares if during the period of the loans the Pilzer brothers withdrew from managing the company. But there was an obstacle to the plan, in that Pilzer's contract as manager of Tobis-Sascha ran until June 1936, and the Creditanstalt insisted on postponing the step until the expiry of that contract. Nonetheless, from the point of view of the Nazis, bent on expansion, prospects had never been better. This was because Austrian film producers were in an impossible financial situation as a result of restrictive German foreign exchange regulations. It now seemed relatively simple to harvest the results of several years of pressure.

In September 1936 Lanske hoped to increase the number of films intended for the German market. He was of the opinion that the 'Aryan Clause' was being applied with such rigidity that there should now be some obvious compensation. He therefore called for an increase in the number of Austrian films which could be distributed in Germany. But this was to become a non-starter when, during the fall of 1936, insurmountable difficulties in transferring revenues back to Austria made it a hopeless task to try and increase production for the German market.

## Technical Details

The proceeds from the showing of German films in Austria could be transferred to Germany without any difficulty whatsoever, but this was by no means the case the other way about. In 1935 this had proved less of a problem, because Austrian earnings from film distribution in Germany were more or less the same as German earnings from film distribution in Austria. So it was possible to settle any small sum owing to Tobis-Sascha internally. However, in 1936 Austria was owed five million schillings, and it looked like reaching seven million in 1937. Production was expected to come to a standstill by September 1936. The high box-office receipts in Germany during the 1930s occurred in part because the number of Austrian films distributed there increased, and in part because Austria produced a number of big successes. On the other hand, German receipts plummeted in Austria, perhaps because there was no 'grand German film,' but perhaps too because attempts were made to get people to boycott German films in Austria. However, in October 1936 it was possible to transfer only 50% of receipts for Austrian films, the rest being 'frozen' in Germany. To quote several Austrian film companies, they were 'swimming in marks and in pawn with schillings.'

From the German point of view there were two ways to balance the accounts. One was to try to get more German films into the Austrian market, and the other was to relocate part of Austria's film production facilities in Berlin. Such a move could easily be financed with the frozen assets which had accumulated in Germany. As an amusing irony, the only German producer who was ready and willing to make use of these assets was Serge Otzoup, the very man who had established his Berlin film company as a kind of watchdog over Austrian film production.

Towards the end of 1936 the Germans let it be known for the first time that they would block any attempt by the Austrians to improve facilities for the transfer of funds, and that one of the reasons for this was the continuing Jewish share in Tobis-Sascha. During negotiations in Berlin about problems of transfer, the

Reich Chamber of Film informed the Austrian delegation that there were still ill feelings about the refusal to approve a capital increase to Tobis (Germany), since this would have given it a decisive influence in the management of Tobis-Sascha. The decision had been made about two years earlier, and the issue had not been raised since. The Reich Chamber of Film now chose to avoid dealing with Oskar Pilzer because he was a 'non-Aryan,' and preferred to negotiate with Lanske because – the pretense was – he represented the Austrian Government.

A piece of confidential information, which probably originated with Lanske himself, is couched in very clear language and differs markedly from earlier statements. What this document shows is that the man in charge of film policy in Austria had accommodated himself to the new situation. He writes of the earlier attempt by Tobis (Germany) to gain possession of the majority shareholding in the Austrian company, and of the blocking action by the Austrian Chancellery. 'Now, however,' he reports, 'there is a new effort being made . . . taking account of the more restrictive foreign-exchange policy which Germany is operating.' He quotes information received from Josef Joham, according to which, 'There can be no solution to the transfer problem for the Austrian film industry, especially for Tobis-Sascha, whilst the Pilzer Group remains essentially in control of this latter company.' The ownership of Tobis-Sascha is now clearly stated to be the stumbling block to solving the transfer problem.

In 1935, Lanske had prided himself on his partial responsibility for blocking the capital increase for Tobis (Germany), but now 'given the present situation,' he proposes 'a more conciliatory attitude.' His impression is that 'because of the cultural importance of the film industry . . . more voices in Austria are being heard publicly pleading for a reduction in non-Aryan influence.' Apparently, Oskar Pilzer had declared his willingness to vacate his position, and at the end of 1936 he gave up the post of Chairman of the 'Gesamtverband der österreichischen Filmproduktion,' the umbrella organisation of the Austrian film industry. He had also expressed willingness to part with his shares, but as Lanske pointed out, 'as the law presently stands, there is no legal procedure which can be invoked against the Pilzer Group.'

Matters had now reached the stage where Tobis-Sascha was on the verge of bankruptcy. It had enormous frozen assets in Germany and no productions planned for 1937. The time was clearly ripe for the transaction proposed. Interest in taking over Tobis-Sascha was being expressed by the trust company 'Cautio,' run by Max Winkler, which was active behind the scenes in acquiring majority shareholdings in all the big German film companies on behalf of the Minister of Propaganda, Josef Goebbels. However, the take-over was not possible in 1936 because of existing foreign-currency regulations.

It was the Austrian Creditanstalt Bank which came to the rescue. The Bank found the financial proposition interesting 'since there were now special transfer measures which permitted the unfreezing of the German assets of Tobis-Sascha AG.' The Bank acted as an agent for Winkler, came to an agreement with Pilzer over the purchase of his shares, and then made a syndicate deal with Tobis (Germany). Although Tobis had once again failed to acquire a majority holding and was merely an equal partner with the Creditanstalt Bank, Winkler was now able to say with some satisfaction that Tobis-Sascha had been 'purged of Jewish influence' (entjudet). The deal led to changes among Tobis' Vienna distributors. Thus, in December 1936 the Dutch distributor 'Intertobis' declared its readiness to cede its two-thirds majority holding in Tobis' Austrian distributing company to the Tobis company in Berlin. Its stated reason was 'the exclusion of non-Aryans from all the Austrian companies run by Tobis.' As was pointed out, this was in fact for the sake of appearances, since the exclusion of non-Aryans 'would clearly look better if it were carried out by Tobis in Berlin than by Tobis in Holland.' As a result, the Jewish lawyer Wilhelm Grüss, who had hitherto represented the interests of Tobis (Germany) in Vienna, was forced to relinquish his post to Fritz Hirt.

## Conclusions

There were further developments following the German invasion of Austria in March 1938. Hermann Paul, director of Patria Films and now a member of the Nazi party as well as President of the umbrella 'Gesamtverband,' was appointed (by Egon Lanske, as it happens) to a newly created post making him in effect the overseer of the entire Austrian film industry (Generalbevollmächtigter der österreichischen Filmwirtschaft). This appointment led to a protest from Fritz Hirt, and the new Minister of Trade, Hans Fischböck, felt obliged to revoke it. Paul's removal from the post cannot obscure the fact that the annexation in March 1938 brought about a large-scale reshuffle only among film producers. Prominent actors and actresses had long been aware of the pressures to which film producers in Austria were being subjected, and even before the annexation had had to define where they stood with respect to the Nazi film industry. Important Austrian figures, like the film director and union official Heinz Hanus, continued to work in and for the Third Reich.

So, the annexation of the Austrian film industry had, at many levels and to varying degrees, already been completed before Hitler's troops entered Austria. A small number of Jewish producers had continued to make films after Jewish influence had been excluded from Tobis-Sascha. This had been possible – as became evident during the German debate about the 'Otzoup Combine' – only because they were prepared to align themselves more or less with Nazi policy on Austrian film production. That a number of them remained active right up to the political Anschluss is shown by the 1938 account sheets of Wien-Film, the Nazi heir to Tobis-Sascha. They list, for example, studio costs incurred by Jewish film companies as 'bad debts,' all of which – and the sums were considerable – had to be written off.

Austrian film policy after 1933 had been concerned primarily with producers and studios. This is explained by the fact that film-exchange agreements with Germany were still being signed in 1934 and 1935 – albeit in conjunction with government officials – by the top film organisations themselves. These organisations had reacted to Nazi film policy essentially in terms of business, but the Government had then had to defend resulting policy at a political level. Lanske had been inclined to play down the problem of 'non-Aryans' as marginal, and until 1936 his policy of accommodation seemed, at least in economic terms, successful. But by the end of the year it had led to total capitulation.

The success of Nazi film policy in Austria is, however, not simply a matter of economics. Many there had for years nurtured hopes of an Anschluss, and the attempt by the Corporate State (Ständestaat) to propagate the concept of an 'Austrian nation' or of 'Austrian man' was in the context of the 1930s artificial and out of touch with realities. A large part of the Austrian bureaucracy saw no alternative to Anschluss, and this state of mind suggested to the Nazis that they could pursue their policy quite cold-bloodedly without fear of serious resistance. Finally, whereas in Germany millions of marks flowed into the Nazi film industry, in Austria the film as a medium had traditionally received little or no support from leading Catholic conservative circles. It had merely served as a welcome opportunity for them to show their teeth in matters of censorship. For her misguided handling of the film industry Austria was to pay a high political price.

## NOTES

1. See Gerhard Renner, *Österreichische Schriftsteller und der National-sozialismus (1933-1940)* (Frankfurt am Main: Buchhändler-Vereinigung, 1986).

2. See Karl Hartl, "Die Situation im Wiener Film" in: *Wien 1938* (Vienna: Verein für Geschichte der Stadt Wien, 1978), pp. 273-276.

3. See Walter Fritz, *Geschichte des österreichischen Films* (Vienna: Bergland, 1969), pp. 118-136.

4. See Jerzy Toeplitz, *Geschichte des Films,* part 3 (Berlin: Henschel Verlag Kunst und Gesellschaft, 1979), p. 313; Jean Mitry, *Histoire du Cinéma,* part 4 (Paris: Jean-Pierre Delarge, 1980), p. 286.

5. Toeplitz, op. cit., p. 315.

6.  See Alexander Jason, *Handbuch des Films 1935/36* (Berlin: Hoppenstedt, 1935); Gerd Albrecht, *Nationalsozialistische Filmpolitik* (Stuttgart: Ferdinand Enke, 1969), pp. 1-27; Wolfgang Becker, *Film und Herrschaft* (Berlin: Volker Spiess, 1973), pp. 32-127.

7.  Becker, op. cit., pp. 76-85; Albrecht, op. cit., p. 23.

8.  The film industry was generally prepared to accept a certain degree of self-censorship, which it regarded as necessary for the security of its invested capital.

9.  Protokollnotiz, 1 March 1934. Österreichisches Staatsarchiv (ÖSta), Archiv der Republik (AdR), Bundesministerium für Handel und Gewerbe (BMHV) Z1. 92.825/34.

10. Letter from the Vienna Chamber of Trade and Commerce to the Trade Ministry, 15 September 1934. Östa, AdR, BMHV, Z1. 104.386-WP/34.

11. Jason, op. cit., p. 50 and pp. 64f.; Becker, op. cit., p. 70.

12. Agreement signed by the Federation of Cinematographic Industries in Austria (Bund der Filmindustriellen in Österreich) and the Federation of Film Producers (Verband der Filmindustrie) Berlin. ÖSta, AdR, BHMV, Z1. 94.825-WP/35.

13. Memorandum to the Federal Minister of Trade concerning Austrian film policy (Lanske), 10 May 1935. Östa, AdR, BMHV, Z1. 100.216-WPA/35.

14. See letters and notes from the German Chamber of Film (Reichsfilmkammer), Bundesarchiv Koblenz, R 56/I and R 56/VI; see also my essay in the volume *Hitlers Propagandisten in Österreich* (Salzburg: Otto Müller, 1988).

15. The following material is based on the archives of the Tobis Company, now deposited with the Bundesarchiv Koblenz, R 109/1; and also on the archives of the Federal Ministry of Trade previously cited.

# Austrian Theatre and the Corporate State

## John Warren

'A future theatre historian will have to dismiss this epoch with a few sad words.' So wrote the young Jura Soyfer in the Viennese newspaper *Sonntag* in 1937.[1] His judgment on dramatic talent in the thirties was shared by many contemporaries, both professional critics and observers like Musil.[2] But if those writers performed in the thirties do not measure up to the great Austrian tradition, their works reflect the problems, tensions and ambivalences of political life in the decade as perhaps at no other time in the history of the Austrian theatre. We see the authoritarian government of the years 1933 to 1938 trying to exercise control over the cultural life of the country, albeit not in so extreme a form as the cultural conformity (Gleichschaltung) insisted upon in the Nazi Reich; and although the Austrian government was able to use the theatre for its own ends, the confused state of Austrian loyalties continues to emerge from many of the key productions. I propose to look at four things: the relationship of the theatre to the political atmosphere prior to 1933; the means of control at the government's disposal; the ways in which the Corporate State (Ständestaat) used the theatre to assist it in its precarious position; the import but also the ambivalence of certain key productions.

It is clear that the extreme political tension of the inter-war years was reflected in Viennese theatrical life, if not as excitingly as in Berlin. To give a few examples: there was violent anti-Semitism in response to Schnitzler's *Reigen;* the Republican Defence Corps (Schutzbündler) had to mount guard for Toller's

*Hinkemann;* there were further anti-Semitic and racial protests at the performance of Krenek's *Jonny Strikes Up (Jonny spielt auf)*; protests and censorship marred performances of Zuckmayer's *The Captain of Köpenick (Der Hauptmann von Köpenick);* screenings of the film *All Quiet on the Western Front (Im Westen nichts Neues)* were banned. Of equal interest is audience reaction to features of the drama: the breathless suspense created by Hofmannsthal's beggar in *The Salzburg Great Theatre of the World (Das Salzburger große Welttheater)*, or the sense that Werfel had represented a proto-communist revolt in 'God's Kingdom in Bohemia' *(Das Reich Gottes in Böhmen)*. Theatre critics of left-wing and right-wing papers recount the same plot from different angles. An example of the way in which theatre could be experienced as the seismograph of bourgeois political opinion occurs in the observations of David Josef Bach, the critic of the *Arbeiter Zeitung,* reviewing Jules Romain's *Der Diktator* on 4 February 1927: there was great applause from an audience seeing what it wanted to see, 'namely a revolt being put down by one who then becomes a dictator.' Here we have to recall that the performance was given only months before the Vienna Law Courts were burned down, an act that intensified desire for the authoritarian government which would become fact in the Austrofascist Corporate State proclaimed by Dollfuss in 1934.

Two changes occurred in Viennese theatrical life in 1932. One was the departure for Berlin of Vienna's most dynamic, talented and progressive director, Rudolf Beer, who had been chosen by Max Reinhardt to take over his Berlin theatres; the other was the appointment of Hermann Röbbeling as Director of the two state theatres, the Burgtheater and the Akademietheater. With the departure of Beer the two theatres, which under his direction had enjoyed both artistic and financial success, reverted to the commercial plane; with the exception of one production by the young Otto Preminger, they made little further contribution to the artistic life of the capital.[3] Beer himself, who as a Jew was forced to leave Berlin in 1933, was unable to regain a foothold in a major Viennese theatre. To use Kraus' cruel and ill-judged words, he was one of the 'unfortunate rats' who 'stepped aboard the sinking ship'; and after suffering fearful ill-treatment at the hands of the anti-Semitic Viennese mob in 1938 he committed suicide. If Beer was a grievous loss, Röbbeling, who came to Vienna with the reputation for sound commercial judgment rather than artistic flair, was to prove the ideal director for a government intent on a theatre able to create an 'Austrian' image and have an influence on potential allies abroad. His appointment might well be seen by the dispossessed Wildgans as 'the victory of the Prater funfair over the spirit of the Burgtheater,'[4] but his services to the Corporate State went well beyond the call of duty.

In 1933 the so-called 'self-closure' of parliament allowed Dollfuss to begin restricting democracy, and on 1 May 1934 he proclaimed the authoritarian Corporate State. The former succession states and National Socialist Germany were hostile neighbours, but Austria also faced dissension within: it is not so much that there were disenfranchised socialists as that Austrians of all political persuasions felt themselves drawn towards the Nazi Reich, partly for reasons stretching back way before 1918, partly in response to the propaganda of the 'master race.' In an attempt to assert Austria's cultural independence the government tried to make theatre an instrument of its cultural policy.[5]

Even without a state policy on the arts, the pressure which could be exercised directly and indirectly on the theatre was considerable. In the first place the directorship of the two national theatres in Vienna was in the gift of the Ministry of Education and Culture, and thus a director wishing to keep his job was unlikely to ignore any hints he was given concerning repertoire; Röbbeling was by all accounts, including his own, a cautious man,[6] and so served his masters well. Secondly, theatre reviews were important to the government, which had the advantage of its own newspapers: the *Wiener Zeitung,* for example, provided good coverage of major productions, whilst Funder's *Die Reichspost* was fervently 'Christian and authoritarian' in tone. The bastion of the 'free liberal press,' the *Neue Freie Presse* had also come under government control, and in any case its readership consisted of people who essentially had to be supporters of government policy. The only left-wing critic of stature, David Josef Bach of the *Arbeiter Zeitung*, was silenced forever when every vestige of the culture of 'Red Vienna' was suppressed in February 1934. Thirdly, the government used Emergency Decrees[7] to indicate to theatres the direction they should take. That of 21 April 1933 exempted the state theatres (Bundes- und Landestheater) from entertainment tax provided that their repertoire was 'culturally or educationally valuable.' The arbiter of the 'value' of the repertoire, it is clear from the second such Decree of 26 January 1934, was 'the Federal Ministry of Education.' Clearly, at a time of high unemployment and economic stringency reducing the price of tickets by removing a tax could be decisive in whether a theatre had an audience or not.

This brings us to the fourth and single most important factor in 'back door' control of the repertoire, the power of what were known as the *Kunststellen*. These were cultural organizations supporting theatre and concert performances by purchasing tickets at block rates for their members. These *Kunststellen* had been established as early as 1919 on the basis of political, religious or employment interests. The largest such was that of the Social Democrats, but there were Christian Social, Civil Servants' and Jewish organizations. The two largest *Kunststellen* sold 1450 tickets daily. In the aftermath of February 1934 the government abolished the Social Democrat organization, which had been run by David Josef Bach, and created a National *Kunststelle* under Hans Brecka, the literary editor and theatre critic of *Die Reichspost* and organizer of the Christian Social *Kunststelle*. The government claimed that the new general organization, following the abolition of the Social Democrat one, was necessary 'in order not to lose the broad mass of workers whom the latter organization had educated into wanting the theatre.'[8] The remaining organizations were then amalgamated with the National *Kunststelle*, which was soon dispensing up to 2000 tickets per day.

However laudable the government's intention might have sounded, in practice it acquired enormous power over any theatre which needed a subsidized audience. The Patriotic Front reported that 'the National *Kunststelle* is all-powerful. Almost every theatre now has to present plays for inspection and approval before they can be performed. Any play not satisfying the *Kunststelle* cannot be performed.'[9] In the contract signed with the Theater in der Josefstadt the theatre agreed to send the text of any new play to the President of the *Kunststelle* five days before rehearsals began; if he rejected it, the *Kunststelle* would have no obligation to buy tickets. Together with the New Life Front (Frontwerk Neues Leben), an umbrella organization on the lines of the Italian *Dopolavoro* and the German *Kraft durch Freude,* the National *Kunststelle* was crucial to the government's attempt to centralize the whole of Austria's cultural and recreational life.

Some idea of the success achieved by Brecka's 'ticket agency' may be gained from a self-congratulatory article published in the *Wiener Zeitung* on 9 March 1938, three days before the Anschluss. Here we learn that at its inception in 1934 the National *Kunststelle* was run by five officials, who shared one telephone; in March 1938 there were sixty-four full-time officials, two thousand advisers and fifty-five telephones. It had raised the circulation of its information bulletin from ten thousand to fifty thousand copies, and it was providing over half a million subsidized tickets, ranging in price from 50 groschen to 4.50 schillings, per year. It had organized theatre visits for one thousand firms and had also issued 200,000 tickets to the socially disadvantaged. Special visits to the theatre were also arranged for the army, the police, the war-wounded and the unemployed: receiving tickets for as little as 30 groschen meant that they paid more for cloakroom charges! All this 'papering the house,' as it is called in England, can clearly have political implications. According to the *Wiener Zeitung* article, the *Kunststelle* saw its task as one of revitalizating the Viennese theatre and maintaining theatre as 'an important cultural factor.' What this meant in practice becomes clearer as we now look more closely at major theatrical productions in the Corporate State.

This process of politicizing the theatre started gradually and was largely opportunistic. Röbbeling's cultural activity, which became part of Austria's foreign policy, was a combination of ideal-ism and political circumstance. Soon after arriving in Vienna he gave a lecture to the League of Nations Association entitled 'The Role of the Theatre in Uniting the Nations' (Das Theater als völkerverbindender Faktor). The lecture was given on 21 February 1932, was broadcast by Austrian Radio and published as a pam-phlet. The lecture is highly rhetorical, drawing its ideals from the German humanist tradition, particularly from Goethe's idea of 'world literature.' It was thus highly suitable as an address to an association of the League of Nations, seeming a beacon of light in a dark and depressing age. One of the seeds planted was to reach fruition in Röbbeling's presentation between 1932 and 1938 of a cycle of major productions. Entitled 'Voices of the Nations in Drama' ('Stimmen der Völker im Drama'), the cycle was made up of fourteen plays from twelve countries.[10] It is doubtful whether there had been direct consultation with the Ministry, and the idea seems to owe more to his strategy for creating interesting publicity and a regular audience. But – as with his cycle 'Austrian Master-pieces' ('Österreichische Meisterwerke') – it is impossible to ignore the cycle's 'political' function within the cultural policy of the Corporate State.

This is very clear with the fourth play, 'The Hundred Days' (*Hundert Tage*), premièred at the Burgtheater on 22 April 1933, shortly after the meeting between Dollfuss and Mussolini in Rome on 13 April, when the latter had declared himself ready if need be to protect Austria's independence with force. Although this 'Napoleon' play, sketched out by Mussolini and written by For-zano, is a mediocre drama the performance by the great German actor Werner Krauss coupled with the clear political interest of the piece ensured its triumph. Following ideas he had expressed in his lecture about uniting nations, Röbbeling arranged for the third act of the play to be broadcast, and this throughout Italy as well as Austria. But this was also in keeping with Austria's foreign policy. Similarly, a special performance was put on for the visiting Italian Foreign Minister, Fulvio Suvich, and was followed by a reception at which government ministers and members of the diplomatic corps fraternized. This sort of social activity, and the concomitant press reports, became usual at all premières but was especially important in respect of countries where contacts needed refurbishment or there were treaties to be signed.[11] In such ways theatre was exploited by the Corporate State.

An attempt was made to re-establish contacts with Hungary by staging the 'Hungarian Faust,' Imre Madach's play 'The Tragedy of Mankind' (*Die Tragödie des Menschen*). Röbbeling later claimed that the renewed diplomatic contact and improved relations between the two countries were directly attributable to this gesture. And this significance was perceived at the time by Felix Salten, for example, who wrote in his review for the *Neue Freie Presse* on 24 January 1934: 'Röbbeling has achieved more than a mere production. By putting Imre Madach on the Viennese stage he has re-opened the door to Hungary which was closed in 1928.' Critics and public were not slow to understand the importance of such productions whether at the Burgtheater or elsewhere, and the foreign press played its part.[12] Similarly, no effort was spared by the Burgtheater in its production of 'The Undivine Comedy' (*Die ungöttliche Komödie*) by the Polish dramatist Count Zygmunt Krasinski. The theatre's leading actors, Werner Krauss and Ewald Balser, took the main roles. Such was the enthusiasm of the Poles for this restoration to the repertoire of a work by a Polish emigré that they awarded the translator, Csokor, a medal[13] (just as Mussolini had the previous year insisted on an interview with Werner Krauss and sent a private plane to fetch him).

In September 1936, as Austria's isolation became ever more apparent, the Comédie Française made a guest appearance at the Theatre Congress in Vienna, but the usual diplomatic gatherings did little to persuade the French that Austria was worth saving. Nor did performances of Shaw's *St Joan* (*Die Heilige Johanna*) influence the English. The critic Oskar Maurus Fontana certainly had high hopes. His review, headed 'Shaw's *St Joan* with Paula Wessely. Vienna, France and England at the Burgtheater,' began as follows: 'An Englishman has brought France's national heroine to life again, and a Viennese girl has produced a beautiful and moving portrayal of her. Three nations have combined their efforts to create a triumph . . .'[14] However, only a few weeks later a British Foreign Office memorandum from Chatfield to Vansittart made it clear that Britain was not prepared to go to war for Austria and that 'we should so inform France confidentially.'

Despite the great success of the Viennese coffee-house in the Austrian Pavilion at the Paris World Exhibition in June 1937, the visit of the Burgtheater failed to influence the French government. Schuschnigg had claimed that 'the Burgtheater was travelling to Paris as the ambassador of the major intellectual power that Austria is today.'[15] The (1931) production of Hofmannsthal's *Salzburg Great Theatre of the World* brought out all the elements of Othmar Spann's influence on Hofmannsthal – in fact, the ideal play to represent the Corporate State. Brecka, Stoessl and other right-wing critics had hailed it as a triumph in 1931, with only David Joseph Bach pointing out in a negative tone the true import of the piece. Despite the strongly right-wing ethos of French politics in the late thirties, with their tradition of anti-clericalism the French were unlikely to be impressed by the play. One by Schnitzler would have been more to French taste but, as Csokor pointed out, Schnitzler, the one name the French might have been expected to recognize, was not even listed among the Austrian writers and artists who had died in the previous thirty years.[16] Clearly the political role of literature had by now become an important concern of the Corporate State.

Stated simply, the development of authoritarian government in Austria from 1933 might be seen in the following terms: firstly the desire to discredit parliamentary democracy; then, after the 'battle for Vienna' in 1934, the need to win back the hearts of the Viennese; next the need to win the ideological struggle with National Socialism; and throughout to stress the importance of the Roman Catholic Church. Encouraged by the National *Kunststelle* and responding to the call for an 'Austria' ideology (see Staudinger in this volume), a large number of dramatists tried to produce plays to meet the needs of the moment. Yet it is also the case that the ambivalences and confused loyalties of these unhappy years were such that many of these works seem uncertain in their message and capable of a variety of interpretations.

To begin before the abolition of democratic government, Richard Duschinsky's 'Emperor Francis Joseph I of Austria' (*Kaiser Franz Josef der Erste von Österreich*), premièred on 24 January 1933, promised to be another of those historical costume dramas, so beloved of the Viennese, in which every Emperor and Archduke of Austrian history had in turn strutted across the stage of the Burgtheater. But those expecting another anodyne creation in the style of the prolific Hans Sassmann were in for a shock. Duschinsky, an actor at the Josefstadt theatre and a writer of minor dramas of contemporary life, had produced a form of historical drama which, as one critic put it, 'struck at the heart of our times.' Here was no sentimental picture of the traditional Viennese 'good old days,' but a rather bitter study of the final years of an Emperor who, although not particularly loved by his people, wants universal suffrage in the face of opposition from his aristocratic ministers, tries to control the militarism of his heir, Franz Ferdinand, and is finally bullied into a declaration of war. Key roles are assigned to the Social-Democrat leader Viktor Adler, to Karl Lueger, to Franz Ferdinand and to the leaders of the 'war party,' Berchtold and Hötzendorff.

The opening scene, set in a turbulent parliament of mixed nationalities, surprised and shocked by its violence, ending with the attack by the Social Democrat deputies and the calling in of the police. This and other such scenes in the play, set in the weeks following the violent disputes over Badeni's language reforms, now reinforced government propaganda that the Social Democrats should be blamed for everything and that parliamentary democracy was a mistake. Indeed, after the abolition of parliament the play was moved to the larger stage of the Volkstheater, where the violent parliamentary scenes could be shown to greater effect, and the work was now recommended for support by Brecka's Christian Social *Kunststelle* (*Die Reichspost,* 23 April 1933). Yet this aspect of the play was counterbalanced by the

figure of Dr Viktor Adler, sane, humane, fighting for universal
suffrage as a way of ending the nationality problems, and in Act
IV speaking out in favour of peace to such effect – Duschinsky had
used excerpts from original speeches – that, as David Josef Bach
reported, 'the actor could not continue, the whole house thun-
dered with applause. . . .'

Dealing with the themes of anti-Semitism, the distinction
between 'the people' and 'the nation' (Volk/Nation), reason of
state, social reform, problems of peace and war, this modest play
clearly caught the mood of the moment. The critics were able to
find in it those qualities which suited their own ends: the *Wiener
Zeitung* wrote of a 'triumph of Austrian acting'; the *Reichspost*,
making a virtue of necessity, saw 'the people's Emperor facing the
people's Mayor'; it was left to the socialist critic Bach to draw
attention to Adler's humanity, the message of peace from Adler
and the old Emperor, and Otto Preminger's arrangement of the
final curtain calls: 'It was intelligent of the producer, Dr Preminger, to allow Dr Adler to appear first alone and then alternately
with the Emperor and Dr Lueger.' Despite his tender years,
Preminger obviously had more feel for the needs of the moment
than most politicians.

It is worth returning to the other successful play of this
moment, the Mussolini/Forzano piece on Napoleon's 'hundred
days' (*Campo di Maggio/Hundert Tage*), whose impact on foreign
policy through its timely première on 22 April 1933 I have already
mentioned. A different matter is raised in considering why it was
necessary to adapt the original German translation by Geza
Herczeg, which had been used in the Weimar production of 1932.
The answer must be sought in Mussolini's close interest in Austria's internal affairs, as can be seen from the secret letters between himself and Dollfuss,[17] and in Röbbeling's being summoned
to Rome to discuss the projected production. Margaret Dietrich
has shown that Hans Sassmann's revised German text sharpens the
attack on parliamentary democracy.[18] Particularly telling were the
lines in which Napoleon justifies setting aside the constitution
(exactly as Dollfuss was planning to do). In the original German

translation of the speech in which Napoleon demands to be made dictator, there is no reference to the constitution; but in one of many changes, Sassmann put the following words into his mouth: 'I was able to abolish the constitution because a constitution is self-defeating as soon as it hinders the actions of those in government.' Here we must recall the historical moment: the Austrian parliament had been terminated and within a few weeks the Patriotic Front (Vaterländische Front), that 'union of all loyal Austrians transcending party boundaries,' would be proclaimed.

David Bach in the *Arbeiter Zeitung* pointed out the falsifications introduced into the original German text by Sassmann, whilst at the other end of the spectrum Hans Brecka praised the new version, specifically linking the play to the situation in Austria, and pointing out that Napoleon's dealings with his deputies ('six hundred fools' in Sassman's version) gave the work its contemporary relevance. Improving even on Sassmann, Brecka clearly approves of Dollfuss' quest for absolute power, stating that in parliament 'the dominance and right of expression of the many, of the all too many, inadequate deputies had led to the paralyzing of the one strong man. Only *one* man, the right man in the right place, can rescue the state in its hour of danger' (*Die Reichspost*, 23 April 1933).

A further and more direct form of government interference in the affairs of the theatre was the commissioned play. The 350th anniversary of the breaking of the Turkish siege of Vienna fell in May 1933. It was clearly time to play 'the Prince Eugene card' again and make him the focus of the celebrations (Türkenbefreieungsfeiern). Eugene had been used by Hofmannsthal during the 1914–1918 War, and he would again be the subject of a play, 'A Cavalry Song' (*Ein Reiterlied*), in 1937. Although not a native Austrian, Eugene of Savoy had, as a nineteen-year-old, been in those forces under Jan Sobieski that had chased the invaders from Vienna, and he had gone on to become Austria's most successful general and statesman.

Isabella Ackerl has documented the use made of the 1933 anniversary celebrations by all political parties,[19] but the group which stood to gain most was the right-wing paramilitary *Heimwehr* under its leader Prince Starhemberg. Hans Sassmann, whose historical 'confections' had dominated one aspect of the Burgtheater repertoire in the late twenties and early thirties, was commissioned to write a play, and his *Prince Eugene of Savoy* was premièred at the Burgtheater on 10 June 1933. As background there were *Heimwehr* rallies, first at Schönbrunn and then at Krems, where Starhemberg, a direct descendant of the garrison commander during the siege of Vienna, spoke of a 'rebirth of Austrian pride and the fight for the Great German Reich (das große deutsche Reich).' He also spoke of the fight against 'the red terror and the brown pestilence.'

It was not easy for right-wing critics to extract political capital out of what was a rather dull play, but Brecka in *Die Reichspost* made much of the storming of Belgrade, where flag-waving and the popular Austrian 'song of Prince Eugene' created what he called 'the mood of Austria.' David Bach of the *Arbeiter Zeitung,* perspicacious as ever, pointed out that the true intention behind plays of this kind was 'to refurbish the old tradition and bring a glorious past back into contemporary consciousness.' This did, in fact, become government policy, and Austrian history was soon to be combed for 'great Austrians.' These were to confirm that Austria represented a second (in Starhemberg's words) 'Great German Reich,' and so create hope for the *Heimwehr* vision that 'the Eastern Marches have awoken' ('die Ostmark ist erwacht').

A new production by Ernst Lothar of Grillparzer's *King Ottokar's Rise and Fall (König Ottokars Glück und Ende)*, premièred at the Burgtheater on 31 October 1933, was very much in line with the government's requirements. This historical tragedy, showing a Bohemian tyrant brought low by the first great Austrian hero, Rudolf von Habsburg, was clearly designed as a morale-boosting experience, with the Austrian flag dominating every scene. This production came at a difficult time in Austrian politics: Dollfuss was still ruling by decree and having survived an assassination attempt on 3 October 1933, was increasing his pressure on all opposition groups. It was in this context that Felix

Salten reviewed the Lothar production in the *Neue Freie Presse* on 2 November, revealing that the paper and the bourgeois theatre-going public were totally behind the government: 'In the same way as we are at last realizing how many of the most precious German contributions to humanity have stemmed from Austrian soil, are Austrian in tone, so today it is the glory of our former dynasty which we celebrate.' Salten then reported the 'tremendous effect' ('tosender Beifallssturm') created by Otto von Horneck's praise of Austria as spoken by the actor Otto Tressler:

> Tressler was surprised and overwhelmed. There were Austrian countryside and Viennese music in his words, not only because of what he said, but also how he said it. With great emotion he reached the closing lines, 'and put right what others have wrongly done,' and again applause thundered through the house. Put right what others have wrongly done – O, Grillparzer! – how that succeeds in the theatre, particularly in this brilliant *Ottokar* production. And, if God wills, may it soon succeed in reality too.

However, even if an emotional appeal to idealize Austria could be made through the works of her great classical dramatist, a more ruthless approach was needed in the war against the last vestiges of parliamentary democracy. The high culture of the Burgtheater public was one thing, the problem (as can be seen from the efforts made by Ernst Karl Winter and Leopold Kunschak) was how to win the hearts of the citizens of 'Red Vienna.' The city's much loved mayor, Karl Seitz, had been dragged from the Town Hall in February and replaced by a Government Commissioner, Richard Schmitz. Even if the citizens had lost all their socialist cultural organizations, the achievements of 'Red Vienna' were still very much present for them, whether physically in the vast housing blocks, welfare centres, shops and various enterprises (now state-owned), or in memory, as in the school reforms of Otto Glöckel, the equitable tax reforms of Breitner, and the health and welfare policies of Julius Tandler.

The 'folk play' (Volksstück) 'Lueger the Great Austrian'
(*Lueger der große Österreicher*)[20] by an obscure writer, Hans
Naderer, must have come as a godsend to the new administration.
From the government's point of view, here was a play that could
scarcely be improved upon: it produced a glowing portrait of one
of those 'great Austrians' so necessary to the implementation of
the new ideology; it paid tribute to the founder of the Christian
Social Party (to which the majority of the government belonged);
and it glorified the positive achievements of one of the great
mayors of Vienna. Indeed, by the end of the play the audience
might have been forgiven for thinking that it was Lueger who had
transformed the slums of 1918 into what had become by 1934 a
model for the rest of Europe; who had waged war on disease and
alcoholism, reduced infant mortality, and kept unemployment
figures consistently below those of the rest of Austria. Albeit he
did none of these things, he is presented in the play as a model
Austrian, with examples of his vigour, humour, 'common touch'
and, yes, anti-Semitism (his infamous utterance 'I decide who's a
Jew' occurs in the text). Naderer's model for his play had been the
Lueger scene in Duschinsky's 'Emperor Francis Joseph I,' and it
was the actor Hommo who again played the Lueger role at the première in the Deutsches Theater on 27 November 1934 before an
audience which included Cardinal Innitzer, Schmitz, Frau Schuschnigg, Fey, Pernter,  other ministers, and relatives of Lueger,
including his aged sister. This gathering of notables from Church
and government at every major première was, of course, an important feature of government policy.

Lueger's final address to his beloved Viennese might have
been written by Guido Zernatto himself. Brecka informed the
readers of the *Reichspost* on 29 November 1934 that there was
nothing surprising in the choice of such a man for the hero of a
drama: 'It is precisely at this time, when old Austrian convictions
are fighting for new expression, that such a hero had to be . . .
His words "remain good Austrians" and "hold together" ring
down into our own age like some sacred exhortation.' Rudolf Hol-
zer, in the *Wiener Zeitung* of the same day, wrote of the misery

which had been inflicted on 'that city of pleasure, Vienna' between 1910 and 1934, and concluded with the statement that 'the
younger generation will now be brought out of the twilight of the
half-forgotten into the bright radiance of a happy, prosperous
Vienna.' The irony of these remarks would not have been lost on
any of the unemployed who were provided by the National
*Kunststelle* with cheap or free tickets to see the play. The *Kunststelle* had been quick in recognizing the play's potential, and had
sent a memorandum to all local HQs of the Patriotic Front urging
them to persuade every Viennese to take advantage of the reduced
prices to see a play 'filled with patriotic Christian spirit' and thus
fulfil the expressed wish of 'our Cardinal and our Chancellor.'[21]

If Naderer was an uncomplicated follower of the Patriotic
Front, the next two productions, strangely, were representative
plays by two members of the illegal Austrian National Socialist
Party. Josef Wenter's drama *The Chancellor of Tyrol,* premièred
at the Burgtheater on 13 December 1934, deals with an episode of
Austrian history far removed from the popular Habsburg themes.[22]
The hero, Biener, Chancellor at the court in Tyrol and a man of
incorruptible character, refuses to be deflected from his duty by
the machinations of the Church and an effete Italian aristocracy.
This makes it difficult to understand why the play was sanctioned
for performance at the Burgtheater, since it was all too easy to see
in Biener a 'Hitler' figure – in the manner of Jelusich's *Cromwell,* a
play not performed until after the Anschluss – whilst Italians and
the Church party are shown in a light hardly compatible with the
ethos of Austrofascism. Even Brecka, writing ecstatically of Wenter as an 'Austrian' dramatist producing a great 'Austrian history
play' is forced to concede that 'it is hardly a very honourable page
in Austrian history that Wenter has opened.'

However, a careful reading of the reviews of Brecka, Salten
and others reveals that it is *Austrian* achievement and *Austrian*
actors that are being praised. Thus Salten in the *Neue Freie Presse*
concludes: 'Josef Wenter's work makes a contribution to that
process which concerns us all today, the discovery of Austria by
the Austrians.' The attempt by government ideologists to empha-

size the greatness in Austria's political past and cultural traditions was bearing fruit. As Salten phrased it, 'only this wonderfully cherished tradition [of the Burgtheater] permits brilliant productions like that of *The Chancellor of Tyrol.*' The sycophantic tones of both reviewers suggest that despite Wenter's membership of the illegal Nazi Party, they had received a forceful memorandum from the Ministry. Perhaps the fact that the government wished to favour the provinces at the expense of Vienna – and provincial dramatists were rare – tipped the scales in the case of the Tyrolean Wenter.

The second of our problematic dramatists, Max Mell, offers difficulties of another kind, with respect to both his person and his play, 'German Forbears' (*Das Spiel von den deutschen Ahnen*), premièred at the Burgtheater on 12 February 1936. Mell had enjoyed the patronage of Hofmannsthal and had great success in the twenties with works like *Apostle Play* and *The Imitation of Christ.* But his sympathies with the illegal Nazi movement were well-known in Austria, and Nazi sympathizers must have had high expectations when the production of *German Forbears* was announced.[23] Few dramas written at the time reveal so clearly not only the economic problems of the day, but also the moral confusion of authors with sincere Catholic convictions who were drawn to political support for Hitler and his followers.

The play presents a typical Austrian farming family, the Hüttenbrenners. Economic circumstances resulting from the First World War and the German economic blockade force the family to consider selling up and take over a guest house in the village. As the second son, Christoph has no share in the family farm[24] and works as a bus driver, but he loses his job as the result of the recession. And so he becomes a member of (in Mell's words) 'the party which has been dissolved' and is responsible for a bomb outrage which costs a child's life. Yet this is no picture of a ruthless Nazi activist such as existed but rather of a tormented self-doubter. At first sight this is a realistic depiction of rural conditions of the period, but we quickly recognize the symbolic intent.

Lacking realist dialect, the play's rich symbolism and literary allusions owe much to Hofmannsthal. Its realism is further undercut by the use of the supernatural: it was labelled a 'fate tragedy' and banned by the National Socialist government after the Anschluss for that reason. Influenced by the return of the 'family ghosts,' Thomas and Gertraud, whose intervention restores simple piety, belief and trust in the old order, and love. Karl Hüttenbrenner decides not to give up the farm: 'My passionate beliefs are: work, hope, the future!' And so the play ends on a positive note. The thrust of the play is, then, those values promoted by the Corporate State: religious belief, love of one's fellows and one's homeland (Heimat). Its appeal to the country's cultural arbiters must have been immediate, since it echoes Dollfuss' famous speech on the Trabrennplatz on 11 September 1933 extolling the restoration of 'Austrian' virtues.[25]

If the conflation of Catholicism and Nazism creates ambivalences in Mell's life and work, there is nothing in the life of Franz Theodor Csokor, apart from his birth in the 'melting-pot of Vienna' (Völkerkessel Wien) to account for the ambivalences in his play November the Third, 1918 (*Dritter November 1918*), premièred at the Burgtheater on 10 March 1937. Worried by possible political implications, Röbbeling had not wanted to stage the work, but Csokor had enlisted the support of Guido Zernatto (who had fought in Carinthia in 1918/ 1919). The play caught the mood of the moment and was a triumph. Clearly, at one level the impact was a nostalgic one, a requiem for the old imperial Austria, when the six or seven peoples comprising Austro-Hungary had formed (in the character Colonel Radosin's words) something 'greater' than the sum of their parts. There was still considerable loyalty to the vanished monarchy, and by stressing the glories of Austria's past the Corporate State had apparently produced an emotional climate, in which the old Empire seemed a paradise of reason and harmony.

But there were other elements in the play. The date in the title, for example, was for Csokor the day on which a large part of the Austrian army laid down its arms and was taken prisoner; it was also the day on which the Austrian Communist Party and the *Heimwehr* had been founded, and on which Vorarlberg had declared its union with Germany. If the setting of the play aroused memories of a past that was gone forever, the characters and the arguments of the piece were a bruising reminder of the present. The most demonstrative response at the première came at Radosin's statement, 'If this Austria ever ceases to exist . . . then there will never be peace in the world.' The critics made much of this — for example: 'No mere prophecy made with hindsight but the bitter truth of experience,' and indeed the newspapers carrying reviews also contained details of arms purchases, the relative armament strengths of various nations, and the like. Fiction and reality had certainly coincided, and not just on the question of peace or war; the problem of the 'people' and the 'nation' was central to both the play and Austria's very existence, since the call for 'One People, one Reich, one Leader!' (Ein Volk, Ein Reich, Ein Führer) was growing louder. In the play the problem of 'people' is personified not so much by the Polish, Hungarian, Czech, Italian and Slovene officers who scurry back to their homes, but by the young Carinthian Ludoltz, who is described as follows: 'a blond Aryan type, standing erect, and with cold grey eyes, looking for all the world like a bird of prey.' He represents the Nazi hero, whose vision of the future echoed Germany's present reality in 1937, a world of which Austria was providing only a pale imitation. Ludoltz, anti-Semite and hater of 'those filthy Viennese,' was played by Fred Hennings, already a supporter and member of the Austrian Nazi Party.[26] Ludoltz's final stand with his machine-gun, fighting for 'German soil,' was prophetic of the end of the 'Thousand Year Reich.'

More sympathetic today is the very human scene between the communist activist Kacziuk, whose ship *Viribus Unitis* has been sunk, and the orderly Geitinger, in civilian life a market-tender from Vienna. This scene was a reminder to the Viennese public of 1937 that the Patriotic Front still had not made its peace with the workers of Vienna. More importantly, Kacziuk represents the other political pole to Ludoltz: the Jewish doctor Grün is asked by

Kaminski whether, if he had to choose, his choice would be Ludoltz or Kacziuk. Grün, who 'represents' Vienna in the play, replies that he does not know. However, this question did not arise in 1937, with the left-wing parties long since banned and the threat of Anschluss increasing daily. Indeed, the representative of the supra-national idea, Colonel Radosin, commits suicide when he fails to persuade his officers to remain true to the ideals of Austro-Hungary. At his burial each of the officers takes his leave of him in the traditional way by throwing earth onto his grave. But Dr Grün's line 'Earth from Austria' was cut by the ever cautious Röbbeling, who feared that Austria's representation by a Jew would cause demonstrations in the theatre. Radosin is buried wrapped in the flag of the defunct Austrian navy, a symbol of the old Austria whose ashes the Corporate State was vainly trying to fan into life. Thus, a play for its time, indeed, and perhaps to be understood only in the light of Csokor's conviction, expressed in a letter to Ferdinand Bruckner whilst he was writing the play, that 'the road which will bring us back to humanity will first have to lead us through a sea of blood.'[27]

If Csokor, the individualist soon to undertake his own 'anabasis' through Eastern Europe rather than exist under a regime he despised, had forced a play out of his own experiences and the issues of the age, others searched through Austrian history for subject matter likely to find favour with the Ministry of Education and the *Kunststelle.* Duschinsky tried the Austrian painter in *Makart,* the National Socialist Ortner produced a vapid *Beethoven,* Felix Braun a passable *Charles V.* Schreyvogl tried his hand at the Boris Godunov material, 'The God in the Kremlin' (Der Gott im Kreml), given its première on 25 December 1937. Like Jelusich's *Cromwell,* the hero could be seen as a 'Hitler' figure.[28]

The last whole-hearted attempt to provide the Austrian government with an 'Austrian' hero was made, appropriately, by one who had served the cultural interests of the Corporate State most faithfully. Rudolf Henz had done this in his work for Austrian radio, on various cultural committees, and in the command structure of *Neues Leben.* His play *Emperor Joseph II* (Kaiser

Josef II), premièred at the Burgtheater on 8 April 1937, deals with the last years of Joseph's life. But as Fontana remarked in his review, however much one may admire this lonely, idealistic figure of the Enlightenment, there was little in the ten years of his reign to provide dramatic interest. Such as there is in this play is limited to a scene set among the populace (Volksszene) at a time of flooding on the Danube, an audience where Joseph shows a wit sadly lacking elsewhere in the work, and the running battle between Joseph and his adviser Kaunitz. The centrepiece of the play is an interview with the Pope, who has made the unprecedented journey to Vienna out of fear that Joseph's reforms were an attack on both Church and the faith. One senses that in the highly clerical atmosphere of Austria in the thirties, Henz might be venturing where few would care to tread.

In his autobiography[29] Henz provides some insight into the problems of the relationship between Church and state at the time (and, amusingly, between actor and his confessor, since Raoul Aslan, who played Joseph, would claim at rehearsal that his confessor had forbidden him to utter this or that line critical of the Church). Röbbeling grew so worried that he asked Hammerstein-Equord, Minister of Public Security, and one Dr Tomek, a Church historian, to attend the dress-rehearsal. This went well, but the practice of allowing the critics to attend dress-rehearsals was to rebound on him, since of the two hundred or so many were Nazi correspondents for German newspapers – this now permitted since the July Agreement of 1936 – and members of the 'illegal' Austrian NSDAP. The situation was further complicated by the presence of Colonel Wolf, a leading monarchist, who had come expecting further glorification of the former imperial house. When he shouted 'bravo,' the Nazis hissed him down; when Joseph directed his barbs against Church and priesthood, the Nazis cheered and were hissed by the supporters of Austrian clericalism. According to Henz, Röbbeling was once again in despair, and the author had to take the text to Cardinal Innitzer himself and obtain his approval before Röbbeling allowed the première to take place.

No scandal spoiled the first night, and the play – with the

actor Aslan in his usual role of Habsburg Emperor—continued to draw packed houses until the Anschluss, when it was banned along with many other works. It was Henz's intention to show Joseph as a reformer and true believer, anxious to renew the Church, and this was certainly acceptable to both Church and government in 1937. On the other hand, the depiction of Joseph's view that the 'subject' races should 'on purely rational grounds' be forced to speak German, and that the training of priests should be organized by the state rather than the Church, may well have given more comfort to the National Socialists and their sympathizers. The austere figure of Joseph, embodying the nobility of duty and self-sacrifice, could easily have been taken for a 'Schuschnigg' figure.

Another topical reference was the 'Reich,' presented far more dramatically, as we have seen, a few weeks earlier on the same stage by Csokor. In Henz's play it is raised in the context of the uprising in Belgium and again related to the problem of 'nation.' It is this question which rouses Joseph to rare passion: 'Surely Belgium cannot expect more freedom than it already receives from Austria? ' he asks, much in the manner of Radosin. He answers his rhetorical question as follows: 'Pieces of bloody flesh, torn from the healthy whole body and easy prey for all sorts of vultures . . . Nations, perhaps, but the Empire [Reich] is larger, the Empire is stronger, my friends, and that they will have to learn in Brussels.' The unfortunate aspect of this speech was that in Vienna in 1937 it was quite clear which nation was an easy prey for all sorts of vultures and which 'Reich' was the stronger. Henz's emotive emphasis of the concepts of 'Reich' and 'Nation' must have given more comfort to the enemy within the gate rather than those vainly trying to believe in the ideology of Austro-fascism.

Critical response was predictable, particularly in the case of Brecka (*Die Reichspost*), who commented on the sensitive nature of the relationship between Church and state. In his review he suggested that only a writer 'about whose religious beliefs and convictions there can be no doubt' might be allowed to treat such matters. He argued that it was Henz's intention to show Joseph's 'tragedy and guilt,' and that he was trying to destroy the popular legend of Joseph as the 'people's Emperor.' His mention of 'allusions to certain events and currents of our time' probably refers to the Concordat with Rome, agreed four years earlier; the question of 'benevolent despotism' as practised in 1937 by the Corporate State; and presumably the new concept of Austria as a second 'German Reich.' I would argue that this play can be seen as a fitting end to four years of attempts by an 'authoritarian and Christian' state to influence the theatre and culture of its subjects, many of whom already had loyalty to the enemy.

My survey is, of course, not entirely fair to Austrian drama during these four years. There were those like Horváth and Soyfer, whose lively and talented work could at best be produced in the cellars of the sub-culture. There was Richard Billinger once seen by Alfred Kerr as a hope for the future, but whose rather uneven work was too near that Nazi doctrine of 'blood and soil.' Franz Werfel and Ferdinand Bruckner did not toe the government line but continued to have their plays produced in Vienna, although they were already exiled in spirit. The majority of Austrian dramatists did conform, and from one point of view it can be argued that the Corporate State (or 'lesser evil,' as it was often termed) fought hard to harness culture to the defence of an Austria threatened with loss of its independence. But the sight of the legatees of a once great dramatic tradition being nudged, bribed and bullied into following the party line is not a happy one. Klaus Mann's description of Vienna at this time is a very fair one: 'The atmosphere was heavy with threat, although not yet lethal, and there were still attractions on offer, both human and artistic.'[30] The attractions of which he speaks were mostly to be found at the opera and in the concert hall, for with the exception of what remained of Max Reinhardt's contribution at the Theater in der Josefstadt Vienna's days as a major theatrical centre were over. When the work of the *Kunststelle,* the Ministry, the government's advisers on culture (Kulturreferenten) and the officials of *Neues Leben* were done, what remained is material fit only for the political historian.

## NOTES

1. Jura Soyfer, *Das Gesamtwerk,* ed. Horst Jarka (Vienna/Munich/Zurich: Europaverlag, 1980), p. 476.
2. Robert Musil, *Tagebücher,* ed. A. Frisé (Reinbek bei Hamburg: Rowohlt, 1976). See such statements as: 'The immortal Austrian . . .could not be less like his present-day counterpart, who wears white stockings and a new cassock' (vol. 1, p. 893). The white stockings refer to members of the illegal Nazi Party, the priest's robes to the dominant influence of the Catholic Church.
3. For a brief account of the achievements of Rudolf Beer as theatre director, see my 'Viennese Theatre in the First Republic,' in: B. O. Murdoch/M. G. Ward (eds.), *Studies in Modern Austrian Literature* (= Scottish Publications in Germanic Studies 1), (Glasgow, 1981).
4. Cited in Fred Hennings, *Heimat Burgtheater* (Vienna/Munich: Herold, 1973), vol. 3, p. 130.
5. Various aspects of the Corporate State's attitude towards culture as a political weapon have received treatment in recent years. The following works are particularly useful: Friedrich Aspetsberger, *Literarisches Leben im Austrofaschismus. Der Staatspreis* (Königstein/Ts: Hain, 1980); Franz Kadrnoska (ed.), *Aufbruch und Untergang. Österreichische Kultur zwischen 1918 und 1938* (Vienna/Munich/Zurich: Europaverlag, 1981); Klaus Amann/Albert Berger (eds.), *Österreichische Literatur der dreißiger Jahre* (Graz/Vienna: Böhlau, 1985).
6. The North German Hermann Röbbeling, who had no enthusiasm for National Socialism, had come from the Thalia Theater in Hamburg. Interesting accounts of him are given in Hennings (note 4 above), by Henz and Csokor, and by his biographer Tekla Kulczicky de Wolczko, 'Hermann Röbbeling und das Burgtheater,' Vienna, diss., 1950.
7. For details of the discovery and implementation of this means to undemocratic rule (Notverordnungen), see Peter Huemer, *Sektionschef Robert Hecht und die Zerstörung der Demokratie in Österreich* (Munich: Oldenbourg, 1975).
8. See Aspetsberger, p. 60.
9. Ibid.
10. For details of these, see Margaret Dietrich, 'Burgtheater und Öffentlichkeit in der Ersten Republik' in: *Das Burgtheater und sein Publikum* (Vienna: Bundesverlag, 1976), p. 696.
11. See Hennings, pp. 174f.

12.  Dietrich, p. 697

13.  See Csokor's humorous account of the affair in a letter to Ferdinand Bruckner of 15 May 1936 in: Franz Theodor Csokor, *Zeuge einer Zeit* (Munich/Vienna: Langen-Müller, 1964), pp. 120ff.

14.  Oskar Maurus Fontana, *Das große Welttheater. Theaterkritiken 1909–1967* (Vienna: Amalthea, 1976), p. 235.

15.  Ibid.

16.  Letter to Lina Loos, 23 October 1937. Csokor, pp. 149ff.

17.  Karl Sailer (ed.), *Geheimer Briefwechsel Mussolini-Dollfuß* (Vienna: Verlag der Wiener Volksbuchhandlung, n.d.).

18.  Dietrich, pp. 687ff. She also includes much of Werner Krauss's account of his visit to Mussolini, but not the comparison which Krauss made between Mussolini and Hitler, for which, see Hans Weigel, *Werner Krauss. Das Schauspiel meines Lebens* (Stuttgart: Goverts, 1958).

19.  Isabella Ackerl, "Die Türkenbefreieungsfeiern des Jahres 1933," *Geschichte und Gegenwart,* Jg. 3 (March 1984).

20.  The complete text of the play is available only in MS in the Stadtbibliothek, Vienna, but many useful excerpts are given in *Hans Naderer. Ein österreichischer Volksdichter,* ed. "Eine Arbeitsgemeinschaft von Freunden des Dichters" (Vienna/Munich: Kurt Wedl, 1961), pp. 30-44. Interestingly, the play seems to have changed its title since 1934 and become (in this volume at least) simply *Lueger.*

21.  Aspetsberger, p. 61.

22.  Wenter was awarded the State Prize for literature, which was then withheld when it became known that he was a member of the NSDAP, but he still received a state grant. After the July Agreement with Germany in 1936 he was awarded both the State Prize and the Distinguished Medal (Ehrenkreuz) for Science and Art. See Aspetsberger, pp. 116ff.

23.  See the comments of Klaus Amann, *Der Anschluß österreichischer Schriftsteller an das Dritte Reich* (Frankfurt am Main: Athenäum, 1988). Amann notes the strange fact that Mell, coming from the Hofmannsthal 'stable' and whose earlier work had been of so pronounced a Catholic flavour, could have become so involved with the illegal party. The play under discussion perhaps reveals some of his own personal problems and doubts through the character of the second brother, Christoph.

24.  See the essay by Helmut Konrad in this volume on the problems of younger children with no claims on the family farmstead. In Mell's

play the third son, Kaspar, a failed painter, equally highlights this situation.

25.  Note these references in Dollfuss' speech: 'In the farmhouse, after a day of joint effort, the farmer eats his soup at the same table and from the same bowl as his labourers. This is where we find the corporate sense of the farming community (berufsständische Zusammengehörigkeit, berufsständische Auffassung).'

26.  See Hennings, pp. 169f. and p. 187.

27.  Csokor, p. 130.

28.  Schreyvogel was 'a man for all seasons,' who produced two versions of a Habsburg play about Archduke Johann Salvator as well as numerous translations, including one for the Jesuit play by Lavery performed at the Josefstadt. Fontana commented laconically on Schreyvogel, 'but what *can't* Freddy do?' On Schreyvogel, see Amann, passim.

29.  Rudolf Henz, *Fügung und Widerstand* (Graz/Vienna/Cologne: Styria, 1981).

30.  Klaus Mann, *Der Wendepunkt. Ein Lebensbericht* (Reinbek bei Hamburg: Rowohlt, 1984), pp. 322ff.

# The Death of 'Austrian Philosophy'

Kurt Rudolf Fischer

*(Paul Stefanek 8.8.1936–19.4.1988 in memoriam)*

I shall begin by defining the concept of 'Austrian Philosophy.' I shall then discuss its 'death' in connection with the murder of Moritz Schlick and the repercussions of this essentially non-political killing. I shall ask what connections there may be between anti-Semitism and Nazism on the one hand and the traditions of philosophy on the other, and proceed to examine the relationship to Nazism of the various philosophies and those professing them at the University of Vienna. Finally, I shall draw some preliminary pessimistic conclusions about such connections and relationships. My discussion will be interspersed, where I consider it appropriate, with remarks from the point of view of a contemporary witness.

By 'Austrian Philosophy' I do not simply mean any or all professional and non-professional philosophical activity in Austria. All that certainly did not end in the 1930s. What I do mean is that a particular kind of philosophy, produced in Austria, came to an end. This I refer to as 'Austrian Philosophy,' an expression coined by Rudolf Haller.[1] One brief characterization of that philosophy is that it is an empiricism rather than an idealism, and it is thus a realistic or positivistic philosophy. Its closeness to science rather than religion makes it a scientific philosophy. And since its concern is with 'Sprachkritik,' that is with logical or linguistic analysis, it is analytic rather than speculative. Although very few, if any, of the thinkers constituting this particular philosophical tendency possess all of the distinguishing marks mentioned, there seems to be sufficient resemblance among them to warrant the characterization proposed by Haller.

The period in question stretches from 1874, when the liberal Minister of Education, Streymaier, appointed Franz Brentano to a chair of philosophy at the University of Vienna, until 1936, when a former student murdered Moritz Schlick. And I refer to this latter date as the death of Austrian philosophy since its demise came about by way of the death of Schlick, its last distinguished representative in Austria. During this period we find in Vienna a string of innovative philosophers, of important philosophical movements and circles constituting *one* of the major roots of that analytical and scientific philosophy which increasingly dominated English-speaking countries and most of the industrially advanced countries of the Western world. It also had some impact in Africa, Asia and South America.

A second major root of this modern movement is embedded in the philosophical culture of turn-of-the-century Cambridge, the Cambridge of Bertrand Russell and G. E. Moore. Like their Austrian counterparts, they too rejected idealism. Such a rejection was, however, no hard task in Austria, since neither the monarch nor orthodox Catholicism found the spirit or letter of idealistic philosophy congenial. Indeed, Francis I once remarked to his university professors: 'I don't need scholars. I need loyal subjects.'[2] As far as the Catholic orthodoxy was concerned, Kant, the founder of modern German Idealism, had been rejected both because he doubted the reality of a world that had, after all, been created by God and – more seriously – because he had assigned to man the autonomy to give himself his own laws. My remarks should be taken only as an intimation of the main cultural and political trend that provided a soil for the growth of an anti-metaphysical philosophy, which was first a handmaiden to Catholic theology and later became – in the eyes of its critics, at least – a handmaiden to modern science.

The most important names and tendencies or schools of Haller's 'Austrian Philosophy' are:

(1) Franz Brentano and his pupils, from whom there evolved the 'Object Theory' (Gegenstandstheorie) of the Graz School, the 'Value Theory' of Meinong and Ehrenfels, the work of

Twardowski and Polish Logic.

(2)   Ernst Mach and Ludwig Boltzmann, who were what one might call philosophizing scientists. With Mach, as with Brentano, it was the liberal Minister of Education who helped to establish the chair to which he was appointed, namely, the 'Chair of Philosophy, with special reference to the history and theory of the inductive sciences.' One reason for the creation of the chair was that Mach could not have a post in physics because the Professor of Physics, Stefan, was an atomist, and Mach, the positivist, had denied the existence of atoms. When Boltzmann, another atomist and realist, was appointed to succeed Mach, the chair had to be renamed so that the successor did not — as custom demanded — have to praise his predecessor. Although Mach and Boltzmann were philosophical arch-enemies, both considered linguistic analysis of the utmost importance to the hygiene of thought. Analysis was to help scientific activity to proceed.

(3)   The 'First Vienna Circle,' a label which we again owe to Haller.[3] The group consisted of Otto Neurath, Philipp Frank, Hans Hahn and others. They were scientists engaging in philosophy, meeting on Thursday evenings in a Vienna coffee-house from 1908 until the outbreak of the First World War.[4]

(4)   The 'Wiener Kreis,' the Vienna Circle proper. The name was invented by Otto Neurath for the group headed by Schlick and having Rudolf Carnap as its most effective and influential analytic and scientific philosopher.

(5)   Ludwig Wittgenstein, a genius, whose only appointment whilst he was in Austria was as a teacher in an elementary school. Wittgenstein cannot be fully subsumed under any of the movements or trends he inspired — the Logical Atomism of Bertrand Russell, the Logical Positivism of Moritz Schlick, the various methods and techniques of Ordinary Language Analysis that swept England and the United States in the 1950s and 1960s. Nonetheless, Wittgenstein is *the* outstanding thinker in the movement I have designated as 'Austrian Philosophy.'

(6)   Karl Popper, a teacher in a 'Hauptschule' (nine-year elementary school), who moved as it were on the periphery of the

Vienna Circle and became a professor first in New Zealand and eventually at the London School of Economics. He achieved world fame both as a philosopher of science and as a liberal critic of totalitarianism. If Wittgenstein did not entirely satisfy the 'requirement' of 'Austrian Philosophy' that endorsement of science was the only or preferred mode of cognition, then Popper failed to satisfy another of its 'requirements,' namely, that the task of philosophy consists in linguistic analysis, in *Sprachkritik*. And so Wittgenstein and Popper, Brentano and Meinong, Mach and Boltzmann, Neurath and Frank, Schlick and Carnap are collected together by Rudolf Haller into one philosophical movement that may well be called 'Austrian,' either because most of the important work of these philosophers was accomplished in Austria, indeed, in Vienna, or because Austria was the land where they started or reached maturity.

And yet there seems to be no connection between the distinguishing marks of 'Austrian Philosophy' and the Austrian national character: that is, there is no equivalent of the 'spiritual depth' of German Idealism, the 'clarity' of French Rationalism or the 'common sense' of British Empiricism. In fact, there seems to be no possible description of the Austrian national character which would establish its connection with 'Austrian Philosophy.' The usual characterization of the Austrian Mind as a mixture of slovenliness, estheticism (sensualism) and 'Protektion'—the attempt to secure personal preferment through the agency of socially influential individuals—in no way helps us to understand 'Austrian Philosophy,' although it may well aid our understanding of the history of Austrian institutions and the way that university appointments are made.[5] The fact, however, that we appear unable to find a connection between Austrian philosophy and an Austrian national character does stand in need of explanation or clarification. My own suggestion is that the philosophy which has achieved world-wide acclaim as *the* modern philosophy and as the philosophical contribution of the golden age of Austrian culture, *fin-de-siècle* Vienna, was produced either by Germans from the Reich or by Jews, and so not by Austrians proper. Brentano,

Schlick and Carnap were Germans from the Reich, whilst Wittgenstein, Neurath, Tarski – and indeed almost all of the lesser figures
who embarked upon important and influential careers in England
and America – were Jews. Only a minority were Austrians proper:
Mach, Boltzmann and the aristocrats Meinong and Ehrenfels.

I am employing the term 'Jew' as defined by the Nuremberg
Race Laws. These Laws seem to express objectively, as it were, the
special place actually assigned to the Jews in and by non-Jewish
society. They tell you who was and who was not to be considered
Jewish. And one might add that subjectively, too, these definitions
were felt to be valid long before the promulgation of the Nuremberg Laws: those with Jewish grandparents *felt* Jewish, no matter
how Christian they and their parents were, albeit the objective
cause for feeling Jewish can no doubt be located in an anti-Semitic
society and the Jewish tradition itself. From my own experience
in Vienna and in the countryside of Austria, I can vouch that
those who had been baptized, as well as their baptized children
and grandchildren, were regarded as Jews by others, and that they
themselves felt that they were Jewish.

I can also vouch – and from most intimate experience – for a
feeling that was later, sometimes as much as a generation or two
later, to be most horribly confirmed, that of 'not belonging.'
Baptized or not, part of the high culture of the *fin de siècle* and
the period between the wars, the Jews in general and Jewish
philosophers in particular, were, ideologically speaking, universalistic. They felt that they belonged to mankind as well as being –
quite compatibly – part of a German scientific and humanistic
tradition. They were members of an international scientific community rather than members of a Jewish religious community or
members of the Jewish tribe.[6] The subjective feeling that one is
Jewish *and* also German can produce tensions that may, of course,
be repressed or resolved in some way or other. Jews in Austria did
not really feel that they belonged, and equally their fellow citizens
did not consider that they belonged. Whereas Englishmen believe
that their Jews belong to the British nation, and, indeed, Americans believe that an Austrian Jew with a foreign accent, like my-

self, is really an American. Austrians never saw their Jews in this way. Ironically, Jews in Austria could show their allegiance to the Emperor and be among those most devoted to the Habsburg State, or later they could identify with or become leaders of the socialist workers. But none of this helped. It used to annoy me when my father said: 'Everything was different under the Emperor,' meaning, of course, that everything had been better then, and I presumed that he meant for the Jews too. But when I asked him who the anti-Semites had been in those days, he replied: 'Everybody.' Even today – and I appreciate how difficult it must be for the most well-meaning Austrian to speak neutrally in matters Jewish – there is talk of 'our Jewish fellow-citizens' (unsere jüdischen Mitbürger), whereas Catholics and Protestants are never 'fellow-citizens' but merely 'citizens.' What all this leads back to is my assertion that there is a discernible philosophy, 'Austrian Philosophy,' as defined and described by Haller; but we can use the term only with the proviso that it does not indicate any connection with the national character in question in the manner of, say, British Empiricism, German Idealism, French Rationalism or American Pragmatism.

In the thirties – in fact, on 22 June 1936 – there was an incident which may be said to exemplify the atmosphere of the Corporate State (*Ständestaat*). It is an atmosphere which could be said to have re-emerged in the past couple of years with the election of Kurt Waldheim as Austrian President, and with the national and international problems associated with that election. At all events, a recent incident connected with philosophy reveals the re-emergence of the atmosphere to which I am referring. Rudolf Haller, to whom I have had occasion to refer several times, was asked by the daily paper *Die Presse* to contribute an article on Moritz Schlick on the occasion of the fiftieth anniversary of Schlick's death. However, Haller's contribution was not accepted; he merely received notification that the paper would not be publishing his article as 'a decision not to do so has been taken at a higher level.' The article has, in fact, since appeared in *Manuskripte* 92/86. But to return to the thirties, Professor Moritz

Schlick had been shot by one of his former students, one Johann Nelböck. As possible motive for the murder – three of the four bullets were lethal – several possibilities have been considered: (1) that Nelböck believed the professor to have written a negative reference for him when he applied for a post at an adult education centre (Volkshochschule); (2) that Nelböck was jealous of his former fiancée and thought, with or without justification, that she was having an affair with Schlick. With regard to either of these possible motives, there was previous psychiatric testimony to the effect that Nelböck was an emotionally unbalanced individual. As a connoisseur of the local scene (and I contrast it to three decades spent in the United States, where everyday life is certainly less corrupt), I am particularly fascinated by what Dr Traude Cless-Bernert reports.[7] She was a student of Schlick's and the last person to whom he talked before he was murdered. She reports that Schlick had attempted to obtain police protection, which he thought he needed because of continued threats, but was informed that he would be asked to pay for the expense of having Nelböck interned in the local asylum, the *Steinhof.*

More significantly, it is sad and shocking to examine the political circumstances in which the murder occurred, the after-effects of the murder in the press, and the reaction of the general public. Indeed, the way the occurrence was *represented* – despite the fact that Schlick was neither a Jew nor a socialist – reveals deep anti-Semitic hatred.

Professor Schlick's name had previously been put on the 'gelbe Liste,' i.e., the list made available to students and giving the names of those who did not really belong, who were – as it was put – members of a 'racially distinct people' (rassen- und wesens-fremdes Volk). The further object of the 'list' was the defamation of that 'people' – meaning, of course, the Jews.[8] The list of names had been put together by professors who were either Christian Socials or German Nationalists, and so contained the names of university teachers who were Jews or thought to be Jews, but also of those who were considered left-wing or liberal. Now Schlick was not only a liberal – albeit a liberal who had pledged his loyalty to the Corporate State – but he also had a suspiciously Jewish first name: Moritz. We may be quite certain that Schlick's first name played no part in the motivation of his killer, but we may be equally certain that it was of importance in the public reception of his killing. Here I quote the leading government newspaper, *Schönere Zukunft*, from an article signed – pseudonymously, of course – by a Professor Dr. Austriacus:

> Chairs of Philosophy at the University of Vienna should be occupied by Christian philosophers. Austria is, after all, a Christian and German country ... We have heard frequently in recent times that a peaceful solution to the Jewish problem in Austria is in the best interest of the Jews themselves, as it will prevent an otherwise inevitable violent solution. It is to be hoped that the terrible murder which has occurred at the University of Vienna will help bring about a truly satisfactory solution to the Jewish problem.[9]

The 'truly satisfactory solution to the Jewish problem' was, as we know, never achieved. Instead there was the violent solution which Professor Austriacus feared, namely, one of the most heinous – if not the most heinous – crime ever committed: the Final Solution. Yet Moritz Schlick actually conformed to the "highest" standards of both Christianity *and* race. Of course, his liberal views may not have met the desired ideals of either Austrofascism or – even less – of National Socialism. But let me here cite the first two paragraphs of the *curriculum vitae* submitted on his graduation from the Luisenstädtisches Realgymnasium, Berlin, in 1900 by Friedrich Albert Moritz Schlick:

> I was born on 10 April 1882 at 49 Prenzlauerstrasse, Berlin, the third and youngest son of Protestant parents. My father is descended from a Bohemian noble family, whose name makes several appearances in history, for example in 1621, when a certain unfortunate Count was

executed in Prague along with 26 other Protestant leaders. The representation of a church in the family crest, even today, is doubtless intended to recall the part played by my forbears in the religious quarrels of that era.
My mother comes from the family of Ernst Moritz Arndt of Rügen Island. It was in memory of the poet that I received the name Moritz.

The public response to the murder of Schlick seems to have been what might be called 'soft' anti-Semitism, whose thesis I take to read: if the Jews are restricted in their public and cultural importance, then this will be not only in the interests of a Christian society but for the good of the Jews themselves, since such restriction will prevent the emergence of 'hard' anti-Semitism. The 'thesis' of 'hard' anti-Semitism consists in the demand that the Jews be expelled and that they leave their property behind, or as the vernacular had it: 'The Jew goes and his cash stays.' Later the Jews could no longer leave, and were bureaucratically and efficiently exterminated. The lust for murdering them has a long tradition in Austria, and there are examples of their being burned at the stake in Vienna five hundred years ago.

It is not my purpose to press the distinction between 'hard' and 'soft' anti-Semitism – in Austria corresponding roughly to the anti-Semitism of Schönerer and Lueger respectively – or, for that matter, to show the continuity between them. More important, it seems to me, is to point up the comparatively liberal attitude of the Nazis towards the deeper recesses of high culture. There is a streak of pragmatism in the thought of Hitler and the practice of Nazism. What seems to have been decisive was whether or not one was of Aryan origin and whether or not one's activities – including, of course, speech – were pro- or anti-Nazi. The truly unshakeable foundations of Nazism were, as I believe we now know, territorial expansion, the elimination of the Jews and, probably, the idea of the Great Leader (Führerprinzip). The cultural policy of 'hard' and 'soft' anti-Semites in some respects coalesces at the highest level of philosophical sophistication; but they differ considerably, for example, with respect to the metaphysical distinction made by naturalism on the one hand and non- or anti-naturalism on the other. Since the 'hard' anti-Semites, the Nazis, were racist and thus biologistic and so ultimately naturalistic, they excluded not only orthodox Jews or those who identified themselves as Jews, but, equally, strongly assimilated, baptized Jews or those who simply had Jewish ancestry. Their concern was a radical demarcation: Jews on one side, the Christian or non-Jewish population on the other.

However irrelevant such a distinction may seem retrospectively, I must, as a contemporary witness and for the sake of the record, emphasize that there is simply no comparison between the country under the rule of the Fatherland Front (Vaterländische Front) and the country under the rule of the Nazis. And I do not say that because of any sympathy towards the corporate state. To explain: soon after my twelfth birthday and about three weeks after 12 February 1934, the date of the outbreak of the civil war that put an end to parliamentary democracy in Austria, I was given in a school examination the essay topic 'The Policeman.' As a result of what I wrote, my parents were summoned by the Headmaster and were informed that if I had been four years older I would have faced a charge in a juvenile court. They themselves were investigated to discover whether they had been members of, or engaged in activity sponsored by, the Communist Party. In fact, my parents were middle-class liberals who voted for the Social Democratic Party because, as my father put it, a Jew could not vote for any other party. The Social Democratic Party had never included anything anti-Semitic in its platform.

In June 1936, when Schlick was murdered – less than two years before the Anschluss – the tradition of Austrian Philosophy in its classical phase, namely the Vienna Circle, was wiped out and was never to regain a foothold at the University of Vienna. For the philosophical insider, it is not immediately obvious whether this was a scandal or a blessing, and some examination and evaluation is required. The examiner's and evaluator's conclusion must and will depend on his philosophical upbringing and conviction. It is nothing new to say that there are different philosophies and that they ignore or are in open conflict with one another. Certainly their different relationships to the ideology and practice of Nazism will be an important issue in our present context. Another relevant matter is the connection of the various professors of the time with Nazism. It is also no novelty to state that power politics plays a role in academic life, albeit this fact is better understood by insiders than outsiders, since the educated public tends to glorify academic life and thought. One must, however, bear in mind that an action motivated by power politics may, in fact, belong to the party political order or may be ideologically grounded. One may instance the fact that Alfred Baeumler was treated as though he was merely being used by the Nazis, whereas he was a Nazi by conviction.[10] After the war many, especially educated, people found it difficult to accept that any educated person, scholar, intellectual or scientist could have been a Nazi by conviction. Everyone had, it was argued, been coerced into pretending to be a Nazi, either to secure an advantage or in order not to get into trouble. It is a matter of opinion which is worse: trying to gain favour with the Nazis without really being a Nazi, or being a convinced Nazi. It seems to me that on an individual level, the factor of decency must be taken into account in assessing guilt, albeit this consideration may – infrequently, to be sure – lead to a paradoxical conclusion: that the perpetrator of a crime stands morally higher than the victim, as when a Nazi saves or helps a Jew who otherwise has no special moral merit; or conversely, a Jew – a victim – may try to save his own life by collaborating with the Nazi.

The relationship of Nazism to the different philosophies, including those espoused at the University of Vienna, is tangled. On the whole, it is easier to find anti-Semitic notions in the religiously inspired tradition of German Idealism than in the scientific tradition of philosophy, including its Austrian variety. And yet, the Nazi view is a scientific view. Just consider a passage from one of Hitler's letters insisting on the primacy of fact over the dictates of feeling, and also a passage from *Mein Kampf* where

Hitler criticizes the Christian Socials for basing their anti-Semitism on a religious idea instead of submitting the 'Jewish problem' to scientific scrutiny:

> (1) Anti-Semitism as a political movement must not and cannot come about as a result of feelings, but only through a recognition of the fact. And the facts are that Jews are not in any ultimate sense a religious community but a race. (2) With superficial arguments like that, there could never have been any serious scientific treatment of the problem.[11]

Nevertheless, it would be difficult to pinpoint a connection between Nazism and any particular naturalistic philosophy like, say, biological evolutionism. The question regarding what part different philosophies play in the ideological foundation of Nazism seems to me somewhat analogous to the question whether Nazism is a totalitarianism or a fascism. The answer to the latter question should be: both, and something else. In terms of its philosophical connections Nazism has features of the German idealistic tradition, but also features of the scientific tradition of philosophy, and yet it belongs in neither tradition, since it is less subtle than any academic philosophy and its appeal is more direct. Academic philosophy may indeed be used to justify Nazism but need not be thus used. We might consider a bizarre example. The emotive theory of value of some Logical Positivists *could* be used to justify Nazism and holistic philosophies of the State, both considered by many to be intrinsically fascist. However, in moral and political matters the emotive theory excludes a final appeal to reason, since this appeal can only be to an emotive expression or attitude no longer subject to rational treatment.

In discussing the relationship of Nazism and philosophies we cannot avoid the closely connected matter of the relationship of the university professors of the time to political ideologies. It is well known that a general, we might call it 'conservative,' attitude existed which contrived to exclude Jews, Liberals and Socialists from university appointments. An anti-Semitic, anti-liberal and anti-socialist camp gained the upper hand in the universities, especially in the humanities, quite soon after the formation of the First Republic. This situation is well documented in a paper published a decade ago by Friedrich Stadler.[12] For instance, in 1922 people seriously discussed whether one's learning or racial origin (Wissen oder Abstammung) should count as the decisive qualification for a university lecturership (Habilitation).[13]

But let us now pass from the Nazi years of the Anschluss or 'war years' – as they are often called, perhaps to justify the extermination of the Jews by invoking the war as extenuating circumstance – and turn our attention to the post-war years. The connection or lack of connection between the years of the Corporate State, the years following the Anschluss and the immediate post-war years has become a matter of considerable concern in Austria since the election of Kurt Waldheim to the Austrian Presidency. In the 1950s and 1960s, two especially powerful professors of philosophy came to the fore in Vienna. Leo Gabriel was a Catholic with scholastic and existentialist leanings, and Erich Heintel was, roughly speaking, a proponent of German neo-Idealism. Indeed, it is Heintel's merit – if merit it be – to have introduced at Vienna a philosophy that has traditionally been rejected there, and whose proponents have even been persecuted in Austria. From philosophical conviction and for philosophical reasons, Gabriel and Heintel between them prevented the tradition of the Vienna Circle from regaining a foothold at the university. That tradition had not been welcome in the Corporate State, and its Jewish proponents were exterminated under Nazi rule. That the survivors were not recalled to university posts is a shame not peculiar to academic philosophy but endemic to the entire situation in Austria after the war. There was a feeling of relief that there were no more Jews, and especially that there were no more Jews in powerful public positions.

The claim that there has been a 'lowering of standards' (Niveauverlust)[14] in Austria is made with some justice, given a general lowering of the level of culture, not to speak of creativity, in all scientific and humanistic endeavors. In one sense this is understandable, since in the three decades before the turn of the century and the three decades after it, Vienna enjoyed a period of productivity that has only few parallels in Western intellectual and cultural history. But this observation should not and cannot serve as an excuse for the Austrian people and the Austrian Government not to invite those who were persecuted, whether famous or not, to return to Austria. In his now classical paper on philosophical developments in Austria at the beginning of the Second Republic ('Die philosophische Entwicklung in Österreich am Beginn der Zweiten Republik'), first published in 1983 and twice reprinted, Rudolf Haller points out how the Ministry of Education, together with Professors Gabriel and Heintel, turned its back on the modern analytical movement.[15] All this said, further work and discussion are certainly required for a more detailed and more complete presentation of the situation before, during and after the 'death of Austrian Philosophy.'[16]

## NOTES

1.  See, e.g., Rudolf Haller, 'Wittgenstein and Austrian Philosophy,' in: J. C. Nyiri (ed.), *Austrian Philosophy. Studies and Texts* (Munich: Philosophia, 1981), pp. 91-112, esp. p. 92: '... there has taken place an independent development of a specifically *Austrian philosophy.*'

2.  Cited by Susanne Preglau-Hämmerle, *Die politische und soziale Funktion der österreichischen Universität. Von den Anfängen bis zur Gegenwart* (Innsbruck: Inn-Verlag, 1986), p. 93.

3.  See his article 'New Light on the Vienna Circle,' in the number of *Monist* entitled 'General Topic: Contemporary Continental Philosophy,' (January 1982, Vol. 65/1, pp. 25-35). See esp. p. 31: 'It was the crisis of natural science which was in the focus of the discussion of the "first" Vienna Circle at that time.'

4.  For the function of the coffee-house in *fin-de-siècle* Vienna see Otto Friedländer, *Letzter Glanz der Märchenstadt. Das war Wien um 1900* (Vienna/Munich: Molden-Taschenbuch, 2nd edition, 1977), esp. pp. 215-219, 'Kaffeehaus.' For its role as the meeting place of the 'First Vienna Circle' see Philipp Frank, *Modern Science and its Philosophy* (New York: Collier Books, 1961), introductory chapter, pp. 13-61.

5. See Peter Kampits, *Ludwig Wittgenstein. Wege und Umwege zu seinem Denken* (Graz/Vienna/Cologne: Styria, 1985), p. 39: 'Even when one gives up any idea of defining an Austrian 'national character' or 'essence'... one might still wish to characterize the Austria of those years (and in some respects the Austria of today) as a mixture of slovenliness, 'Protektion,' estheticism and pleasure-seeking on the one hand, and a nihilism that moves between black farce, the demonic and a lurking despair on the other.' (Editors' translation.)

6. See Steven Beller, '*Fin-de-siècle* Vienna and the Jews: the dialectics of assimilation,' *The Jewish Quarterly*, Vol. 33/3 (123), 1986.

7. In: *Zeitgeschichte* (Institut für Zeitgeschichte), Vol. 7, no. 9, April 1982, pp. 119–234, esp. 233.

8. See Michael Siegert, 'Der Mord an Professor Moritz Schlick,' in: Leopold Spira (ed.), *Attentate, die Österreich erschütterten* (Vienna: Löcker, 1981), pp. 123–131, esp. the section on the 'gelbe Liste,' pp. 125–127.

9. Ibid., p. 126.

10. See R. J. Hollingdale, 'Introduction' to his *Friedrich Nietzsche: Thus Spake Zarathustra* (Baltimore, Maryland: Penguin Books, 1961). For a general discussion of the tangled relationship between Nietzsche and Nazism, see my 'Nazism as a Nietzschean "Experiment"' in: Mazzino Montinari/Wolfgang Müller-Lauter, Heinz Wenzel (eds.), *Nietzsche-Studien. Internationales Jahrbuch für die Nietzsche-Forschung*, Vol. 6 (Berlin/New York: Walter de Gruyter, 1977), pp. 116–122, esp. p. 117 concerning Baeumler.

11. Letter to Adolf Gemlich, Munich, 16 September 1919 in: Eberhard Jäckel with Axel Kuhn (eds.), *Hitler. Sämtliche Aufzeichnungen 1905–1924* (Stuttgart: Deutsche Verlagsanstalt, 1980), pp. 88–90; quotation pp. 88f. And Adolf Hitler, *Mein Kampf* (Munich: Zentralverlag der NSDAP, 1939), p. 126. (Editors' translations.)

12. Friedrich Stadler, 'Aspekte des gesellschaftlichen Hintergrunds und Standorts des Wiener Kreises am Beispiel der Universität Wien' in: Hal Berghel/Adolf Hübner/Eckehart Köhler (eds.), *Wittgenstein, the Vienna Circle and Critical Rationalism. Proceedings of the 3rd International Wittgenstein Symposium, 13th to 19th August 1978/Kirchberg am Wechsel* (Vienna: Hölder-Pichler-Tempsky, 1979), pp. 41–59.

13. Ibid., p. 45.

14. See Eckehart Köhler, 'Niveauverfall der Philosophie seit 1934/38 an der Wiener Universität,' unpublished paper, read (in part) at the 'Arbeitsta-

gung: Die Philosophie an der Universität Wien in den Dreißiger Jahren, nach dem 'Anschluß' an das Dritte Reich und in der Zweiten Republik bis in die Sechziger Jahre,' held on 30 April 1988 at the Institut für Wissenschaft und Kunst, 1090 Vienna, Berggasse 17.

15. *Manuskripte* 23 (1983), 57-68; included in Rudolf Haller, *Fragen zu Wittgenstein und Aufsätze zur Österreichischen Philosophie* (Amsterdam: Rodopi, 1986), pp. 219-245. Here we read: 'The younger generation at Vienna University, not least in its substantial protection from outside influence, seemed (and indeed seems) bent on pursuing the philosophy which came back after the war (Restaurationsphilosophie)' (p. 239). To this passage the book adds a footnote, 39a: 'Happily there are some clear signs of change even in Vienna.' (Editors' translations.) This added footnote is omitted in the third printing of the paper in: Friedrich Stadler (ed.), *Kontinuität und Bruch 1938-1945-1955. Beiträge zur österreichischen Kultur- und Wissenschaftsgeschichte* (Vienna/ Munich: Jugend und Volk, 1988), pp. 157-179.

16. Since the Oxford symposium, a workshop has been conducted in Vienna on the topic of philosophy at the University of Vienna during the past half century (see above n. 14). This has brought further clarification of the issues and problems involved in the relationship between philosophy and politics during that period. The workshop was organized by Franz M. Wimmer and myself, and included several short papers by Eckehart Köhler, Klaus Dethloff, Gernot Heiss, Georg Graf, Otto Pfersmann, Rudolf Ekstein (a moving personal recollection of how studying at Vienna University in the 1930s was experienced by Jewish students); and two longer papers read by Cornelia Wegeler and Frank Hartmann. The round-table discussion had contributions from Rudolf Burger, Rainer Hegselmann, Peter Kampits, Hans-Dieter Klein and Friedrich Stadler. The workshop had also invited Erich Heintel and Reinhold Knoll. The former accepted and then refused to attend because he felt that Rudolf Haller had insulted him in print. Reinhold Knoll simply did not appear. In the volume *Verdrängte Schuld. Verfehlte Sühne. Entnazifizierung in Österreich 1945-1955* (Bad Vöslau: Verlag für Geschichte und Politik, 1986), Knoll's contribution ('Die Entnazifizierung an der Universität Wien,' pp. 270-280) contains very serious attacks on Heintel—referred to as 'H'—on the basis of minutes and notes by the author's father, Professor August M. Knoll, a member of the University's committee on denazification. Because the date of the workshop had to be changed suddenly, Professor Rudolf Haller

could not attend. Professor Werner Leinfellner also had to withdraw because of the change in date of a conference at which he had a function. An 'Arbeitsskriptum' had been prepared as a basis for discussion and included particularly important papers. In addition to those already cited by Haller, Knoll and Stadler, there were: Rainer Hegselmann, 'Alles nur Mißverständnisse? Zur Vertreibung des logischen Empirismus aus Österreich und Deutschland,' and Hans-Dieter Klein, 'Philosophischer Idealismus und Nationalsozialismus.' For further relevant literature, see Rudolf Haller's short report 'Philosophie in Österreich nach 1945' in: *Was wird Zählen? Ein Rechenschaftsbericht über die 2. Republik* (Vienna: Literas-Universitätsverlag, 1988), pp. 114–116. Also the following papers published in an issue of *Forum* (Vienna, May/June 1988), Nos. 413/414: Reinhold Knoll, 'Der infame Mensch'; Gernot Heiss, 'Arnold Gehlen'; Frank Hartmann, 'Die Nazisophen,' (34–36). Finally, cf. Frank Hartmann's report shortly to appear: 'Geistiger Anschluß: Die Wiener Philosophie und der Nationalsozialismus' *Information Philosophie* (Basel, 1988).

# The Jewish Intellectual and Vienna in the 1930s

## Steven Beller

The 1930s saw the disappearance of the Jewish intellectual from Vienna, and the result has been catastrophic for the cultural life of what was once one of the leading centres of cultural and intellectual innovation in Europe. This will be the central theme of this essay, but this bald statement of intent immediately raises a number of questions, not least of which is what is meant by the term 'Jewish intellectual.'

Friedrich von Hayek, in his introduction to the memoirs of his mentor, Ludwig von Mises, revealed his definition of this slippery term:

> A Jewish intellectual who advocated socialist ideas had a recognized rôle to play in the Vienna of the first third of this century, and this was naturally allowed to him. The Jewish banker or businessman who, bad enough, defended capitalism also had an unquestioned right to do so. But a Jewish intellectual who defended capitalism seemed to most a monstrosity, something unnatural, which could not be put into the order of things and which one could not begin to comprehend.[1]

In this version the Jewish intellectual was a recognized figure in Viennese cultural life who was on the Left. There are, however, other versions of the Jewish intellectual, which fly in the face of this definition.

Claudio Magris, for instance, wrote the following concerning the Habsburg myth in the literature of the 1930s:

> To these Jewish intellectuals, such as Werfel, Roth and Zweig, who were witnessing the emergence of a Europe governed by racial hatreds, the old Habsburg Monarchy, despite herself not being totally free of the blight of anti-semitism, appeared as an ideal homeland, which had guaranteed a happy, secure life. It is because of this that it was from their pens that the most heartfelt, loving reminiscences of the empire flowed.[2]

This view, in its identification of Jewish intellectuals with a nostalgic yearning for the old empire, seems to fly in the face of the version given by Hayek. On one level, of course, this is because the two are talking about quite different matters. On another, however, the fact that they both use the term 'Jewish intellectual' can be seen as neither absurd nor coincidental. Rather their apparently casual use of the same term points to a real phenomenon, which is the fact that Jewish intellectuals did play an enormously large part in Viennese culture, the culture of fin-de-siècle Vienna.

One way of approaching this central question is by asking another, tributary question, a deceptively simple one: when did 'Vienna 1900' end? At first sight it would not appear particularly important or difficult to choose a suitable point of caesura, yet when one looks at the various suggestions problems arise. This can be seen by considering the dates chosen for the many exhibitions on 'Vienna 1900' held in the last few years. One such obvious point is 1914, the outbreak of the First World War, and the beginning of the end of Vienna's role as capital of the Habsburg Monarchy. This was the date chosen by the exhibitions in Edinburgh and New York.[3] Yet many people, among them Friedrich Torberg, have been at pains to point out that much of what we consider the culture of 'Vienna 1900' only came to fruition after the war.[4] One might say that it was a 'golden autumn,' but the inter-war period produced Schoenberg's *Moses und Aron,* Wittgenstein's *Tractatus Logico-Philosophicus* and Musil's *Der Mann ohne Eigenschaften.* Indeed in the cultural life of Vienna there was a great deal of continuity between the prewar and postwar periods.[5]

Another suggestion for a cut-off point was that made by the Vienna exhibition, *Traum und Wirklichkeit,* which had as its end date 1930.[6] This date neatly avoids any discussion of the embarrassments of Austrian history in the 1930s, which in itself makes it suspect as an historically acceptable date, and indeed it has nothing much to recommend it apart from a spurious mathematical cogency.

The date which, after all, seems the most sensible is that chosen by the Paris exhibition: 1938.[7] Yet the reason why this is so is not so much because 1938 marked a caesura in the history of Austria, as rather that it marked the effective end of the large Viennese Jewish community and of the role played by Jewish intellectuals in Vienna's cultural life. That is to say that the cogency of 1938 as an end point for 'Vienna 1900' rests largely on the claim that the Jewish role in cultural life was so central that the disappearance of the Jews set in train by the events of 1938 was the event which has left Vienna without the cultural zest which had marked it even in the inter-war period.

Such claims rest on an interpretation of the cultural flowering of 'Vienna 1900,' which has as its central motivating force the Jewish assimilation.[8] According to this interpretation, the Jewish assimilation brought to Vienna a group of people, imbued with the ideology of emancipation and intent on the pursuit of *Bildung* and other liberal, Enlightened principles, people who saw in Vienna a centre of German liberal civilization in which they could realize these goals. Yet the actual Vienna was far from this ideal and instead harked back to a pre-modern, Baroque tradition, with church and emperor at its centre. Jewish immigrants, with their faith in the power of education, and an emphasis on individual ethical responsibility, did not fit in at all well with this other 'Baroque' Vienna, with its stress on obedience to the established social and religious order, and the aesthetic celebration thereof.

Nor could they reconcile themselves easily with other time-honoured principles of this traditional Vienna, such as *Schlamperei* and *Gemütlichkeit,* which, in their denial of the rule of law and the implied rejection of the uncomfortable search for truth, flew in the face of Jewish value systems, whether they be traditional or emancipationist.

Traditional Vienna was, in addition, endemically hostile to the Jews, and it is not coincidental that it was anti-Semitism which proved to be the magic key by which Lueger was able to unlock the anti-liberal masses to overwhelm the liberal patriciate in the 1890s. As a result liberalism virtually disappeared as an effective political force, leaving the liberal bourgeoisie, but especially its Jewish contingent, politically impotent in a hostile environment. They were, ironically, forced to seek the protection of their old enemy, the Habsburg state, from the Viennese electorate. An even greater irony was that Jews sought refuge in the world of culture, where they could still act without being attacked as Jews, but by so doing essentially repeated the strategy of their forbears, who had sought solace in the world of the mind, against the onslaughts of their persecutors.

Out of the clash of cultures and out of the turmoil caused by the collapse of liberal hegemony in Vienna arose the critical modern culture which has made 'Vienna 1900' so famous. This was the culture of Kraus, Weininger, Freud, Schnitzler, Schoenberg and even Wittgenstein, in other words primarily the achievement of intellectuals of Jewish background: in that sense Jewish intellectuals. Yet it was also the primarily Jewish audience, in the salons and the coffee houses, the liberal press and the theatres, in the liberal educated class in general, which contributed so greatly to Vienna's cultural dynamism and made the 'Jewish intellectual,' better perhaps: the intellectual Jew, such a significant figure in Vienna's cultural life.[9] This is what is usually meant when we talk of the 'Jewish intellectual' in Vienna, and as such there was not one type of 'Jewish intellectual' so much as many Jewish intellectuals. They might often be at variance with each other (sometimes with themselves) in their responses to their situation, but they nevertheless had in common the fact of that situation, the fact of being Jewish, from a Jewish background, and the effect of that was such as to have an often decisive impact on the way they thought, and hence on the culture to which they contributed so much.

This cultural world was so rich and varied that it could produce not only left-wing Jewish intellectuals of the type Hayek describes, but also von Mises and the writers Magris is concerned with. How well, however, did this great cultural flowering survive in the 1930s, and was 1938 the great caesura which it is claimed to be? Was it the destruction of the Jews and of the Jewish intellectuals, which led to the subsequent provincialization of Vienna?

Such a view receives emphatic confirmation by a book published as early as 1922, by a man, Hugo Bettauer, who was dead before the 1930s could realize his uncanny prophecies. Bettauer's *Die Stadt ohne Juden,* sloppily written and full of second-rate kitsch as it is, is nevertheless a remarkably prophetic novel.[10] He envisaged in this novel a time when a Christian Social chancellor of Austria, Schwertfeger, would order the expulsion of the Jews (racially defined), and showed through the devastating results of this exodus on the remaining Aryan population the central role played by Vienna's Jews in the city's life.

There are, of course, some positive results. The workers are now very happy to be rid of their Jewish leadership; the housing problem in Vienna is solved overnight.[11] Yet the woes caused by the absence of Jews far outweigh these fringe benefits. The banks are taken over not by native Austrians, who are not prepared to invest enough capital, but rather by complete foreigners.[12] Theatre life, excluding the opera, deteriorates to a pitiful level, as does the world of operetta, for there is no one to write the hit tunes or witty libretti.[13] Elegance disappears as the new inhabitants of the city, from the countryside, have no requirement for Paris fashion, and Christian ladies do not any longer have to compete with the fashion-conscious Jewesses. Just as all the fashionable ladies' couturiers are about to go out of business a shop assistant has an inspiration; he suggests that his shop go over to selling Loden clothes as high fashion and is rewarded by immediate success. After a while Loden is being sold as the latest Paris fashion.[14]

Among other details Bettauer describes how the once great literary coffee houses in the centre of Vienna are empty, the intellectual life of Vienna effectively dead.[15] Worst of all, as far as the Christian Socials are concerned, the absence of Jews means that they no longer have a ready scapegoat for the failures of their policies, and appeals to some sort of world Jewish conspiracy only make the impotence of the Austrians more painful, as they realize they can do nothing about such things.[16]

Thus Schwertfeger's dream of a state which would be 'free from the spirit of usury, from Jewish skepticism, from disintegrative qualities and elements, . . . which represent Jewry' collapses, and there is a 'happy ending' in which one sly Jew hoodwinks the whole of the Austrian populace.[17] (It is an ending which could easily have been written by an anti-Semite without many changes.) In real life there was no such happy ending, and much of Bettauer's prophecy is way off the mark, especially as concerns economics. Yet there is to my mind a remarkable accuracy in his descriptions of what cultural life in Vienna would be like without Jews, for it seems to me fairly clear that the provincialization which he is describing has gone on by leaps and bounds in postwar Vienna, right down to the astounding prevalence of loden cloth in the fancy stores on the Kärntnerstrasse and Am Graben. What, however, did Bettauer base his prophecies on, and how vital were the Jews in fact to Vienna as a cultural centre between the wars?

One of the ironies of using 1938 as the great caesura in the history of the Jewish intellectual in Vienna is that, if one were to concentrate purely on 1938, then the Jewish role in Viennese culture would not seem all that spectacular. To do this, however, would be to distort the picture greatly, for in fact 1938 did not happen in a vacuum, but was rather preceded by a catalogue of events which saw the gradual diminution of the Jewish role in Vienna. The situation, described by Bettauer and others, of the Jews as the central actors in Vienna's intellectual life, was disrupted not all at once in March 1938, but rather was the final stage in a dispossession of the 'Jewish intellectual' which had started as early as the late 1920s.

The 1920s can be seen as the heyday of the Jewish intellectual as Hayek understands the term. If one had looked at Viennese modern culture in the late 1920s the Jewish presence would indeed have seemed immense. One can see this from a contemporary and quite humorous account of Vienna in that era, *Was nicht im Baedeker steht,* by Ludwig Hirschfeld. Hirschfeld describes the leading groups in the world of literature and theatre and the names he mentions are largely those of Jewish individuals.[18] The author himself comments elsewhere in the text on a peculiarity of the Viennese, shared by everyone, from Nazi to Jew, of only deciding on a person's ability or character after knowing the answer to the question: 'Is he a Jew?' Hirschfeld then offers the following piece of advice: 'Be careful during your stay in Vienna not to be too interesting or original, otherwise you might, behind your back, suddenly be called a Jew.'[19]

The irony of such attitudes was that it was, as Hirschfeld himself hints, all too easy to confirm them on the basis of the actual situation in Vienna. One can illustrate this by looking at some of the most important cultural and intellectual movements in Vienna in this period. The first person Hirschfeld mentions in connection to this little Viennese peculiarity is, inevitably, Freud. The pejorative nature of the term 'Jewish science' should not stop us recognizing the fact that, especially in Vienna, psychoanalysis continued to be dominated by Jews. Indeed, Jewish individuals were very prominent in most of the schools of psychology in Vienna. There was Alfred Adler and his school of Individual Psychology, with pupils such as Manès Sperber, and others such as Charlotte Bühler (though her husband Karl was not of Jewish descent) and Paul Lazarsfeld who developed their own fields. Psychology in Vienna thus had a very large Jewish presence.[20]

In philosophy the Vienna Circle was officially launched in 1929, although it had been meeting informally for a long period before that. In the pamphlet which marked the launch, *Wissen-*

*schaftliche Weltauffassung: Der Wiener Kreis,* there was a list of fourteen members.[21] Of these eight were of Jewish descent. Of the rest two were from Germany, and two others named had not wanted to be on the list. One other, Viktor Kraft, was born in Vienna and was an enthusiastic member of the circle. It is hardly surprising, therefore, that people thought he was Jewish, even though, in reality, he was not.[22]

The archetypal 'Jewish intellectual,' Hayek's version, was in the socialist movement. Here the number of Jewish intellectuals prominent in the intellectual leadership of the party was very great indeed. Otto Bauer, the leader of the inter-war Austrian socialist party was Jewish, as was the leading socialist theorist, Max Adler. David Josef Bach and Joseph Luitpold Stern, leading figures in the movement of socialist *Volksbildung,* Oskar Pollak, the editor-in-chief of the socialist daily, the *Arbeiter Zeitung,* Julius Tandler and Hugo Breitner, who together restored the bodily and financial health of 'Red Vienna,' and many more prominent socialist intellectuals were Jewish. Indeed in his account of the socialist debacle in the 1930s Joseph Buttinger saw the Jewish intellectuals as an overwhelming presence in the educated leadership of the party.[23]

It is perhaps ironic that at the other end of the political spectrum – of Western politics, it should be said – among the defenders of the capitalist system, people of Jewish descent were also very numerous. This is hinted at in the quotation with which this essay began, for Ludwig von Mises was a Jewish intellectual who did the unspeakable and defended the market economy. His private seminar became the major vehicle between the wars for developing the theories of the Austrian school of liberal economics, and was the proving ground for Hayek. Roughly 80% of the participants in that seminar were people of Jewish descent.[24]

In the field of music there was also a large Jewish presence, although not perhaps as dominant as in others. Schoenberg was far and away the most important figure here, but from 1926, with his appointment in Berlin, he can hardly be counted as part of Viennese cultural life.[25] After him there were composers of the caliber of Berg, Webern and Krenek, who were not of Jewish descent. On the other hand there were many composers who were, including Egon Wellesz, Erich Wolfgang Korngold, Paul A. Pisk and Rudolf Réthi.[26] Thus there was a considerable presence of Jews in modern music in Vienna.

In art there was a similar situation at perhaps a lower level of Jewish participation. There were many Jewish artists, such as Max Oppenheimer (MOPP), Georg Ehrlich, Rudolf Ray-Rappaport and Georg Mayer-Marton, who became the secretary of the *Hagenbund*.[27] Yet for all their great talent they did not constitute a particularly significant contribution to modern art, but then neither did inter-war Austrian art in general. In architecture, on the other hand, there was the important work of the *Österreichische Werkbund*, whose leading figure was Joseph Frank, the brother of the philosopher Philipp Frank, both Jewish.[28]

It was in literature, however, that the Jewish presence was at its most prevalent. It is perhaps ironic that the most famous work of fiction in this period, *Der Mann ohne Eigenschaften*, was written by a non-Jew, Robert Musil. Yet he was exceptional in more ways than one. The Austrian literary scene was dominated by the work of such as Broch, Werfel, Roth, Kraus, Polgar, Friedell, Anton Kuh, Otto Soyka, Felix Salten, Leo Perutz and all those other Viennese Jewish writers who provided Vienna with its literary life.[29] The world of the literary coffee houses, as described in the works of Friedrich Torberg or the memoirs of such as Milan Dubrovic, was essentially a Jewish one, as indeed Torberg's use of 'Tante Jolesch' as a symbol of that life would indicate.[30]

Thus there was an extraordinarily large role for Jewish intellectuals in Vienna in the period up to 1930. The 1930s, however, saw a progressive disappearance of much of this world. Some losses were cased by death, due either to natural causes, as in the cases of Hofmannsthal (1929), Schnitzler (1931) and Kraus (1936), or to murder, as in the case of Hugo Bettauer (1925).

The most significant way in which Vienna's cultural life suffered losses, however, was emigration. There was a great exodus of talent around 1930. Some had left even earlier. Schoenberg had been called to Berlin; Joseph Roth had also moved to Berlin and then to Paris; Stefan Zweig had moved to Salzburg (which he left in 1934).[31] Hans Kelsen, the great theorist of legal positivism, left for a post in Germany in 1930.[32] Emigration before 1930 was the choice of relatively few and did not have too large an effect on the general cultural life of Vienna. The problem of emigration became very serious, however, in the period 1933–1934, which saw a disastrous turning of the tide for Jewish intellectuals in Vienna.

The destruction of parliamentary democracy in Austria, and the subsequent civil war resulted in the disappearance of a great part of the social and political environment in which left-wing Jewish intellectuals, indeed all sorts of Jewish intellectuals, had flourished. To start with, the Jewish intellectuals in the socialist leadership, chief among them Otto Bauer, had to flee to avoid arrest after the debacle of February 1934. Similarly, anyone who was sympathetic to their cause or refused to join the *Vaterländische Front* came under intense pressure. A case in point is that of Heinrich Gomperz, who refused to join, and in September 1934 was pensioned off from his professorship at the university, emigrating in 1935 to California.[33] It was in similar circumstances that individuals such as Otto Neurath, Manès Sperber, and Joseph Frank left.[34]

Many up-and-coming young Jews also left because there appeared to be no options open to them in the new clerical and corporate Austria. Ernst Gombrich, for instance, left in 1936 for a position in the Warburg Institute in London, with the strong encouragement of his friend Ernst Kris. With all academic jobs in the hands of the *Vaterländische Front* it did not appear at all likely that someone such as Gombrich, of Jewish descent, would be able to get a job in Austria.[35]

Emigration was the most practical answer to a bad situation. Austria was in the throes of a terrible economic depression, which inevitably had its material effects on cultural life, and made the chances of earning a living as an intellectual of any sort in Austria scant. Then there was the fact of Hitler's seizure of power across the border, which was felt as a constant threat, and, as several essays in this volume show, had a direct effect on career prospects in Austria as well. Of course the Austrian *Ständestaat* was also against Hitler, but an additional incentive to emigration was the consideration that just because Austria was against Hitler, this did not mean that it was on the side of the Jews. Far from it: Austro-Fascism, as we have seen, did not exactly encourage the usual politics of Jewish intellectuals, or even Jews generally. Indeed it was precisely the Jewish intellectual who, as Peter Pulzer among others has pointed out, had replaced the Jewish capitalist as the bête noire of Austrian anti-Semitism, had come to represent that 'Jewish spirit' which the fictional Schwertfeger, and the all too nonfictional Bishop of Linz, attacked so strongly.[36]

While nothing to compare with what was happening in Germany, there was in the Austrian *Ständestaat* discrimination against Jews, which amounted to a 'genteel apartheid,' and it was the 'intellectuals' who particularly suffered from this. In the university there was much violence among the studentship against Jewish colleagues, which encouraged a marked decline in the numbers of Jewish students.[37] In any case, the career prospects of students, once they had qualified, were not at all good. Jewish physicians were not promoted, because promotion required evidence of a certificate of baptism; the extent of discrimination can be gauged by the fact that in 1934 many Jewish doctors in state pay had been sacked for being socialist members, while most non-Jews in the same situation had not been. Jewish lawyers were less exposed to such practices, as their position was inherently more independent. Nevertheless, here too there was little prospect of promotion to the bench without conversion. Corporatist Austria was thus not a very favourable environment for Jewish intellectuals.[38]

Murray Hall's essay illustrates graphically the kinds of problems which Austria's absorption into the Nazi economy posed for Jewish writers in Vienna. Kurt Fischer has shown what pressure Jews in the academic world were under; all in all the period 1934–1938 was one which saw the gradual disintegration of the world of the Jewish intellectual. There is no more graphic illustration of this than the fate of the *Neue Freie Presse,* the lynchpin of the cultural world of 'Vienna 1900.' Financial and political pressures meant that in 1931 Ernst Benedikt had sold half of the newspaper's equity to someone who turned out to be an agent for the Austrian government. In 1936 Benedikt sold the rest of the equity to the same person. By 1938, therefore, the *Neue Freie Presse,* once the flagship of the liberal bourgeoisie, was a mouthpiece of the clerico-fascist regime.[39]

The Jews who did not emigrate reacted to all these problems and pressures in various ways. As will have become apparent from the discussion of the nature of the 'Jewish intellectual' above, there was not one response of the 'Jewish intellectual,' but rather many responses from all the different sorts of Jewish intellectuals, each addressing essentially the same problem in their own way.

One reaction was the rediscovery of the Jewish self. In the 1930s the Zionists gained power in Vienna's Jewish community, and an increased sense of Jewish identity can be seen in many prominent cultural figures.[40] Schoenberg completed a long process of return to Judaism by being formally accepted back into Judaism in Paris in 1933.[41] In *Warum die Fackel nicht erscheint,* published in 1934, Kraus made a remarkable confession, stating that he owed his intellectual disdain and his admiration for language and nature, to an uncompromisable Jewishness which he loved above all else: 'as something that was untouched by race or money, by class or background, in short by any type of hatred between the troglodytes and the racketeers.'[42] Even Wittgenstein felt the need to confess to his friends in Cambridge in 1937 that he was three-quarters Jewish, and this reflected a concern with his Jewishness which went at least as far back as 1931, when, in a note, he refers to himself as a 'Jewish talent.'[43]

Closely related to this response was that of other Jewish individuals, such as Stefan Zweig, who fell back on the kind of humanism on which the ideology of Jewish emancipation had been founded, and continued to defend this by now apparently anachronistic world-view.[44] Or there were those such as Broch and Canetti who saw all too clearly the amoral power of the crowd, the masses, and attempted, in comprehending this power, to make people aware of it, so that it could be controlled, and the freedom of the world of the mind preserved.[45] Another option, in the face of an authoritarian state, and the threat of Nazism, was to continue to believe in the power of emancipation, in the form of a workers' revolution, and this is what many Jewish individuals, such as Käthe Leichter and Manès Sperber did, involving themselves in the socialist or communist underground.[46]

On the other hand, many Jews and Jewish intellectuals ended up supporting the Catholic conservatism of the *Ständestaat*. The emancipation was far enough in the past for some Jews, it is not clear how many, to regard themselves by 1934 as a fully integrated part of the Establishment. This may well have been especially prevalent in the assimilated haute bourgeoisie, where Christian Social acceptance of Jewish money (Fritz Mandl) and financial advice (Gottfried Kunwald), and the common goal of the defence of property, may have given the impression of an identity of interests. In addition, the *Ständestaat*, to the extent that it represented the idea of an independent Austria, could be seen as a bulwark against Hitler.[47]

In this context, and only in this context, the rebirth of the Habsburg myth among Magris's 'Jewish intellectuals' such as Werfel, Roth, and Ernst Lothar, or Kraus's vain support for Dollfuss, can be truly understood.[48] The confusion created by this situation is made plain by the case of Egon Friedell. Friedell is often seen as a Jew at ease with his Jewishness, what in German is called a 'bewußter Jude.' He was in reality what one might term a Jewish anti-Semite, and officially a Protestant. His *Kulturgeschichte der Neuzeit* (1927), wittily written though it is, included in it a vicious attack on the corrupting nature of the 'Jewish spirit,' which any anti-Semite would have been proud to have written. It is thus not so surprising that in 1935 Friedell attempted to reach agreement with the German Nazi regime, only to be rejected out of hand with the simple explanation that he, Friedell, was a Jew. From then on Friedell inevitably became an ardent 'Austrian' and anti-Nazi.[49]

It is unclear just how widespread this, as it were, right-wing Austrianism was among Vienna's Jews and indeed how right-wing it really was. Mixed up in the identification with the *Ständestaat* was that hankering back to the 'Austrian idea' of a perfect liberal, and pluralistic state, which had never really existed except in the minds of many Jews and some Josephinist bureaucrats.[50] That many saw Schuschnigg and his regime as the heirs of that tradition shows just how desperate the situation was.

The reaction of most Jews and many Jewish intellectuals was, to carry on as if nothing had really happened. The very feeling of belonging, of being part of Viennese society, made someone such as Lili Schnitzler or George Clare largely oblivious to any danger, or else persuaded them into suspending their sense of any threat.[51] Canetti's memoirs show a cultural circle which is carrying on as usual, more or less devoid of any political content or involvement. It is a world of salons, whether it be that of Alma Mahler-Werfel, the Zsolnays, or the Schwarzwalds, and of coffee houses, especcially the Café Museum. Here Canetti talked about virtually everything to Dr. Sonne, not so much a Jewish intellectual as a Jewish secular scholar.[52] Torberg's world is also that of the coffee house, carrying on regardless of the world beyond the lace-curtained windows. It is perhaps the final symbolic irony that Ernst Lothar should, as is described elsewhere in this volume, be making theatre up until the very last moment – intent on suspending disbelief as long as was humanly possible.[53]

Yet this state of affairs, in which cultural life can be said to have been merely ticking over, with little new produced, was far from the golden age of the critical culture of the Jewish intellectuals discussed earlier. By 1938, in other words, a great deal of the substance of Vienna's cultural life had already been lost. So we are left with the question of what Vienna actually did lose in 1938. The answer is, that despite the ground being prepared by the *Ständestaat*, Vienna still had a great deal to lose in 1938.

Despite attempts to change matters, in 1938 a remarkably large part of Vienna's liberal educated class was still Jewish. In 1936 62% of Vienna's lawyers were Jewish, 47% of the city's physicians, 28% of its university professors. These people were sacked after 1938.[54] This is only part of the story, however, for the criterion for these figures must have been religion. If one looks at the criterion of descent, which was the relevant one after 1939, then the results are even more dramatic. One example to hand is that of the medical faculty of the university, where of the total teaching faculty of 153 personnel, 118 (77%) were sacked in 1938 because of their Jewish racial origin.[55]

Vienna also lost the younger generation, who might under more favourable circumstances have been the successors to the tradition of Jewish intellectuality but who instead went abroad, their potential never realized in Vienna itself. Then there were those non-Jews in the intelligentsia who nevertheless had to leave for the sake of their Jewish wives; Musil is the most important example of this, though there were others. In this context one might remark that Hitler's Nuremberg Laws were, whether one likes it or not, remarkably efficient in weeding out Vienna's intelligentsia, one way or another.

Therefore much was lost in 1938. One can conclude, however, that 1938 was only the climax to a long drawn out process, which at the latest from 1933 had spelt doom for the role of the 'Jewish intellectual' in Vienna. Yet that does not mean that the role of the Viennese Jewish intellectual had come to an end. If one looks at 1938 in another way, one can claim with some justification that 'Vienna 1900' in one sense never really died but was instead continued abroad, in American and English philosophy or English art history, for instance. Is it any wonder that among the nine more prominent names on Perry Anderson's list of the foreign maîtres d'école of England's national culture, published in 1968, one can find those of Wittgenstein, Gombrich, Karl Popper, and Melanie Klein?[56] In a sense 'Vienna' just moved away with the people who were the inheritors of the people who had created that cultural phenomenon in the first place. If you like: is not London, N.W.6 one of the last bastions of the Habsburg Monarchy?

Seen in longer perspective, 1938 was only a stage in an historical development going back to the eighteenth century, of the assimilation into, and cultural response to, Western, Enlightened culture of Central European Jewry. In that light it is heavily ironic that the one place where *that* culture finds so little echo is Vienna itself. Hans Thalberg, one-time colleague of Bruno Kreisky and Kurt Waldheim, has in his memoirs made the following remark: 'The Jews in Austria were always the pike in the carp pond. Now the carp have killed and eaten up the troublesome pike. Without pike around the carp are, it is true, fatter; but in the pond something is missing.'[57] When one realizes just what the Jews and Jewish intellectuals meant to the cultural life of Vienna, one can see his point.

## NOTES

1. Ludwig von Mises, *Erinnerungen* (Stuttgart: Fischer, 1978), p. xv.
2. Claudio Magris, *Der habsburgische Mythos in der Österreichischen Literatur* (Salzburg: Otto Müller, 1966), p. 267.
3. Cf. the catalogues, Peter Vergo, *Vienna 1900: Vienna, Scotland and the European Avant-Garde* (Edinburgh: H.M.S.O., 1983); Kirk Varnedoe, *Vienna 1900: art, architecture and design* (New York: MOMA, 1986).
4. Friedrich Torberg, *Die Tante Jolesch oder Der Untergang des Abendlandes in Anekdoten* (Munich: DTV, 1975), p. 220.
5. Cf. Hilde Spiel, *Vienna's golden autumn 1866-1938* (London: Weidenfeld and Nicolson, 1987), pp. 193-236.
6. Cf. the catalogue, Robert Waissenberger, ed., *Traum und Wirklichkeit: Wien 1870-1930* (Vienna, 1985).
7. Cf. the catalogue, *Vienne 1890-1938, l'apocalypse joyeuse, sous la direction de Jean Clair* (Paris, 1986).
8. For an elaboration of the following view, see my article: "Fin de siècle Vienna and the Jews: the dialectics of assimilation," *The Jewish Quarterly*, vol. 33, no. 3 (123), 1986, pp. 28-33. This is itself a summary; a detailed version is forthcoming from Cambridge University Press, under the title *Vienna and the Jews 1867-1938: A Cultural History*.
9. For an indication of the extent of Jewish involvement in fin de siècle Viennese modern culture, see my article: 'Class, culture and the Jews of Vienna 1900,' in Ivar Oxaal, Michael Pollak and Gerhard Botz, eds.,

*Jews, Antisemitism and Culture in Vienna* (London: Routledge and Kegan Paul, 1987), pp. 39-58.

10. Hugo Bettauer, *Die Stadt ohne Juden* (Vienna, 1980, reprint). A new edition is soon to be published by Ullstein, Berlin.

11. Bettauer, *Die Stadt ohne Juden*, p. 49.

12. Ibid., pp. 43-44.

13. Ibid., pp. 71-73.

14. Ibid., pp. 73-79.

15. Ibid., pp. 81-82.

16. Ibid., p. 124.

17. Ibid., p. 139.

18. Ludwig Hirschfeld, *Was nicht im Baedeker steht: Wien und Budapest* (Munich: Piper, 1927), pp. 43-47, 88ff.

19. Ibid., pp. 56-57.

20. Cf. Erika Weinzierl, Kurt Skalnik, eds., *Österreich 1918-1938: Geschichte der Ersten Republik,* vol. 2 (Graz: Styria, 1983), pp. 565-566.

21. The pamphlet and list are reproduced in Otto Neurath, *Empiricism and sociology* (Dordrecht: Reidel, 1973), pp. 299-318, with the list being on p. 318.

22. Information on Viktor Kraft courtesy of Paul Neurath, Vienna.

23. Joseph Buttinger, *In the Twilight of Socialism* (London: Europa, 1954), pp. 80-81. Also see Henriette Kotlan-Werner, *Kunst und Volk: David Josef Bach 1874-1947* (Vienna: Europa, 1977); Ernst Fischer, *An opposing man* (London: Allen Lane, 1974), pp. 134-135; Ernst Glaser, *Im Umfeld des Austromarxismus: ein Beitrag zur Geistesgeschichte des österreichischen Sozialismus* (Vienna: Europa, 1981).

24. The list is in Mises, *Erinnerungen*, pp. 65-66.

25. H. H. Stuckenschmidt, *Schoenberg: His Life, World and Work* (London: John Calder, 1977), pp. 303ff.

26. Weinzierl, Skalnik, *Österreich 1918-1938,* pp. 663-665; Sylvia Maderegger, *Die Juden im österreichischen Ständestaat 1934-1938* (Vienna: Geyer-Edition, 1973), pp. 263-264; Norbert Leser, ed., *Das geistige Leben Wiens in der Zwischenkriegszeit* (Vienna: Österreichischer Bundesverlag, 1981), pp. 295-299.

27. On Mayer-Marton, see Johanna Braithwaite, 'George Mayer-Marton (1897-1960),' *The Wiener Library Newsletter,* Vol. 2, no. 3 (May 1987).

28. Leser, *Das geistige Leben Wiens,* pp. 286-292.

29.  Cf. Maderegger, *Die Juden im österreichischen Ständestaat*, pp. 257ff.

30.  Milan Dubrovic, *Veruntreute Geschichte: die Wiener Salons und Literaturcafés* (Vienna: Zsolnay, 1985); Torberg, *Die Tante Jolesch;* Friedrich Torberg, *Die Erben der Tante Jolesch* (Munich: DTV, 1981).

31.  David Bronsen, *Joseph Roth: eine Biographie* (Munich: DTV, 1981), pp. 208ff.; D. A. Prater, *European of yesterday: a Biography of Stefan Zweig* (Oxford: Oxford University Press, 1972), pp. 120ff.

32.  R. A. Métall, *Hans Kelsen: Leben und Werk* (Vienna: Deuticke, 1969), p. 56.

33.  R. A. Kann, H. Gomperz, eds., *Theodor Gomperz: ein Gelehrtenleben im Bürgertum der Franz-Josefszeit* (Vienna: Österreichische Akademie der Wissenschaften, 1974), pp. 27-28.

34.  Weinzierl, Skalnik, *Österreich 1918-1938* pp. 645, 675.

35.  Interview with Sir Ernst Gombrich, Cambridge, 2 March 1988.

36.  Peter Pulzer, 'The development of political antisemitism in Austria,' in: Josef Fraenkel, ed., *The Jews of Austria: essays on their life, history and destruction* (London: Vallentine Mitchell, 1967), p. 441; Fischer, *An opposing man*, p. 134-135.

37.  Maderegger, *Die Juden im österreichischen Ständestaat*, pp. 152-156.

38.  Ibid., pp. 224-240.

39.  Adam Wandruszka, *Geschichte einer Zeitung: das Schicksal der 'Presse' und der 'Neuen Freien Presse' von 1848 zur Zweiten Republik* (Vienna: Neue Wiener Presse, 1958), pp. 144-146.

40.  Maderegger, *Die Juden im österreichischen Ständestaat*, p. 47.

41.  Stuckenschmidt, *Schoenberg*, pp. 365ff.

42.  Karl Kraus, *Warum die Fackel nicht erscheint*, in *Die Fackel* (Munich, 1973, facsim. reprint), vol. 39, end of July 1934, XXXVI, no. 890-905, p. 38.

43.  Rush Rhees, ed., *Recollections of Wittgenstein* (Oxford: Oxford University Press, 1984), pp. 34-36; Ludwig Wittgenstein, *Culture and value* (Oxford: Basil Blackwell, 1980), pp. 18-19.

44.  See Donald Daviau's article in this volume; also George E. Mosse, *German Jews beyond Judaism* (Bloomington, 1985), the chapter on Zweig and Ludwig.

45.  On Broch, Erich Kahler, *Die Philosophie von Hermann Broch* (Tübingen: Mohr (Siebeck), 1962), pp. 58-76.

46.  Buttinger, *In the twilight of socialism*, pp. 81-87; Herbert Steiner, ed., *Käthe Leichter: Leben und Werk* (Vienna: Europa, 1973), pp. 152-175; Manes Sperber, *Bis man mir Scherben auf die Augen legt* (Vienna:

DTV, 1977), pp. 51ff.

47.  Maderegger, *Die Juden im österreichischen Ständestaat*, pp. 82-101;
     G.E.R. Gedye, *Fallen bastions: the Central European tragedy* (London:
     Victor Gallancz, 1939), pp. 73ff.

48.  Magris, *Der habsburgische Mythos*, pp. 265-267; Maderegger, *Die Juden
     im österreichischen Ständestaat*, pp. 257-262.

49.  Gordon Patterson, 'Race and antisemitism in the life and work of Egon
     Friedell,' *Jahrbuch des Instituts für deutsche Geschichte, Tel-Aviv
     University*, 1981, pp. 319-339.

50.  For an extraordinary example of this see Ernst Lothar, *Der Engel mit
     der Posaune: Roman eines Hauses* (Salzburg: Verlag: 'Das Silberboot,'
     1947), pp. 643-644.

51.  Interview with Lili Schnitzler, Vienna, 27 October 1988; George Clare,
     *Last waltz in Vienna: the destruction of a family 1842-1942* (London:
     Macmillan, 1981), pp. 126ff.

52.  Elias Canetti, *Das Augenspiel: Lebensgeschichte 1931-1937* (Munich:
     Karl Hauser, 1985), passim, esp. pp. 155, 206-207, 225.

53.  Cf. Hans Thalberg, *Von der Kunst, Österreicher zu sein: Erinnerungen
     und Tagesbuchnotizen* (Vienna: Böhlau, 1984), p. 58.

54.  Maderegger, *Die Juden im österreichischen Ständestaat*, p. 220.

55.  Weinzierl, Skalnik, *Österreich 1918-1938*, p. 584.

56.  Perry Anderson, 'Components of the national culture,' *New Left
     Review*, no. 50 (July-August 1968), 17.

57.  Thalberg, *Von der Kunst Österreicher zu sein*, p. 80.

'My True Enemy':
Freud and the Catholic Church 1927–1939

Ritchie Robertson

In 1937, a few months before the absorption of Austria into Greater Germany, Freud told a visitor, René Laforgue, that he was not afraid of the Nazis. 'Help me rather,' he said, 'to combat my true enemy.' When Laforgue asked who this 'enemy' was, Freud astonished him by replying: 'Religion, the Roman Catholic Church.'[1]

Moreover, Freud believed himself to have a dangerous enemy in the person of one Father Wilhelm Schmidt, who is mentioned in the correspondence with Arnold Zweig, once as Freud's enemy and once as a person of great power in the Austrian Corporate State. This paper is intended to suggest Schmidt's importance in the culture and politics of Austria in the 1930s and earlier; to account for Freud's antipathy to him; and to argue that Freud's last major work, *Moses and Monotheism,* is a covert and complex response to Schmidt's own theory of monotheism.

Freud's antipathy to religion in general is well known. Growing up as a Jew in a largely Catholic country, he absorbed many secular and anticlerical ideas. Some of these influences have recently been mentioned by Peter Gay, who points out how much Freud was pursuing the ideals of the Enlightenment through his scientific career.[2] His youthful heroes were scientists like Darwin, Huxley and Tyndall. He read the anticlerical historians Lecky and Buckle. He first declared his open opposition to religion in *Totem and Taboo,* where it is explained as originating, along with all other cultural achievements, in the Oedipus complex. He explored the topic further in *The Future of an Illusion,* proposing an evolutionary view of religion as a primitive survival to be replaced by science, and ending his peroration with a quotation from Heine: 'Den Himmel überlassen wir / Den Engeln und den Spatzen.'³

The delusions of religion were once more set against the concrete achievements of science in 1932, in the last of Freud's second series of *Introductory Lectures on Psychoanalysis.* Here he notes that psychoanalysis is not just a technique of research and therapy. It presupposes a Weltanschauung, namely that of science. Freud sums up the scientific world-view as a programme of rigorous scepticism which dismisses revelation or intuition as sources of knowledge. He acknowledges that science most often has no answer to suffering. But then neither has religion, except a delusory one which must always be contradicted by harsh experience. Freud hopes that mankind will mature enough to discard religion and submit to the dictatorship of reason: 'Our best hope for the future is that the intellect—the scientific spirit, reason— will in time establish a dictatorship in man's psychic life.'⁴

Given these views Freud could hardly be at ease in the actual dictatorship ruled by Dollfuss. The Austrian Corporate State represented an extreme reaction against the period of Liberalism in which Freud had grown up. It was dominated by the Catholic Church and drew on long-established conservative and anti-Semitic traditions. Its corporatist programme was an amalgam of traditions of Catholic and conservative political thought, opposed to what was seen as the atomizing and secularizing influence of liberal capitalism. One such tradition was 'social policy' (*Sozialpolitik*), represented by the Papal Encyclical *Rerum novarum,* which accepted the existing social order but wished to modify it by legislation to remove its harshness. The other was 'social reform' (*Sozialreform*), represented by the reactionary thinker Karl von Vogelsang and his successor Othmar Spann, who wanted society to be reorganized on feudal lines, all economic activity to be brought under state control, and the state to be closely linked with the Church.⁵ At the first mass rally of the Fatherland Front (*Vaterländische Front*) on 11 September 1933, Dollfuss proclaimed the corporatist reorganization of the state and contributed to a conservative and Catholic definition of Austrian identity that implicitly excluded Jews. After glancing over the glories of Austrian history, he deplored the decline of feudal society and the rise of liberalism, soulless materialism, and unrestrained capitalism. He promised to roll back liberal democracy, replacing the ineffectual hegemony of political parties with the mass movement represented by the Vaterländische Front. He concluded: 'We want the social, Christian, German state of Austria on a corporate basis and under strong, authoritarian leadership!'[6]

The *Ständestaat,* however, avoided explicitly endorsing anti-Semitism, partly in order to distance itself from National Socialism. Moreover, the anti-Semitism current in Austria was not of the National Socialist variety, based on pseudoscientific theories of race. It was primarily a Christian abhorrence of Jews as the people responsible for Christ's death, overlaid with the hostility of peasants and urban petty-bourgeois to the Jew seen as the embodiment of capitalism, and combined, at a higher social level, with resentment against Jewish competition for professional appointments.[7]

The Catholic and anticapitalist version of anti-Semitism was formulated on 21 January 1933 in a pastoral letter from the Bishop of Linz. He condemned the racial doctrines of the National Socialists as well as all pogroms and other manifestations of anti-Semitism and disrespect for the Jewish religion. But he was also roused to anger by 'the international Jewish spirit,' which, he said, dominated modern cultural and commercial life. 'Degenerate Jewry in alliance with world Freemasonry,' he proclaimed, 'is also the principal bearer of mammonistic capitalism and the principal founder and apostle of Socialism and Communism, the harbingers and pace-makers of Bolshevism.' To destroy the harmful influence of the Jews was the duty of every Christian. The Bishop referred with evident approval to the ghettos which had been set up in Italian cities during the Counter-Reformation and recommended that his contemporaries should 'erect a strong legislative and administrative barrier against all the spiritual filth and the immoral slimy flood, emanating principally from Jewry, which threatens to overwhelm the world.'[8]

Such public utterances help to explain why Freud was reluctant to publish his essay in Biblical criticism, *Moses and Monotheism*, for fear of arousing Catholic enmity. He gives his reasons in a letter to Arnold Zweig on 30 October 1934: 'We live here in an atmosphere of Catholic orthodoxy. They say that the politics of our country are determined by one Pater Schmidt, who lives in St Gabriel near Mödling. He is a confidant of the Pope, and unfortunately he is himself an ethnologist and student of comparative religion, whose books make no secret of his abhorrence of analysis and especially of my totem theory.'[9] Freud added that the journal of psychoanalysis recently founded in Rome had suddenly been banned, and that the ban was thought to have come direct from the Vatican and to have been instigated by Father Schmidt. If Freud were to irritate this person further, his influence in Austria might be used to outlaw psychoanalysis on its home ground. Later, in the prefatory note to part III of *Der Mann Moses*, Freud explained that he had withheld the work from publication because the Catholicism of the Austrian corporate state was the last bulwark against the various barbarisms of Germany, Italy and Russia, and since Catholicism already viewed psychoanalysis with distrust he could not risk strengthening its suspicion.[10] In a later letter to Zweig he again referred to Schmidt: 'And I count it to my credit that our arch enemy P. Schmidt has just been awarded the Austrian decoration of honour for his pious lies in the field of ethnology. Clearly this is meant to console him for the fact that providence has allowed me to achieve the age of 80.'[11]

Although Father Schmidt's name will be familiar to many Austrians, few people in the English-speaking world are likely to have heard of him. Yet in his time he was an anthropologist of worldwide reputation, and the few available glimpses of his political career suggest that he wielded considerable backstairs influence as early as the last years of the Habsburg Empire.

Wilhelm Schmidt was not an Austrian, but a German. He was born at Hörde, in industrial Westphalia, in 1868, the son of a factory worker. While still in his teens he joined the missionary society called the Societas Verbi Divini, and much of his life was spent studying and later teaching at its seminary in St Gabriel on the edge of Mödling, near Vienna. From 1925 to 1938 he was also professor of anthropology at Vienna University. He founded the Anthropos Institute for anthropology, and was also involved in establishing the Museum für Völkerkunde in Vienna. In 1925 he helped to organize an exhibition of missionary work in Rome, and was appointed by the Pope as Director of the Museo missionario etnologico. In 1928 he was honoured by a huge Festschrift composed by an international array of authors, including the eminent American anthropologists A. L. Kroeber and Robert Lowie, as well as the social reformer Othmar Spann.[12]

Despite his training, Schmidt seems not to have done any missionary work or anthropological fieldwork. Although he organized many expeditions, he himself never left Europe until 1935, when he went on a lecture tour of the United States, China, Japan, Korea, and the Philippines. His researches into Australian languages, on which he was an authority, were based on published accounts and on information sent him by missionaries. His productivity was awe-inspiring. Besides his linguistic publications, his main work was *Der Ursprung der Gottesidee* ('The Origin of the Idea of God'), in twelve massive volumes which cannot contain less than five million words. A bibliography of his works (not quite complete) lists 647 items, besides over sixty pieces of sacred music. His biographer tells us that Schmidt used neither a typewriter nor a card-index, and describes his working methods in a manner reminiscent of Kafka's Castle officials: 'His great ideas forced him to keep writing furiously. Thus in the course of his long life he wrote tens of thousands of pages in his own hand; as his works appeared in print, their manuscripts gradually grew into stacks a yard high beside his desk, and their blank sides served to draft new works.'[13]

Before giving some account of the anthropological theories contained in his voluminous works, I want to glance at Schmidt's political activities, hard though they are to make out. In 1916 Schmidt was appointed chaplain to the Imperial headquarters, which brought him close to the Imperial family. In 1918 he was

active in the International Catholic Union, which organized conferences to discuss the social reconstruction of postwar Europe
and forestall the influence of international Socialism on the peace
settlement. He figures in the diary of Ignaz Seipel, who was soon
to become leader of the Christian Social Party in the First Republic. On 11 January 1918 Seipel was summoned by telephone to see
Schmidt at Mödling. When Seipel arrived, Schmidt gave him
instructions from the Emperor to attend a conference which the
Catholic Union was planning at Zürich.[14] This suggests that
Schmidt was already a grey eminence of considerable standing.
Seipel's diaries contain some tantalizing entries mentioning heated
discussions with Schmidt, who was visiting him at the time of the
Emperor's abdication. On 7 November 1918 Seipel warned
Schmidt against 'imprudent actions.' The Emperor abdicated on
11 November, and on the following day Seipel and Schmidt had a
'violent dispute' about Schmidt's politics.[15] Clearly Schmidt, like
many of the Austrian clergy, was a loyal monarchist who found
the prospect of a republic difficult to accept.

Schmidt's conservatism is made plain in his publications and
sermons. In 1920 he issued a book, *Der deutschen Seele Not und
Heil* ('The Plight of the German Soul and its Salvation'), in which
he maintained that the War had revealed the bankruptcy of modern secular civilization and that mankind's only hope was to return
to the Church. On 26 September 1920 Schmidt delivered an
address to the Vienna Catholic Congress, which was published in
the conservative Catholic weekly *Das Neue Reich* ('The New
Empire'). Schmidt's address referred to the elections scheduled for
17 October. The previous elections, in February 1919, had left the
Social Democrats the largest party in Parliament, with just over
40% of the vote. Hence the title of Schmidt's speech: 'Befreiung
Wiens vom jüdischen Bolschewismus!' ('The Liberation of Vienna
from Jewish Bolshevism!') In this speech he denounced Social
Democracy as 'a regime alien to our people and imposed by
force,' dominated by Jews who were plotting to destroy religion.
By the end of his speech he had come to equate Socialism with
Bolshevism, speaking of 'the shameful alien rule of the Jewish

Bolsheviks.' The Jews are described in bold type as 'inferior members of an alien race.'[16]

At the same time Schmidt believed in social reform in the sense defined above. He agreed with the Christian Social Party in opposing liberalism, deploring its atomizing effect on society, and urging that capitalism should be controlled. Accordingly, Schmidt was among the founder members of the Catholic Bund Neuland, which aimed to bring Christianity to the modern urban masses and thus remove them from the temptations of atheism and Social-ism.[17] Resting on conservative anticapitalism, the Bund Neuland identified capitalism with the Jews, and its periodical, *Neuland,* contains several articles denouncing Jews as a 'race of Cain' ('Kainsvolk')[18] and warning Austrian Catholics to practise 'racial conservation' ('Rassepflege') and combat 'Judaization' ('Ver-judung').[19]

Since Schmidt was an anthropologist, it was easy for him to put forward theories of race. He was concerned first of all to condemn the racial theories of National Socialism. He rejected the National Socialists' genetic determinism, on the grounds that in Catholic doctrine the soul was an integral entity which could not be affected by the genes. Instead, Schmidt's mentor was his colleague at Vienna University, the prehistorian and racial theorist Oswald Menghin. Menghin criticized the National Socialists for confusing the materialistic concept of race with the cultural concept of 'Volkstum.'[20] But his book *Geist und Blut* ('Spirit and Blood') shows Menghin himself to be confused: he maintains that the Jews are culturally unassimilable because they have become an urban people while the Germans are basically a peasant people; but he also wants to deny on racial grounds that a Jew, however thoroughly he may have absorbed German culture, can ever be accepted as a German.[21]

Schmidt follows Menghin in both these ways. For him, 'Volkstum' is primary, while race is secondary; the German 'Volkstum,' a cultural entity, comprises a number of races, such as the Nordic and Ostic races. Along with the National Socialists' racial materialism, Schmidt rejects their programme of 'Nordification' ('Aufnordung') on the grounds that it may discriminate against one of Germany's racial minorities – the Westphalians, who according to Schmidt belong to the 'Dalic' race. And, like Menghin, he wants to fuss or confuse racial and religious categories in order to keep the Jews separate from the Germans.[22] The crucial difference between Jews and Aryans, he explained in an article in the Catholic journal *Schönere Zukunft* ('A Fairer Future'), lies in the 'psychic structure' of the Jews. Since rejecting the Messiah they have been 'a people who, in the deepest region of their souls, have lost contact with their national roots.'[23] The Jews are not mentioned in his treatise *Rasse und Volk*, which is an essay on German 'Volkstum' and its need to be rooted in the soil of Germany. Schmidt's insistently organicist imagery strongly recalls the influential book by Julius Langbehn, *Rembrandt als Erzieher* ('Rembrandt as Educator,' 1890), which provided an influential definition of 'German-ness.'[24]

It is not surprising that Schmidt enthusiastically supported the Corporate State. In 1934 he commended it for upholding the family and demanded that it should introduce further measures. Any defamation of the family in the media should be punished. People should be legally forbidden to live together outside wedlock. Girls should be educated for motherhood. Education should include eugenics. Religious intermarriage should be severely prohibited. The employment of women in offices and factories should be reduced to a minimum. And the tax laws should favour the fathers of large families, who should also be given jobs in preference to childless men.[25] He was the chairman of a commission set up in 1936 by the Austrian episcopate to establish a Catholic university at Salzburg, a project to which he was intensely committed.

Although Austria under Dollfuss largely avoided anti-Semitism, we have already seen that there were exceptions. The Bishop of Linz was one; Schmidt was another. In December 1933 Schmidt gave an address to the Catholic Congress in the First District of Vienna under the title 'Zur Judenfrage' ('On the Jewish Problem'). He condemned the overrepresentation of Jews in the professions and the media, and deplored the corruption which had overtaken the Jews since their failure to accept Christ:

> As punishment for this crime, this people, as Christ himself prophesied, was expelled from its native soil and has wandered about ever since as a rootless people deprived of the soil of the homeland in which it was rooted. The distortion of its character and its severance from its roots, which have lasted for almost two millennia, have also affected its physical race, secondarily, but none the less effectively. If a Jew whole-heartedly and sincerely enters the Catholic Church, he has removed the strongest reason separating him from us and surmounted the true and deepest cause of his otherness. But the racial effects of this cause which have made themselves apparent in the course of these two millennia cannot be removed all at once, even by baptism; that requires much time and inward labour, so that he is indeed one of us, but not in the same way as our German kinsfolk.[26]

As this passage, combined with his publications on the racial question, may demonstrate, Schmidt came closer than perhaps anyone else in Austria to grafting a new racial anti-Semitism onto the traditional religious and anticapitalist anti-Semitism. The social implications of his views are indicated by his approving reference to a recent book by Emmerich Czermak and Oskar Karbach, *Ordnung in der Judenfrage* ('Dealing with the Jewish Problem'), which begins by declaring: 'Nowadays we can see with absolute clarity that liberal, socialist, Bolshevist Jewry is a degenerate Jewry.'[27] They do not propose to exclude the Jews from economic and cultural life, but rather to confer upon them the status of a recognized minority. Yet, since the authors also reject the possibility of Jewish assimilation, it is difficult to see what this would have achieved except singling the Jews out as targets for discrimination.

All this gives ample reason for Freud to dislike Schmidt.

They had already crossed swords, however, as a result of Freud's venture into anthropology in *Totem und Tabu*. Schmidt himself held strong views on anthropological questions. He belonged to the diffusionist school, which attempted to explain cultural similarities (in institutions and material products) as resulting not from independent invention but from diffusion from an original centre. The German school of diffusionists tried to identify a number of 'Kulturkreise' ('cultural circles'), areas within which such diffusion had taken place.

Schmidt was particularly interested in the most primitive peoples, such as the Congolese Pygmies, the Andaman Islanders, the Australian Aborigines, and the inhabitants of Tierra del Fuego. Using data collected by explorers, mainly missionaries, Schmidt began by studying these peoples' languages and then passed to their religions. He established to his own satisfaction that all these peoples shared a primeval monotheism. All believed in a Supreme Being who was the author of good. In addition, they led peaceful lives, were monogamous, cared altruistically for children, old people and fertile mothers, and had a clear concept of private property. So perfect was their social order, in fact, that Schmidt found himself driven to conclude that these peoples must have received a direct revelation from God. To have made such an impression on them, God must have appeared in person, in physical form. This conclusion forms the climax of the first six volumes of *Der Ursprung der Gottesidee*, and Schmidt leaves the reader in no doubt that his supernaturalism is absolutely literal:

> It was the really existing Supreme Being, the actual Creator of heaven and earth and, in particular, of mankind, who appeared before His most excellent creatures, mankind, and revealed Himself, His own being and workings, disclosed Himself to their minds, wills and emotions immediately after Creation, when He dwelt familiarly together with mankind.[28]

Hence myths about the primeval paradise must be true, and so must the creation myths of the most ancient peoples. After all, as Schmidt observes, they derived their information from God, the most reliable witness to an event which was still recent. Subsequently, however, this happy state was disrupted by sin. Schmidt considers it most probable that the Fall resulted from the excessive pride of the tribal leader who communicated with God on behalf of his followers. Thereafter the male-dominated society of primeval mankind gave way to a matrilocal and matrilineal society, and all the troubles of history followed. Only in remote spots like the Andamans and Tierra del Fuego did remnants survive of man's original paradisal state.

It hardly needs to be said that Schmidt's anthropology has not worn well. For one thing, it is based on methods and assumptions which, however respectable in their time, have since been decisively rejected. Like the almost equally prolific British armchair anthropologist Sir James Frazer, Schmidt reached his conclusions by comparing multifarious data. This 'scrap-book treatment, which was dignified by being labelled the "comparative method,"' as Sir Edward Evans-Pritchard later described it,[29] risks misunderstanding ethnographic facts by considering them in isolation from their social context. Data can thus easily be marshalled to support the anthropologist's pet theory. Another method employed by anthropologists who were unable to make field trips was to draw up detailed questionnaires for travellers. This was a well-tried method, going back to the ethnography of the late Enlightenment. It was used at the beginning of the twentieth century as a means of collecting information about peoples under German colonial rule, and Schmidt was among the anthropologists employed by the Imperial Colonial Office to draw up the questionnaire. But, as the unorthodox anthropologist and missionary Bruno Gutmann pointed out, the questionnaire method tends to force the ethnographic data into a rigid set of preconceived concepts which cannot be modified by first-hand experience in the field.[30] Diffusionism, long an anthropological orthodoxy, is now out of favour: cultural similarities are now thought to be adequately explained by independent invention in response to similar material environments. Schmidt's theory of primeval monotheism has antecedents going back to the eighteenth-century Jesuit missionary Lafitau, whose *Moeurs des sauvages américains comparés aux moeurs des premiers temps* (1724) was a path-finding exercise in ethnographic comparison and diffusionist theory.[31]

Schmidt was patently biased in his use even of the data available to him. For example, in crediting the Andaman Islanders with a highly ethical monotheism, he was following a late nine-teenth-century study which had been contradicted by the British anthropologist Radcliffe-Brown. After prolonged and careful enquiries, Radcliffe-Brown found that the Andamaners believed in several divinities and that their principal divinity was thought to be indifferent to moral offences, even murder and adultery, and to be angered only by such actions as melting wax, killing a cicada, and digging up yams. In *Der Ursprung der Gottesidee* Schmidt compares Radcliffe-Brown's account of the Andaman Islanders with earlier accounts at considerable length, but his criticism is directed exclusively at Radcliffe-Brown, and his show of im-partiality is unconvincing.[32] Schmidt's supernaturalism makes it clear that despite his pretence of objective research he was guided by his own fantasies. In particular, his account of primitive society sounds much too good to be true. Schmidt's primitives (whom he had never seen in the flesh) seem already to have attained the social harmony which the Austrian Corporate State was striving to restore. And by blaming women for the loss of this primeval harmony, Schmidt has translated the myth of the Fall into terms that are anthropological, yet no less mythical.

Ironically, Schmidt's work is now held by anthropologists in even lower esteem than Freud's. Yet in their time Schmidt was in the scientific mainstream, while Freud was regarded as an imperti-nent amateur. Accordingly, the manual of anthropology for students, *Ursprung und Werden der Religion,* that Schmidt pub-lished in 1930, contains sharp attacks on Freud and Durkheim — both amateurs and, not coincidentally, both Jews. Schmidt op-poses the argument by Freud that totemism is the basis of religion. He maintains that among the most primitive peoples such practices as parricide and cannibalism are unknown, and defends primitive men against Freud's slanders: 'To bring such men into connexion with modern sex-ridden neurotics, as he [Freud] would have us do, and from this connexion to deduce the alleged fact that all thought and feeling, especially subliminal, is founded on and saturated with sex, must remain lost labour. Thus Freud's hypothesis loses its last shadow of hope ever to corroborate or establish any single part of itself, for every part collapses in ruin.'[33] Durkheim's *Les Formes élémentaires de la vie religieuse* is likewise condemned as 'purely speculative.'[34] That anti-Semitism was among Schmidt's motives is clear from his attack elsewhere on the Jewish anthropologist Salomon Reinach, whom he accuses of adopting the theory of totemism from Robertson Smith's *Religion of the Semites* solely in order to undermine the pre-eminence of Christianity in the history of religions.[35]

The enmity between Freud and Schmidt was no mere scholarly disagreement. Each man held to his convictions the more strongly for their lack of scholarly foundation. Their beliefs were founded, rather, on incompatible ideologies – progressive liberalism versus Catholic conservatism – and on opposed historical myths. Freud sees human history as a slow and painful struggle from primitive animism through theology and philosophy up to the highest stage of consciousness, science, which can at last begin to confer some real instead of illusory benefits upon mankind. For Schmidt, on the other hand, history is a process of loss and decline. A primeval revelation by God himself showed the earliest men the essence of religion and the ideal social life. There could be no compromise between Freud's belief in progress and Schmidt's belief in decline.[36]

But this of course is an incomplete account of Freud's social thought. In his late works his belief in progress is counterpointed and indeed contradicted by an increasing cultural pessimism which brings him closer to Schmidt. His doubts about the value of civilization are clearly stated in *Civilization and its Discontents*. It also appears, more obliquely, in *Moses and Monotheism*. Though hardly to be taken seriously as Biblical criticism, this book is fascinating if seen as an exercise in myth-making.[37]

Very obviously, *Moses and Monotheism* opposes all that Schmidt stood for by describing Christianity as a neurosis and contrasting it with both Judaism and the modern scientific spirit. But in another way it resembles Schmidt's work. Both Schmidt and Freud are concerned with the transmission of a doctrine. In both cases the doctrine is monotheism. It is transmitted, in Schmidt's account, by diffusion; in Freud's, by repression. Schmidt asserts that God appeared in person to primitive man and taught him a monotheism which was diffused over the globe and, in the process, corrupted and forgotten, except in the refuges of primitive humanity. Freud maintains that the monotheism of the Pharaoh Akhenaten was transmitted by Moses to his followers the Jews, and, though repeatedly forgotten, it survived securely in the unconscious. Thus both Schmidt and Freud were constructing myths of decline, and both were concerned with how doctrines survive – a very understandable concern at a time when civilization seemed likely to be defeated by either Nazism or Communism. And Schmidt's work needs to be seen as the context in and against which Freud's last major book was written.

The end of the story is quickly told and establishes a strange parallel between the two men. After the Anschluss both went into exile. Because of his forthright and outspoken condemnation of National Socialism, Schmidt was arrested on 13 March 1938, the day after the Anschluß, kept under guard for several days, then released after Mussolini, prompted by the Pope, had intervened on his behalf. In April he was forbidden to teach. He went to Rome and arranged for the Anthropos Institute to be transferred to Fribourg in Switzerland, where he continued his anthropological work until his death in 1954. Freud meanwhile remained in Vienna till June 1938, then managed to leave with his immediate family for Britain. There he completed and published *Moses and Monotheism,* an exploration of religion which is, among many other things, a covert and ambiguous reply to Schmidt.

NOTES

1. René Laforgue, 'Personal Memories of Freud,' in *Freud as we knew him,* ed., Hendrik M. Ruitenbeek (Detroit: Wayne State University Press, 1973), pp. 341-349 (quotation from p. 344).

2. See Peter Gay, *A Godless Jew: Freud. Atheism, and the Making of Psychoanalysis* (New Haven/London: Yale University Press, 1987). Schmidt's importance to Freud is acknowledged by several references in Ernest Jones, *Sigmund Freud: Life and Work* (3 vols., London: Hogarth, 1953-1957), III, but goes unmentioned in Professor Gay's recent biography *Freud: A Life for Our Time* (London: Dent, 1988).

3. 'Heaven we'll leave to the angels and the sparrows' (from Heine, *Deutschland: Ein Wintermärchen,* Caput 1); *The Standard Edition of the Complete Psychological Works of Sigmund Freud,* trans. James Strachey et al. (24 vols., London: Hogarth, 1953-1974), XXI, p. 50.

4. Ibid., XXII, p. 171.

5. See Alfred Diamant, *Austrian Catholics and the First Republic: Democracy, Capitalism, and the Social Order, 1918-1934* (Princeton: Princeton University Press, 1960).

6. 'Wir wollen das neue Österreich' in *Dollfuß an Österreich: Eines Mannes Wort und Ziel,* ed. Hofrat Edmund Weber (Vienna: Reinhold, 1935), p. 31.

7. See John Bunzl and Bernd Marin, *Antisemitismus in Österreich: Sozialhistorische und soziologische Studien* (Innsbruck: Inn-Verlag, 1983); Ivar Oxaal, Michael Pollak and Gerhard Botz (eds.), *Jews, Antisemitism and Culture in Vienna* (London: Routledge & Kegan Paul, 1987).

8. 'Hirtenbrief des Bischofs Gföllner' in Emmerich Czermak and Oskar Karbach, *Ordnung in der Judenfrage* (4. Sonderheft der *Berichte zur Kultur- und Zeitgeschichte,* ed. Nikolaus Hovorka, Vienna: Reinhold, 1934), pp. 138-139. On Catholic anti-Semitism, I have found the following indispensable: Hermann Greive, *Theologie und Ideologie: Katholizismus und Judentum in Deutschland und Österreich, 1918-1935* (Heidelberg: Schneider, 1969); Erika Weinzierl-Fischer, 'Österreichs Katholiken und der Nationalsozialismus,' *Wort und Wahrheit,* 18 (1963), 417-439, 493-526.

9. *The Letters of Sigmund Freud and Arnold Zweig,* ed. Ernst L. Freud, trans. W. and E. Robson-Scott (London: Hogarth, 1970), p. 92.

10. *Standard Edition,* XXIII, p. 57.

11. *The Letters of Freud and Zweig,* pp. 130-131.

12. Biographical data on Schmidt are taken from Joseph Henninger, *P. Wilhelm Schmidt S.V.D., 1868–1954: Eine biographische Skizze* (Fribourg: Paulusdruckerei, 1956), and the obituary by Wilhelm Koppers in *Mitteilungen der Anthropologischen Gesellschaft in Wien,* 83 (1954), 87–96. Koppers also edited *Festschrift P. W. Schmidt: 76 sprachwissenschaftliche, ethnologische, religionswissenschaftliche, prähistorische und andere Studien* (Vienna: Mechitharisten-Congregations-Buchdruckerei, 1928). For Schmidt's bibliography see Fritz Bornemann, 'Verzeichnis der Schriften von P. W. Schmidt S.V.D. (1868–1954),' *Anthropos,* 49 (1954), 385–432. For his place in the history of anthropology, see the detailed account in Marvin Harris, *The Rise of Anthropological Theory* (London: Routledge & Kegan Paul, 1969), pp. 382–392.

13. Henninger, pp. 41–42.

14. Friedrich Rennhofer, *Ignaz Seipel, Mensch und Staatsmann* (Vienna/Cologne/Graz: Hermann Böhlaus Nachf., 1978), p. 115.

15. Ibid., pp. 727, 155.

16. 'Befreiung Wiens vom jüdischen Bolschewismus! Eine Katholikentagsrede von Professor Dr Wilhelm Schmidt S.V.D.', *Das Neue Reich,* 3, 10 October 1920, pp. 42–43. Quotations from p. 43; Schmidt's words are 'der schmachvollen Fremdherrschaft des jüdischen Bolschewikentums' and 'minderwertige Fremdstämmlinge.' This item is not listed in Bornemann's bibliography.

17. See F. M. Kapfhammer, 'Die katholische Jugendbewegung,' in Erika Weinzierl et al. (eds.), *Kirche in Österreich, 1918–1965* (2 vols., Vienna: Herold, 1967), II, pp. 23–53. Schmidt contributed 'Der Neulandtechniker in seiner sozialen Stellung,' *Neuland: Blätter jungkatholischer Erneuerungsbewegung,* 1, iii (Christmond 1923), pp. 49–55, setting out his anti-Socialist view of industrial relations.

18. Alfred Missong, 'Was sollen wir zum deutschen Faszismus sagen?', *Neuland,* 1, viii (May 1924), 173–179 (quotation from p. 178).

19. Hans Dibold, 'Die Juden,' ibid., 4, i (Hartung [sic] 1927), pp. 9–15; quotations from pp. 11–12.

20. Oswald Menghin, *Geist und Blut: Grundsätzliches um Rasse, Sprache, Kultur und Volkstum* (Vienna: Schroll, 1934), p. 53.

21. Ibid., pp. 171–172.

22. Wilhelm Schmidt, *Rasse und Volk: ihre allgemeine Bedeutung; ihre Geltung im deutschen Raum,* 2nd edition (Salzburg: Pustet, 1935). Menghin is quoted on p. 51; the races composing the German people are listed on p. 99.

23.  'Das Rassenprinzip des Nationalsozialismus,' *Schönere Zukunft,* 7 (24 July 1932), 999–1000 (quotation from p. 999). Schmidt's words are 'ein im tiefsten Seelengrunde ihrer Nation entwurzeltes Volk.'

24.  *Rasse und Volk,* p. 216.

25.  'Die Familie im katholischen Staate,' in *Der katholische Staatsgedanke: Bericht über die katholisch-soziale Tagung der Zentralstelle des Volksbundes der Katholiken Österreichs am 29. und 30. April 1934 in Wien* (Vienna: Volksbundverlag, 1934), pp. 41–51. See also his 'Freiheit und Bindung des Christen in der Gesellschaft,' *Allgemeiner Deutscher Katholikentag Wien 1933* (Vienna, 1934), pp. 91–96.

26.  'Zur Judenfrage,' *Schönere Zukunft,* 9 (21 January 1934), 408–409.

27.  Czermak and Karbach, p. 9. Schmidt refers to this book in 'Zur Judenfrage,' p. 408.

28.  *Der Ursprung der Gottesidee* (12 vols., Münster: Aschendorffsche Verlagsbuchhandlung, 1926–1955), VI, p. 493. This passage is also quoted, but misattributed, by Harris, p. 391.

29.  E. E. Evans-Pritchard, *Theories of Primitive Religion* (Oxford: Clarendon, 1965), p. 10.

30.  J. C. Winter, *Bruno Gutmann, 1876–1965: A German Approach to Social Anthropology* (Oxford: Clarendon, 1979), pp. 52, 62–65.

31.  See W. E. Mühlmann, *Geschichte der Anthropologie,* 2nd edition (Wiesbaden: AULA-Verlag, 1984), pp. 44–45, 206.

32.  See Schmidt, *Der Ursprung der Gottesidee,* III, esp. pp. 53–60; A. R. Brown [sic], *The Andaman Islanders: A Study in Social Anthropology* (Cambridge: Cambridge University Press, 1922).

33.  Schmidt, *The Origin and Growth of Religion,* trans. H. J. Rose (London, 1931), p. 115. (The original was not available to me.)

34.  Ibid., p. 117.

35.  *Der Ursprung der Gottesidee,* I, pp. 39–40.

36.  A brief comparison between Freud and Schmidt is drawn by Walter Burkert, *Homo Necans: The Anthropology of Ancient Greek Sacrificial Ritual and Myth,* trans. Peter Bing (Berkeley/Los Angeles: University of California Press, 1983), p. 73.

37.  For a fuller interpretation of *Moses and Monotheism* see Ritchie Robertson, 'Freud's Testament: *Moses and Monotheism,*' in Edward Timms and Naomi Segal (eds.), *Freud in Exile: Psychoanalysis and its Vicissitudes* (New Haven and London: Yale University Press, 1988), pp. 80–89.

# Kraus's Shakespearean Politics

## Edward Timms

Culture and politics: what kind of 'and' is that? It was not the connections between culture and politics, but the disjunctions – the tragic dichotomy – that shaped German and Austrian affairs during the first half of the twentieth century. The special significance of the Viennese satirist Karl Kraus is that he addressed this dichotomy so directly. Through his journal *Die Fackel*, published from 1899 until his death in 1936, he engaged with public affairs more intensively than any other Austrian writer of his generation. But the qualities of imagination he brought to bear on politics reflected an essentially literary disposition – a mind nurtured not on Karl Marx or Theodor Herzl, but on Goethe and Shakespeare.

It was this traditional conception of culture as a source of humanistic values which sustained Kraus's satirical enterprise. His essential technique was subversive intertextuality – the juxtaposition of documentary material, culled from the columns of newspapers, with an extraordinary range of references from literary sources: from the Bible, from Kant and Schopenhauer, from Goethe, Schiller and the German classics, from the comedies of Nestroy and the operettas of Offenbach, above all from Shakespeare in German translation. This intertextuality is one of the characteristic features of early twentieth-century modernism, exemplified by T. S. Eliot's *Waste Land*. Responding to what Eliot called 'the immense panorama of futility and anarchy which is contemporary history,' Kraus too used 'fragments' from literary tradition to shore civilization up against its 'ruins.'[1]

For Kraus as a satirist working against authoritarian ideologies, this intertextuality had the additional advantage of being a

345

device for outwitting the censorship. It would not have been possible for him to conduct his memorable campaign against the dehumanizing effects of the First World War, if he had not been such a master of satirical quotation. Juxtaposed against the German of Kant, Goethe or Hölderlin, the chauvinistic pronouncements of the Austrian Foreign Minister or the German Kaiser could be trenchantly exposed, at a time when the censorship inhibited more explicit forms of pacifist protest. In this sense Kraus's approach to politics was non-political – inspired by ethical humanism rather than party-political allegiance. And even during the 1920s, when Kraus threw his moral authority behind the Austrian Social Democratic Party, he still insisted on the primacy of cultural values. The German language (he insisted), especially the language of the classics, should supply the norms for a civilized society.

Here we encounter Kraus's central problem: how are cultural values to provide guidelines for political conduct? To this problem Kraus responded with a series of interlocking strategies. The first was to turn the concert halls of Vienna (and of other central European cities) into a cultural-political forum – through his celebrated readings from his own work and recitations from the works of others. By this means he transformed the public platform into a kind of tribunal, from which to pronounce judgment on the crimes and follies of his contemporaries. But he spoke not simply in his own voice but as the conscience of a great cultural tradition.

Behind this strategy we may detect the Schillerian conception of the theatre as a moral institution. Kraus's personality was shaped during his impressionable early years by the Vienna Burgtheater, whose repertoire gave prominence to ethically elevating forms of drama. And he explicitly aligned himself with the Burgtheater tradition when he instituted his own 'theatre of poetry' ('Theater der Dichtung') – those recitations of great works of the European theatre with which he delighted his audiences for so many years.

Kraus was, however, aware that in a fragmented modern society the theatre can no longer have the redemptive mission assigned to it by Goethe and Schiller. When he addresses the problem of connecting culture with politics more realistically, it is not through the theatre but in the courts of law. Kraus is often seen too exclusively as a critic of the Austrian legal system, particularly of the oppressiveness of the Habsburg penal code during the final years of the Austro-Hungarian Empire. This disregards his affirmative attitude towards the law, especially during the early years of the Austrian Republic.

The law in this affirmative perspective synthesizes the moral and imaginative insights of humanistic culture with the practical requirements of modern society. The poets may indeed become the unacknowledged legislators of mankind when their finer perceptions—for example, of the vagaries of human behaviour in the sexual sphere—provide the inspiration for more enlightened legislation. Kraus himself invoked precisely this conception when—in the context of an early satire on sexual hypocrisy—he defined the ideal legal system as 'Shakespearean ideas couched in legal terms': 'Dort ist Kultur, wo die Gesetze des Staates paragraphierte Shakespearegedanken sind, wo mindestens, wie im Deutschland Bismarcks, Gedanken an Shakespeare das Tun der leitenden Männer bestimmen' (F 115, 4: September 1902). ('True civilization is to be found where the laws of the land are Shakespearean ideas couched in legal terms or where at least a knowledge of Shakespeare guides the actions of men in leading positions, as in Bismarck's Germany.')[2]

This conception of literary culture as a source of guidance for enlightened legislation and policy was clearly over-optimistic. But Kraus was able to test the theory out in practice through the innumerable actions he initiated in the courts of law. He achieved his greatest practical success when the pronouncements of his imaginative tribunal were reinforced by legally binding judgments in court. His most remarkable feat during the 1920s was his campaign against the newspaper magnate Imre Bekessy. This culminated—after a crescendo of attacks by Kraus both in *Die Fackel* and on the public platform—in Bekessy having to flee the country in order to avoid arrest. Significantly, this success was not achieved simply through the power of impassioned discourse. Equally important was the remorseless pursuit of Bekessy through the courts, conducted on Kraus's behalf by his indomitable advocate, Dr Oskar Samek.

Kraus's triumph over Bekessy was achieved in 1926, at a time when the political situation in Austria was relatively calm. The question during the final decade of his career was whether such successes could be repeated in a country that was becoming so unstable that the rule of law was itself under threat. In July 1927 a Viennese jury acquitted three members of a right-wing paramilitary organization (Frontkämpfervereinigung) who had shot and killed two participants in a left-wing demonstration at Schattendorf in the Burgenland. This court decision provoked mass protests in Vienna by left-wing sympathizers, which culminated in the burning of the Palace of Justice. As the demonstration turned into a riot the police opened fire, causing a total of ninety deaths.

Kraus's reaction was to hold the Chief of Police, Johannes Schober, responsible for this slaughter of civilians, which included women, children, and innocent bystanders. For over two years, from the summer of 1927 through to autumn 1929, he campaigned by every conceivable method to force Schober to resign. His tactics provide a model for the intervention of a public-spirited writer in political life – a model both through the merits of his campaign and in its limitations. In September 1927, one month after the shootings, Kraus had hundreds of copies of a poster pasted up throughout Vienna, calling on Schober to resign. This was followed by a sequence of four numbers of *Die Fackel* which documented the police atrocities in horrifying detail and intensified the attack on Schober's integrity. Kraus discovered that Schober had also been implicated in the earlier Bekessy affair and may even have helped the newspaper magnate to avoid arrest. His next move was to attempt to draw the Police Chief into a court action that would finally discredit him, by accusing him of forgery and abuse of his official powers. But Schober, supported by a chorus of adulation from conservative politicians and in the bourgeois press, refused to budge.

Kraus then changed his tactics, switching the focus of his campaign from the courts to the theatre. In May 1928 he published *Die Unüberwindlichen* ('The Invincibles') – one of the most powerful plays ever written for a specific political purpose. In this documentary play Schober (thinly disguised as Polizeipräsident Wacker) is portrayed in a series of compromising situations. The play culminates in a scene in which Schober's conservative political rhetoric is juxtaposed with horrifying details of the massacre of 15 July 1927. Kraus also uses the Brechtian technique of interpolated songs, above all the celebrated 'Schoberlied' in which the Police Chief proclaims that his whole life long he has done nothing but his duty: 'Ich kann wahrlich von mir sagen, daß ich mein ganzes Leben lang nichts als meine Pflicht getan habe, weil dies und nichts anders meine Pflicht ist.'[3] ('I can truly say of myself that I have done nothing but my duty my whole life long because this and nothing else is my duty.')

This play, particularly the self-righteousness of its hero who denies all responsibility for crimes committed under his authority, has not lost its topicality – even in the Austria of the late 1980s. The thinly disguised documentary characters, transfigured by Kraus's linguistically sensitive imagination, embody recurrent human attitudes: above all, the deviousness of conservative politicians who beat the patriotic drum when their personal integrity is challenged. It is a play which is ripe for revival. Kraus repeatedly read scenes in public and arranged for the play to be staged – in Germany, of course, not in Austria (the première was in Dresden in May 1929). He had not abandoned his aim of mobilizing public opinion against Schober in order to force his resignation.

Kraus's crusade against Schober was the most explicitly political campaign he ever fought; political both in the sense that it had a clearly defined practical goal (Schober's resignation) and also in the party-political sense. By taking up the cause of the socialist demonstrators of July 1927, Kraus closely aligned himself with the Austrian Social Democratic Party. All the more spectacular therefore was Kraus's defeat. For Schober's strong stand on law and order, the ruthlessness with which he had put down a socialist insurrection, made him the hero of the Austrian middle classes and the bourgeois press. It transformed him indeed into the rising star of the conservative coalition in the Austrian parliament.

On 14 July 1929, in a public reading which marked the second anniversary of the massacre on the streets of Vienna, Kraus denounced Schober once again (coupling his name with that of a German Police Chief, Zörgiebel, who had been responsible for the shooting-down of left-wing demonstrators during a Berlin May Day parade). Kraus denounced Schober as a 'mediocre civil servant,' parading around the streets of Vienna – that 'imbecile city' – as if he were a 'generalissimo inspecting the front' ('. . . [einen] mediokren Konzeptsbeamten . . ., der als Generalissimus die Front einer verblödeten Stadt absschreiten wird,' F 811–819, 5). ('[a] mediocre petty official . . ., who like a generalissimo is inspecting the front-line of a benumbed city.') In August 1929 this denunciation was published in *Die Fackel*. Scarcely a month later, on 29 September 1929, Schober was appointed Austrian Bundeskanzler.

There can be few moments in the history of the first Austrian Republic which so graphically illustrate the disjunction between culture and politics. Seen within the framework of Kraus's cultural and ethical ideals, Schober was totally discredited. For confirmation of this viewpoint, we need only turn to the memoirs of the most notable independent witness of the riots of 15 July 1927, Elias Canetti. Canetti was by no means entirely in sympathy with the behaviour of the demonstrators. The blend of fascination and horror with which he responded in July 1927 to the irrationality of the mob were to inspire his great work on the theme of *Crowds and Power*, published over thirty years later (*Masse und Macht*, 1960). But Canetti could recognize the ethical principles which had inspired Kraus's action. In his autobiography Canetti describes how in September 1927 he walked from one of Kraus's anti-Schober posters to the next, pausing in front of each one, 'als sei alle Gerechtigkeit dieser Erde in die Buchstaben seines Namens eingegangen.' ('as if all the justice on earth had entered the letters of Kraus's name').[4]

In terms of practical politics, however, it was Schober who was triumphant. Despite the instability of the Austrian economic situation (after the Wall Street crash of November 1929), he remained Bundeskanzler for over a year and achieved some notable successes, above all the renegotiation of the financial indemnity clauses in the Treaty of St. Germain, which had placed such a burden on Austria. This success transformed Schober into a national hero. He was also widely admired abroad as a strongman capable of maintaining the social and financial stability of the Republic (the British *Daily News,* a liberal paper, called Schober 'the best policeman outside London') (F 838–844, 2). Even from the Austrian Social Democrats, Schober received grudging support (not least, because he was making efforts to bring the right-wing paramilitary Heimwehr under control). And on 15 July 1930, the third anniversary of the massacre, Schober received an official welcome from the Social Democrats when he paid a conciliatory visit to a working-class district of Vienna (Arbeiterheim Favoriten).

Registering all of this in *Die Fackel,* Kraus conceded defeat. He realized that he was capable of gaining victories only in the imaginative sphere – through the transposition of Schober into a literary figure in *Die Unüberwindlichen.* In the sphere of practical politics Kraus acknowledged that he had become powerless. Deprived of the support of the Social Democrats, who seemed to him to have betrayed their own principles, he felt increasingly isolated. And this feeling was intensified as in the autumn of 1930 the political storm clouds gathered. In September 1930 the National Socialists made their sensational electoral breakthrough in Germany, increasing their representation in the Reichstag from 12 seats to 107. In the Austrian general elections a month later, Schober consolidated his position, although as leader of a minority group in the right-wing coalition he switched to the position of Deputy Bundeskanzler and Foreign Minister.

This double blow left Kraus totally disenchanted with politics. He had hitherto looked to Berlin for political and moral support, not least for his campaign against Schober. The Berlin audience for one of his public readings in April 1928, which had included an attack on Schober, had responded with such enthusiasm that Kraus even noted in *Die Fackel* (in a rare expression of political optimism): 'Bei solcher Teilnahme wäre selbst ein Sieg innerhalb dieser trüben Zeitlichkeit erdenkbar' (F 781–786, 82). ('With this support it would even be possible to conceive of victory within the murky realm of contemporary life.') And the Berlin production of *Die Unüberwindlichen* in October 1929 had been greeted in the German press with tremendous enthusiasm, as a pioneering form of political theatre (F 827–833, 11–36). A year later all these hopes were dissipated.

This disheartening sequence of events led Kraus in October 1930 to announce his 'Abschied von der Politik' ('withdrawal from politics'). The Austrian election results, which had enabled Schober to consolidate his position, prompted Kraus to declare himself 'an den Wirrungen dieses miesesten Staatswesens vollständig desinteressiert' (F 845–846, 1), ('totally uninterested in the confusions of this most dismal of political entities.') This signaled a decisive shift from the sphere of practical politics into what may be called 'Shakespearean' politics. Commenting on the electoral success of the Schober-bloc, he writes: 'About Schober I could still have composed many a rhyme, but things are now becoming Shakespearean' ('jetzt aber geht es ins Shakespearesche.' F 845–846, 2). The word 'Shakespearean' here serves to signal the approach of a cataclysmic tragedy. And rather than define his political position in his own words, Kraus borrows lines from the final act of *Timon of Athens.* Timon, totally disillusioned with human civilization, has turned his back on the city of Athens and taken refuge in the woods. But Athens is now threatened by the military power of Alcibiades, and two senators come to plead with Timon to return and organize the defence of the city. Timon replies (in words which stand for Kraus's attitude towards Austria): 'If Alcibiades kill my countrymen, / Let Alcibiades know this of Timon, / That Timon cares not.' (F 845–846, 3; *Timon of Athens,* Act V, Sc. 1). Kraus's comments make it clear that the Alcibiades who is about to 'sack fair Athens' is intended as a reference to Prince Starhemberg, leader of the Heimwehr.

During the last six years of Kraus's life, from 1930 to 1936, his main creative energies were devoted not to politics but to translating, editing, and giving public readings from the works of Shakespeare. A total disillusionment with practical politics underlies his perplexing responses to the catastrophic events of the day. His reactions, after the Nazi seizure of power in Germany in 1933 and the collapse of democratic government in Austria, are well known. He switched his allegiance from the Social Democrats, whom he accused of betraying their own cause, to Dollfuss, whose authoritarian regime he saw as the last line of defense against Nazi dictatorship.

To the horrifying events in Germany he responded by writing an exceptionally powerful polemic, *Dritte Walpurgisnacht*. It is a trenchant and indeed prophetic work, which identifies – on the evidence available in 1933 – the totally destructive tendencies of Nazism. But Kraus refrained from publishing this work (it did not appear until 1952). He decided not to publish, partly because he feared that the publication of such an outspoken anti-Nazi polemic, written by a Jewish author in Austria, might provoke retaliation against defenseless Jews in Germany; partly because he was overwhelmed by his sense of the ineffectiveness of the written word in the face of unmitigated tyranny. Kraus's 'cultural' approach to politics presupposed the rule of law and the freedom to appeal to enlightened public opinion. The collapse of that framework left him no alternative but to withdraw into 'silence' – signalled by the eight-line poem, 'Man frage nicht' ('Don't Ask'), which he published in October 1933. His position was summed up in a celebrated phrase which he used in *Die Fackel* the following year, after a silence which had lasted for a further nine months: 'Mir fällt zu Hitler nichts ein' (F 890–905, 153): 'When I think of Hitler, my mind goes blank.'

The rights and wrongs of Kraus's change of political stance – and of his decision not to publish *Dritte Walpurgisnacht* – have been endlessly debated. My aim in this paper has been to shift the focus of the debate by showing that Kraus's strategy of silence does not date from 1933. It began three years earlier, after the triumph of Schober in Austria had caused him to despair of the possibility of a politics based on ethical principle.[5] But it is also important to recognize that this withdrawal from politics was not simply a form of fatalism. It was counterbalanced by a programme of cultural retrenchment centred on the revival of Shakespeare.

Shakespeare was important for Kraus precisely because his plays seemed so prophetically to interact with the follies and disasters of the twentieth century. Throughout his career Kraus interwove his commentary on contemporary life with literary allusions, creating a complex system of intertextuality. Shakespeare's plays, with their extraordinary range of situations and characters, seemed to provide a kind of master plot, linking political conflict with moral retribution. They abounded in 'vorahnende Beispiele' (F 65, 28–29: 'premonitory examples'), in terms of which Kraus could interpret the behaviour of his contemporaries. 'Shakespeare had foreknowledge of everything,' he had proclaimed during his early crusade against sexual hypocrisy ('Shakespeare hat alles vorausgewußt,' F 115, 3). From Shakespeare Kraus derived not merely a set of psychological types and moral categories for the evaluation of human conduct, but a comprehensive explanatory system – indeed a form of secularized holy writ, analogous to the kind of universal explanatory system which an earlier age had found in the Bible.

During the 1930s the need for this kind of explanatory system had become more urgent than ever before. For the events of his decade led to a crisis in historiography – the collapse of the progressive view of human history which had shaped western thought since the Renaissance. Both liberalism and Marxism, in their different ways, presupposed an evolving pattern in human affairs. With the collapse of the European economy and the triumph of the dictators, all of this was thrown into question. The crisis was memorably recorded in the Preface to the *History of Europe,* published in 1936 by H.A.L. Fisher: 'One intellectual excitement has been denied me. Men wiser and more learned than I have discerned in history a plot, a rhythm, a predetermined pattern. These harmonies are concealed from me. I can see only one emergency following upon another.'[6]

Kraus's intensified preoccupation with Shakespeare was a response to precisely this dilemma – an attempt to discern a 'plot' or a 'rhythm' in history. But at different stages in his career he placed different Shakespeare plays in the foreground. Around 1905, during his campaign against sexual hypocrisy, he had fore-grounded *Measure for Measure*, a play which, being set in Vienna, provided him with particularly apt analogies. Kraus identified him-self with the words of the disguised Duke, who returns in Act V to pass judgment on the wickedness and hypocrisy of the Viennese:

> My business in this state
> Made me a looker-on here in Vienna,
> Where I have seen corruption boil and bubble
> Till it o'er-run the stew: laws for all faults.
> But faults so countenanced, that the strong statutes
> Stand like the forfeits in a barber's shop . . .
> (Act V, Sc. 1; F 115, 1; cf. F 845–846, 5)

During the First World War, it was again Shakespeare who provided Kraus with an answer to the anguished question which he formulated in May 1917, as the mass slaughter of the war con-tinued without any conceivable end:

> Um nicht rasend zu werden, sage dir immer wieder, daß das Sterben einen dir vorläufig verborgenen Sinn gehabt hat, weil doch so viele Menschen nicht ausschließlich deshalb gestorben sein können, um ein Hinterland von Schreibern und Wucherern zurückzulassen. (F 457–461, 97) (In order to retain your sanity keep telling yourself that these deaths must have a meaning which for the present is concealed from you, because so many people cannot have died solely for the purpose of leaving behind a hinterland of propagandists and profiteers).

Shakespeare (for Kraus) most memorably states the problem, with his image of:

> Man, proud man,
> Drest in a little brief authority,
> Most ignorant of what he's most assured –
> His glassy essence – like an angry ape,
> Plays such fantastic tricks before high heaven,
> As make the angels weep.
> (*Measure for Measure*, Act II, Sc. 2; F 457–461, 98–99)

But when in autumn 1918 the forces of military tyranny were defeated by the western democratic alliance, Kraus was able to reaffirm Shakespeare's vision of a moral universe in which human crimes are subject to cosmic retribution. The key text is now *Hamlet*, the tragedy of a state so corrupt that the royal house must be overthrown and order restored by Fortinbras, the representative of a new power. Kraus hailed the collapse of the Austro-Hungarian monarchy in precisely these terms, assigning the role of Fortinbras to the statesman who seemed destined to create a new democratic order amid the ruins of Europe: the President of the United States of America, Woodrow Wilson. And *Hamlet* also provided Kraus with his own role-model, as Horatio who at the end of the drama bears witness 'to th'yet unknowing world / How these things came about' (F 499–500, 4; *Hamlet*, Act V, Sc. 2).

Around 1930, as we have seen, it was *Timon of Athens* which enabled Kraus to express his complete disillusionment with Austrian politics and his forebodings about the overthrow of the state. But the misanthropy of Timon does not provide the final word in the evolution of Kraus's Shakespearean politics. The tragic role played by Dollfuss on the Austrian political stage prompted Kraus to invoke the most sombre of Shakespeare's political tragedies.

In a number of *Die Fackel* published at the end of July 1934, Kraus spoke out openly in support of Dollfuss – 'der kleine Retter in großer Not' ('the diminutive saviour in a great emergency'). The fact that Dollfuss was resolutely defending the independence of Austria against the Nazi threat was for Kraus so important that he was willing to disregard the Dollfuss government's use of force to suppress the Socialist rising of February 1934. But the publication of this number of *Die Fackel* almost exactly coincided with the abortive Nazi coup of 25 July, which resulted in the assassination of Dollfuss.

When almost four months later on 9 November Kraus gave his next public reading, the text he chose was *Macbeth*. When Kraus entered the concert hall (Mittlerer Konzerthaussaal), his audience rose and stood in silence – a unique occurrence. They must have realised that this reading of *Macbeth* was intended as a tribute to Dollfuss. Kraus introduced the tragedy as 'Shakespeares und der Weltdramatik größtem und leider gegenwärtigstem Drama' (F 912–917, 70–71): 'Shakespeare's and world-drama's greatest and sadly most topical play.' And he explicitly associated the killing of Dollfuss with Macbeth's awesome crimes, the murder of the noble Banquo and of Duncan, King of Scotland. It was certainly Dollfuss that he had in mind when he read the lines:

> Besides, this Duncan
> Hath borne his faculties so meek, hath been
> So clear in his great office, that his virtues
> Will plead like angels trumpet-tongued . . .
>
> (*Macbeth*, Act I, Sc. 7)

And it was this tragedy which provided a summing-up of Kraus's sentiments in 1934: 'O horror! horror! horror! Tongue nor heart / Cannot conceive nor name thee!' (Act II, Sc. 3)

But Kraus, as we now know, did not abandon the task of 'naming' the horror of Nazism. *Dritte Walpurgisnacht* achieves precisely this by juxtaposing the documentation of Nazi atrocities against the most inspired achievements of German culture. The German of Hitler and Goebbels is confronted with that of Goethe (in *Faust* II) and of Schlegel-Shakespeare (above all, *Macbeth*).

Kraus never abandoned the quest for meaning – for a moral meaning – in political events, even after he acknowledged his own powerlessness to affect the outcome. His consolation (again derived from Shakespeare) was expressed in the words: 'The worst is not, / So long as we can say, "This is the worst"' (*King Lear,* Act IV, Sc. 1). 'Saying the worst,' 'naming the horror' was Kraus's final contribution to the culture of his time. But he knew that culture could no longer alter politics. The Nazi political tyranny could be defeated only by force. And despairing of the appeasement policies of France and Britain, Kraus at the end of his life turned his gaze (as he had in 1918) to the only country capable of saving democracy. The political solution he envisaged is expressed not in cultural terms, but in the emphatic abbreviations of ultimate emergency. There was only one solution (Kraus wrote after the Nazi seizure of power in Germany): 'ein SOS bis nach USA'[7] ('an SOS to the USA').

## NOTES

1. *Selected Prose of T. S. Eliot,* ed. Frank Kermode (London: Faber, 1975), p. 177; T. S. Eliot, *Collected Poems 1909-1935* (London: Faber, 1958), p. 77.
2. References to *Die Fackel,* ed. Karl Kraus (Vienna, 1899-1936) are identified in the text of this article by the abbreviation 'F', followed by the number of the issue and the page reference.
3. Karl Kraus, *Die Unüberwindlichen* (Wien: Verlag 'Die Fackel', 1928), S. 112.
4. Elias Canetti, *Die Fackel im Ohr: Lebensgeschichte 1921-1931* (Frankfurt am Main: Fischer, 1982), S. 232.
5. Schober was forced out of office in 1931, after the collapse of the Creditanstalt and the failure of negotiations for a customs union with Germany. By this date the Austrian political situation had become so unstable that it was no longer possible for Kraus to celebrate a moral victory (cf. F 864-867, 1-4; December 1931).
6. H.A.L. Fisher, *A History of Europe* (London: Edward Arnold, 1936), p. v.
7. Karl Kraus, *Die dritte Walpurgisnacht* (München: Kösel, 1952), S. 114.

# EPILOGUE

## Austria in the Thirties: Reality and Exemplum

### Kenneth Segar

### I

Given their diversity, it may appear rash to claim that the essays in this volume offer any particular focus on Austria in the thirties. Nonetheless this epilogue highlights the two themes which for me emerge as central. The first is how Austrian high culture helped foster ideologies inimical to its nineteenth-century liberal tradition; and how these ideologies created power structures which destroyed that culture, in large measure by silencing its foremost representatives, the Jewish intelligentsia. The second theme is the extent to which one is justified, despite Hitler's invasion, in speaking of March 1938 as an Anschluss. These two themes are related, but they will be seen to have something further in common, namely, that in each case an examination of the relevant historical material has implications for the Austria of the 1980s. One Austrian historian, indeed, claims that the Austrian people are today living in a false relationship to events of the thirties, and that this is responsible for their most urgent social and political problem.[1] Seen thus, righting the record is not merely a historiographical, but also a moral task. The final section of my epilogue deals with the content of and scandal surrounding Thomas Bernhard's play *Heldenplatz* (1988), a work strongly supporting the view that failure to master the thirties is the source of Austria's deepest social ill.

### II

Peter Pulzer has written that 'with the end of the multi-national empire, the Catholic Greater German tradition, linguistic and cultural and deriving from the Romanticism of a hundred

359

years earlier, was revived.' He explains: 'Catholic reactionaries were as deeply imbued as nationalist ones with the theories of the "organic" state, the corporate society, and the folk community which had always been stronger in Austria than in Germany . . . Both camps were attracted by the corporatist theories of Othmar Spann, Professor of Sociology at the University of Vienna, and bodies like Richard von Kralik's *Gralbund* (League of the Holy Grail) which combined Catholicism with pan-Germanism . . . .'[2] Anton Staudinger's paper on the 'Austria' ideology further lists: Josef Eberle's Catholic right-wing journal *Schönere Zukunft* (Brighter Future); Richard Schmitz's anti-democratic and racist commentary on the 1926 Christian Social Programme; the writings of the Christian Social legal historian Hugelmann, of the historians Hantsch, Hirsch and Srbik, the geographers Machatschek and Hassinger, the Germanist Nadler.

It is regrettable that the name of a major artist from Vienna's liberal cultural tradition, Hugo von Hofmannsthal (1874–1929), also belongs in this list. He was a co-founder and the theorist of the Salzburg Festival, and in his writings promoting the Festival he articulates a cultural myth foreshadowing ideological aspects of the coming authoritarian and totalitarian societies. This myth replaces the older one of the Habsburg dynasty as the emblem of unity and harmony in the Empire. With the collapse of that Empire, Hofmannsthal substitutes the idea of an Austria which is no longer a political entity, but the repository of three thousand years of Western culture, to be worshipped as at a shrine, but also to be constantly revitalized by its artists. This pious act of preservation and vivification will give Austria a new meaning in terms of a civilizing European mission. In Hofmannsthal's essays written between 1911 and 1928 to explain the spirit of the Salzburg Festival, we are given the major components of this heady vision — to allude to Musil's parody, 'that the genius of Europe may discover its true home to be Austria.'[3] Yet what purports to be an idealist cultural vision — and for Hofmannsthal culture essentially inhabits a 'mental and spiritual space' (geistiger Raum)[4] — in fact contains political sub-texts crucial to the direction shortly to be taken by Austrian society. These are to be found in the Festival's 'sacral' aspect;[5] its celebration of the folk theatrical tradition of Southern Germany and Austria; its rural setting.

Firstly, the sacral aspect is most apparent in the mystery play written specifically for the Festival, *The Salzburg Great Theatre of the World (Das Salzburger große Welttheater)*, performed in the Catholic Collegienkirche. Through Catholic baroque images, the work preaches medieval hierarchy as a response to the 'spectre of Bolshevism.'[6] It is the preservation of 'the world order of a thousand years'; the beggar drops his revolutionary axe in a moment of 'mystical illumination,' and the feudal order of Europe is sustained.[7] Visitors from all over the world and from every class of Austrian society are asked to participate, more as congregation than as audience, in a celebration of this age-old order. Drama as sacral festivity (rather than secular conflict) is the conservative dramaturgy *par excellence;* and Hofmannsthal's mystical leanings in a Catholic context and setting, supportive of the hierarchical order of society, create artistic legitimation of the reactionary political Catholicism of his time.

Secondly, in his depiction of the opening performance of *Everyman* Hofmannsthal eulogizes the South German and Austrian 'natural predisposition to theatre': 'From Brixen and Sterzing [since 1919 the German-speaking Bressanone and Vipiteno of Alto Adige] northwards to Nuremberg, from western Bavaria across to the borders of Hungary . . . the native folk have kept folk theatrical traditions alive.'[8] The Festival is an emanation and stylization of 'German folk' culture. Like Hofmannsthal's collaboration on festival opera with the Bavarian Strauss, it flows across artificial political frontiers and is thereby clearly in tune with German National tendencies in Austria at the time.

Finally, Hofmannsthal's praise of Salzburg as an ideal setting for his representation of German, Christian and conservative values contains clear indications of another tendency. Salzburg is 'not the big city'[9] (read: Vienna) with its 'separate stratum of restless intelligentsia'[10] and its 'journalism, which especially insinuates novelty and things alien into the way we think and talk.'[11] Salzburg has all the vitality of the 'folk' and the 'lasting reality of a rural community close to nature'; since 'festival performance is the essential art form of the Bavarian-Austrian tribe (Stamm),' and 'Salzburg is at the heart of the Bavarian-Austrian region (Landschaft),' the farmers from the surrounding area come 'quite naturally' to watch theatre when *Everyman* is performed in the cathedral square.[12] Equally, whilst Vienna represents a public which is 'unstable, capricious, bent on novelty,' the folk form a community that is 'old and wise,' harbouring 'in its rich depths the mystery of German nature';[13] indeed, the intelligentsia represent things 'alien' to the power of 'folk tastes and instincts.'[14] The qualities Hofmannsthal here associates with 'big city' are those most clearly associated in the public mind with Jews, who are central to Vienna's intellectual life, to its liberal Enlightenment culture, to its press;[15] they appear to be the antithesis of Salzburg's Christian, conservative, German-folk ethos. At all events, the Jews of Austria are marginalized by any contemporary Austrian theory of culture which is provincial rather than metropolitan, Catholic-conservative rather than liberal or avant-garde,[16] 'instinctively' German as opposed to intellectually 'alien.' Perhaps it is not entirely fortuitous that the theme of the keywork of the Salzburg Festival, *Everyman,* is the defeat of Mammon, another potent association in the anti-Semitic mind.

So, the genuflexion before reactionary Catholicism is clear. The map drawn of the incidence of natural 'folk' theatre is of the kind which Pan-Germans of the period were and would be drawing (Aspetsberger); and the baleful mental posture of 'blood and soil' is present with the description of culture in terms of 'the tribe in its landscape'[17] and 'alien' intrusion. The Salzburg Festival as part of Hofmannsthal's culture mythology clearly has socio-political sub-texts: promotion of Austrian society as Christian, German and corporatist; adherence to a pseudo-scientific racial theory; insinuation of a covert anti-Semitism. Their camouflaged presence in a programme of high culture at the least facilitates subliminal receptivity, and may ultimately give moral standing, to sinister ideas that were already political dynamite. It seems appropriate that Salzburg was where the Corporate State and the German Reich fought for cultural dominance in the thirties.

The Corporate State of 1934–1938 is – with the necessary substitution of Austro-Germanism for Pan-Germanism after the creation of a Nazi Reich – the political realization of Hofmannsthal's hierarchical, Christian and German cultural vision. Indeed, his *Salzburg Great Theatre of the World* was the regime's chosen work to represent its image at the Paris World Exhibition of 1937 (Warren). The cultural policy of the corporate state was, as one might expect, to give moral and financial support to (1) work whose aesthetic underpinned the religious, ethical and political *status quo* (Fuhrich-Leisler); (2) work with a patriotic Austro-German bias, i.e., voicing the 'Austria' ideology. In fact, this amounted to manipulation of repertoire and box-office by the national *Kunststelle,* the cultural organization which functioned more and more as a state board of censors (Warren).

It is clear that a regime with an authoritarian, Christian and Austro-German ideology would be hostile to the variegated liberal culture of an essentially open society. And since this culture was still in large measure 'promoted, nurtured and even created' by a highly assimilated Austrian Jewry,[18] the policy of the regime was bound to be inimical to Jewish artists and intellectuals. They would suffer increasing marginalization and crises of cultural identity (Beller).[19] Albeit the regime did not officially support anti-Semitism as such,[20] its authoritarianism could not fail to challenge the Jews along with the culture they represented. Moreover, the Catholic Church dominated and in some respects controlled the cultural policy of the Christian Social regime, and the thirties did see examples of a new scope and virulence in anti-Semitic statements from its hierarchy.

Thus, in 1933 Bishop Gföllner of Linz, who was actually censured by the Episcopate, went far beyond traditional religious anti-Semitism, blaming 'degenerate Judaism' (along with freemasonry) for the spread of Bolshevism, socialism and 'mammonistic' capitalism, but ultimately for its harmful influence on all aspects of life. He declared it an 'Aryan and Christian' duty to

stop the spread of the 'Jewish spirit.'[21] Whilst Bishop Gföllner
stopped short of allowing those who claimed to be good Christians to become Nazis, Bishop Hudal in 1937 argued that Nazism
was compatible with Christianity as long as fundamental Christian
dogmas were not violated (Pauley). There are, then, examples in
the Catholic hierarchy of the increasing collusion of the Church
with German racism, which might be pagan but was at least not
communist. And racist tendencies found support elsewhere within
Catholic culture. For example, the racist anthropologist Father
Wilhelm Schmidt, whose influence is traceable back to the Vatican
itself, 'came closer than perhaps anyone else in Austria to grafting
racial anti-Semitism onto traditional religious and economic anti-
Semitism' (Robertson). The effect of such attitudes in the hierarchy of State and Church meant that penetration of the prevailing culture by one or other strand of anti-Semitism became a
further instrument in the erosion of that culture.

In that enterprise, however, something far more ominous was
achieved by the illegal Austrian Nazi Party, whose strategy was
completely to undermine the restricted freedoms enjoyed by
Austria's cultural institutions in the Corporate State: the independent authors' associations were infiltrated by writers sympathetic to Nazism and manipulated to the point where they were
little more than instruments of cultural policy of the Nazi Reich;
NSDAP propaganda, pressure and terror, massively supported
from the Reich, ensured that liberal culture was on the defensive
in an increasingly Pan-German, racist (völkisch) climate. For all
that, it was the economic pressure that was decisive. The Reich
attacked the Austrian tourist trade in general and the Salzburg
Festival in particular with the imposition of a Thousand Mark Visa
(Tausend-Mark-Sperre) for visits to Austria (Prossnitz). Publishing
and the sound-film industry needed the larger German market to
be economically viable. We now know of the difficulties under
which Austria's most famous publishing house functioned, until it
was under the control of the Reich in all but name (Hall); and the
same applies to the film industry (Renner). Both succumbed to
pressure, and their 'Anschluss' was virtually completed by the

mid-thirties. As Hall puts it, the swastika flying over the publishing house of Paul Zsolnay on 12 March 1938 was purely symbolical; it had been reality for years.

However, it would be wrong to overlook the ground that was already sown amongst the intelligentsia. There is an extended list of Pan-German writers, who showed their hand at the Ragusa PEN meeting of May 1933 (Amann, Hall). And here, as the insistent repetition in the Symposium papers makes so clear, the appeal of anti-Semitism is central. It was, in fact, the major reason for the Nazis' political success after 1930: they exploited to the full the classless appeal of anti-Semitism, which in its new and violent guise absorbed all previous forms – religious, economic, pan-German, ultra-right racist. Pauley states that it is doubtful whether any other issue so united the Austrian people, not even the Versailles Treaty. Thus it was that Austria's cultural institutions could lend a powerful voice to the newer, more intensely propagated ideology of race and obliterate the intellectually variegated culture of a liberal past.

A depressing story is told, then, through the essays of Fischer on Austrian philosophy and anti-Semitism at the University of Vienna, Robertson on anti-Enlightenment anthropology, Prossnitz on the Salzburg Festival, Fuhrich-Leisler and Warren on theatre, Renner on the film industry, Amann and Hall on the writers' organizations and the book market. The 'blood-and-soil' direction of literature became modern, relevant and powerful (Amann, Aspetsberger), whilst the famous 'golden age' of Viennese creativity was labelled biologically decadent. Culture was now the propaganda of the Catholic authoritarian society, racist Pan-Germanism, or else a backwater. Outside the official culture of the thirties the 'merely aesthetic' writers like Zweig or Auernheimer seemed irrelevant to the dangerous currents of the age (Daviau), and the moralists like Kraus, Horváth, and Soyfer found too little or no public resonance (Timms, Jarka).

Beller finds it 'ironic' that Vienna of all places should be where the liberal emancipatory culture of the eighteenth century found so little echo. Perhaps the Enlightenment had never penetrated Austrian culture deeply enough, either through Joseph II's attempts to impose wholesale reform or through the later brilliance of its (so frequently Jewish) literati and thinkers. Be that as it may, the forces that conspired to control and redefine culture in the Austria of the thirties were massive: the dictatorial power of the Corporate State; economic and political pressure from the German Reich; the ability of the Austrian Nazi Party, with support from the Reich, to infiltrate, subvert and terrorize cultural organs and institutions. Unlike the corporatist and Nazi ideologies, liberal culture found itself without a power base to promote or even tolerate it and so failed to enter into that political transaction which Peter Pulzer has described as 'the conjunction of facts and ideas.'[22]

### III

History tells us that in March 1938 Austria was invaded by a foreign power. Yet the situation already outlined suggests that an 'Anschluss' had been taking place at a cultural level throughout the years 1933 to 1938. And was this collusion not, in fact, a reflection of attitudes at less exalted levels of the social scene? We know that 60,000 people awaited Hitler on the main square at Linz, and 200,000 people acclaimed him on the Heldenplatz in Vienna as he announced the integration of his homeland into the Greater German Reich. Here we have the second thrust of what the historians at the Oxford Symposium were doing: together their papers amount to a detailed examination of the attitude of the Corporate State to the Reich, and of the attitude of Austrians to the Corporate State and to Nazism.

The picture is complex. Binder examines the 'legitimist' position, documenting the acts by which the Corporate State tried, right up to Schuschnigg's acceptance under duress of Hitler's ultimatum, to fend off the attentions of the Reich; and also the acts by which the corporate state tried to draw the teeth of the Austrian Nazi party. It is a substantial list. However, Staudinger's discussion of Austrofascism – the amalgam of nationalist ideology and authoritarian rule which lasted from 1933 to 1938 – claims not only its palpable resemblances to (and so in a sense preparation of) the totalitarianism which replaced it, but argues that the 'Austria' ideology and pipe-dream of a twentieth-century Danubian Confederacy created longings among Austrians which only the Nazi Reich could now satisfy. Konrad's dissection of support for the Corporate State, Social Democracy and National Socialism in the weaker social groupings in the provinces shows the economic roots of political fluctuations – if one likes, a left-wing attempt to 'understand' popular reaction comparable to the right-wing attempt made elsewhere by Ernst Hanisch.[23] Pauley has shown the significance of anti-Semitism throughout Austrian society, in which there was clearly a sense that the Reich was dealing with Jews more efficiently than was the corporate state. The extent to which Anschluss was welcome to large sections of the Austrian population thus further complicates the simple political fact of Hitler's invasion on 12 March 1938.

Nonetheless, to understand this complex social picture we really need to consider what 1918 meant for Austria. Until then Austria's German-speaking population had identified more with the Habsburg dynasty than with anything as disparate as the multi-racial Empire; with the collapse of the Empire they still did not become a nation but rather formed a number of 'camps,' Christian Social, Social Democrat, German National. Moreover the idea of integration into the German Reich appealed, on economic or ideological grounds, to large numbers in all three groupings. When the Fatherland Front seized power in 1933, it was a case of one 'camp,' the Christian Social, out-manoeuvering its two major opponents, Social Democrats and German Nationals. It is the contention of Anton Pelinka that dictatorship of the corporate state created internal strife tantamount to civil war among these three groupings, leading to a second 'civil war' from 1938 to 1945.[24]

But Pelinka's historical analysis goes further than this and examines what he considers to be a conspiratorial silence since 1945 about Nazism and the internecine struggles in the Corporate State. Indeed, he goes so far as to speak of 'the great taboo,' a concept with which he attempts to identify the source of modern Austria's political malaise. He admits that 'it would have been impossible to stabilize Austrian democracy with clear antagonism towards such a large part of the population (former National Socialists)' (p. 78), and that the 'covering up of the merciless hostility of the past eased coexistence' (ibid.) in the Second Republic. Unfortunately this suppression (or repression) of the realities of the thirties allowed the major political parties, conservative and socialist, 'to attract (former) National Socialist voters at the expense of anti-Nazism' (p. 77).

Scandals have occurred as a result of this attitude: the Reder, Reinthaller and Borodajkewycz *affaires* (ibid.); Chancellor Kreisky's defence of the former SS-officer Friedrich Peter, without any perceptible reservation, against Simon Wiesenthal (p. 79); the Freedom Party leader Jörg Haider's anti-Slovene slogans in Carinthia, and the large landed property which, before Haider acquired it, had been Aryanized – a procedure defended as a legal transaction. 'Neither Jörg Haider nor the majority of the Austrian public was sensitive enough to recognize the inevitable connection between native anti-Semitism, the Nuremberg race laws, and such "legal transactions"' (p. 80). Pelinka concludes his argument as follows:

> It might have been reasonable in the short run to respond to the Austrian civil war, to the large-scale murderous rioting of Austrians against Austrians, with this sort of integration strategy. Yet in the long run this strategy proved to be harmful, because integration forgets its own object – what the republic is supposed to be reconciled with . . . There can be no reconciliation with a spirit dividing human beings into those of higher value, lower value and nonvalue; which opposes any form of pluralism in principle; which scorns tolerance as sentimentalism; which is fundamentally antithetical to all values advocated by the Enlightenment and the – bourgeois – revolution . . . ; reconciliation cannot occur with the spirit for which these people once stood. The Second Republic is a product of war – of the world war from 1939 to 1945 as well as the Austrian civil war from 1938 to 1945. This Second Repub-

lic, this Austria, must be conscious of these origins, and must draw the required consequences. Only then can Austria regain international respect (pp. 81f.)

During the last decade Austrians have numbered among historians willing to ask appropriate questions about the Anschluss and internecine strife of the period 1933–1945. Whether as 'understanding' or critique, their work on this period offers an exemplum of the moral function of historiography: the nation must know the truth about the thirties in order to participate in breaking the 'great taboo.' For as a cultural historian has elsewhere noted, 'reflection on the past is not just an activity to be permitted to a few learned mandarins on the margins of . . . society, but a vital part of what a nation knows, feels, and is.'[25] Like Anton Pelinka historians at the Oxford Symposium clearly recognized that such reflection can have political implications.

## IV

In one sense Thomas Bernhard's play *Heldenplatz* (1988) reworks his well-known existential pessimism, with Austria serving as a magnifying glass simply because it is 'absurdity to the power of ten.'[26] But the theme of the work also ties it to the function of historiography discussed in the previous section: Austria must face up to what happened if the present is not to remain victim of an unmastered past and herald a bleak future. For his 'plot' is centred around the meaning of the Heldenplatz on 15 March 1938, and its destructive intrusion into Austrian life in March 1988. And here Bernhard places the Jews, rightly as we have seen, at the centre of the problem. The relationship of the two dates is figured in the fates of the two émigré Jewish brothers, upper middle-class academics, invited in the fifties to return to the posts they had been forced to vacate in 1938. And because of the suicide of one of the brothers in the anniversary month of the annexation, leading to speculation – on stage and off – that anti-Semitism resurfacing in the Waldheim era is responsible for his death, *Heldenplatz* is undeniably also a meditation on Austria, its Jews and the legacy of an unregenerate past.

It is not in any way sentimental, and for two good reasons. Firstly, the dead brother appears to have been no paragon of virtue: a household tyrant, egotist and pedant, with many and as appalling prejudices as the one from which he was forced to flee – he can refer to members of his family as 'sub-human types' (p. 50). But the play makes the more powerful case for that, since our honesty and humanity cannot depend on our predilections. Secondly, the play is unsentimental in using a comic reversal: instead of permitting contemporary Austrians to make anti-Semitic utterances, thereby generating pathos, Bernhard lets the Jews themselves speak satirically against everything Austrian – the Church, the theatre, the press, the provinces, the Austrian President, the Chancellor, politicians, political parties, old anti-Semites, neo-Nazis.

The utterances of the Jewish figures reveal continuous violent mistrust: 'the Viennese hate the Jews / and they will always hate the Jews / into all eternity' (p. 84); 'hatred of the Jews is the purest absolutely unadulterated nature / of the Austrian' (p. 114); 'there are more Nazis in Vienna today / than in thirty-eight' (p. 63); 'in the National Library I have the feeling / that they are all Nazis around me / they are all waiting for the signal / to attack us openly' (ibid.). As in the thirties, the Jews sense that they do not belong: 'In Austria you have to be either Catholic / or National Socialist / nothing else is tolerated / everything else is destroyed' (p. 63). In particular, there is fear of the political possibilities: 'the most dangerous of all European states' (p. 148); 'the Socialists today are nothing other / than Catholic National Socialists'; 'in this most terrible of all states / you have only one choice / between conservative swine and socialist swine' (p. 164); 'the socialists and the conservatives are playing into the Nazis' hands' (p. 135). And, finally, there is straight vituperation: 'the city of Vienna is the epitome of mindlessness and vileness' (p. 66); 'the mass of Austrians are in their entirety / a brutal and stupid nation' (p. 88); 'six-and-a-half million feeble-minded people, raving lunatics' (p. 89); 'mindless mountain-dwellers' (p. 147), 'idiots from Styria, morons from Salzburg' (p. 66); Austria is 'an intellectual and cultural sewer' (p. 97); 'this little state is one large dung heap' (p. 164).

At one level this is theatrical enactment of fears felt by Austria's Jews, of retaliation for the hatred they have suffered and are again suffering,[27] an artistic procedure not without danger. But it is also a continuation of the Austrian satirical mode of Nestroy and Karl Kraus. Did not Kraus in the thirties write of Austria as 'this most dismal of all states' and Vienna as 'that imbecile city'? (Timms). Bernhard certainly intensifies the scurrility of the 'raisonneurs,' carpers and grumblers of Austrian comedy, but he is, after all, tackling what his characters see as the resurgent spirit of 1938. His trick is to stylize 'beer hall' obscenity, and thus artfully mirror the mentality of those he wishes to provoke into declaring themselves.

Bernhard has certainly succeeded in provoking. Several of the above quotations were leaked to the press—by actors, it was suggested, refusing to perform in the play—long before the première or publication of the text. There was intense reaction in newspaper articles and correspondence, in parliament, on radio and television, in violently abusive private letters and, finally, in and outside the theatre itself. There were demands that the play be banned, that the Burgtheater director and play's producer, Claus Peymann, be deported back to his native Germany, and vastly cruder responses still. In exaggerated indignation, xenophobia and viciousness, those so reacting helped Bernhard to make his point. And, of course, his provocation similarly turns the theatre audience into participants in the play. As bitter insults come from the stage, knee-jerk ripostes go back from the auditorium. At the première the concluding hallucinatory 1938 crescendo of 'Sieg heil,' apparently rising from the 1988 Heldenplatz outside the windows, gave way to an aggressive chant in rhythmic counterpoint from a group of protesters: 'Peymann raus' (Peymann out).[28] Where did theatre end and reality begin?

In the volume of 'Documentation' published by the Burgtheater,[29] we are given an assemblage of newspaper cuttings from the period August to December 1988 (the première was on 4 November), from which it is possible to reconstruct the 'scandal' and general reception of the play. Every politician, journalist, individual or group reacting to Bernhard and Peymann revealed the forces of reactionary or liberal thinking ranged against each other. Whether the anti-Semitic 'Staberl' of the *Neue Kronen-Zeitung*[30] (the Austrian tabloid which campaigned throughout the land against a play no one had yet been able to read, let alone see), together with the right extremism of a Jörg Haider, will win the day, or whether those who want clarity about the past and social sanity for the future will do so is certainly one question posed by Bernhard's play. Whereas Hofmannsthal presents the myth of a good Austria, in which the Beggar raises an axe 'against everyone and everything' but lowers it in pious submission,[31] Bernhard's comic grotesque theatre offers the subversive myth of an evil Austria, and his figures strike everyone and everything. Instead of harmlessly celebrating the one-hundredth anniversary of the Burgtheater, *Heldenplatz* raises ghosts, talks of the devil, cries havoc, unleashes emotion, and yet ultimately craves contradiction.

In this post-Brechtian theatre, what cannot come right on stage is presented to the public as its problem. Can that public prove Bernhard's appalling vision of Austria 1988 wrong? Have they, indeed, an answer to the writer in the *Jüdische Rundschau,* who says of the call to censor or otherwise suppress *Heldenplatz:*

> In the composition of those objecting, in the arguments used, in the methods employed, and in the demands made, (I am reminded) of precisely that coalition of the thirties under Chancellors Dollfuss and Schuschnigg, who with their Austrofascist Corporate State prepared and made possible the seamless, frictionless transition into Hitler's Reich. The recent coalition consisted of President Waldheim, the entire leadership of the [conservative] Austrian People's Party, the Viennese Bishop Kurt Krenn, considered reactionary even within Catholic circles, the

right-wing leader of the Austrian Freedom Party Jörg
Haider, various duelling fraternities and extreme right-wing
student organizations. Before this political interest group
gave up its battle so fraught with danger for political
democracy . . . it called in the usual jargon for the public
to boycott the play.[32]

The usual self-defence of Bernhard's countrymen when confronted
by his 'hate tirades' against Austria has been that he is 'sick'; this
time (to quote President Waldheim) 'the entire nation has been
insulted.'[33] Innumerable responses of this kind suggest that March
1938 and Austria's Jews have been less bearable subjects for many
Austrians than other vehicles for Bernhard's similar savagery.

However, in the Burgtheater volume of 'Documentation' we
also find the views of enlightened people. Educators, their pupils,
professional men and women, intelligent theatre-goers and at least
one politician[34] respond positively to Bernhard's and Peymann's
Theatre of Provocation and Scandal. In disapproving of the many
calls to ban the play or dismiss the Director of the Burgtheater,
such critics of bigotry are denying that those 'disjunctions' of
culture and politics characteristic of the thirties (Timms) have yet
recurred; and the reactions of these people also suggest the presence of another Austria, one not in mental slavery and not afraid
of the unnerving experience of national self-examination. In all
this Bernhard and Peymann have proved to be masterly publicists
in the task assigned to present-day Austria by its taboo-breakers.

> Postscript:
> 'the Oxford of nineteen-eighty-eight is not the
> Oxford of nineteen-fifty-seven / fascism is a minor
> premise of English society too / people always for-
> get / the English too have their own brand of
> fascism.' (Thomas Bernhard: *Heldenplatz*)

NOTES

1.  See Anton Pelinka, 'The Great Austrian Taboo: The Repression of the Civil War,' *New German Critique*, 43 (Winter 1988), 69–82. This article is an enlarged, translated version of the author's 'Der verdrängte Bürgerkrieg' in: Anton Pelinka/Erika Weinzierl eds., *Das große Tabu: Österreichs Umgang mit seiner Vergangenheit* (Vienna: Verlag der österreichischen Staatsdruckerei, 1987), pp. 143–153.

2.  Peter G.J. Pulzer, *The Rise of Political Anti-Semitism in Germany and Austria* (New York: John Wiley & Sons, 1964), p. 318.

3.  Robert Musil, *Der Mann ohne Eigenschaften* (Hamburg: Rowohlt, 1952), p. 231.

4.  See Hugo von Hofmannsthal's essay 'Das Schrifttum als geistiger Raum der Nation' (1927), *Prosa IV* (Frankfurt am Main: Fischer, 1955), pp. 390–413. This lecture was directed at young university graduates and propounded the idea of 'a conservative revolution' (p. 413).

5.  Hugo von Hofmannsthal, 'Das Publikum der Salzburger Festspiele' (1928), *Prosa IV*, p. 470: 'What the Festival excludes, to be plain, is gloom without hope or uplift, the commonplace without depth, complete absence of the sacral (das völlig Weihelose).'

6.  Hugo von Hofmannsthal, *Aufzeichnungen* (Frankfurt am Main: Fischer, 1959), p. 304.

7.  Ibid., pp. 297f.

8.  Hugo von Hofmannsthal, 'Das Salzburger große Welttheater' (1925), *Prosa IV*, pp. 266ff.

9.  Hugo von Hofmannsthal, 'Das Publikum der Salzburger Festspiele' (1928), ibid., p. 467.

10. Hugo von Hofmannsthal, 'Zum Programm der Salzburger Festspiele 1928,' ibid., p. 472.

11. Hugo von Hofmannsthal, 'Das Salzburger große Welttheater' (1925), ibid., p. 268.

12. See Hugo von Hofmannsthal, 'Deutsche Festspiele zu Salzburg,' *Prosa III* (Frankfurt am Main: Fischer, 1952), p. 441; and 'Festspiele in Salzburg' (1919), ibid., pp. 444ff.

13. Hugo von Hofmannsthal, 'Das Spiel vor der Menge. Eindruck und Überlegung' (1911), *Prosa III*, pp. 63f.

14. Hugo von Hofmannsthal, 'Das Salzburger große Welttheater' (1925), *Prosa IV*, p. 267.

15. For the Nazis' railing against the 'Jewish press' in the twenties and thir-

ties, see Pauley in this volume, p. 35.

16. See Sander L. Gilman, 'Strauss, the Pervert, and Avant-Garde Opera of the Fin de Siècle,' *New German Critique,* 43 (Winter 1988), 35-68: 'There is a strong, popular image of Jewry as the bastion of the cultural avant-garde, an image shared by some Jews, as well as much of the German anti-Semitic literature of the period' (p. 65).

17. See Walter Muschg, *Die Zerstörung der deutschen Literatur* (Bern: Francke, 3rd edition, 1958). Muschg applies the phrase (pp. 290f.) to Josef Nadler's theory of literature propounded in his 'Literary History of the German Tribes and Regions' (*Literaturgeschichte der deutschen Stämme und Landschaften*), the first volume of which appeared in 1912. Nadler's denial of individual creativity and insistence on 'tribal blood' (Muschg, p. 289) as well as on 'birthplace and homeland' (ibid., p. 290)—all these factors indissolubly linked—turns 'the history of the mind into geography and nature mythology' (ibid., p. 292). In his writings on Salzburg, Hofmannsthal draws heavily on the language and thought of Nadler' actually citing him in 'Festspiele in Salzburg,' *Prosa III*, p. 448.

18. Stefan Zweig, *Die Welt von Gestern* (Frankfurt am Main: Fischer, 1962), p. 32.

19. In debate from the floor concerning the 'Jewish' aspect of being a 'Jewish intellectual,' the question was raised whether this was not tantamount to playing the anti-Semites' game. Surely one was either a good or a bad intellectual, and what had Jewishness to do with it? Whilst Beller amply demonstrates that there is nothing monolithic in the cultural or political posture of Vienna's Jews, he does consider their origins to have a 'decisive effect' on their thinking. His case has been given theoretical grounding by Michael P. Steinberg: 'In seeking a method for discussing the relationship of Jewishness and intellectuality in Austrian modernist culture, we must steer between a deterministic ethnic maximalism on the one side, and an ethnic minimalism perhaps indeed based on a denial of the intellectual relevance of Jewish identity on the other side. Jewishness in Austrian culture is a question of meaning, not cause. Critical intellectuals who saw themselves in opposition to the social and political structures and the ideological systems of self-representation in Austrian society certainly integrated their perceptions of themselves as Jews into their intellectual personae. And, the more problematic the intellectual opposition to the society and its forms of self-representation, the more the constitution and intellectual integration of Jewishness

became problematic as well' ('Jewish Identity and Intellectuality in Fin-de-Siècle Austria: Suggestions for a Historical Discourse' in: *New German Critique*, 43, Winter 1988, p. 15). What was true of an earlier decade is still 'more problematic' in the ideological conditions of the Corporate State.

20.   It was, however, true that lower organs of state could show anti-Semitic prejudice with impunity, and Jews were subjected to constant hostility in pamphlets and the press, which was almost entirely in government hands by 1934. For a brief account of the state's attitude to its Jews, see Sylvia Maderegger, 'Die Juden im österreichischen Ständestaat,' *Emuna*, 2 (1972), 104–110. The author's full-scale study is *Die Juden im österreichischen Ständestaat 1934–1938* (Vienna/Salzburg: Geyer Edition, 1973).

21.   See Pulzer (note 2 above), p. 321.

22.   Pulzer, ibid., p. 330.

23.   See Ernst Hanisch, 'An attempt to "understand" National Socialism. The provincial experience,' *Austria Today*, 2 (1987), 9ff.

24.   See Pelinka, 'The Great Austrian Taboo.' Page references appear in brackets in the text.

25.   T. J. Reed, 'A Piece of History,' *Oxford Magazine*, 44 (1989), 2. The author's comment relates to modern Germany, but appears precisely to apply to Pelinka's view of Waldheim's Austria.

26.   Thomas Bernhard, *Heldenplatz* (Frankfurt am Main: Suhrkamp, 1988), p. 118. Further page references are given in brackets in the text.

27.   For Viennese Jewry's present fears of persecution, see 'Jetzt trauen sie sich wieder! Umfrage unter Wiener Juden über Pogromangst in Österreich,' *Der Spiegel*, 51 (19 December 1988), 130. Reproduced in *Heldenplatz. Eine Dokumentation* (Vienna: Burgtheater, 1989), p. 289. Typical reactions of Viennese Jews: 'I keep thinking about when I ought to get out of Austria, and whether I'll be able to choose the right moment.' 'Of course [we will leave Austria] . . . given the present situation, we should have gone already.' It is reported, among other disturbing statistics, that only 10% of the present-day Viennese Jews questioned would not be frightened to travel by subway if they thought they might be recognized as Jews.

28.   Review in the *Frankfurter Allgemeine* (7 November 1988). Reproduced in *Heldenplatz. Eine Dokumentation*, p. 230.

29.   For details, see note 27 above.

30.   See *Heldenplatz. Eine Dokumentation*, p. 288.

31.  Hofmannsthal, *Aufzeichnungen,* p. 297.

32.  Robert Singer, *Jüdische Rundschau* (10 November 1988). Reproduced in *Heldenplatz. Eine Dokumentation,* p. 264. It should be noted that the socialist Federal Chancellor Vranitzky and his Education Minister Hilde Hawlicek refused to be drawn towards any act of censorship. The former socialist Federal Chancellor Kreisky, interviewed by the journal *profil,* let it be known that he thought it 'stupid' of Waldheim to speak against performance of the play, but he considered it 'cowardly' of Vranitzky to say nothing at all. He himself would like to 'tell Bernhard to his face that it is a particularly vile act' to make a Jew say things about Austrians which 'he was not prepared to say in his own voice' (ibid., p. 94). These comments were made in October 1988 before it had been possible to read or see the play.

33.  *Volksstimme* (12 October 1988). Reproduced in *Heldenplatz. Eine Dokumentation,* p. 49.

34.  See Vienna City Councillor Ursula Pasterk's statement of 12 October 1988, reproduced in *Heldenplatz. Eine Dokumentation,* p. 50. She writes among other things: 'We are going to make complete fools of ourselves. It does not bear thinking what people abroad will say and write after the première when it is clear that Conservative [ÖVP] and Freedom Party [FPÖ] politicians wanted to ban a play critical of Austria's attitude to those who were forced to flee in the thirties. We will simply have wasted all the efforts made during this commemorative year to reappraise our past ... Anyone who refuses to face up to the theme of this play and simply wants to turn its performance into a scandal is guilty of using rough media justice against an artist and his art. And that can only damage our claim to be considered a cultured nation.'

# CONTRIBUTORS

KLAUS AMANN studied at the University of Vienna, gaining his doctorate in 1976. He has since taught at the University of Klagenfurt (*Habilitation* 1986). He has published on the interaction of literature and society in nineteenth- and twentieth-century Austrian literature, most recently producing *Der Anschluß österreichischer Schriftsteller an das Dritte Reich* (1988). (Institut für Germanistik, Universitätsstraße 65–67, A-9010 Klagenfurt, Austria.)

FRIEDBERT ASPETSBERGER studied at the University of Vienna. He holds the Chair of German at Klagenfurt University and is Director of the Robert Musil Archive. His publications on German and Austrian literature from Hölderlin to the present day are numerous. Of special interest in the context of this volume are his work on Arnolt Bronnen and his book *Literarisches Leben im Austrofaschismus* (1980). (Institut für Germanistik, Universitätsstraße 65–67, A-9010 Klagenfurt, Austria.)

STEVEN BELLER is Research Fellow in History at Peterhouse, Cambridge. His publications centre on the Jewish role in Viennese culture at the turn of the century. His book on that subject is to be published by Cambridge University Press in 1989. (Peterhouse, Cambridge CB2 1RD, U.K.)

DIETER A. BINDER studied history and German literature at the Universities of Vienna, Graz and Bonn, gaining his doctorate in 1976. He teaches contemporary Austrian history at the University of Graz (*Habilitation* 1983). He has published widely on Austrian history and culture of the thirties. Since 1982 he has been a member of the editorial team of the Graz periodical *Geschichte und*

*Gegenwart.* (Institut für Geschichte, Schubertstraße 23, A-8010 Graz, Austria.)

DONALD G. DAVIAU was a Fulbright Student at the University of Vienna in 1953–1954. He has been Professor of Austrian and German Literature at the University of California at Riverside since 1955, where he is currently Chairman of the Department of Literatures and Languages. He has written books and articles on Auernheimer, Bahr, Hofmannsthal, Kraus, Schnitzler and Stefan Zweig. He is President of the International Arthur Schnitzler Research Association, and since 1971 has been editor of *Modern Austrian Literature*. Since 1980 he has been President of the American Council for the Study of Austrian Literature, and is a member of the Austrian P.E.N. Club. In 1977 he was awarded the Austrian Cross of Honour for Science and Art. (Department of Literatures and Languages, University of California, Riverside, California 92521, U.S.A.)

KURT RUDOLF FISCHER was born in Vienna and emigrated to the U.S.A. in 1938. He studied philosophy at Berkeley and Vienna Universities, gaining his doctorate with work on Franz Brentano in 1964. He has taught widely in the U.S.A., returning to Vienna as Fulbright Research Professor and since 1978 as Guest Professor. He has published on contemporary philosophy and nineteenth- and twentieth-century intellectual history. (Institut für Philosophie der Universität Wien, Universitätsstraße 7, A-1010 Vienna, Austria.)

EDDA FUHRICH–LEISLER studied theatre and art history at the University of Vienna, where she took her doctorate in 1967. Since 1968 she has worked at the Max Reinhardt Research Institute. Her main interests are German-speaking theatre from the late nineteenth century to 1945, with special reference to Max Reinhardt and his associates. She has been responsible for major exhibitions, produced books and catalogues (several jointly with Gisela Prossnitz), and contributed numerous articles to journals and works of reference. (Max Reinhardt Forschungsinstitut, Hofburg, Batthyanystiege, A-1010 Vienna, Austria.)

MURRAY G. HALL studied French and German at Queen's University at Kingston, Ontario, before taking a doctorate at Vienna University in 1975, where he now teaches (*Habilitation* 1987). He has published on Musil and many aspects of Austrian literature between the wars, including the book *Der Fall Bettauer* (1978) and his two-volume study of Austrian publishing 1918–1938 (1985). (Kulmgasse 39/12, A-1170 Vienna, Austria.)

HORST JARKA studied German and English literatures at the University of Vienna, where he took his doctorate in 1955. Since 1959 he has taught German language and literature at the University of Montana. He has edited the complete works of Jura Soyfer (1980) and published a critical biography of the writer (1988). (Department of Foreign Languages and Literature, University of Montana, Missoula, Montana 59812, U.S.A.)

HELMUT KONRAD studied history and German literature in Vienna before teaching at the University of Linz (*Habilitation* 1980). He was appointed professor there before moving to the Chair of Contemporary History at Graz in 1984. He has published four books and almost one hundred articles on wide-ranging aspects of Austrian and European history. His main interests are the history of the working-class movement, contemporary history and the theory of history. (Institut für Geschichte, Abteilung Zeitgeschichte, Albrechtgasse 7, A-8010 Graz, Austria.)

BRUCE F. PAULEY took his doctorate at the University of Rochester, U.S.A., in 1966 and is at present Professor of History at the University of Central Florida. Among his many publications are three books on Austrian history, including *Hitler and the Forgotten Nazis*. He is writing a history of the Jews in Austria 1914–1938. (Department of History, University of Central Florida, Orlando, Florida 32816, U.S.A.)

GISELA PROSSNITZ studied German literature and theatre at the University of Vienna, where she took her doctorate in 1966. Since then she has been Director of the Max Reinhardt Research Institute in Salzburg. She has organized major exhibitions, and produced numerous books and catalogues (several jointly with Edda Fuhrich-Leisler) on Reinhardt and his associates, as well as on various aspects of the Salzburg Festival. Her main research interest is German-speaking theatre of the first half of the twentieth century. (Max Reinhardt Forschungs- und Gedenkstätte, Schloss Arenberg, Arenbergerstrasse 8–10, A-5020 Salzburg, Austria.)

GERHARD RENNER studied at the University of Vienna, taking his doctorate in 1981. He works at the Documentation Centre for Modern Austrian Literature, and has published widely. His main research interest is the interaction of culture and politics in the thirties. He is at present compiling a detailed list of all unpublished collections of authors' and artists' works held in Austrian libraries and museums. (Palffygasse 5, A-1170 Vienna, Austria.)

RITCHIE ROBERTSON studied English and German literature at the University of Edinburgh, and took his doctorate at the University of Oxford. In addition to numerous articles on German and Austrian literature he has published books on Kafka and Heine. He edits, with Edward Timms, *Austrian Studies,* a yearbook whose first number will appear in 1990. He is at present Fellow in German at Downing College, Cambridge, but has been appointed Fellow and Tutor in German at St John's College, Oxford, from October 1989. (St John's College, Oxford OX1 3JP, U.K.)

KENNETH SEGAR studied French and German at the University of Oxford, and took his doctorate in 1972. Since 1966 he has been Fellow and Tutor in German at St Edmund Hall, Oxford, has published on Schnitzler and Hofmannsthal, and is co-organizer (with John Warren) of the Oxford Austrian Study Group. (St Edmund Hall, Oxford OX1 4AR, U.K.)

ANTON STAUDINGER studied history and German at the University of Vienna, where he took his doctorate in 1969. He has taught at the Institut für Zeitgeschichte, Vienna, since 1966 (*Habilitation* 1980), becoming Professor of History there in 1983. He is a member of the Austrian Association for Contemporary History, as well as the Centre for Research into the Austrian Resistance. He has published very widely, particularly on the history of the Austrian First Republic. (Institut für Zeitgeschichte, Rotenhausgasse 6, A-1090 Vienna, Austria.)

EDWARD TIMMS studied at the University of Cambridge, where he took his doctorate and now teaches as a Fellow of Gonville and Caius College. In addition to publications on comparative literature, he has written widely on Austrian subjects. The first volume of his biography of Karl Kraus appeared in 1986, and he is currently completing the second volume, which deals with Austrian culture and politics of the period 1919–1938. He is (with Ritchie Robertson) the initiator of a new international yearbook, *Austrian Studies,* to be published by Edinburgh University Press. (Gonville and Caius College, Cambridge CB2 1TA, U.K.)

JOHN WARREN studied at the University of Bristol. He has taught German and Austrian studies at Oxford Polytechnic since 1965, and has published on the German theatre of the inter-war years. He organized the Oxford Symposium on Max Reinhardt in 1985, the papers of which he edited together with Margaret Jacobs in 1986. He is co-organizer (with Kenneth Segar) of the Oxford Austrian Study Group. (Oxford Polytechnic, Gypsy Lane, Headington, Oxford OX3 0BP, U.K.)

# NAME INDEX